You Cannot Send an Innocent to Life in Prison and Get Away With It

The vanishing of Peter Falconio

by

Gerard Catherin

You Cannot Send an Innocent To Life in Prison and Get Away With It

All Rights Reserved

Copyright © 2024 Gerard Catherin

Printed in Australia

Reproduction in any manner, in whole or in part,
in English or any other language, or otherwise,
without the written permission of the copyright holder is prohibited

First Printing 2025

ISBN: 978-0-7638043-3-3

Dedications

This book is dedicated

- to Bradley John Murdoch an Innocent Man and his family
- to my friends, helpers and researchers
- to Gregory Dick owner of the Aileron Roadhouse
- to Andrew Fraser who passed away on the 3rd of August 2023
- to Victor Susman
- to Judge Mildren
- to Keith Noble
- to Robin Bowles
- to Richard Shears
- and to all people who like myself, always believed that Murdoch was innocent.

Other books by Gerard Catherin

38 Specks: The proposition. Can an Aussie prospector solve the mystery of Rennes le Chateau? Gerard Catherin,. South Australia Ginninderra Press 2021

***

Mentioned in the literature are numerous names. All found and taken from books already published, articles from journalists, videos on the internet, documentary about the case, not forgetting the officials –certain witnesses –forensic scientists –certain members of the police force and all the disinformation from the media purposely thrown at the public with the intention to deflect from the truth.

I have the courage of my convictions. I commented about anything that didn't comply with the truth –common sense –integrity –honesty and justice.

I haven't been defamatory towards anyone. I am just reporting, questioning what people wrote and said including my views and comments.

It never had the intention to be soft on certain topics, simply reporting the truth as any journalists would. I firmly believe in the reliability of facts. Yes, I have been aggressive and sarcastic at times with my comments, but that's me.

All words or sentences in italic in this book are not my own, sometimes I forget but I always mention the source of the information. I have tried my utmost to report accurately what was illogical –bias and totally unfounded about the case and the trial based on what I collect, copy and paste.

IMPORTANT NOTICE
It is imperative that since the death of Bradley John Murdoch on the 15 of July 2025 the Social-Media has had a feast releasing woke information. As a result, it is necessary for me to add a new chapter which I will be inserting after chapter 96 Conclusion page 463

Contents

Foreword	1
Author's Note	2
1- Somebody Knows	5
2- Some People are Making a Lot of Noise	10
3- There Is Nothing More Deceptive Than an Obvious Fact	13
4- Think	16
5- How I Got Interested in The Case	17
6- This Book	20
7- Warning	21
8- Source Of My Information	23
9- What Do We Need to Understand	26
10- What Do We Know? [1]	28
11- What We Know, What We Don't [2]	30
12- What We Need to Challenge and Prove	46
13- The Judge	50
14- The Jury	54
15- Let Us Be Clear about The Word Conspiracy	58
16- There Cannot Be a Proven Murder Without a Dead Body	59
17- What Would You Answer?	60
18- Is/Was It a Murder Case?	63
19- Honi Soit Qui Mal y Pense	65

20-This Is Important	70
21-Legalese The Lawyers' Language	73
22-What We Need to Prove [2]	74
23-Coincidence?	75
24-Murdoch, Joanne Lees, Peter Falconio in Alice Springs	79
25-According To Joanne Lees and The Prosecution	84
26-Time of the Alleged Death [1]	86
27-Time Of the Alleged Death [2]	88
28-The Reason Why Joanne Lees Was Found Warm And Clean When Rescued	101
29-Did Joanne Lees Really Drive Slowly From Alice To Ti Tree?	104
30-6.10pm At Ti Tree [1]	113
31-Footprints –Shooting	119
32-Most Of What the Jury Knows	124
33-How Did Joanne Lees Escape –Did She Really Escape?	127
34-Re-Enactment	134
35-Cable Ties	136
36-One Fact That Nobody Can Deny	140
37-Toyota Land Cruiser	141
38-Oh! La La! The Front Teeth	147
39-Cigarettes	149
40-Murdoch Interviewed	152
41-The Kombi –CCTV Man –DNA	157

42-Important –Interesting –Truly Funny	166
43-Murdoch Looking Different Depending And According to Lees	173
44-Up Until Now What Have We Got?	174
45-Plan And Strategy	182
46-Newcomer…New Suspect	187
47-Turbulent Waters	190
48-The Road Train Driver Vince Millar	195
49-First Obvious Fact	203
50-Three Men in a Red Japanese Car	216
51-The Land Cruiser Man	219
52-Monsieur Malouf and His Cruiser	227
53-Some Plan….	235
54-Short Chapter	240
55-Still Debating	241
56-Four Years Later	244
57-Ballistics	252
58-Bradley Murdoch –Peter Falconio –Joanne Lees	260
59-From The Daily Mail	263
60-Did Lees Make Money from The Story and How Much	267
61-Monsieur Murdoch and The Tanami	270
62-The Key Assumptions Underpinning the Prosecution's Case	271
63-Distances (Internet –Hema Maps)	274

64-Calculation And Choice	276
65-We Definitely Have…	279
66-For Your Perusal	283
67-The Fuel Factor	284
68-The Court of Criminal Appeal	286
69-Who Will?	308
70-The Obvious Fact –The Race Is On	313
71-Second Choice of Route…	315
72-R Vs Murdoch –The Falconio Case – A Study In Identification By Dean Mildren Retired Judge	319
73-Monsieur Hall Is Being Challenged	327
74-As I Said Previously…	333
75- First Proof Beyond Reasonable Doubt	334
76- Second Proof Beyond Reasonable Doubt	342
77-Third Proof Beyond Reasonable Doubt	344
78-Fourth Proof Beyond Reasonable Doubt	352
79-I Am Sorry to Disappoint You	358
80-About Billiluna	360
81-Closing Argument	361
82-Closing Argument [2]	365
83-Ah! The Missing Dollar	377
84-Closing Argument [3]	378
85-Up To Here	384

86-The Prosecution Never Believed Joanne Lees 'Story	385
87-Murdoch's Brother Gary and His DNA	393
88-The High Court Said…	402
89-The Sentencing of Murdoch	404
90-More From Murder in The Outback Documentary	410
91-The Meaning of The Word Disappearance According to Lees	415
92-Extra: An Analysis of DNA Evidence, Must Be Read	421
93-The Barrow Creek Abduction –Missing Person $250,000 Reward Poster July 2001 *515*	454
94-Key Event	459
95-My Lust for Justice Is Such…	462
96-Conclusion	463
97-Now that is dead Murdoch	466
98-Refences	469

+

The Vanishing of Peter Falconio

Foreword

Ladies and Gentlemen, This Is an Easy Case!

According to the Prosecution, Bradley John Murdoch a drug dealer and Peter Falconio with girlfriend Joanne Lees both drug users were seen in a restaurant in Alice Springs allegedly some hours apart on the 14th of July 2001.

According to the Prosecution, Murdoch feared they were spying on him, so he followed them, stopped them at Barrow Creek, Northern Territory Australia, shot Peter Falconio in cold blood with a big silver gun then abducted Joanne Lees binding her hands behind her back with some handmade cuffs. He then pushed her in the back of his Land Cruiser through a passage between the seats and the back of the car. Then according to Joanne Lees, he moved their car a Kombi a short distance to avoid suspicion. After moving the Kombi I assume that he had to come back to the alleged crime scene which was only a short distance away to clean the mess after shooting Falconio. In the meantime, Joanne Lees escaped. So, he apparently searched for her with his light torch and his beautiful Dalmatian dog, but failed to find her after five hours. Then according to Chief Justine Martin Brian in his sentencing, **[Murdoch]** *put the body of Mr Falconio to the rear of his vehicle…*

Then in great hurry after loading the body of Peter Falconio to the rear of his vehicle he drove to Alice Springs where he was picked up by a CCTV camera at a truck stop where he refuelled after doing little shopping. Then again in great hurry after taking drugs he drove towards Broome in Western Australia but was seen at Fitzroy Crossing **1,412km** away refuelling at 8.00pm on the 15th of July 2001.

Arrested in 2003 for the alleged crime, Murdoch was found guilty on all charges in 2005 four years after and sent to prison for life. That is basically the story.

Up until now the Dead Body has yet to be found, meaning he just vanished!

The Vanishing of Peter Falconio

Author's Note

If you think Bradley John Murdoch received a fair trial, THINK TWICE.

A true crime is something very serious indeed. A staged crime is even worse, it is beyond comprehension.

Accusing someone of murder needs evidence and proofs beyond any reasonable doubt.

Australian law requires that every person accused of a crime is deemed innocent until proven guilty in a court of law.

The burden of proof rests upon the Crown. Proofs must be 'beyond all reasonable doubt'. It requires a higher standard of proofs than just a 'satisfaction' that the accused is more likely guilty than not.

We all know that justice is not infallible and innocent people have spent lengthy periods in Australian prisons.

On 13 December 2005, in the Northern Territory Supreme Court, a jury found Bradley John Murdoch guilty of the alleged murder of Peter Falconio on the 14th July 2001. Their verdict was unanimous…GUILTY ON ALL CHARGES!

It didn't comply with the rule of law: Beyond any reasonable doubt, but to the satisfaction that the accused was more likely guilty than not… That is what I really believe.

The community could now feel safe, another 'bad guy' was safely locked away in prison serving a life sentence with little chance of parole.

The case was 'done and dusted'.

But right from the very beginning serious doubts about the case were raised from across the spectrum including the media, legal circles, journalists, concerned citizens, police, even the Prosecution (as you will discover further on) involved in the case renewing the appeal to locate Peter Falconio; not to forget the accused, who maintained his innocence from day one.

The Vanishing of Peter Falconio

Not long after the verdict was announced words such as 'kangaroo court', 'setup' and miscarriage of justice appeared in the media. Books have been written, blogs, films based on the case, TV series etc.

According to the 'system' the accused had received a fair trial. Justice had been delivered.

So why has the case remained in the media after twenty years. Why are the authorities some months ago asking for anyone having any information about the case to come forward? ...REMORSE? Or worried that the truth will resurface and that perhaps the guillotine will be reset after long inaction [reminding you that the guillotine is a French invention by Monsieur Guillotin]

Why should we care so long after the case? Because, as His Honour Judge Stephen Norrish QC writes: *"When [justice] is denied we are somehow all diminished. "*

Anyone can be in the wrong place at the wrong time. Under the right set of circumstances, it could happen to anyone.

Justice Norris encourages everyone who participates in the justice system and the community *"to exercise the enduring vigilance needed to prevent the mistakes of the past occurring in the future, even for those accused of involvement in unspeakable crimes that seize the public imagination and cause revulsion in reasonable minds"*.

This book is somehow a detailed account of the Falconio case. Several other authors have analysed the case in great depth and details, especially the book by **Dean Mildren** retired Judge**; R v Murdoch the Falconio Case a Study in Identification and Circumstantial Evidence –Find Falconio Dead or Alive by Keith Noble a 504 pages book, more like a thesis than a book –not forgetting Dead Centre the book by Robin Bowles** and many more including startlingly **No Turning Back** the book by the [accuser] **Joanne Lees.** All highly recommended, but none of those authors ever mentioned the obvious fact, a fact that everybody missed to recognise and if some did recognise it, they sure kept their mouths shut for good reasons. No attempts by anyone, was ever made to clear the innocent.

Here, we need to question everything that needs and must be questioned as well as all the assumptions put forward by the Prosecution. We need to know and comprehend why a guilty verdict in all charges?

It is my contribution to that enduring vigilance.

"From time to time, innocent people are convicted. That is the flaw in our system of justice. There can be no greater injustice than a person being convicted of a crime they did not commit...When an innocent person is sent to gaol, justice is truly denied, and there have been far too many instances of that in Australia."

His Honour Judge Stephen Norrish QC. *Justice denied.* 2017

There are more important things than finding the murderer. And justice is a fine word, but it is sometimes difficult to say exactly what one means by it. In my opinion, the important thing is to clear the innocent." (Agatha Christie death in the Clouds)

The Vanishing of Peter Falconio

1 - Somebody Knows

Somebody knows what happened that night—really knows.
(Andrew Fraser)

Peter Falconio was a British tourist from Hepworth, Huddersfield West Yorkshire who vanished in the Australian outback whilst travelling with girlfriend Joanne Lees. Although his body has never been found, Bradley John Murdoch was convicted of his murder on December 13, 2005 four years after the alleged offence.

On the evening of 14 July 2001, British backpacker Peter Falconio and Joanne Lees, his girlfriend, were driving in their old orange Kombi heading for Darwin on the Stuart Highway. They had left Alice Springs around (nobody knowns). Darwin is around 1,500 km from Alice Springs; a trip that would normally take one day even longer had they reached their destination.

They had been warned that it was dangerous to drive through these remote parts at night, unprepared especially in a vehicle on its last leg. I myself do travel a lot and I would call it lunacy. Believe me I know. But Peter Falconio and Joanne Lees were on the last leg of their big Outback adventure and, it seems that aborting the trip was not part of the agenda.

According to Joanne Lees, at about 8.00pm, and ten km north of Barrow Creek, a man driving a four-wheel drive pulled level with the Kombi and indicated that there was something wrong with the back of the vehicle. Apparently, Joanne Lees didn't want Peter Falconio to stop. Did she know something we don't?

Peter pulled over and left the motor running—the four-wheel drive pulled up behind him. Peter went to the back of the van, Joanne shuffled over to the driver's seat. She could hear the men talking about sparks coming from the exhaust. Peter knew there was a problem with backfiring—a mechanic had told him as much when he serviced the Kombi in Alice Springs hours earlier. Peter Falconio returned, grabbed his cigarettes and asked Joanne Lees to rev the motor, then went to the back to talk to that stranger. Everything seemed to be fine, but that was to be the last time Joanne Lees saw Peter Falconio—dead or alive.

***

The Vanishing of Peter Falconio

Joanne Lees heard a bang then 'the man' appeared at her window pointing a big silver gun to her head. The man managed to restrain her hands behind her back and unsuccessfully attempted to tape legs together and gag her with electrical tape. She ended up in the back of his land cruiser and somehow managed to escape, running into the bush where she remained hidden for a good five hours (according to her story). The man searched for her but eventually gave up, or so the story goes according to her. (You will find this in the transcript of the Appeal).

On the same night truckie Vince Millar was travelling south on the Stuart Highway heading for home in Alice Springs when he got a call from his boss to return to Darwin. His co-driver Rodney Adams was asleep in the cabin of the road train—a beast of a vehicle. Around thirty minutes after midnight, Vince saw something he will never forget.

He saw in the distance the headlights of a vehicle making strange manoeuvres. Minute before arriving at the alleged crime scene then he saw two men pushing a third one (the jelly man) into a small Japanese car and by the time he arrived at the alleged crime scene he saw the car passing him at high-speed heading north towards Darwin with the three men on board. Within minute, he saw a distraught woman in shorts and a light T-shirt coming out of the bush onto the road flagging him down.

Travelling at about 85 km/h Vince reported that it took him some distance to pull the rig to a halt.

At first, he thought he'd run over the woman and as he searched under the trailers with his flash light he expected to see body parts. But instead, he saw the young woman. "Eh, come here" he said. Joanne Lees flew from under the trailer and latched hold of Vince. In between sobs she told Vince a terrifying story.

Vince calmed Joanne Lees and bundled her into his rig. They spent some time searching up and down the highway for the Kombi and Peter Falconio but when she told him the man had a big silver gun Clint Eastwood type and had killed her boyfriend, he quickly decided to get the hell out of there—drove to the Barrow Creek Pub and called police.

The Vanishing of Peter Falconio

On the same day John Bradley Murdoch was seen dinning at the Red Rooster restaurant in Alice Springs, and "par un fait du hazard", call it luck or synchronicity Joanne Lees and Peter Falconio were there also but at an interval of two hours (Ref: Andrew Fraser)

This is how the story starts but ending with the condemnation for life with a 28 years non-parole of a man for the murder of Peter Falconio. This was an easy case Your Honour: Guilty!

The trial by Jury began on October 18, 2005 in the Darwin branch of the Northern Territory Supreme Court, where Bradley John Murdoch from Western Australia was tried for the murder of Peter Falconio and the abduction of Joanne Lees. The trial concluded on December 13 with the conviction of Murdoch on all counts. He was sentenced to life imprisonment with a minimum non-parole period of 28 years –conditional upon Murdoch revealing where he had buried Peter Falconio's dead body. Given that Murdoch had maintained his innocence from Day One it is likely that he will die in prison.

On December 12, 2006 Murdoch appealed against his conviction and his sentence. On 10 January 2007, the Northern Territory Court of Criminal Appeal dismissed his appeal.

Murdoch applied for Special Leave to appeal to the High Court of Australia. On 21 June 2007, the High Court refused to grant Special Leave. Under the Australian judicial system Murdoch has now exhausted all opportunities to appeal.

Even his request to attend his mother's funeral was denied.

From the moment the incident became public the press was all over it. Another backpacker murder in Australia attracted international press particularly from the UK. Hundreds of journalists descended on the Northern Territory.

Like the Azaria Chamberlain case, the disappearance of Peter Falconio became one of the most controversial cases in Australian legal history. Peter Falconio's dead body has not been found.

The Vanishing of Peter Falconio

Outback murders are the stuff of horror stories. Innocent young tourists travelling through a vast alien landscape set upon by a lunatic no-one to help. Wolf Creek [the movie] is said to be based in part on the Peter Falconio case is perhaps the most known.

From the heart of the Australian outback, the inside story of the terrifying murder that shocked the world:

- Did the attack even happen?
- What really happened on that night in the outback?
- Did the police get the wrong man?
- Is there more to this story?
- Contaminated evidence?
- Identification?

Over the next few weeks every second person I spoke to had seen the program. Some were intrigued, some dismissed it as a media beat-up, but many, like me, were furious at the possibility that an innocent man has already been in prison for so many years. It did happen before.

As I began researching the literature I became increasingly concerned to learn more about the inconsistencies the TV program had identified. The case did not come to trial until four years after the alleged events.

The case should have relied on real evidence and identification. Both of which were not cleverly challenged, even not challenged at all. It became the subject of two appeals.

There was no Dead Body found and no eyewitness to the actual alleged murder/killing, only Joanne Lees the accuser. However, Joanne Lees never saw the accused killing her boyfriend, she never saw the body drop on the ground even being metres away from Falconio while speaking to the accused.

- No weapon or spent bullet cartridges had been found.
- There were witnesses who claimed to have seen Peter Falconio alive a week after his alleged shooting.
- The reliability of the DNA evidence was [NOT] challenged. It cannot be explained, therefore it is very suspicious and doesn't comply to the rule beyond reasonable doubt

The Vanishing of Peter Falconio

- Statements from reliable witnesses were ignored –dismissed – and ridiculed.
- By the time the case came to trial witness statements changed, mostly by witnesses deeply involve but the main one is undeniably Joanne Lees who believed that she is the only authority because she was there.
- The truth –integrity of forensic evidence was not properly challenged.
- Conflicting evidence upon which the whole trial was based etc.

The Vanishing of Peter Falconio

2 - Some People Are Making a Lot of Noise

Is/was Murdock really a bad boy and a murderer?

Well, knowing the man is not what we could say a good role model being a drug dealer, his accuser Joanne Lees, the only witness is also a drug user and so is/was Peter Falconio the man she said she care so much about. Why is it that some people are now making a lot of noise? Is it because people realised after all that time that the trial was in fact not a fair trial, but a trial by media conducted by I believe a misleading Judge followed by a Prosecution surfing on the same wave.

Is there new information now coming to the surface, information which may have been purposely dismissed or unknown at the trial, mostly by the Jury who was kept in the dark?

Yes, right now, on ATN 7 Television, some people are making a lot of noise. The case is somehow back on the agenda, people like me will watch the show and ATN 7 will make more money. Nothing wrong with that, thanks to Victor Susman and Andrew Frazer, ex-Defence Lawyer who seems to play a big part during the whole show, simply because like me, he believes Murdoch is and could [NOT] have been the murderer.

The paramount thing which has not yet been achieved at the time of the trial was to tell the Jury the truth. Most of the important facts were ignored, dismissed or kicked under the table.

I feel we have been, [us] the masses, the media, the photographers, the journalists, we all have been interfering with the case when it first hit the news, like the Azaria Chamberlain case in the 80s. Because of the immense publicity Bradley John Murdoch had [no] chance to have a fair trial. He was guilty even before entering the courthouse. The officials could not afford a second Azaria Chamberlain Case… Bad for business and the officials – police –judges –prosecution –experts –tourism industry –the economy –our trust and faith in our judiciary system etc.

People like blood. Some of us thrive on people's misfortune, we all seem to have the answer when in fact we know absolutely nothing. We constantly assume.

The Vanishing of Peter Falconio

A murder case if well published and advertised before a trial is always under the influence of the masses and the publicity always works against the accused...always.

Murdoch didn't get a fair trial. Presumption of innocence was ignored. It is a success story for the ones profiting from it and they were man - like Joanne Lees as you will discover.

It seems that Murdoch's accuser Joanne Lees did just that! Why is that Murdoch' accuser Joanne Lees did just that! Why is that?

At the time of the alleged offence everybody was talking about it, it was real big news. Rumours and assumptions were running faster than the bullet train. True news, fake news, the media was interfering, manipulating the whole system. Our faith in the justice system had been put to the test. "*In Good Faith*" was no more, nobody seemed to care as long as it sells. Gosh why are people so complaisant and so gullible?

We should all feel guilty for being the participants, but we don't until it happens to us.

Remember The Azaria Chamberlain case in 1980? Well, Lindy Chamberlain was crucified from day one by people who knew nothing about the bush –the outback –the dingoes, and Australia and much more. She was innocent but found guilty from the first hour of the morning. She spent some years in jail. It was a total injustice, a miscarriage of justice, a total failure of our judiciary system, she lost everything, thanks to the media, television, newspapers and all the journalists and the ones who knew nothing about Australia, and DINGOES.

The alleged murder case of Peter Falconio seems to be no different. I myself and others believe the man is innocent, NOT because I say so, but because there are too many things wrong and suspicious with the case and the evidence presented as true facts. I feel a culprit, a scapegoat had to be found regardless of the lack of evidence beyond reasonable doubt. If there was no culprit, one had to be found, and I believe that is what took place. We need and must understand that: A scapegoat had to be found, it had to be Murdoch.

The Vanishing of Peter Falconio

Beyond a reasonable doubt is the highest standard of proof that must be met in any trial.

The Vanishing of Peter Falconio

3 - "There Is Nothing More Deceptive Than an Obvious Fact"

(Sir Arthur Conan Doyle)

The obvious fact in my personal opinion is the total lack of proven facts indicating beyond reasonable doubt that a crime was committed and also the fact that it was more like a 'satisfaction' that the accused was more likely guilty than not. The obvious fact is evidence beyond reasonable doubt that cannot be argued because it is The Proof. It is evidence that nobody can deny therefore it is THE PROOF. Two plus two equals four in my world. Try proving me wrong!

The most difficult evidence to challenge in the case is the DNA evidence about the test results and how the experts came to such conclusion not even knowing where a small bloodstain found on the back of Lees 'T-shirt come from. Nobody can challenge the test results unless working for the laboratory and even so if the evidence is suspicious or corrupted, the only person who may come to the rescue is a whistle blower…This is what's happening lately with Government labs in Queensland and most probably in other states.

And also, why did police use Murdoch's brother (Gary) DNA after Murdoch was questioned by Western Australia police earlier in the peace then released after accepting his alibi, alibi which later on was classified information not to be released. What was so secretive about his alibi? (You will read about this later on).

We need real proofs beyond reasonable doubt

It is like having to return an item to a shop because the item is faulty. The first question the salesman or woman will ask you is:

"Do you have your receipt Sir?...

Oh, I am sorry I lost it".

Well, you know the answer! Unless you have the receipt, you cannot prove anything. The receipt is the absolute proof.

"This is what really happened."

These were the Prosecution's words? The absence of proven facts? The Prosecution has constantly assumed things that should have never been taken seriously as facts. The doubt is constantly present, every single evidence put forward by the Prosecution is doubtful.... WE DON'T KNOW. At times when reading the amount of data, it felt like watching a play on Broadway, but the most distressing result was the guilty verdict. Evidence [?], what evidence, including the DNA trump card put forward of course by the Prosecution, even if it had been tampered with.

It is the agenda, [Murdoch must be found guilty]? When no evidence indicates that a crime was committed beyond any reasonable doubt...On the contrary.

The first example that comes to mind are words like:
This is what really happened

Addressing someone using the words **THIS IS** what really happened is intended to deceive and influence.

This is what really happened means what it means: It did take place. But is that a true fact when there is no dead body –when Joanne Lees is/was the only witness knowing that she even didn't witness the shooting of her boyfriend when she was only couple of metres away from him and the alleged killer. Sorry to say but the Prosecution was not a witness, the Prosecution was not at the alleged crime scene at the time (nor was the Defence and the Judge). The only witness present at the alleged crime scene was Joanne Lees the accuser. Yes, she was there because she was rescued there so to speak by the road train driver Vince Millar. But didn't actually saw her boyfriend dropping dead nearly at her feet (she heard the sound from an exhaust or a shotgun) she didn't see Falconio drop dead between the two cars (the Kombi and the Cruiser). She was metres away from the Cruiser herself being in the Kombi sitting behind the wheel. So please, let's be fair.

The correct words should/could have been: This is what may have happened. It is only the Prosecution's words claiming facts that cannot be proven beyond reasonable doubt. The Prosecution was not a detective, was not there to witness, was not at the alleged crime scene etc. This is not beyond reasonable doubt. The Prosecution could have said: I think this is what happened. Saying I think has a different meaning altogether, but even so, it would have sent a message of doubt (not sure, not knowing). The

The Vanishing of Peter Falconio

Prosecution I feel was a bully! Lawyers cannot use these words when not knowing or assuming. "This is what really happened", means what it means: It did happen, it took place. The Prosecution was not a witness. Lawyers should know better. Justice –truth –integrity must be understood.

Having reflected on this, can you imagine what went on during the trial…I can't. Unfortunately, there is more to come.

The trial of John Bradley Murdoch could be seen as a farce but definitely not a fair trial. Bradley John Murdoch never received a fair trial.

4 - Think!

A long time ago I read somewhere that in all offices and factories of IBM (International Business Machines 1924) signs were on display that read: THINK. I feel this could well be appropriate to what I am trying to solve –the innocence of Bradley John Murdoch.

***

SO G'DAY *"MES AMIS"*…THINK and please pay attention this Aussie alleged crime caused a lot of ink to flow…. It is twisted and frustrating.

***

Bradley John Murdoch was accused and convicted of the alleged murder of Peter Falconio on the night of the 14th of July 2001 at Barrow Creek in Northern Territory Australia four years after the alleged event, on the accusations and claims of Joanne Lees his girlfriend who described her attacker on the 15th of July 2001 the morning after the alleged offence, confirmed by police report but giving a different description of her attacker later on and most probably after seeing a photograph of her attacker published in newspapers when she was in Sicily and which was well advertised regarding a rape case involving Murdoch, who was found not guilty on all charges. (That was already the beginning!)

Yes, I know, I have said it, sent to life imprisonment with a 28 years non-parole. People need to understand what life in prison means and does to you and your loved ones if you were in the same situation and innocent. How would you feel?

There will be many repetitions about facts –time –locations –people etc. They are necessary for the comprehension of this incredible "farce" Please don't forget a man's life depend on it. We need to check –double check –triple check…The German way of thinking.

The Vanishing of Peter Falconio

5 - How I Got Interested in The Case

I have been living in Australia for 56 years. In 1970 I travelled extensively, went all around the continent for nine months following the coastline then travelling inland with my girlfriend at that time, in my Brand-New Renault 10 costing me $3,500 bought in William Street Sydney pulling a box trailer which I bought after a lottery win of $200 in the Sydney Opera House lottery…Times have changed. The trailer was carrying all the junk we didn't need.

I have been a full-time prospector for now over twenty-five years. I am an amateur photographer, chef by trade and for the last nearly ten years I have tried my hands at writing. My first book written with my co-writer and friend Jennifer Sinclair, *"38 Specks."* The proposition was released on the 8th of March 2021 by a very respectable and reputable Australian publisher: Ginninderra Press of South Australia.

Being a chef (a good one of course) and a prospector (not a fossicker) I am a very good observer. To compliment this quality, I am also a good judge of character. I don't get influenced by people very often. I always seek advice when needed. I have a mind of my own, my mind belongs to me. I always pursue whatever project I am involved with, and I always ask too many questions…However with caution!

I know the bush and the outback. For the last 45 years I went on many road trips for work but also for pleasure. I am a Land Cruiser man. I have always been travelling solo most of the time.

I know what the roads or tracks are like; very tough treacherous and extremely dangerous at night, Australia is a tough and rough continent.

In 2017 and 2018 I travelled the Tanami twice. I spent three days at Wolfe Creek Crater (it's Wolfe for the Crater but Wolf for the movie). Corrugations are a nightmare, so is the bulldust, the sharp rocks, the potholes, the high grass like spinifex, the wildlife like kangaroos, emus, boars, sheep, stock and even wild camels. You can't get fuel at night you're facing punctures at any time with sharp rocks. Because of the corrugations one needs to drop the tyre pressure by half, down to 10/15 pound per square inch in my case.

Road trains have normally a tyre pressure up to 95 lb /square inch which they have to drop to 50 or 45…ASK ANY TRUCKIES. It's a really nightmare even worse if you break down as there is no one to help. Hardly any network for mobile phone if you know what I mean. In other words, it is not life threatening if you are well prepared but it is nonetheless very challenging.

On my way back from Halls Creek I went across Australia via the Plenty Hwy all the way to North Queensland. I also drove on the Sandover, the Oodnadatta track, the Birdsville track many times, the French line and many more… I can assure you that in 56 years I travelled more than anybody I know.

In June 2018 I had left Canberra on the 1st of May heading to Adelaide where I stayed three days at Jennifer and her husband Mario. From there I drove solo all the way to Darwin following the iconic train "The Ghan" driving 3,000 km [NOT] on the Stuart Hwy but on the dirt track that runs along the railway line through a continent unknown to most of us (I have uploaded 259 video clips on you Tube of the trip that can be watched at: The Ghan with Truckasaurus 2018.

Obviously when I got to Darwin I had to turn back and I travelled on the Stuart Hwy. I stopped at Larrimah another puzzling little hamlet where nothing happens at the exception lately of the disappearance of Patrick (Paddy) Moriarty and his dog on December 2017.

Then further down the Hwy I stopped at Aileron a roadhouse 180 km from Barrow Creek the alleged crime scene.

I spent one day and one night there. The Aileron Roadhouse is 132km from Alice Springs. There I spoke to Gregory Dick the owner. After dinner I took some photos of old photographs which were on display in the room adjacent to the dining room. One attracted my attention: The reward poster – Northern territory – Barrow Creek Abduction Reward $250,000

After having done so, I went to the bar and spoke to Gregory telling him that the poster was interesting and added "I always felt something was wrong about the case. I found strange that the woman escaped but I am amazed that the dog didn't find her"

His answer came as a shock "Mate, he is alive and doing well"

I replied, "What do you mean?"

"Well, she told a big lie at the trial, she denied being here just hours before the alleged offence. Me and my staff we remember them very well, we served them food, even my manager spoke to them… Some drug business, some drug lords……"

From that moment I got interested, but it took me some time to get going and do something about it. Since that day, I among all people believe that Bradley John Murdoch is innocent. People are screaming for the truth to come out of the woodwork, people are questioning. His trial was not a fair trial, that's the least I can say. It was definitely a BIG FARCE. We must fight for his release, a retrial –a new appeal –even a pardon must take place as new evidence are popping up (the reason for this book): Justice must be done.

How can we make it happen? I don't really know but I like to believe in one of my favourite Idiom; What goes up must come down. I trust that, [IF] all honest and intelligent people of this country get together and fight this Evil thing, our small and combined effort and tenacity should be influential. I believe when public opinion starts questioning, things will start moving in the right direction…We should win. The truth and justice must and will prevail. An innocent man cannot spend his entire life in prison for a crime he has not committed.

6 - This Book…

- Is for me and others to understand why the trial of Bradley John Murdoch received a guilty verdict on all charges in 2005 four years after the alleged crime,
- Is also an attempt to finding if an alleged crime was committed

I must admit, the majority of us think that we, including the jurors do understand how criminal laws work, but truly we know very little about these things. We always assume even if we know nothing about a case. I know there are more honest than dishonest people, but what do you do when the system is corrupt?

We are definitely influenced by publicity: social media –newspapers – television –talkback radio –even our friends and peers etc.

This book reflects also my views and opinions. I am entitled to such views and opinions as long as they are not defamatory. I am only trying to understand the reason behind the final decision: Guilty on all charges. I believe the received verdict was inappropriate knowing the trial was pre-set in very turbulent waters. As Keith Noble wrote in Find Falconio Dead or Alive:"

- *"Northern Territory officials have done everything they can to denigrate all verbal and written statements about Falconio which do not conform with the official narrative "*

It concerns all people involved, all the unfounded facts described as evidence and misleading information, definitely the lack of evidence, the dismissed claims from genuine witnesses but most importantly the end result and the unanimous verdict of guilt when there are I believe absolutely no proven facts, no evidence beyond reasonable doubt that a crime was committed even if the DNA test results showed otherwise. The test results were not challenged but the time will come proving otherwise.

The Vanishing of Peter Falconio

7 - Warning

*Note

I started writing this book unaware of the messy case. Messy is a better description than complicated because the case is straight-forward: Was Murdoch at the alleged crime scene? The case is based entirely on what information I could find on the internet and upon the declarations and claims by Joanne Lees "THE ONLY WITNESS" and the Prosecution bewildering attitude.

- That on the 14th of July 2001 Bradley John Murdoch was the man who stopped Joanne Lees and her boyfriend Peter Falconio north of Barrow Creek.
- That after stopping them, Murdoch (according to Lees and the Prosecution) shot Peter Falconio in a pre-meditated way and then abducted Joanne Lees.
- That after escaping her attacker by hiding in the bush for around five hours on a cold winter night, she was rescued (rescued from what I don't know) by the road train driver Vince Millar between midnight and 00:30 on the 15th of July.
- She had to be rescued there for people to believe that the alleged offence truly took place.

Four years after the alleged crime in 2005 Lees identified and claimed for the second time that the man seen on a CCTV film at a truck stop in Alice Springs was Bradley John Murdoch when in fact this second description and identification is the opposite of her first description and identification of the man given to police on the morning after the alleged crime at Barrow Creek.

You must understand that, as I was writing along, more information started to fall into my lap in an unexpected way.

***

The Vanishing of Peter Falconio

The story is not about a crime but an alleged crime. It is about the vanishing of Peter Falconio…. Nothing else, he just disappeared in thin air like a puff of smoke… That is the Sixty-Four-Dollar question.

The Dead Body has never been found or recovered therefore it cannot be proven beyond reasonable doubt that a crime had been committed.

The only witness is Joanne Lees "THE ACCUSER simply because she was at the alleged crime scene. She didn't actually witness the killing of her boyfriend when in fact Peter Falconio and the alleged accused killer were metres away from her speaking to each other (according to her story). I find this extremely remarkable (repeat I know).

Nothing beyond reasonable doubt proving that a crime had been committed. NO proofs beyond reasonable doubt that Bradley John Murdoch was at the alleged crime scene at the time.

It is very difficult to comprehend. But yes, I know you will point out at the DNA card or proof (according to the Prosecution). In fact, for the last twelve months, things don't seem to be going well for some Government Laboratories involve in the DNA business here in Australia and abroad (extreme corruption/lies etc.). Just in the state of Queensland 20,000 cases have to be reviewed because of the corruption involving DNA. This will be discussed further on.

The Vanishing of Peter Falconio

8 - Source of My Information

Most of my information comes from:

- The book by Joanne Lees No Turning Back published 2006
- The book by Dean Mildren (retired Judge) AM RFD QC; R v Murdoch: The Falconio Case, A Study in Identification and Circumstantial Evidence.
- Books/papers by Dr Moles which are mainly in the areas of miscarriages of Justice
- The book by Robin Bowles Dead Centre 2022.
- The book by Keith Noble: Find Falconio Dead or Alive.
- The book by Roger Maynard: Where's Peter 2005
- The transcript of the appeal 2007 NTCCA1 Murdoch v The Queen 10 Jan 2007
- The transcript 2005 NTSC76 –2005 NTSC77 –2005 NTSC78
- The book by Richard Shears: Bloodstain.
- The book by Sue Williams: And then the Darkness.
- From the internet –newspapers like Daily Mail etc.
- Some are from brief telephone conversations with Gregory Dick the owner of Aileron Roadhouse and emails and text messages with Andrew Frazer and victor Susman.
- Jeremy Gans
- Robert Watts
- Also;

From watching the first show 18 July 2020, when Seven News, aired the first of the four- part true-crime series *Murder in the Outback:*

The Falconio and Lees mystery, and presented by former high profile criminal defence lawyer Andrew Fraser and his longtime mate, TV producer, Victor Susman. It promised a comprehensive re-investigation of the case against Bradley John Murdoch, found guilty in 2005 of the murder of British backpacker Peter Falconio on a lonely stretch of the Stuart Highway in 2001 (Murder in the outback).

The Vanishing of Peter Falconio

Why is it that after 20 years police is asking for anybody having information about the disappearance of Falconio to please, come forward? Don't you find this strange? Was a mistake made somewhere along the way? Is it a replay of The Azaria Chamberlain Case or is it related to drugs and drug lords. After all, as you will find out, James Hepi the ex-business partner of Murdoch in the drug business, one of the witnesses at the trial testified against Murdoch. He testified against Murdoch saying that he knew Murdoch did it and giving police some cigarettes butts apparently from cigarettes smoked by Murdoch in an attempt (most probably) to frame Murdoch hoping to eliminate his partner and competitor from the lucrative drug business by killing two birds with one stone.

How can anyone involved in selling drugs would have testified against his ex-partners if it's not for his own benefit or perhaps hoping to become a police informer? Perhaps he was already an informer [?] Since Murdoch's incarceration, James Hepi must have had a good run, sales must have improved exponentially…But that is me thinking! Would you trust such witness?

***

In the Supreme Court of the Northern Territory Justice Martin Brian sentenced Murdoch to life imprisonment with a 28 years non-parole period – conditional upon Murdoch revealing where he had buried Falconio's body. Given that Murdoch has maintained his innocence from day one, it is likely that he will die in prison.

The documentary promised 'powerful first-hand accounts of those closest to the case', with exclusive access to the never-before-seen original defence case documents and startling information in the police files, that was never shown to the jury. The first two episodes attracted about 1.6 million viewers.

In 2009 after two appeals had failed, Murdoch approached Fraser to re-evaluate his case and see if there was any hope of further appeal. Fraser had, in his own words, "defended every type of crook you could imagine—drug barons, businessmen and murderers."

He'd also had his own experience as a felon spending years in prison for drug offences. In

2011 Andrew Fraser was confident that Murdoch should get a retrial, if not a pardon. He told the media: "It's the greatest legal railroading in this country since Lindy Chamberlain". Fraser and his longtime mate Victor Susman have been working on the case ever since.

The Vanishing of Peter Falconio

9 - What We Need to Understand

In a criminal cases and trials, six definitions need to be understood, and they are:

- 1- Beyond Reasonable Doubt;
- 2- Circumstantial evidence;
- 3- Unanimous verdict;
- 4- Majority verdict;
- 5- Hung verdict; and
- 6- Who has the right of veto?

1a- Beyond reasonable doubt

In a criminal case, the prosecution bears the burden of proving that the defendant is guilty beyond all reasonable doubt. This means that the prosecution must convince the jury that there is no other reasonable explanation that can come from the evidence presented at trial.

2a- Circumstantial evidence

Circumstantial evidence is indirect evidence that does not, on its face, prove a fact in issue but gives rise to a logical inference that the fact exists. Circumstantial evidence requires drawing additional reasonable inferences in order to support the claim.

3a- Unanimous verdict:

The jury are asked by the judge to reach a unanimous verdict - that means, they should all agree on whether the defendant is 'guilty' or 'not guilty'. If they can't do that after carefully considering and discussing the evidence, the judge can allow them to reach a majority verdict of at least ten people.

4a- Majority verdict:

'Majority verdict' is defined as: a verdict agreed to by 11 jurors where the jury consists of 12 persons, or a verdict agreed to by ten jurors where the jury consists of 11 persons.'

5a- Hung verdict:

If the answer to that enquiry is [no], then likely, the judge will discharge the jury on the basis they could not reach a verdict, unanimously or by majority. The result is what is called a 'hung jury'

As a result:

A hung jury, also called a deadlocked jury, is a judicial jury that cannot agree upon a verdict after extended deliberation and is unable to reach the required unanimity or supermajority. Hung juries usually result in the case being tried again.

This situation can occur only in common law legal systems, because civil law systems either do not use juries at all or provide that the defendant is immediately acquitted if the majority or supermajority required for conviction is not reached during a single, solemn vote.

(Wikipedia)

6a-The meaning of VETO

To refuse to admit or approve. The judge is the ultimate decision maker. He has the right of Veto meaning he has the right to overturn a jury's verdict if there is insufficient evidence to support the verdict.

The Vanishing of Peter Falconio

10 - What Do We Know? [1]

When I started this book, beside the preliminaries and the introduction, I wanted first to discuss the DNA trump card used by the Prosecution. The DNA trump card as I call it, is the only evidence with no real proofs as nobody knows where the small bloodstain found on the back of the accuser's T-shirt came from which has contributed to the unanimous received guilty verdict. Nothing could have done it better.... But there is more to it regarding the Jury...The book is only starting.

- However, the case still needs to be challenged again and investigated. It is a very suspicious and murky area;
- Where did the bloodstain found only on the back of Joanne Lees 'T-shirt come from? and
- <u>Why was no DNA found on Lees when Murdoch was desperately trying to restraint her feet or legs? Closed contact took place unless I am stupid!</u>

Please give me some answers if you can. Impossible to be challenged by anyone simply because you haven't got the formula or the recipe use for the fabrication, just like the Covid 19 vaccine or Coca-Cola, nobody knows what's in it.

The bloodstain patch on Lees T-Shirt was found on the back, a spot where it would be so unlikely to be found. Nobody knows how it got there [?] The testing for DNA on the steering wheel –the gear stick –on the cuffs taken in a paper bag by police etc. is more than suspicious. Anyone can smell a rat miles away –corruption by excellence if you ask me.

I like to use one of my favourite quote by Gary G.Kohls MD. I found it very relevant to the case; it goes like this:

"What good fortune for those in power that people do not think...It gives us a very special, secret pleasure to see how unaware the people around us are of what is really happening...."

Please take time to reflect on this. THEY must think that we are all stupid!

The Vanishing of Peter Falconio

Having said that, to successfully arrive at a conclusion beyond reasonable doubt, we need to challenge every single word spoken and written. It cannot be: Maybe –perhaps –possibly –similar –nearly identical –if you are satisfied –please ignore etc. To achieve that we need to establish beyond reasonable doubt; what we know –and what we don't. Among what we know –and what we don't, we should be able to find some obvious facts.

It is a long list. What we know is mostly from Joanne Lees 'own story –the Prosecution –from Murdoch –the police –the investigators –the experts – articles from the press –books written about the case –transcripts –but and unfortunately not much from the Defence team.

It is a part of the brainstorm of things I had to analyse.

- Inconsistencies in witness evidence
- Circumstantial evidence
- The effect of prejudicial and adverse publicity
- The right to a fair trial and fair hearing
- The presumption of innocence
- The role of the DNA trump card
- The no dead body
- The role of the jury –judge –and counsel –witnesses etc.
- Books –blogs – TV series – and many non-sense stories you will find on the internet and elsewhere.

The Vanishing of Peter Falconio

11 - What We Know What We Don't [2]
with comments

Following the journey and steps of our two holiday makers not forgetting Murdoch:

Did a crime really take place?

To prove anything in life like in mathematics one needs facts to come up with "The Proof". I know it's a long list. It is somehow the introduction to the story. Reading along you will get familiarised with the case. You will refer to it often. Don't forget that I made it my mission to clear an innocent man. If you were Bradley Murdoch, wouldn't you be pleased to know someone is desperately trying to get you free? Yes, this list is necessary.

1. Chief Justice Brian Ross Martin was the trial Judge
2. Chief Justice Martin's daughter, Joanna Martin was in a relationship with a juror who sat on Murdoch's trial – a boy was born to the couple five months after the trial (Robin Bowles author; Dead Centre). As it takes nine months from conception to birth, I let you do the calculation. Bowles spent over 60 hours interviewing the accused.
3. Rex Wild QC was the Prosecutor
4. Grant Algie was the Defence lawyer
5. Peter Falconio is/was the alleged victim
6. Joanne Lees Falconio's girlfriend is/was the only witness at the alleged crime scene simply for the fact that she was rescued there (from what we don't know [?]).
7. Joanne Lees did not see the actual killing of her boyfriend even being metres away from both men (the accused and boyfriend)
8. All she claimed is/was hearing a bang but didn't see her boyfriend dropping dead on the ground near her.
9. The accused killer Bradley John Murdoch and the accuser Joanne Lees and boyfriend Peter Falconio were apparently seen at a restaurant hour at different time in Alice Springs on the 14th of July 2001

10. We know at what time Murdoch was at the restaurant according to his claim in the transcript but, the time for Lees and Falconio is unknown.
11. Andrew Fraser ex-convicted Lawyer claimed the time apart was two hours [?]
12. Murdoch claimed that yes, he went to the restaurant and gave the time
13. The accused is a drug dealer –the accuser is a drug user – Falconio the alleged victim is/was [?] a drug user.
14. Joanne Lees and Peter Falconio left Alice Springs towards Barrow Creek on the 14th of July 2001 but the time is unknown.
15. According to Sue William (author) they departed Alice Springs around 5.00pm on the 14th (need proofs). How did she arrive to such conclusion [?]
16. According to the Prosecution, Murdoch felt that Lees and Falconio were spying on him, (of course Lees agreed) so HE followed them until reaching Barrow Creek where the alleged crime took place (hard to believe).
17. Alice Springs to Ti Tree is 195km. Leaving at 5.00pm to be in Ti Tree at 6.10pm (70 minutes) watching the sunset requires a speed of 195km ÷ 70 = 2.78km/per minute x 60 = 167kmh. It is not possible
18. We know they had to travel from Alice to Aileron 134km –then Aileron to Ti Tree 62 km –then Ti Tree to Barrow Creek 119km
19. According to Sue Williams;" *Lees fails to state the time when she, and allegedly Falconio, left Alice Springs. But in And then the darkness; 2006: p. 98, Sue Williams says:*

"[T]hey realised it was nearly 4 pm. They both climbed into the Kombi and raced back to the caravan park to have a final shower before they left. Then they drove to the chicken fast food *chain Red Rooster.... Peter bought pizza and Joanne picked at his leftovers." (added emphasis)*

20. *So according to Williams, they drove from Blatherskite to Stuart Park where they showered without paying. Then they drove to Red Rooster where they sat down to eat.*

That would have taken until c.5 pm/17:00. Then, according to the literature, Lees drove to Ti Tree, a distance of 195 kilometres, where she viewed the sunset

21. The first stop was at Aileron roadhouse where Joanne Lees and Peter Falconio stopped, arriving at 3.30pm departing at 4.30pm according to the owner and his staff, five people in all.
22. They were at the roadhouse according to Gregory Dick the owner and four members of his staff including the manager. They were served food and drinks while looking at brochures as if they were planning a holiday trip.
23. While at Aileron according to the manager and staff, Lees went out and spoke to a man for a short time near the fuel pump.
24. Again, according to the staff, they knew each other. Each member of the staff testified that the man had no resemblance to Murdoch but Lees and the man knew each other.
25. Again, according to the staff, the man looked more likely Chris Malouf. (Malouf will be introduced in the course of the book further on). He also owns a Land Cruiser.
26. None of the staff members saw the man leave nor they saw Lees and Falconio (both) getting into the Kombi and drive off towards Ti Tree.
27. Gregory Dick testified at the trial but his declaration was ignored and dismissed.
28. Joanne Lees always denied having stopped at Aileron…Up until the trial in 2005 (I wonder why?).
29. Gregory Dick and his staff remembered Lees very well being…She is/was a "Good Looking Sheila" (their words).

The Vanishing of Peter Falconio

30. 62 km further on at Ti Tree Lees was seen watching the sunset [alone] at 6.10pm but we truly don't know at what time she and Falconio arrived at Ti Tree (there is a lack of compatibility regarding the unknown time of arrival and the time (6.10pm), because we don't know the departure time from Alice.
31. According to a witness Joanne Lees was alone but Lees denied the fact claiming Falconio was with her.
32. Questioned by police detective Kerr, Lees unfortunately gave two [2] wrong answers. As a result, the witness declaration (apparently) prevailed.
33. Lees departed Ti Tree at 6.30pm aiming for Barrow Creek. Alone or with Falconio makes no difference as explained further on.
34. Joanne Lees arrival time at Barrow Creek is not known but it can be calculated if you believe her story.
35. Leaving Aileron at 4.30pm driving at 60kmh takes one hour (60minutes) therefore arriving at Ti Tree at 5.30pm (14th).
36. Leaving Aileron at 4.30pm driving at 80kmh takes 45 minutes, therefore arriving at Ti Tree at 5.15pm (14th).
37. Arriving at 5.15pm till Lees watching the sunset at 6.10pm the time difference is 55 minutes and one must wonder what did Lees do during those 40 minutes and where was Falconio?
38. Arriving at 5.15pm the time difference is 55minutes. Ask yourself the same question as above]
39. At Barrow Creek the alleged accused stopped Lees and Falconio who miraculously is back in the picture.
40. The alleged killer stops Lees and Falconio at: [a] 6.30pm + two hour = 8.30pm (driving at 60kmh the distance of 119km arriving 8.30pm
41. [b] 6.30pm + 1 hour and 35minutes = 8.05pm on the 14th of July 2001(driving at 80kmh) arriving at 8.05pm
42. At Barrow Creek assuming that from the time the alleged killer stopped the Kombi, it would be fair to assume that a 15 minutes

conversation must have taken place. Meaning the killing time had to be (8.30pm + 15 minutes = 8.45pm) or (8.05 + 15 minutes = 8.20pm). So, the alleged accused must have shot Peter Falconio in cold blood at: 8.45 pm or 8.20pm. That is if Joanne Lees' story is true [?]

43. Of course, [IF] the 15 minutes conversation took place between the two men who were metres away from Joanne Lees sitting behind the Kombi's steering wheel.
44. THE TIME OF THE ALLEGED DEATH IS: 8.45pm or 8.20pm
45. As I said if the killer shot Falconio, it is/was with a big silver revolver Clint Eastwood type as claimed by Lees.
46. Then the accused abducted Lees.
47. We need to ask ourselves how long after allegedly shooting of Falconio (who must have dropped dead, still warm, meters away from the Kombi and Lees) did the killer appeared at the window of the Kombi threatening Lees with [A] big gun? Half minute –one minute –two -or less than one minute? I am asking this because….
48. From the transcript: The Queen vs Murdoch [2005] NTSC 75
49. "Opportunity to observe offender [8] page 3: "Ms Lees said in evidence at the preliminary hearing that at the time of the events it was PITCH BLACK…."
50. So, immediately after the shooting, Falconio dropped dead on the ground –then the offender goes to the Kombi threatening Lees with the Big gun and below is what he does according to the transcript
51. "The offender forced LEES over towards the passenger side of his vehicle and removed a canvas sack from under the canopy over the tray of the utility. He then placed the sack over LEES 'head and pushed her into the front passenger side of the vehicle. During the process the sack was dislodged from LEES 'head. At this time LEES observed the dog in front of the

driver's seat. LEES described the dog as being a medium sized, shorthaired, brown and white blue heeler. LEES attempted to get out of the driver's side door but was blocked by the dog. The offender forced LEES over the seats into the back of the utility."

52. This is confirmation Lees saying that she was pushed into the back of the Cruiser via a passage between the seats and the back of the Cruiser. (Toyota has never manufactured a Land Cruiser with a passage between the cabin and the back).
53. It also tells you that she gave the description of the dog as Blue Heeler. (Murdoch's dog is a Dalmatian not a Blue Heeler hey!)
54. Then according to the transcript below:
55. "The offender came to an opening in the back of the utility and stated, "Shut up and I won't shoot you." The offender then walked away…**She never saw him again**…. Relates to 51 and 52 further down.
56. Then Lees escaped and hid in the bush or scrub for five hours (her claim) until rescued by a road train driver Vince Millar and his co-driver around 0.15am on the 15th July 2001
57. Lees said that she escaped with her hands tied up. She claimed that she escaped [not] from the sides (left or right) of the Land Cruiser but from the back.
58. Murdock's Land Cruiser did not have an opening at the back (because of a cage).
59. The Land Cruiser on the CCTV film is not the accused's Cruiser. The Cruiser and the driver have never been identified by police. The Cruiser on the CCTV film has an opening at the back but there is no cage.
60. The only people who did identify the Cruiser and the driver are/were: Joanne Lees –the Prosecution –and of course our dear Mister Hepi who is no less than Murdoch's associate in the

drug business. (Mr Hepi will be introduce in due course) and the Judge who did agree.

61. Murdoch was towing a campervan trailer. The Land Cruiser on the CCTV film has no camper trailer attached. We don't even know if it was fitted with a towbar (poor photograph).

62. We don't know how long after being pushed in the Cruiser Lees escape, but it had to be before 9.00pm (calculated time) because it is the time the killer had to leave Barrow Creek to be seen at the truck-stop in Alice at 0.30am on the 15th and I don't think she would have been stupid to stay in the Cruiser when the killer moved the Kombi according to her story. I also don't think for one minute the killer would be that stupid not to check if Lees was secured after moving the Kombi…meaning nothing fits according to her story.

63. Which means the time spent by Lees in the back of the Cruiser is; a- from 8.45pm to 9.00pm = 15 minutes and b- from 8.20pm to 9.00pm = 40 minutes

64. While Lees was hiding, the alleged killer or someone else moved the Kombi [?]

65. We don't know how long after being pushed in the cruiser the alleged killer or someone else moved the Kombi [?]

66. All we know is that Lees claimed that when the offence took place it was pitch black and very cold.

67. When Lees found herself in the back of the Cruiser after being pushed in by the killer, she again confirmed that her environment or the space she was in was pitch black and very cold meaning she could not see anything at all.

68. During that time Lees claimed that the killer search for her with a torch light but no mention the dog.

69. The above contradict her claim that she never saw him again

70. But we know that according to my calculation the killer had to leave at 9.00pm to be seen in Alice at 12.30pm on the 14th or

0.30am on the 15th. It takes three hours and 30 minutes to do the drive between 95 and 100kmh for a distance of 305km.

71. So really if you do the calculation as I said above, Lees only spent:

72. [a] 15 minutes in the back of the Cruiser (9.00pm – 8.45pm =15 minutes) [b] 40 minutes in the back of the Cruiser (9.00pm – 8.20pm = 40 minutes)

73. Therefore, she had to escape before the killer left at 9.00pm. Knowing that she claimed hiding five hours on a pitch black and cold winter night doesn't fit because when rescued, Vince Millar said that she was warm and clean. The temperature on that night was between ten and 13 degrees. (I like to know how someone would feel wearing only a light T-shirt and shorts after spending five hours in a ten to 13 degrees environment, but coming out nice and warm. I imagine when the re-enactment took place police didn't ask or forced Joanne Lees to stay the full five hours in the bush, at the location as per her claim. That would be too easy hey!

74. If she escaped while the killer was moving the Kombi, it had to be between 8.20pm or 8.45 (including the 15 minutes conversation) and 9.00pm, which is not possible

75. Because [if] and when the killer came back from moving the Kombi, he would have realised without any shadow of a doubt that she was no longer in the Cruiser …Are you okay with that?

76. But remember the transcript says: **She never saw him again.**

77. So, there is definitely more than one way to understand the situation.

78. [1] She escaped while he was moving the Kombi which is not possible because she knew he had to come back, and the killer wouldn't be that stupid not to search for her but, knowing she claimed she never saw him again raises few questions.

79. [2] Lees could have escaped after the killer moved the Kombi and after the killer left the crime scene BUT she couldn't otherwise she would be still in the Cruiser hey! However, according to the judge (<u>our third witness</u>) who claimed the dead body was in the back of the Cruiser means that Lees and Falconio were both in the back of the cruiser (clapping in the background). Whichever way you look at it, NOTHING FITS.
80. TO PUT IT SIMPLY…sounds like a FAKED STORY but we will rehearse this later on.
81. According to Lees, she came out of her hiding place after five hours.
82. To be rescued by a road train between midnight on the 14th and 0.30am on the 15th of July. (Apparently around 0.15am on the 15th)
83. Just minute before being rescued by the road train, driver Vince Millar, saw two men pushing a third one into a small red Japanese car.
84. The Jury was never told about the three men at the trial.
85. The road train driver and his co-driver took Joanne Lees to Barrow Creek. From there police was called.
86. Early in the morning Lees gave the first description of her attacker.
87. Lees changed her description of the killer later and also at the trial in 2005.
88. Early on the morning the day after the alleged offence according to the transcript below:
89. Even more suspicious, when reading the transcript 2007NTCCA1 –Murdoch vs The Queen 10 January 2007
90. After the police had arrived, Ms Lees identified a standard white Toyota Land Cruiser utility with a green canvas cover as being somewhat similar to the vehicle driven by her assailant. However, she said that there were some differences. For example, in the vehicle looked at by her it was not possible to

go through from cab to the tray at the rear. The canopy also seemed to be a different colour on the inside
Also, on the morning the day after the alleged offence according to the transcript below, according to her first description police started erecting roadblocks.

91. This will be discussed in details in one chapter but knowing it was pitch black when she was in the back of the cruiser, how did she come to such conclusion (different colour of the canopy on the inside)?
92. In the meantime, at 0.30am at Alice Springs an unknown Land Cruiser was seen entering a truck stop (Shell) recorded on a CCTV camera film.
93. According to the Prosecution, Lees, and our dear Monsieur Hepi, the man on the CCTV film was definitely Murdoch the killer.
94. The man was similar to Murdoch, the Land Cruiser also was similar to Murdoch's Cruiser.

    However, only and strangely, it is only Joanne Lees -the Prosecution and Mr Hepi who could identify the mystery man and Land Cruiser (as I mentioned before)

95. Police nor anyone else could identify the man or the Cruiser. It remains a mystery!
There was no camper trailer attached to the mystery Cruiser
The Cruiser seen on the CCTV film has an opening at the back contrary to Murdoch's Cruiser which in some way had none because "the cage" is/was in the way blocking it.

96. The man on the CCTV film left the truck stop at 1.00am after refuelling aiming for an unknown destination. I said unknown because if we don't know who he is (never been identified), it's impossible to tell where he was going. Not knowing the identity of

the man and his Cruiser, it is impossible to know of his destination. (Just trying to prove my point again))

97. Murdoch claimed that on the 14th of July before noon he refuelled at a BP Service Station in Alice Springs (transcript).

98. Murdoch claimed that at 3.30pm on the 14th of July he was at the turn off at the start of the Tanami 20km north of Alice Springs.

99. Murdoch claimed that at the time of the alleged offence he was near Yuendumu.

100. Murdoch claimed that between midnight and 1.00am on the 15th of July he was near the Granites on the Tanami (the Granite mine).

101. Murdoch was seen refuelling at Fitzroy Crossing in Western Australia around 8.00pm Northern Territory time on the 15th 1,412km away by Mr Jamieson

The real time of the real death is unknown (no dead body)

102. Murdoch's footprints were no found, nothing belonging to him was found.

103. Peter Falconio's footprints were never identified at the alleged crime scene.

104. Joanne Lees had a lover named Nick who was in Australia at the time of the alleged crime.

105. The only identified footprint found at the alleged crime scene belongs to Joanne Lees

106. Another four unidentified footprints were found according to the experts/investigators.

107. The only items found at the crime scene three months later were some black tape and a tube of lip gloss. Some blood apparently a mixture of animal blood and human blood was found under a small mound

of dirt which looked like a decoy because it was too obvious like a pimple on your nose.

108. Gregory Dick (owner of Aileron Roadhouse) testified at the trial but his claim was dismissed.

109. Vince Millar (road train driver) was questioned by police on the morning after the alleged event. He signed his first declaration at that time.

110. From his first signed declaration two pages went missing or purposely destroyed [?]

111. A new declaration was drafted by police but Vince Millar refused to sign it (didn't comply with his first declaration).

112. When Vince Millar rescued Lees, he found her nice and warm, clean and unbruised.

113. On the morning the day after the alleged offence and according to the transcript of the appeal (also mention on p 119) below:

114. After the police had arrived Ms Lees identified a standard white Toyota Land Cruiser utility with a green canvas cover as being somewhat similar to the vehicle driven by her assailant. However, she said that there were some differences. For example, in the vehicle looked at by her it was not possible to go through from cab to the tray at the rear. The canopy also seemed to be a different colour on the inside

115. We know that, the (PARKED) standard white Toyota Land Cruiser was NOT LIKE the offender's Cruiser because the offender's Cruiser HAD A COMMUNICATION between the cabin and the back (according to Lees).

116. Also, because the canopy of the offender's Cruiser seemed to be a different colour on the inside which is strange because she told police that when locked in the back of the Cruiser it was pitch black (sorry for being sarcastic).

117. On the morning the day after the alleged crime police arrested Chris Malouf, but police eliminated him after the scanning of the man by Lees with her eyes closed. Lees failed to recognise him as well as his Land Cruiser and after DNA test were carried out [?]

118. We don't know the meaning of: DNA tests were carried out [?].

119. DNA tests were carried out on Lees T-shirt after an alleged bloodstain was found on the most unlikely place for the bloodstain to be found and that is on the back of Lees 'T-shirt on the shoulder

120. The source of the bloodstain is unknown and has never been elucidated.

121. DNA tests were carried out on the Kombi steering wheel and the gear stick

122. The test results were not properly accurate and challenged, for reasons you will read further on. They also had been tampered.

123. The definition of "carried out" is unknown or not specifically precise in relation to Chris Malouf [?].

124. It took 28 months for the carry out test to be sent to the lab for analysis

125. Joanne Lees gave a phone call to New Zealand offsetting the time line by two hours

126. On 14 August 2002 police took a blood sample from Murdoch's brother Gary in Perth. That is 13 months after the alleged crime…Why? Don't you think that in possession of Lees' shirt for all that time THEY could have tested that small bloodstain… But NO!

127. Why getting Murdoch's brother blood sample?

128 Initially WA cops didn't interview Murdoch as a suspect.

129. Cops interviewed Murdoch and accepted his alibi but refused to reveal what it is. WHY?

130. What did they already know about Murdoch to warrant testing his brother's blood?

131. THEY didn't have Hepi statement then (It is Hepi who dobbed Murdoch)

132. 28 August 2002 Murdoch arrested for rape in South Australia, but found not guilty.

133. 24 October 2003 the samples/swabs were sent to Dr Whitaker in the UK

134. At the trial after hearing all evidence the jury retired for final deliberation as to; Guilty or not guilty.

135. After deliberation the jury couldn't come up with a YES or NOT guilty verdict. So, the judge asked the jury to go back giving them extra time to come up with a unanimous verdict. However, it looked like it was going to be a 'Hung" verdict.

136. The judge did not inform the jury that a majority verdict legal in the Northern Territory was available and that it would be accepted.

137. Joanne Lees –the Prosecution –and Mr Hepi, all three identified Murdoch and his Land Cruiser from the video footage when even police was unable to do so (no number plates BUT;

138. At the trial all the calculations trying to prove that Murdoch was the man on the CCTV footage were done assuming the man on the CCTV video was Murdoch as well as the killer who left the truck-stop at 1.00am. This was contrary to Murdoch's claims mentioned above (90 –91)

139. Nobody and I like to repeat it; NOBODY did the calculation according Murdoch's claim that he departed Alice Springs at a different time which was nearly ten hours earlier. Knowing this; who do you think was the man on the CCTV video footage?

140. In Robin Bowles's book Dead Centre who has had a good relationship with Murdoch, interviewing him so many times and who also

was at the trial all along, in her epilogue page 411 she wrote about Rex Wild (the Prosecution) who told the court in his summing up that;

141. Miss Lees's identification hadn't be central to the overwhelming case against Murdoch, which had hinged upon DNA evidence linking him to the crime. Her evidence was ancillary and additional, Mr Wild told the High Court; in our submission, there was no miscarriage of justice. High Court Justices John Heydon, Murray Gleeson and Ian Callinan agreed. Within five minutes they had dismissed the application as having insufficient prospects of success."

142. Well, we'll see about that!

143. Also on page 411/412, she wrote; another issue raised its head less than six months after Murdoch was sentenced, but before his attempts to appeal. Murdoch was asking Robin Bowles to come to Darwin as he couldn't discuss anything on the phone. Murdoch information was explosive. Put bluntly, he alleged that his judge's daughter, Joanna was in a relationship with a juror during the trial. Murdoch wanted me to confirm this rumour, brought into prison and told to a fellow inmate by a visiting social worker.

144. Readers need to know that it is an offence for people like me to know the identity of a juror. Or to attempt to discuss the trial with them, during or after…Then further on… I was more concerned about the impact such a relationship may have had on the outcome of the trial. The opportunities of "pillow talk seemed obvious and damaging."

145. Then the explosive part;

146. Joanna Martin had worked in a community legal service near the Supreme Court…Joanna's boss, an older Aboriginal woman, knew quite a bit about Joanna's friendship with Joanne Lees. This was even more disturbing news…Joanna's boss told me she'd had to reprimand Joanna on several occasions for spending too much time at the court and neglecting her workload……She spent time sitting in court with that Joanne Lees…Gave her presents. Lees wanted T-shirts to give her UK friends, so

Joanna got her some with Aboriginal designs on, from our supply…She confirmed Joanna was on maternity leave but didn't want to discuss the details. Too frightened she might lose her job….

147. After three days of research, I was able to establish the following facts:

148. Chief Justice Martin's daughter, Joanna Martin was in a relationship with a juror who sat on Murdoch's trial.

149. A boy was born to the couple, allegedly in the first week of May 2006. The trial ended on 13 December 2005. Another child, a girl, has been born since and the Chief Justice has retired.

150. NO WONDER! But further on page 413 Robin wrote;

151. A journo I tipped off sought an interview with the Chief Justice who asked for questions in advance. The journo provided them, to be told the Chief Justice knew nothing and that a relationship, [if] it existed commenced after the trial" So that was it until 2007

152. Well, I think that's enough, I recommend our readers to buy Robin's book.

153. One police officer told Robin during an adjournment, in the presence of the head of Supreme Court security that, "We know Murdoch wasn't the shooter, but he's going down for it…." page 426 of her book.

154. Finally, Joanne Lees has always claimed from day one that Peter Falconio had been shot by the accuser. However much later on when questioned by police about her lover Nick Reilly, unprepared about the question she contradicted her own claim

155. I may have forgotten a few but, for the time being. I think the list is long and explicit enough. There are more of what we know but I will deal with it during the course of this book relevant to the appropriate chapters. Now we can start working!

156. From this chapter we assumed: The calculated time of death is 8.20pm –or 8.45pm.

The Vanishing of Peter Falconio

12 - What We Need to Challenge and Prove

As you know it is necessary for the investigation to assume that a crime took place. We need to ask questions, questions that needs to be answer by YES or NO but not answers like: Perhaps –maybe –it could be –I think –I suppose – it is similar –if you are satisfied etc.

For example, it is not because they were seen at the same restaurant some hours apart that anybody can say or confirm that Murdoch is/was the man who shot her boyfriend beyond reasonable doubt…Please, I would like this to be clear and understood.

On the other hand, if I may suggest, perhaps the test results from the DNA investigation were based purely on the word commonly and often used by the Prosecution and Ms Lees and that is: Maybe **THE TEST RESULTS WERE *"SIMILAR"* TO MURDOCH'S DNA**

***

- Was John Bradley Murdoch at the alleged crime scene? [1]
- Why no footprints or anything belonging to Murdoch including his dog and his car could not be identified at the alleged crime scene? [2]
- Who owns the four unidentified footprints? [3]
- What is the time of arrival of the Kombi at Barrow Creek? Lees may well have picked up Falconio somewhere after leaving Ti Tree and arrived around 11.00pm or even 11.30pm then sat in a car to keep warm till the road train arrived? [4]
- What is the real time of alleged killing? [5]
- Who was the man seen talking to Joanne Lees at Aileron? [6]
- Where was Joanne Lees' lover at the time of the alleged offence and who is he? [7]
- Was the man seen on the CCTV film in Alice Springs really Murdoch? Was the man investigated as well as his Land Cruiser? [8]
- Did Murdoch change his appearance to commit the alleged offence according to the Prosecution? [9]

The Vanishing of Peter Falconio

- Was Joanne Lees' telephone call to New Zealand investigated? [10]
- Why is the testimony of the owner of Aileron Roadhouse and his staff dismissed and somehow ridiculed? [11]
- Who were the two men pushing a third one (jelly man) into a small Japanese car? [12]
- Who is/was the third man pushed into the Japanese car by two men? [13]
- Why did drug dealer James Hepi take cigarette butts to police? [14]
- Why did police accept the butts? [15]
- Why did police take the cuffs allegedly used by Murdoch to restrain Joanne Lees in a paper bag to Murdoch when in jail accused of rape but found not guilty on all charges? [16]
- What was Joanne Lees' first description of Murdoch given to police in 2001? [17]
- Why did Joanne Lees claim differently at the trial in [2005] four years after the alleged crime? [18]
- What is the source of the very suspicious patch of bloodstain supposedly from Murdoch found on the back of Joanne Lees T-Shirt only? [19]
- Why was the Defence team unable to challenge the DNA investigations? [20]
- Why was Joanne Lees warm and clean when rescued by the road train driver? [21]
- How long did Joanne Lees hide in the bush? [22]
- Is the CCTV man truly Murdoch? [23]
- Is Murdoch truly the CCTV man? [24]
- Did Murdoch Land Cruiser have an opening at the back? (remember the cage) [25]
- Was Murdoch towing a trailer/campervan? [26]
- Is the Land Cruiser on the CCTV at the truck stop Murdoch's Cruiser? [27]

The Vanishing of Peter Falconio

- Why is there no photograph of Murdoch's Cruiser on the internet? **[28]**
- What are the differences between the Cruiser seen on the CCTV film and Murdoch's Cruiser? **[29]**
- How many fuel tanks were fitted on the Land Cruiser seen on the CCTV film? **[30]**
- How many fuel thanks were fitted on Murdoch's Cruiser? **[31]**
- How did Murdoch manage to push Lees in the back of his Land Cruiser? **[32]**
- How did Lees escaped from the Cruiser having her hands tied up in her back? **[33]**
- When did Lees escape? **[34]**
- When did Lees leave her hiding position? **[35]**
- Why was Lees warm and clean when rescued? **[36]**
- How long before rescuing Joanne Lees did Vince Millar witnessed the two men pushing the third one into the Japanese car? **[37]**
- At the time of the alleged offence was the night clear, dark and pitch black? **[38]**
- At what time did the Land Cruiser seen on the CCTV film enter the truck stop? **[39]**
- At what time did the Land Cruiser seen on the CCTV film left the truck-stop? **[40]**
- What breed of dog was Murdoch's dog? **[41]**
- To put the icing on the cake, why claims by some witnesses who saw Falconio alive days after his alleged killing ignored, dismissed and ridiculed? **[42]**
- Et cetera........!

To put it simply: **When –where –why –**and **how?** These are the four and most important questions that needed answers.

The Vanishing of Peter Falconio

These were the favourite questions Napoleon Bonaparte Emperor of France 1769-1821 always asked before entering into battle…However, he was stupid enough to invade Russia in winter…I thought I mention it!

We need proof beyond reasonable doubt……Without any doubt!

13- The Judge

To say the least, this piece of information is one of the most important.

The Judge's daughter Joanna Martin was in a relationship with a juror who sat on Murdoch's trial. This is truly compelling evidence of misinformation and corruption. This information is from Robin Bowles found in the epilogue of her book "Dead Centre" page 410 to 427. I wonder why the Judge retired after the trial [?] Does it means that anybody in a position of power and control is no longer liable for their past actions as soon and as long as they are retired?

***Note**: If a boy was born in the first week of May 2006 and knowing that the trial ended on December 2005, it is less than six months after the trial. Knowing that it takes nine months from conception to birth, you must admit that the relationship at the time of the trial was in fact more than real, meaning that Joanna Martin at the time of the trial was in her fourth month of pregnancy. Nobody needs a calculator to work this out (laughter and clapping in the back)

***

It is said that a judge who do not instruct a jury honestly, properly and correctly is unfit for purpose. It could be seen as an insurance scam, hoping that you won't read the small prints!

Some people go further by saying: "HE or SHE should be fired and never re-hired."

Well, I wouldn't go that far but knowing that the jury was not told of a Majority verdict is reprehensible and punishable by law. It has influenced the verdict it was meant to deceive. It was meant or designed to deflect attention away from the actual facts and the involvement/whereabouts of others involved in the case at the time of the alleged events.

The judge must have had some good reasons for not telling the jury about the majority verdict. As a result, beyond reasonable doubt was not going to be part of the agenda. I don't believe that all members of the jury would have been in agreement if it had been a majority verdict.

The Vanishing of Peter Falconio

The final decision in these matters should have been with the Jury. After all, judges are appointed nearly for life without having their own performance judged.

Further down from FFDA we read: "*...even more so given the jury was kept in the dark*". The jurors were told by the judge that the verdict had (must) to be **unanimous**" **it was an order mind you, not an option or suggestion.**

Again, I need to copy and paste from **FFDA p135** for the comprehension of the word **instructions.**

*"Instructions are what a judge is said to give a jury before they retire to deliberate. For some judges, however, those instructions can become directives and go beyond what is **legally permitted.** Verdicts being overturned on appeal due to faulty instructions given to the jury by a judge are not uncommon. In the Murdoch trial, the instructions given by Judge Brian Martin are reprehensible. At the end of the trial, he stated the following to all 12 jurors: "The verdicts, whether they be guilty or not guilty, must be unanimous. Would you please retire to consider your verdict"7*

Can you believe that?

"Then, a short time later, Martin stated something else. In the words of Lees, the judge made a statement in the courtroom that included the following facts. "There was a discussion between counsel and the Chief Justice as to a unanimous verdict and a majority verdict.

In the Northern Territory, in the event of a hung jury, the law enables a conviction through a majority verdict. The Chief Justice explained his view that a majority verdict should not be considered inferior to a unanimous verdict."8

"Martin's instruction to the jury was that the members must come to a "unanimous" verdict. But this is not what Martin himself declared later when he started talking about the acceptance of a majority verdict. In the Criminal Code Act of the Northern Territory, section 368 on majority verdicts states: "Where upon a trial a period of not less than six hours has elapsed since the jury retired and the jurors are not unanimously agreed

upon their verdict the court shall: (a) if the jury consists of 11 or 12 jurors and ten of those jurors are agreed upon a verdict to be given, take and enter that verdict as the verdict of the jury; or (b) if the jury consists of ten jurors and nine of those jurors are agreed upon a verdict to be given, take and enter that verdict as the verdict of the jury."

"Legally, majority verdicts are permitted in the Northern Territory. (Whether this is a good or bad thing is another matter.) But this fact was not conveyed to the jury in Martin's instructions. He told them their verdict had to be unanimous – that was a lie which Martin told every juror. It is what Martin wanted, but it is not the law. Martin should have informed the jury of section 368 which permits majority verdicts. But that devious JUDGE kept that fact from the jurors because Martin wanted a unanimous verdict. He and other officials of the Northern Territory would have been roundly condemned by the public if Murdoch was not convicted. So, Martin would not take the risk. It only would have required three jurors to vote not guilty and Murdoch could have walked away – a free man."

"If there were members of that jury who did not believe the case against Murdoch was proved beyond a reasonable doubt, those jurors could have acquiesced and reluctantly gone along with the other jurors just to get the hell out of there – because they did not know a majority verdict was acceptable.

If, before their deliberations, all jurors had been instructed correctly by Martin that a majority verdict was permitted, some of the jurors might have voted not guilty because a unanimous verdict was not required." (FFDA p135)

This is quite unbelievable to say the least. Knowing this, I believe that it could have been a heavy weight in favour of the accused. The verdict was definitely influenced (purposely) by the action of a judge not instructing the jury honestly.

Here, the Judge and the Prosecution are to blame and so is the Defence for not mentioning the fact. The Defence team could have challenged the matter.

The Vanishing of Peter Falconio

- Yes, it was definitely conspiracy (or plot if you prefer) but, what about the Defence, what was the Defence thinking?
- Was the Defence aware of the replication between unanimous and majority verdict? Of course, the Defence was aware of it they are lawyers are they not?
- How was this possible, how could this happen? Who can we trust? It seems that nobody can be trusted. They called this a fair trial! Was this a fair trial?

***Note**. When using the word "conspiracy" for some people it is synonym to terrorist – racist –and white supremacist etc…A boy is a boy and a girl is a girl unless some people may know better!

Well, further on I give a number of synonyms for the word "conspiracy ". There are quite a few and I ask anyone who is not in accordance with my views to check the definition of the word "synonym and conspiracy on the internet…They might learn few things. It was definitely the case of; *show me the man and I'll show you the crime"*

14 - The Jury

Here we have a list of people in relation to the trial:

Ian Barker QC addressing Appeal Court about issues regarding evidences given by Joanne Lees – former Northern Territory DPP **Rex Wild** who retired after Murdoch's trial (I wonder why?) –**Joanna Martin** who worked in a community legal service near the Supreme Court Her boss confirmed Joanna was on maternity leave –a boy was born to the couple first week of May 2006, the trial ended on 13 December 2005) – **Legal Aid Lawyer** – **Sean Hoey** (a man charged with the Omagh bombings Ireland) – **Dr Jonathan Whitaker** of Britain's Forensic Science Service –**Professor Allan Jamieson** (forensic expert) –**QC Tom Percy** from Perth – **Gary (Murdoch's brother)** – **Geoffrey Gerard Atkins** (article in the Age newspaper) –**Frank Thorne** (UK Sun) – **Phil Cook** (track Driver interviewed in Murder in the Outback program) – **Deputy DPP Tony Elliot** – **Chris Malouf** (claiming he camped metres away at the alleged crime scene on the day of the alleged events)– **Gregory Dick** (from Aileron Roadhouse) – **officer Libby Andrew** (under the guise of chaperone) – **Joanne** Lees and Jess [?] assumed Lees 'sister – **Liz Hayes** (from 60 minutes) –**Colleen Gwynne** (police) –**John Elfernick** Attorney General – **Stuart Tipple** Lindy Chamberlain's Barrister (extremely important as you will read further on in this book) –**Professor Paul Wilson** and **academic Juliette Landon**.

***

Speaking of the jury, jurors don't seem to ask questions. Are they allowed to speak in a trial, are they allowed to ask questions?

They sit frozen in a court room, trying to absorb mostly what the Prosecution is feeding them with. As far as the Defence is concerned, nothing much to say or read. Most of the time no one can tell if the presented facts are true or false and why some truly and important evidence are ignored, dismissed and ridiculed. Using the Prosecution's language, [NO], I am not satisfied with the words: *Please disregard –ignore –similar –if you believe etc.* and many more which you will discover during the course of the story.

The jury was not told the truth regarding the majority verdict. I don't even know if the Jury was told about the many changes made by Lees during the four years investigation. These changes were ignored, swallowed by such mountain of prejudices. It is an absolute preconceived opinion that is not based on reason –facts –and even actual experience. There is/was only one witness and that is Joanne Lees who never saw the actual killing of Peter Falconio. It is bias –it was meant to influence –to prejudice Bradley John Murdoch. The jury was not told too many things –the jury was not properly instructed by the judge and I believe it was for too many bad reasons: Murdoch is a bad boy, he sells drugs, he must be found guilty. This was the main priority because the Northern Territory officials didn't want a bad boy roaming the streets and nobody wanted a repeat of the Azaria Chamberlain case. The verdict had to be unanimous. Murdoch had to be found guilty for unknown reasons to most of us.

It was not a question of: Could Murdoch be innocent? But rather: **YES, HE IS GUILTY!**

Yes, it is true, even his accuser Joanne Lees introduced here as the good girl and the victim, is really not much better. She and Peter Falconio are drug users could also be drug dealers involved with drug Lords. …Who knows? But I am only assuming and assuming doesn't prove anything.

Being a drug dealer doesn't mean that you are a **"METICULOUS KILLER".** You simply sell drugs for profit. There is a great difference between selling, using and killing.

If people believe that a drug dealer is automatically wearing the killer tag, well there are millions of killers walking the street…So watch out!

I know jurors can be wrong, but they must be properly and honestly instructed by the judge.

Nevertheless, if a juror is in relationship with [A] Judge's daughter who is also as well in a close and friendly relationship with the main and only witness (also the accuser), <u>I believe people will start asking questions.</u>

The Vanishing of Peter Falconio

Unfortunately like any human being they are not infallible, far from it. In Bradley John Murdoch's trial the jury was definitely mislead and deceived. The six men and six women were oblivious of too many very important information…<u>At the exception of the one involved in the relationship</u> [?]

Anyway, who cares: HE is/was guilty…HE had to be. Imagine that instead of Murdoch, it could be you –your son –daughter –or a friend. I would love to know your thoughts on that…Sorry if I sound sarcastic.

Good read below by Graeme Crowley/Paul Wilson:

"It is our view that the adversarial system gives police enormous discretion over what evidence is followed up or ignored and which suspect is eventually interrogated, detained and charged. Unlike the system…in most European nations, where independent oversight is provided by a judge or non-police official. Australia's adversarial procedures allow the police to cull the evidence they collect.

Unless the defence is able to pour enormous resources into their own investigation, the jury will have no idea that what is presented to them by police and prosecution is potentially distorted. The worst-case scenario is where evidence has been illegally obtained or fabricated." **Graeme Crowley; Paul Wilson Who Killed Leanne** [Holland]? 2005: P3 FFDA p131

"The ancient right to have a criminal case ultimately decided by 12 good men' is not what it originally was, when jurors could ask witnesses and defendants questions. It has evolved into another part of this elaborate adversarial system whereby the best performing barristers can be the difference between conviction and acquittal, regardless of truth and justice Trial by jury: Is an ancient right being diluted to save money?guardian.co.uk 11 January 2010 (FFDA p.132)

"The show trial was in its ninth week when the jury commenced its deliberations. It is reasonable to believe that after two months of jury duty, the jury was concerned about being sequestered until all the verdicts for all

the specific charges were finalized. Such sequestration might have gone on for days, and there were only a few shopping days to Christmas. Imagine how some jury members must have felt – especially those with children or grandchildren, and those who had other family commitments and responsibilities, and those who held views contrary to the majority. The thought of being locked up with other jurors, they might not have even liked personally, to discuss verdicts with those whose decisions were based on Lees' emotions would have seemed pointless.

It might well have been a case where jurors, who really wanted to vote not guilty, did not see any possibility of their position being accepted.

So, they just held their noses and voted guilty – even more so given they were mis-instructed by Martin who told them all the verdicts had to be unanimous (FFDA p132)

So, that was the situation at that time…Put yourself in their shoes!

15 - Let Us Be Clear About the Word Conspiracy…

In my previous chapter I used the word "conspiracy"

When using the word "conspiracy" for some and for most of the people (nowadays) it means: terrorist – racist –and being some kind of white supremacist and who knows what else.

The definition from the internet of the word conspiracy is:

- *"A secret plan by a group to do something unlawful and harmful. The action of plotting or conspiring.*

"She served five years in prison for taking part in in a conspiracy to sell stolen art work"

Similar: Plot –scheme –stratagem –plan –machination –cabal – intrigue –deception –play trick –ruse –dodge –subterfuge – sharp practice –frame up –fit-up –racket complot –fraud.

- The action of plotting or conspiring: *"They were cleared of conspiring to pervert the course of justice"*

Similar: Plotting –collusion –intrigue –connivance –machination – collaboration –treason.

The problem nowadays is that people don't read, people are too lazy to open a dictionary. I find this amazing because now with the help of the internet anyone can find anything just by the click of a button on a keyboard. It's all there to be found nearly instantly.

The assassination of J.F Kennedy –Pearl Harbour – 9/11 were planned, each of the event was a conspiracy (doing something unlawful and harmful)

But as we know now, a boy can no longer be called **A** boy and a girl **A** girl. The Peter Falconio Case is/was **A CONSPIRACY** aiming at protecting and profiting someone or a group of people for reasons which will be difficult to prove.

The Vanishing of Peter Falconio

16 - There Cannot Be a Proven Murder Without a Dead Body

Our planet earth, our little paradise is not flat but round. On a map, yes, it is flat, but in space it is spherical. Nevertheless, there are thousands of people if not millions who still believe otherwise and if you don't agree with me, then we have a serious problem!

If there is no Dead Body in a murder case what can be said and deducted?

- The supposedly victim is really dead and buried somewhere.
- The victim has vanished, is in hiding for personal reasons unknown to us and may reappear at a later date.
- It is a fifty –fifty chance and, it certainly doesn't apply with the rule "beyond any reasonable doubt. **WE JUST DON'T KNOW**. This alone should have been a heavy weight in favour of Murdoch, not prejudicial.
- Especially if the only witness is the accuser
- If a person is killed it has to take place somewhere, usually the crime scene. Of course, the murderer may take the body somewhere else to be buried just to cover his tracks, but nonetheless when a crime takes place, there is always some evidence and definitely more than one.
- When murder is committed there could be some witnesses or not. The case is much easier if there are witnesses. In this case it doesn't look good for Murdoch but OK for the Prosecution…The only witness is the ACCUSER Joanne Lees. It is her words against the accused. This is important, I already smell a rat!
- When murder is committed there is always a weapon, a tool used in the killing. Usually, a search is done hoping to find it, irrelevant what tool was used even poison.
- When murder is committed **TIME** is important because if one cannot say **WHEN**, it is impossible to establish **WHERE –WHY**.

The Vanishing of Peter Falconio

17 - What Would You Answer?

If I ask you who is right: Joanne Lees or Murdoch? Well, you will have no answer because you don't know and mostly because you know nothing about the case...You haven't read anything about the case and......<u>You were not there.</u>

Don't forget, here the accuser is the only witness.

The first task and the only one really is to establish [if we can].

- If Bradley John Murdoch [was] or [not] at the alleged crime scene. It appears that he may not have been there on the night of the alleged abduction, because, there are no evidence that he was. No footprints –no items belonging to him –no evidence of his dog being there –no evidence of his car-trailer –gun etc. was found;

- According to his claim (transcript of the appeal) at 3.30pm on the 14th of July he was at the junction of the Stuart highway and the Tanami 20km north of Alice Springs

- At the time of the alleged crime, he was near Yuendumu (time of the alleged crime needs to be calculated if you believe Lees' story)

- Also, according to the transcript, he claimed that between midnight and 1.00am on the 15th of July he was near the Granites (granite gold mine) on the Tanami;

- <u>The best evidence of all is NOT what the investigators have found but what they haven't found.</u>

- No evidence found: No motive –no footprints –no footprints of his dog –no wheel marks of his car and trailer and more......and of course no Dead Body!

The Peter Falconio case and trial seems to be no different to the Azaria Chamberlain case. Murdoch didn't receive a fair trial because of all the publicity and more importantly because his photograph was published when accused of rape, but found not guilty on all charges. I strongly believe it was a trial by media. Everybody, people were brainwashed to hate Murdoch, he was guilty like Lindy Chamberlain because: NO DINGO could have or would take a baby! Murdoch's alleged murder trial is similar: No proofs, no evidence and no facts proven correct... Not a fair trial if you ask me. Even before the start, he was Guilty! Guilty your Honour... Guilty! They wanted blood, thanks to the damning media coverage and some corrupt officials, [NOT] forgetting the accuser Joanne Lees.

Please never forget: The only witness is Joanne Lees and no one else... The bigger the lies the more people believe it!

You have read only a few chapters and I hope that you are truly starting to understand the situation that, to prove that a crime was committed you need a motive –evidence –witnesses -a dead body –time of death –what type of weapon or *"l'arme du crime"* –and more! Any facts –statements from witnesses –time of certain events – locations etc. must be beyond reasonable doubt. It cannot be: May be –I don't know –I think etc.

Here the accuser is the only witness. How can anyone prove that Joanne Lees is telling the truth? It is mission impossible, it's her words against anybody's words.

The accuser identified the alleged murderer three times.

- The first time in 2001when she gave her first description of the killer the morning after the alleged offence.
- The second time when she was in Sicily when told by a friend that the photo of Murdoch was on the internet...I recognised him instantly she said!
- And the third time in 2005 at the trial four years after the alleged crime as well as her own abduction, after changing many of her claims more than once and as a matter of fact always using the word; Similar (the man description is similar so is the dog –the car – the silver gun etc.).

Speaking of the word "similar" do you think that people who were involved with the DNA investigations may have thought that; the word "similar" would be good enough if used?

***

Every claim made by Joanne Lees is doubtful and could be interpreted as; I don't know or I think or maybe or I will look for more opportunities?

The Vanishing of Peter Falconio

Joanne Lees has changed her claims too many times. Nothing of what she claimed complies with the rule of law: Beyond reasonable doubt…Why?

As we all know, anybody can accuse anyone. It is always the accused who has to defend himself or herself. The end result: it can't be proven nor disproved beyond reasonable doubt. The accused is most of the time found guilty…Unless you have real proofs.

Now, reading from Find Falconio Dead or Alive:

"As has been stated correctly by observers of the Falconio case, Murdoch was tried and convicted in the media long before the sham show trial (October-December 2005). In part, there are examples of headlines which are worded so specifically and so negatively, that anyone reading them would immediately conclude that he was guilty. With such damning media coverage, it was impossible for him to have a fair trial. And that a jury was selected from a contaminated pool of Territorians, which had been exposed to many negative messages about Murdoch for more than four years, confirms how corrupt the whole kangaroo-court process was." (FFDA p.279)

The Vanishing of Peter Falconio

18 - Is/Was It a Murder Case?

Most of the people believe the case is a murder case. Well, it's not.

You must understand that Peter Falconio's case, is not a murder case but a disappearance case, he vanished... Even Joanne Lees said it when questioned about her lover Nick when she said; *"I had nothing to do with Pete's DISAPPEARANCE neither has Nick"* (as you will find out further on).

A murder case requires a Dead Body and proofs beyond reasonable doubt. Peter Falconio's body up until now has never been found, proofs beyond reasonable doubt failed. Until the body is found, **DEAD OR ALIVE** it will remain a disappearance case.

Even more astonishing, alleged evidence by some eye witnesses that Falconio was seen alive after his alleged death is more than interesting, don't you think?

Dead people don't walk the streets incognito days after their death. We are not watching a science-fiction movie, this is serious business!

- This is an alleged murder case where there is no dead body and where the accuser the prime witness is Joanne Lees.

What we need to sort out among all the data collected is to prove beyond reasonable doubt if the accused was truly at the alleged crime scene at the time when this alleged crime was supposedly committed.

If the accused was not at the alleged crime scene, logic beyond reasonable doubt tells us that the accused could not have committed the alleged crime.

The accused was found guilty basically on the facts (unproven) that;

- He was the man at the Shell truck-stop in Alice springs,
- And the fact that his DNA according to some experts did match the DNA results from a blood stain found on the back of the accuser Joanne Lees where it would be questionable and unlikely to be found.

If the accused was not at the alleged crime scene, physically unable to commit the crime simply means that all the assumptions pointing to the DNA indicates: Fowl play –fabricated –concocted –forged –falsified etc. and who knows what else [?]

The Vanishing of Peter Falconio

- We need to know that western Australian police did questioned Murdoch but he was released because he had an alibi. This alibi has since been classified as **NOT TO BE DISCLOSED**. Also, police were desperately seeking for Murdoch's DNA as a result they asked his brother Gary if he was willing to be tested for DNA as you will read further on.

Can a man be sent to prison for life because [someone] just disappeared, and when the only witness is the accuser, and no proofs beside the DNA results which are very suspicious as well, because nobody knows the source of the bloodstain found on the back of Lees, a very unlikely place to be found as well as the suspicious test result and as well as the time it took **(more than 28 months)** for the alleged evidence to arrive at the lab to be analysed.

I know time is the essence if the intention was to pervert the course of justice (plotting etc.) Do you find this fulfilling the requirement?

By constantly using the word **crime** we are conditioned to believe that **crime** it is. In people's mind, the man is guilty, he is a drug dealer…. Everybody hated his guts, <u>**he is the killer,**</u> he is a very bad boy. He must be guilty! The Prosecution won the argument, the received verdict proved it…**GUILTY** on all charges.

There cannot be murder beyond reasonable doubt if there is no Dead Body and if the accused was not at the alleged crime scene. I don't think anyone can disagree even if believing that the DNA trump card said so.

Please think: What happen regarding the DNA test samples **between the 17th of July 2001 and the 24th of October 2003?** (Please keep on reading).

We just don't know. All we know is that Peter Falconio may have been killed and the only fact beyond reasonable doubt is; that he vanished… Nothing else!

The word disappearance of Falconio instead of murder points to one direction and one only:

Where is Peter Falconio?

Is he dead and buried, is he alive, hiding? Where is he, does anyone knows?

The Vanishing of Peter Falconio

19 - Honi Soit Qui Mal y Pense

"Honi soit qui mal y pense is a maxim in the Anglo-Norman language, a dialect of Old Norman French spoken by the medieval ruling class in England, meaning "shamed be whoever thinks ill of it", usually ..." <u>Wikipedia</u>

I am still reading, wondering and try to get my head around about everything I can find about: **Murdoch –his brother Garry –Joanne Lees –the Judge –the Prosecution –the Defence Lawyer –the Jury –the Experts –the Media –the Police –the dog –the trailer** etc. and much more. I watched any video clips I can find. Many relevant evidences have been supressed, dismissed or tampered with. Well, are we all blindfolded including members of the Jury?

But has the jury been told about certain things that they should have known?

Was the jury told that in the Northern Territory there can be two types of verdicts: **Unanimous** or **Majority** verdict: If a majority verdict had been delivered (six men and six women), I believe Murdoch would be free now simply because to deliver a guilty verdict it must be: Beyond reasonable doubt. There cannot be any doubt like: It can't be; 'perhaps Murdoch is guilty' or 'I think that he must be guilty'. It is not a choice depending on someone mood, narrative or agenda. Proof is needed and it must be beyond reasonable doubt. (I know it's a repeat)

- Knowing this, did the judge do his job?
- Was the Prosecution looking for justice?
- Was the Defence up to the job?
- What was the reason for not instructing the jury about Majority verdict?
- What was the agenda?

The judge failed to instruct the Jury; a man's life depended on it. It cannot be said that Bradley John Murdoch received a fair trial. Do you agree with me?

This is only a very short book, from a story teller if you like…<u>But I made it my mission to clear the innocent</u>.

The Vanishing of Peter Falconio

I want to make it easier as possible for people to read. I have no intention to write a thesis about the case. I like people to realize: The man may or may not have committed the alleged crime, we don't know. No evidence proving that a murder took place on the 14th of July 2001: **NOTHING** at all, **[NO]** evidence found. I must admit this is quite remarkable!

From the start there is no Dead Body, then, there is no evidence whatsoever that Murdoch was at the alleged crime scene. Please, don't tell me that the Dead Body will be found, sorry but it has already been 21 years and I don't think people have been looking for it.

Murdoch allegedly committed the crime. Well, the Dead Body if Falconio was murder has/had to be buried close to the alleged crime scene, not miles away knowing that if Murdoch is/was the killer he was in great hurry after searching for Lees for nearly around five hours <u>as per her</u> <u>claim</u> (clapping in the background) meaning burying the body had to be very close to the alleged crime scene...We don't even know if he had a shovel! Murdoch could not afford the time driving somewhere else to do it, even stopping on his way to Western Australia...Too much in a hurry according to the Prosecution –Joanne Lees –and Mr Hepi (Murdoch ex- partner in the drug business).

Don't forget the killer had to be seen at 0.30am on the 15th in Alice Springs because Joanne Lees –the Prosecution – Mr Hepi –and few others including the staff from the Shell stop (who were not sure) claimed the man on the CCTV film is/was Murdoch (according to the transcript of the appeal as you will read further on).

Was the CCTV man truly Murdoch at the truck stop? According to Lees *"Yes that's him, he is the man"* (her words). Mind you after changing her claims twice.

Is Murdoch truly the man on the CCTV film? It has never been proven beyond reasonable doubt. He would not have the time to bury the body and else, then drive to Alice at an average speed of 90/100km/h, which takes three hours and 30 minutes.

- <u>To bury the body can only be achieved after Murdoch stopped searching for Lees,</u>

The Vanishing of Peter Falconio

- If he did and if Lees 'story is true [?]
- But not when searching for her with his dog and his torch light after she escaped.

It had to be before midnight because Lees claimed she escaped after Murdoch left the alleged crime scene after his five hours search which doesn't fit according to her story (it should be 9.00pm on the 14th). We know that it is absolutely not correct because if it was him, [HE] had to enter the Shell truck-stop at 0.30am on the 15th.

- Therefore, it had to be before leaving the alleged crime scene. if [**NOT**], meaning the body must be buried near the alleged crime scene and, if [**NOT**] it simply means that the alleged killer arrived at the truck-stop with the body of Falconio on the back of the Land Cruiser which was confirmed by our dear Judge during his sentencing of Murdoch…Can you believe that? What a farce!
- Then herself flagging down the road train between midnight and 0.30am on the 15th of July [**NOT**] before, [**NOT**] after. Contradiction between Lees and the Prosecution.
- Which is not true because if Murdoch left the alleged crime scene after and around midnight means he would arrive in Alice around 3.00am, not 0.30am which is not the case, because the Land Cruiser did enter the Shell truck-stop at 0.30am on the 15th as I said above.

Don't be ridiculous, this is a real FARCE! A miscarriage of justice. It has never been a fair trial. This took place twice in Northern Territory (could be more) and I wonder why; coincidence?

The received verdict was guilty on all charges (meaning the killing and the abduction) with no proofs or facts beyond reasonable doubt. Murdoch is rotting in jail and no one cares! Perhaps the only hope is for the technology using facial recognition that someday, somehow, somewhere Peter Falconio will be picked up. Would that be great, the body has been found…Alive and doing well…I wish –you wish –we wish!

- There hasn't been one piece of evidence regarding Lees' story up until now proving that Murdoch was at the alleged crime scene and killed Falconio.

- However, he was found guilty **because of the DNA trump card** so they said!

Everyone: The Judge, the Prosecution, the Jury, the Experts, the Police, the Northern Territory Officials, Joanne Lees, the media all were against Murdoch from day one. They hated his guts, he is/was a bad boy, a drug dealer. **BUT** hey, can Joanne Lees be trusted? She is a drug user. Is she a good girl? Do you believe Peter Falconio was a good boy? He is a drug user. Did this really take place? Who can you trust?

Both are drug users and perhaps drug dealers. They cannot be trusted and the main argument is that Joanne Lees is the only witness, she can claim whatever she wants. She should have been thrown out of the witness box and put on stage instead of Murdoch……Definitely.

But then as you will read further on, Monsieur Hepi also a drug dealer who did business with Murdoch has the audacity to say that it was Murdoch and to make things worse gave police some cigarette butts three months after the alleged offence to frame Murdoch, and the police has the audacity to accept the butts. James Hepi must have been hoping to get a piece of the cake, the $250,000 reward or perhaps a favour from police? Was he already a police informer and if he was, what would be the reason, drug business from both side, dealer/s and police? What a disgrace!

Can Monsieur Hepi being <u>a drug dealer and a criminal</u> be trusted testifying against another drug dealer and ex-partner? Yes, total trust as far as this witness is concerned. Who is conspiring against who? Would you trust a criminal and an obvious liar?

I found this remarkable indeed. Don't you think this could really be a farce? Well, I think this was a repeat of the Azaria Chamberlain case or the Shandee Blackburn case. It has somehow the same characteristics. The State could not afford another failure. A repeat of the Azaria Case, still in the same state? **YES**, we definitely need a retrial. Why? Because there is more to come, we are only at chapter 19.

So dear readers, I need you to be the new Jury. Please, try using some logic, seek the truth and may God bless Australia and our Justice System…. Keep on reading and listen to me carefully. Don't ignore my plea.

The Vanishing of Peter Falconio

Having said that, I am the only one who can give myself a pat on the back if no one else does! After all, why not if it makes me feel good. I remember when I was young reading the San-Antonio novels written by that incredible Monsieur Frederic Dard a humorous crime writer (fiction series) where the main character a French Secret Service detective named San-Antonio narrates his adventures with great verve and sarcasm. The only difference between him and I is that I like Justice to be real and done with. [I] haven't been over 300 novels, each of them fascinating fiction stories including 175 adventures of San-Antonio, always fulfilling impossible missions given by the "old man", a true James Bond. His novels were published from 1949 to 2001. Born 1921 died 2000 (Wikipedia). I thought I mention it.

***

The Peter Falconio Case is a true story that needs to be told because it is a miscarriage of Justice of incredible proportion. Bradley John Murdoch must and has to be cleared of the crime he could not have committed.

"There are more important things than finding the murderer….it is to clear the innocent "

Remember: "*Dieu et mon droit –Honi soit qui mal y pense! (God and my right –shame on anyone who thinks evil of it)*

The Vanishing of Peter Falconio

20 - This Is Important

Things that are paramount in the case:
- No Dead Body
- Only one witness Joanne Lees <u>if you exclude the Prosecution and the Judge.</u>
- Real time of the alleged crime unknown, (no dead body, no witnesses, only Lees).
- Was the accused at the alleged crime scene? Unknown, (no footprints, no dead body, no witness only Lees).
- Was Murdoch the CCTV man, was the Land Cruiser seen on the film Murdoch's Land Cruiser? (both never identified by police)

Does this look like beyond reasonable doubt? No, it doesn't, I put money on it, nobody can deny the fact that the trial was already starting on the wrong foot and that Bradley John Murdoch was guilty because he was a drug seller and a very bad boy but I believe that this is not the only reasons.

Locations

It is a topic well debated and they are:

Alice Springs –Aileron roadhouse –Ti Tree –Barrow Creek -the Tanami – Tilmouth Well –Yuendumu – The Granite –Rabbit Flat Roadhouse – Halls Creek –Fitzroy Crossing…Eventually Broome.

Below are the most important locations and distances between each location. We shall need it further on and they are:

Alice Springs to Fitzroy Crossing **1,412km** –Alice Springs to Broome **1,702km**

Alice Springs to Aileron **134km** –Aileron to Ti Tree **62km** –Ti Tree to Barrow Creek **119km** –Barrow Creek to Yuendumu **318km** (via Aileron, turning right via Pine Hill & Mount

Denison meeting the Tanami at Yuendumu).

Alice Springs to Tilmouth **190km** –Tilmouth to Yuendumu **145km** –Yuendumu to The Granite **254km** (57km before Rabbit Flat)–Yuendumu to Rabbit Flat Roadhouse **311km** –Yuendumu to Bililuna **591km** –Rabbit Flat to Bililuna **280km** (fuel stop) –Bililuna to Halls Creek **196km** –Halls

The Vanishing of Peter Falconio

Creek to Fitzroy Crossing **290km** –Alice Springs to Fitzroy Crossing **1,412km**

Barrow Creek to Fitzroy Crossing via Yuendumu (via Mount Denison turning right before Aileron then towards Yuendumu then Yuendumu) **1,404km**

The alleged crime scene.

Where is that? Well, the name as you know is Barrow Creek (it was actually 10km north of Barrow Creek) a small dot on the Stuart Hwy in Northern territory. Having said small dot, it means small dot. There is nothing around. It's not Ship Creek but the back of whoop-whoop.

Fitzroy Crossing is in Western Australia **1,412km** from Alice Springs where Murdoch was seen refuelling at around **8.00pm on the 15th of July 2001** (Northern Territory time).

Time

IT SEEMS that time has also been and mostly well debated. <u>WELL, that is not true at all</u> as you will learn...Time is paramount because if you cannot tell **when,** it is impossible to tell **where** – **why** – **how** (that is pure logic already discussed).

Facts: Can be true –false –or fabricated).

There are a number of facts, but the most extensive work and unmatched source is the book by **Judge Dean Mildren**: **R v Murdoch: The Falconio Case – Study in identification** and **books by Dr Moles –the book by Keith Allan Noble: FIND FALCONIO Dead or Alive** (free if ordered on line) **and of course the book by Robin Bowles.**

Undeniably, and among all that mountain of data (to be proven or disproved) there are many contradictory claims, (not about the mentioned authors above) but by all parties involved in the case concerning all evidences and claims presented to the jury, like Joanne Lees –the Judge – the Prosecution – police –forensic experts –witnesses etc.

The Vanishing of Peter Falconio

The best way to sort out this mess, is to address each one by one when possible, and see what can be fished out. Don't forget my aim is not to find the killer but to clear the innocent. Nothing but the truth, meaning <u>we need real facts</u> beyond reasonable doubts!

21 - Legalese The Lawyers' Language

When someone is lying in a murder case irrelevant if it is the accuser or the accused, there will always be at some stage a simple answer or an obvious fact revealing the lie. Most of the time people can't remember fully the answers they may have given when interrogated.

In every language there are different types of communication:

- The everyday language or colloquial is the language used in ordinary or familiar conversation; not formal or literary. It is the unofficial – conversational –everyday –casual –natural –formal –unpretentious –familiar –chatty –friendly –idiomatic –slangy –vernacular –popular -demotic etc.).

(Yes, it's all from the internet…So the choice is nearly unlimited).

Then you have the language spoken by the academics like lawyers; The Legalese language which of course includes writing as in Academic writing type like in Law.

- Legalese refers to contract language that lawyers use. This legal terminology or legal-speak typically refers to words a specific word, therefore having a specific and indicative meaning like for example
- "Henceforth" meaning from this or that time on
- And "stipulation" from the verb stipulate meaning demand or specify (a requirement typically as part of an agreement –a bargain –proviso –or condition.
- Essentially "legalese" is lawyers' lingo that may be difficult for people outside of the industry to understand.

However, the language will not stop someone seeking the truth. Yes, it will take longer to comprehend but if there is a will there is a way. So, put yourself in the jurors' shoes

The Vanishing of Peter Falconio

22 - What We Need to Prove [2]

Transcripts are truly big bags of words for the one not used to the lawyers' language

We don't need to investigate the complete list (page 26-28) but the most important and vital claims are claims by Joanne Lees and the Prosecution and some criminals like Mr Hepi.

In chronological order we need to question a great amount of data. To each action is a reaction. Here is a brief list for the time being.

- 1 - Murdoch –Falconio –Joanne Lees seen at the same restaurant in Alice Spring.
- 2 -Departure time from the restaurant for each of them on the 14th.
- 3 -Murdoch's departure time from Alice on the 14th.
- 4 -Falconio and Lees' departure time from Alice on the 14th.
- 5 -The CCTV man arrival time in Alice on the 14th/15th.
- 6 -The CCTV man departure time from Alice on the 15th.
- 7 -Falconio and Lees' arrival time at Aileron.
- 8 -Falconio and Lees 'departure time from Aileron.
- 9 -Falconio and Lees' arrival time at Ti Tree
- 10 -Falconio and Lees' departing time from Ti Tree
- 11 -Lees' arrival time at Barrow Creek the alleged crime scene allegedly alone [?]
- 12 -Time of Peter Falconio's killing (time of death) –time of Lees' abduction –time of her escape –time spent by Lees hiding.
- 13 -Time spent by the killer searching for Lees after her escape.
- 14 -Time of the killer departing the alleged crime scene.
- 15 -Time of Lees' rescue –time of Chris Maloof arrest at Barrow Creeck and more…

23 - Coincidence?

[1a] *"Murdoch – Falconio – Lees were all positively identified at the same fast-food restaurant in Alice Springs on the day of the alleged attack which the Prosecution argued accounts for some DNA match."*

This is very interesting. We shall talk about this later on also when debating the first identification by Joanne Lees given to police on the - morning after the alleged murder and abduction…Very interesting indeed. Apparently, they were at the fast-food restaurant some hours apart…According to Andrew Frazer two hours [?]

I don't see any problem with that, it could be true, but there would be insufficient evidence and explanation as to why and how the patch of Murdoch's bloodstain [if his], landed on the back of Lees' T-shirt and nowhere else? …How did it get there? Please explain!

On the other hand, being at the same restaurant could imply some coincidence or assuming some business deal between the three of them. One selling and two buying. Who knows? But then why some hours apart? Two bad boys and one bad girl doesn't make it right.

- Maybe a deal went wrong at the time or before even after. Everything is possible.
- But being at the restaurant at different time doesn't mean that Murdoch's intention was to kill Falconio later on at Barrow creek in cold blood with a big silver gun which has never been found, **[BUT]** then downgraded to a smaller calibre by the **OFFICIALS** (more about it later on).
- Unless you give me a good reason, being at the restaurant on that day at different time is no evidence that Murdoch is the alleged killer.
- <u>Can this be used as evidence</u>?
- You've got to be joking, you can't be serious

If a deal didn't take place according to plan, Falconio and Lee may well have thought and decided that Murdoch will be their scapegoat…Payback time? But this is not the reason. As far as the reason is concerned, we will never know the link regarding their relationship if any?

- This alleged crime may have taken place if you believe Lees story but then at the time, what happen?
- If Murdoch knew what Joanne Lees and Falconio looked like, the same applies to Lees and Falconio:
- They had to know what Murdoch look like.
- **SO WHY** did Joanne Lees give a description of Murdoch that didn't match his true physic on the morning the day after the alleged event?
- So why is Lees' description of Murdoch to police on the morning after the alleged offence totally the opposite?

REMEMBER, one bell one sound, two bells two sounds. What I am saying here is purely based on Lees claiming that the alleged crime and her abduction took place like in the movie. If nothing took place, the question remains: Where is/was Falconio instead of where is the Dead Body?

If a crime did take place, the three of them at the restaurant in Alice could be related and important, but we truly don't know if they were at the restaurant some hours apart. They may have had a talk/confrontation of some kind before or after being at the restaurant, we just don't know, all this is pure supposition for someone having a good imagination. Again, we don't know! This is truly pure fiction.

- However maybe nothing happened [?]
- According to Lees our reliable witnesses and the Prosecution; yes of course, Murdoch was at the restaurant because he said so and gave the approximate time and yes of course Falconio and Lees were at the restaurant, but the time is unknown/not mentioned, not given.
  - But who claimed that they were at the restaurant at different times besides Andrew Fraser? Is there any recording taken by a CCTV camera? The proof has to be on [a] film if true of course [?]
  - So, is there a CCTV film proving they were seen at the restaurant some hours apart and how far apart?
  - Any witness or witnesses?

The Vanishing of Peter Falconio

- The whole situation would definitely be different if they had been seen at the same time……Do you agree?
- This is like writing a novel, changing the story as you go along to fit the ending.

The sketch artist used by police was inexperienced in police work.

- Why using such a person?
- Was the artist chosen by the police for a particular reason?
- Anyhow, [HE] did a very good job because upon the information given by Lees to the artist what came out was enough for Lees…She recognised the accused hey!
- She identified Murdoch from the drawing and that was good enough.
- The proof is that police arrested Chris Malouf on the morning because he looks like the man described by Lees. (you will know about Malouf further on)
- That was the first description given to police on the morning of the day after the alleged offence [15th July 2001].
- It is after the description given by Lees that police started to erect roadblocks hoping to catch the attacker fitting Joanne Lees description. Police cannot deny that… But everything failed to arrest a killer…Obviously!
- All police did was to arrest Chris Malouf and then releasing him after Lees failed to recognize him and his car and after DNA tests were carried out. I/we still don't know the meaning of "were carried out", but I go along. To me sounds like taking a swab…If they did [?]
- DNA tests were carried out could have dual meaning. It could be interpreted as
- Tests were negative (no match or similar) or awaiting results [?]
    - It could also mean that swabs had been taken as I said above.
    - But for someone with bad intention…Swabs can be disposed of or destroyed or simply not sent to the lab. The whole exercise is widely open to corruption or for the purpose of perverting the course of

justice if you ask me…Tests were carried out is a very suspicious information.
- The release of Chris Malouf is very suspicious. How did they get to him so quickly?
- Arresting an undercover agent to make it look real [?]…Unfortunately no proofs.

The Vanishing of Peter Falconio

24 - Murdoch, Joanne Lees, Falconio in Alice Springs

[2a] *Murdoch saw Lees and Falconio while in Alice Springs, and believed that they were following him. So, he drove behind them as they travelled on the Stuart Hwy, and then stopped them as to get rid of them, because he feared that they may be spying on him and may contact police in relation to drug running.*

- Firstly, where does this come from? Who is speaking for Murdoch?
- The words are made to insert the little worm not into the apple but into the Jurors' Brain.... If you do not share my views, please say so......
- That is all very well, so Murdoch, Lees and Falconio were seen in Alice.
- At the same restaurant but some hours apart (according to transcripts and Andrew Frazer).
- And who else saw them if I may ask? Who is/are the witnesses?
- Was this information captured on the CCTV camera of the restaurant at different time during the day? (Um!)
- Then, how could a small microscopic patch of bloodstain (at this stage, not DNA) be from Murdoch miraculously landing on the back of Lees' T-shirt?
- Was Murdoch dancing with Lees to the tune of "ASSASIN TANGO"? (Mr and Mrs Smith –Cinematic –by John Powell) powerful piece of music
- So, if Murdoch "feared that they may be spying on him"
- It truly means they knew each other without any doubt (drug dealer--drug users, no explanation needed). Of course, according to the Prosecution our second reliable witness.
- Lees –Falconio –Murdoch at the Red Rooster (that is probably where police got the burger to accompany the cuffs in that paper bag (You will read about it further on) coincidently or not, it means –indicates –tells you –shows, which ever words you like to use,

The Vanishing of Peter Falconio

- That someone is assuming that Murdock knew what Lees and Falconio looked like and if he did the other way around or vice versa should apply. Monsieur the Prosecutor doesn't seem to understand that, assuming a fact is one thing, proving it is another.
- If he feared they were spying on him truly means they knew each other. This of course is only an assumption which need to be proven beyond reasonable doubt. (Those are/were not the words of the Defence, but mine).
- What is the Prosecution trying to say?
- It means Murdoch saw Lees and Falconio while in Alice Spring or Lees and Falconio saw Murdoch while in Alice…That is what it means…
- It doesn't mean that Murdoch is the alleged killer and, that it was an alleged premeditated crime.
- [NO]; it only means what it means even according to the Prosecution who introduced the words "he feared" pretending that they saw each other. It is [A] created fact meant to influence and deceive the jury. It has to be proven…If I am not correct, God help me please!
- When Lees gave her first description to police of the alleged offender who stopped them on the morning the day after the alleged offence….
- The description should have been the description of the real Murdoch, [NOT] the one with long hair –long moustache etc. [BUT] the one they saw in Alice, but [NO], it wasn't. Do you get my message? Please don't say yes just to make me feel good.
- It should have been the DESCRIPTION of Murdoch who feared that they were spying on him.
- Is that the reason and the motive why he would kill Falconio in cold blood and then let Joanne Lees go free? Just like that? ..Simply and fearlessly.
- So, Murdoch eating at the restaurant had to sit on a chair, a chair that Lees made sure she would remember at all cost, so she could sit

exactly on the same one (if available) so that the patch of bloodstain would be transferred to the back of her T-shirt…What a laugh! (Clapping in the background).
- That is clever from her, she has definitely a good imagination
- Planning to sit on the same chair (that is if no one is sitting on it),
- But how did she know what chair Murdoch was sitting on? That is the $64 question hey" I had to mention this because some people have suggested that the bloodstain was transferred because they sat on the same chair…How funny is that?
- So, using some politician favourite words: PLEASE EXPLAIN!

But then how do you explain the hours apart? He feared that they were following him, gosh the Prosecution is truly a good mind reader. Murdoch does not look like her first description to police and Murdoch doesn't look like the CCTV man in 2005. Were these the Prosecution's words and thoughts? What do you think, who is lying, who's dreaming?

Please, I Beg You…. Think!

If this alleged crime is a creation of Peter Falconio –Joanne Lees –and their partners is crime, all what I am writing or saying can be put in the bin or burned because you will never find an answer regarding events that never took place, unless writing a fiction book. You will become senile and the end result…Well you will end up in an asylum for the rest of your life and it will be THEM who will make a movie about YOU. However, keep on reading.

Don't forget they're all involved with drugs, Lees is the accuser –the only witness and to put the icing on the cake, in 2005, four years later (and also in between) she again changed the description of the man who stopped them, killing her loved boyfriend with a big Silver Clint Eastwood type gun claiming he was the man on the CCTV film…. Really…Do you believe that?

Please give me some answers, this is more than a farce, this is a disgrace, this is an insult to anybody's intelligence, a miscarriage of justice…Perhaps the earth is flat after all hey!

The Vanishing of Peter Falconio

Furthermore, upon the description given by Lees, as soon as police got the sketch from the artist police was setting up roadblocks, meaning:
- They were not looking for Murdoch, not the man seen at the restaurant nor the CCTV man, but for man fitting the description given by Lees: A man with long hair, moustache, a man of medium build with an Australian accent driving a <u>similar</u> four-wheel drive accompanied by a <u>similar</u> dog. We don't know about the gun which has never be found

But now we have a newcomer!

At the time of the alleged crime according to FFDA a man by the name of Chris Malouf was allegedly camping 55 metres from where the alleged crime is supposed to have taken place but saw nothing and heard nothing…We shall come to it further on, so please don't jump to conclusion, be patient.

According to our unreliable witness who changes things all the time, her first description of her attacker was not a man nearly as tall as a door frame, with a beautiful short haircut, with no moustache, with no bags under his eyes, didn't have a thin long face, don't know about the deep voice, but he was wearing a cap for sure with a little logo, a logo that Monsieur James Hepi Murdoch's ex-partner recognised on the CCTV film of course after dobbing him.
- If you can see the logo from the CCTV footage, make sure you ring me please….
- Yes of course, because the man on the CCTV was wearing a similar cap, so it had to fit, not the description but the cap!
- Also, nobody knows if at the UNKNOWN time of this alleged crime Murdoch was wearing a cap?
- All we know is that YES, the man who has never been identified (including his Land Cruiser) was wearing one…A cap that is.

I don't believe that Lees had lost her memory, same with Monsieur James Hepi, but I believe that their reliability needs to be questioned and clarified. Both could be wolves dressed in sheep 'clothing roaming the prairies.

The Vanishing of Peter Falconio

25 - According To Joanne Lees and the Prosecution

An alleged crime was committed. That is very well but…Where is the Dead body?

On one side we have the Prosecution full on prosecuting and on the other side we have the Defence pretty much at sleep (assuming) when the debate is mostly about: where – when – why –and how

The only two facts that both the Prosecution, the Defence and Joanne Lee were forced to agree on, were:

- There is no Dead body
- Murdock has been seen refuelling his car in Fitzroy Crossing in WA around 8.00pm **1,412km** from Alice Springs on the **15th of July 2001** (the day after the alleged crime).

These are the only two facts. Anything else is pure unfounded supposition, meaning it has to be proven beyond reasonable doubt. In other words, that's not much at all.

Questioning someone like Joanne Lees is not something I wish onto anyone because you would get a different answer to the same question more than once.

She has changed her claims and declarations so many times which puts her into the category of truly "unreliable witness". Ironically and I said it many times, and I will repeat it again as we go along: She was the only witness, not to the actual alleged killing but because she was rescued there. After all she could also be the prime suspect.

- Is/was she involved in the vanishing of Falconio, a fact which cannot be proven beyond reasonable doubt?

Many people have asked too many questions…Unfortunately unanswered. Anybody has the right to ask questions especially in an alleged murder case…The truth must be told irrelevant of people's opinion and agenda. Unfortunately, we all know that it doesn't work like that.

There are many unanswered questions about both their whereabouts…. She is the main shareholder in the case …She apparently made a lot of money out of it, but denies that she did…**WHY?**

The Vanishing of Peter Falconio

NOW before reading the next chapter and the ones after and until the end of this manuscript, you must remember the route taken by the Alleged Killer – Murdoch –Joanne Lees –and Peter Falconio from Alice Springs to the Alleged Crime Scene of Barrow Creek.
It is **Alice Springs – Aileron Roadhouse –Ti Tree –Barrow Creek**.

Then later on, please refer to chapter 63 - DISTANCES page 228 of the manuscript. This will help, as we all get confused sometimes.

The Vanishing of Peter Falconio

26 - Time of the Alleged Death [1]

1) Time of death

Logically the time of death is unknown because of the lack of a Dead Body.

What follows below is necessary to go through again regarding the time of death.

- We know according to Joanne Lees that she was watching the sunset at 6.10pm at Ti Tree on the 14th of July 2001the day of the alleged offence. She claimed she was not alone but with Peter Falconio.
- But for you the reader, contrary to her claim, a witness confirmed that she was alone watching the sunset (accepted by police).
- Being alone or not makes no difference anyway because <u>I am only interested from her time of departure from Ti Tree towards Barrow Creek 119km away.</u>
- Joanne Lees left Ti Tree towards Barrow Creek at 6.30pm on the 14th
- Knowing that the old Kombi maximum speed was 80km/h full throttle, it took her 95 minutes (1 hour and 35 minutes) to reach Barrow Creek the alleged crime scene using an average speed of 80km/h.
- Traveling 119km at 60kmh you need 1km x 119 = 119 minutes (say 120) or two hours

As a result, we should have two times of death:

- First arrival time at Barrow Creek is 8.05pm
- Second arrival time at Barrow Creek is 8.30pm

However, choosing 80km/h a top speed knowing the state of the old kombi which was on its last leg would have been a dangerous exercise.

If you were driving it, wouldn't you be worried that you may kill the engine and rather than going full throttle you would rather drive at a slower pace say 60km/h especially if you are not in great hurry? Yes, I think you would and I am pleased with your answer because some authors used the 80km/h. For me it sounds more like 60km/h. It is more logical and I am going to use a speed of 60km/h (so that the engine can be saved).

So, to answer the question, the alleged time of death is 8.05pm or 8.30pm

Falconio being back in the picture, the killer stopped Lees and Falconio at 8.05pm or 8.30pm (I didn't say Murdoch because it has to be proven). As I said, Falconio is back in the picture according to Lees' book; Falconio was with her…Of course! That's her story hey!

- Then after stopping the Kombi, both men Falconio and the killer got out of their car,
- Then a small conversation took place (I assume in all fairness that a 10/15minute conversation took place, could be less [?]).
- Then the killer shot Falconio in cold blood without any hesitation and permission (laughter in the background!) **Motive unknown [?]**

So, we can deduct that the killing time including the 15 minutes conversation is:

8.05pm + 0.15 = 8.20pm or 8.30pm +0.15 = 8.45pm on the 14th of July 2001

THE ALLEGED TIME OF DEATH IS OR COULD BE: 8.20PM or 8.45PM

- That is when Falconio should have dropped dead falling on the ground near or between the two parked cars, the Cruiser behind the Kombi as seen in the re-enactment (Murder in the Outback first documentary, a re-enactment which is by the way a big farce) and also metres from Lees who strangely couldn't see them but could hear them…She heard a BANG!

That is if the story is true according to Lees our only witness …But we shall see.

27 - Time of the Alleged Death [2]
According to Lees' book No turning back page 53/54

She described the moment on these terms:

"Pete stopped Taz (Taz is the name of the Kombi) on the left-hand side of the road, partly on the gravel and partly on the tar. The four-wheel drive pulled up and parked behind us. Pete got out and I moved across into his seat and began to climb out. Pete stopped me and told me to wait inside, where it was warm...

This is important but I like to remind everybody that in Australia we drive on the left so, it would be normal to stop on the left (clapping in the background).

- This tells you that it was very cold outside. Please remember she was only wearing a very light T-shirt the one with a bloodstain found at the back on the shoulder (Um!), when she was rescued by Vince Millar the road train driver who still can't believe that she was warm and clean. (I wonder if he ever found out why)

Then,

"I position myself in the driver's seat and left the door slightly ajar so I could try and see and hear what was happening..."

Then further on she wrote:

"Pete came back to the driver's side and told me everything was okay, that the man had seen sparks flying from our exhaust. He picked up his cigarettes from the shelf below the dash and asked me to rev the engine...I revved the engine and listened out, with the door slightly open, for further instructions from Pete. ...I did this a few time...There was a bang and my first thought was that it was the exhaust backfiring.

I sat up straight and looked out of the driver's side window to my right. The man filled up the window and stared back at me...I stared back into his cold eyes, paralysed. My focus was drawn to the big silver revolver he held in his right hand...I managed to stutter, why? Why are you doing this? **The man was huge** *and I felt his deadly presence all around me..."*

- As you can tell, the conversation between Falconio and the alleged killer was short. It must have taken no more than 10/15 minutes at the most as I said.

From this we can already deducted few things:
- After hearing the "bang" it certainly didn't take long for the man to appear at her window pointing a gun at her. Would half a minute or perhaps less be a fair estimation?
- <u>The man was huge</u> she said.
- The man had **a big silver revolver**. (I said big because later on, it was going to be downgraded to a smaller calibre by the Officials).

Lees –Falconio –and the man were very close to each other according to the position of the cars –Lees could hear them talking – Lees couldn't see the man –and she didn't see Falconio been shot –she only heard a bang. Do you find this realistic and logical, [NO] I don't, because if one looks at the photo of the Kombi, the Kombi has large windows all around. Even sitting behind the steering wheel, Lees would have had the full panoramic view (360 degrees) from where she was sitting, + two rear vision mirrors…Think about that!

- From here we know the alleged time of death, it is **8.45pm** on the 14th of July **(8.30pm + 15 minutes = 8.45pm on the 14th**.

This should also confirm if the story is true and if the alleged crime took place, but we don't know yet [?]. Obviously, this is all according to Joanne Lees' story the only witness of this alleged crime.

- However, Lees didn't actually saw the killing. She heard a bang yes, but didn't see Falconio drop dead on the ground metres away from her and the killer.

From the moment Falconio got shot to the moment the man filled the window pointing the gun at her, the laps of time must have been or should have been no more than say thirty seconds, but I would say half the time more like fifteen seconds. The killer has now to deal with Lees.

- Falconio is now dead on the ground

- Then the abduction of Lees takes place. It is most interesting to read the transcript of the appeal, which tells you how difficult it must have been for the alleged killer to handle Lees and also according to the experts on DNA, the body contact between the alleged killer and Lees must have left a lot of DNA on Lees' clothing. In fact, none was found….

The killer after restricting her mobility by binding her hands behind her back, then tried to restrict her feet or legs but was unsuccessful (imagine the struggle and body contact but no DNA of the alleged killer found on Lees later on, as shown in Murder in the outback)) then he pushed her into the back of his Land cruiser <u>from the cabin via a passage between the seats</u> <u>and the back of the Cruiser</u> (that is what she claimed also mentioned in the transcript below).

- Which we know is a total lie. Please ring Toyota Australia if in doubt.
- During Lees 'abduction I presume the Dead Body is/was still on the ground.
- But Lees escaped…When? How long after being pushed did she escape; we don't know [?]

From the transcript The Queen vs Murdoch [2005] NTSC 75
"Opportunity to observe offender
[8] page 3…….
"Ms Lees said in evidence at the preliminary hearing that at the time of the events it was PITCH BLACK…." (Very important)

"IN THE SUPREME COURT OF THE NORTHERN TERRITORY OF AUSTRALIA AT DARWIN The Queen v Murdoch [2005] NTSC 75 No. 20215807 BETWEEN: THE QUEEN Plaintiff AND: BRADLEY JOHN MURDOCH Defendant CORAM: MARTIN (BR) CJ REASONS FOR JUDGMENT (Delivered 15 December 2005)

The Vanishing of Peter Falconio

Introduction

[1] The accused is charged that on 14 July 2001, near Barrow Creek, he murdered Peter Marco Falconio. He is also charged that on the same occasion he deprived Joanne Rachael Lees of her personal liberty and that he unlawfully assaulted Ms Lees in circumstances of aggravation.

[2] Early in the evening of Thursday 14 July 2001, Ms Lees and Mr Falconio were travelling north in a Kombi van on the Stuart Highway approximately ten kilometres north of Barrow Creek. Mr Falconio was driving. A vehicle pulled alongside, and the driver gestured to Mr Falconio to pull over. It is the Crown case that the driver of the other vehicle was the accused. 2

[3] After Mr Falconio stopped the vehicle on the side of the highway, he walked to the rear of the Kombi van where he met the driver of the other vehicle. Ms Lees could hear the men talking about sparks coming from the exhaust. Mr Falconio returned to the driver's side door and asked Ms Lees to rev the engine. That was the last time that Ms Lees or anyone else saw Mr Falconio alive.

[4] While Ms Lees was revving the engine, she heard a loud bang. It is the Crown case that the driver of the other vehicle shot Mr Falconio… (UM! straight like that and no proofs…no worries)

[5] Ms Lees ceased revving the engine and turned to look out the window. She observed a male person standing at the driver's side window with a gun pointed at her.

[6] On two occasions Ms Lees has identified different photographs of the accused as depicting the offender. She also identified the accused in court during the course of the preliminary hearing.

[7] The Crown proposed to lead evidence of those acts of identification and to ask Ms Lees to identify the accused in court at the trial.

The accused objected to the admission of all evidence of identification by Ms Lees.

The Vanishing of Peter Falconio

I ruled that the evidence could be led and I now set out my reasons for that ruling. three Opportunity to observe offender

[8] Ms Lees said in evidence at the preliminary hearing that at the time of the events it was "pitch black". As to what occurred after Ms Lees saw the male person pointing the gun at her, the following is a convenient overview taken from a Crown summary of facts provided to the court by way of assistance for the purposes of the pre-trial objections:

"The offender told LEES to switch the engine off and moved inside the vehicle, pushing LEES to the passenger seat. The offender directed LEES to put her head down and arms behind her back. LEES screamed and struggled with the offender and put her feet up on the dash board. The offender placed the gun at LEES' temple. LEES acquiesced removing her feet from the dash and placing her hands behind her back. The offender placed cable ties (hand made from cable ties and electrical tape) around LEES' wrists and forced her out of the vehicle. LEES fell onto the gravel injuring her knees.

HERE, NO METAL IN THE CUFFS Therefore not difficult for any rescuer to free Lees from the cuffs (I like to mention it before I forget).

The offender got out of the vehicle and lifted LEES' legs up by the ankles and attempted to put electrical tape around her ankles. LEES struggled and the offender was unable to securely tighten her ankles. The offender then punched LEES to the right side of the temple. The offender lifted LEES to her feet and placed tape around her mouth and head. LEES struggled with the offender which loosened the effect of the tape. The offender forced LEES over towards the passenger side of his vehicle and removed a canvas sack from under the canopy over the tray in the utility. He then placed the sack over LEES' head and pushed her into the front passenger side of the vehicle. During this process the sack was dislodged from LEES' head.

Here I need to stop and ask:
- Why would the offender put a paper bag on her head?

The Vanishing of Peter Falconio

- To prevent Lees from identifying her offender...She had already seen his face, heard his voice and witnessed how **huge** he was (her words) during the whole struggle...Didn't she? So, what is this all about, are we all stupid?

At this time LEES observed the dog in the front driver's seat. LEES described the dog as being a medium sized, shorthaired, <u>brown and white, blue heeler</u>. LEES attempted to get out of the driver's side door but was blocked by the dog. <u>The offender forced LEES over the seats</u> into the back of the utility. Whilst LEES was in the back of the utility she screamed out to the offender, "What do you want? Is it money? Is it the van? Just take it. Are you going to rape me?

The offender came to an opening in the back of the utility and stated, "Shut up and I won't shoot you." The offender then walked away. LEES screamed out, "Have you shot my boyfriend? Have you shot Pete?" Again, the offender came to the back of the utility and said, "No." LEES heard the offender walk down the side of the vehicle on the gravel."

[9] *In evidence Ms Lees said a light was on in the offender's vehicle when she was forced into that vehicle.*

- <u>This is definitely an incredible farce.</u>

Subsequent Events

[10] On the Crown case, Ms Lees then escaped from the back of the utility and hid in the surrounding scrub. She did not see the offender again.

Ah, okay, she escaped and hid in the bush for around five hours. Let me tell you, dear reader, that on the evening and the night of the alleged offence according to the weather bureau, the outside temperature was between ten and 13 degrees Celsius.

[11] Approximately five hours later Ms Lees left her hiding spot and waved down a passing truck. The driver of the truck observed that Ms Lees was fearful and upset. Her wrists were bound by ties and she had tape around her neck and left ankle.

[12] Ms Lees was taken to Barrow Creek. At about 6am police officers arrived at Barrow Creek and took a statement from Ms Lees. She gave a

The Vanishing of Peter Falconio

description of the offender which, speaking very generally, was not inconsistent with a description of the accused. (WOW!)

Identification

[13] It is the Crown case that after the events described by Ms Lees the accused travelled to Alice Springs where, in the early hours of the morning, he stopped at the Shell truck stop and purchased fuel and other items. Images captured by a security camera at the Shell truck stop were shown to Ms Lees on 4 August 2001… (NO mention of BP where Murdoch refuelled).

Indicating an image of a person who the Crown asserts was the accused, Ms Lees said: "That man is too old, he's too old."

[14] The security film was subsequently enhanced. In evidence given at the preliminary hearing in May 2004 Ms Lees was shown the enhanced film. She said the picture she observed in August 2001 was of poorer quality than the picture she was shown in court. She said that in August 2001 she was not able to say anything about the identification of the person depicted in the video… (Here, definite contradiction, the artist employed by police, drew a sketch according to Lees 'Lees'description).

[15] As to the identity of the person shown in the enhanced film, Ms Lees said: "He's somewhat of a man I described". (here again contradiction) Ms Lees also said that the vehicle depicted was similar to the one she had described and she was unable to pick out any dissimilarity."

- Here again contradiction regarding the vehicle, because on the morning after the alleged offence after spotting a similar vehicle and most probably wanting to outwit police, she made the comment that the vehicle even being similar was not the same because the vehicle she was pushed in had a connection between the cabin and the back…It's all in the transcript as you will see later on. Therefore, lees saying that she was unable to pick out any dissimilarity is **A BIG LIE.**

From [1] to [15] above is given by the transcript.
WHAT CAN WE DEDUCT?

The Vanishing of Peter Falconio

From **[8]** –It was pitch black.

From **[10]** –After escaping she did not see the offender again. So, how is it possible for Lees hiding for five hours to witness the offender searching for her with his dog and a hand torch when in fact SHE didn't see him again, [and] that offender had to be seen in Alice Springs at 0.30am at the truck stop when claiming 'she never saw him again?"

From **[11]** – Lees hid for five hours. Do you believe Lees would come out warm –clean –and unbruised after five hours?

From **[13]** –the man is too old speaking of the offender but the Crown contrary to Lees claims that he is the man (2001)

From **[14]** –But in 2004 Lees is claiming that; "he is somewhat of a man I described "

From transcript: The Queen v Murdoch [2005] NTSC 76 No. 20215807

[7] "The details of subsequent events relied upon by the Crown for the purposes of the pre-trial objections are set out in my reasons for judgment in R v Murdoch (No 1) [2005] NTSC 75.

"In substance it is the Crown case that the accused forced Ms Lees into his vehicle from where she escaped into the scrub. While Ms Lees was hiding in the scrub the accused shifted the (3) Kombi van and left it in the scrub on the western side of the Stuart Highway."

- This tells us that, while in hiding the alleged killer had the possibility to move the Kombi **[BUT]** according to **[HER]** claim she didn't see the offender again means that after shifting the Kombi,
- The alleged killer left the alleged crime scene having no fear whatsoever by letting the prime witness to a crime he just committed go free. I find this very puzzling to say the least [?]

Of course, if you believe Joanne Lees 'story, the alleged killer had to leave at 9.00pm on the 14th July 2001 because he had to be seen at 0.30am on the 15th of July otherwise the story wouldn't stand a chance. I will be saying this again many times for people to understand that nothing fits, and she had only fifteen minutes to organise her escape...Brave woman

ALSO, from the transcripts above imagine the alleged killer struggling to restrict Lees's hands –feet –and mouth? [BUT NO DNA FOUND] on Lees's clothing later on...Amazing!

Now do you also believe that Lees had the intention of escaping from the driver's side after seeing the dog sitting behind the wheel knowing also that the alleged killer could easily stop her just by going around the front of the car...She would not have gone very far knowing it was pitch black.

- However, she gave a good description of the dog. Unfortunately, it didn't fit the description of Murdoch's dog...We all know that.
- Then it says clearly that she was pushed by the offender through a passage between the seats and the back of the utility (clapping in the background!)

After Lees being pushed and secured in the back of the Cruiser, what would be the main alleged killer's preoccupation?

I believe that he would be preoccupied with the disposal of:

The Dead Body –the burial –the cleaning of any mess –the removal of any evidence, but according to the transcript below, when Lees escaped, the killer is not preoccupied by her escape, NO, HE JUST LEFT. Wow, I find this extremely remarkable indeed!

.... While Ms Lees was hiding in the scrub the accused shifted the three Kombi van and left it in the scrub on the western side of the Stuart Highway.

- This sentence must be from the second witness: The Prosecution...AMAZING!

Well of course no mention in the transcript of the appeal about how she escaped.

- It doesn't seem that the killer is preoccupied with her escape. Instead of searching for her, he prefers and chose to move the Kombi when in fact nobody knows who moved the Kombi, how and when. (Clapping in the background).
- Nothing truly took place but now to fit the plot, **the ALLEGED KILLER** has to be seen entering the truck stop in Alice at 0.30am on the 15th the day after the alleged.

I find extremely remarkable that an alleged killer not even on the run kills Falconio in cold blood in a premeditated manner, then abduct his girlfriend, then just letting her go without any worries at all. I hope they're going to make a good movie out of it.

DO YOU SHARE MY VIEWS ON THIS?

Well, I don't buy it. The only witness to the alleged crime was Lees and Lees only.

- The alleged killer would not have moved the kombi knowing that Lees could escape.
- He could not lose her; his life would depend on it… <u>Would that be logical?</u>
- Difficult to believe that moving the Kombi was his prime preoccupation. This sounds like pre-fabricated by our only and very unreliable witness supported by our second witness; the Prosecution, including the Judge later on.

In this story everything is SIMILAR; similar look, similar four- wheel drive –similar DNA –similar dog –similar cap –similar everything. Well, they will need to modify the definition of similar in the dictionary and on the internet.

Now, what we know from the transcript is very interesting and I think you are going to laugh.

The alleged killer had only 15 minutes from the time Falconio got shot to move the Kombi – clean the mess and leave the alleged crime scene with the dead body in the back of the Cruiser (according to the Judge in his sentencing)

Do you think the alleged killer would put the dead body on the back of his vehicle and leave? I am waiting for your answer or any answer for that matter.

REHEARSAL OF THE ABOVE

The alleged killer according to Joanne Lees –the Prosecution –Mr James Hepi a drug dealer, Murdoch ex-partner –and few other people, the CCTV man is Murdoch because he looked similar and the Land Cruiser is also similar to Murdoch's one].

Similar must be the only word in the dictionary meaning… The same! So, for the moment the CCTV man seen on the film is Murdoch.

- So, the CCTV man, the alleged killer must leave the alleged crime scene at 9.00pm.
- Why 9.00pm?
- Because the CCTV man arrived at the truck stop in Alice at 0.30am on the 15th
- To arrive at 0.30am at the truck stop the CCTV man driving say 90/100km/h km/h would need between **3hours** and **30 minutes** to drive from Barrow Creek to Alice. Also, 20km before Alice it is a winding road and there are quite a few speed limits to take notice of. How do I know that? Because I drove on that road many times. So, three hours and 30 minutes is a fair estimation…Could be a bit less.
- If we deduct three hours and 30 minutes from the arrival time in Alice (0.30am). The time as I said is 9.00pm (as above).

So, 9.00pm being the departure time of the CCTV man (the alleged killer or Murdoch according to the Prosecution's crystal ball) from Barrow Creek should ring the bells: The danger bells…It should…… Why?

- Simply because the Kombi departing Ti Tree at 6.30pm
- Arriving at Barrow Creek at 8.30pm –then time of the killing 8.45pm –then the CCTV man (the killer) departing again the

alleged crime scene at 9.00pm. **That is fifteen minutes** after the alleged shooting of Falconio….
- Does this sound right? Please give me your thoughts on that?
- Knowing the killer first has to kill –then the abduction of Ms Lees –then the shifting of the Kombi –then search for Ms Lees <u>on a cold and pitch- black winter night</u> with his flash light and his cattle dog (Murdoch's dog is a Dalmatian) – the cleaning of the mess –then the removal of all evidence –and finally the burial of Peter Falconio, when Lees said that SHE NEVER SAW HIM AGAIN. Wow, remarkable. I hope they are going to make <u>another good movie</u> out of that…A real one!

Truly, what do you think? Are we all stupid? No crime was committed on that day.

BUT

Between midnight and 0.30am, just minutes before stopping to rescue Joanne Lees, the road train driver Vince Millar saw two [2] men pushing a third one (the jelly man) into a Japanese car, just before rescuing Joanne Lees around 0.15am on the 15th.
- Could this be a good decoy or could it be reality?
- Who do you think the third man could be? Falconio or his twin brother?

Strange as it may seem, Falconio re-appears in Bourke NSW a week later according to more than one witness (allegedly ten witnesses came forward) in good shape and alive! (Please read below).

The declaration of **Robert Browns** & **Melissa Kendall** who saw Falconio after his disappearance in Bourke is astonishing to say the least – (radio times also as seen on ATN 7 19-07-2020), why would they say something untrue? Keep on reading please…

"(Peter Falconio sighting Radio Times documentary series Murder in the outback)

The Vanishing of Peter Falconio

"Then we learned two witnesses claimed to have seen Falconio days after his appearance. Robert Brown and Melissa Kendall believe the backpacker is still alive after seeing him in Bourke, a remote town in New South Wales, 2,000km from where he went missing.

"I'm 200 percent sure it was Peter Falconio," said Brown in the documentary. "I will undergo any lie detector test, anything anybody wants me to. I was a metre away from him."

Walking the cameras through what happened he said: "I was reading the race results in the paper and I heard the door squeak, and Melissa was on the other side and she's yelling out to me.

"She yelled at me again and then the next minute she turned the paper over and on the front page there was a picture of a gentleman down in the bottom right-hand corner and she tapped it.

"I put the paper down and walked around the corner and then bang I am looking straight at this bloke I saw in the paper. I was sort of in shock."

He then added: "I didn't go to the police straight away because it was none of my business.

Melissa said: "I personally believe he is alive, where he is I don't know." She also explained that the police found out about the 'sighting' when an officer overheard her talking to a colleague in her former workplace.

Well dead people don't walk the streets incognito days after their death.

Would you agree that nothing took place at the alleged crime scene? And that Joanne Lees is an incredible liar. But wait there will be more.

28 The Reason Why Joanne Lees Was Found Warm and Clean When Rescued

We can see according and knowing from previous chapters that:

- The time of the arrival of the Kombi at the alleged crime scene if we believe Lees 'story is/was **8.05/8.30pm** on the 14th of July 2001.
- We don't know if Joanne Lees was alone when she arrived at Ti Tree meaning she could have dropped Falconio before arriving at Ti Tree. All we know is that police favoured the witness 'claim that she was alone watching the sunset.
- The time of death (the alleged killing) occurred at **8.45pm** (15 minutes after the arrival of the Kombi at the alleged crime scene). So, being a normal person, you would believe that Falconio was with Lees?
- I would say yes, because it is so easy for "The Officials" to dismiss a witness 'claim if the claim doesn't fit the agenda.
- But even so, we don't know if her arrival (8.05/8.30 pm) is real [?]
- She could have arrived at 10.00pm or 30 minutes before the road train driver saw two men pushing a third one into a Japanese car... Everything is possible!
- Believing Lees 'story, I calculated that from 8.45pm to 9.00pm on the 14th of July.
- The offender had only 15 minutes after the killing and the abduction of Ms Lees well secured in the back of his Cruiser; to bury the Dead Body –to clean any relevant mess –to remove any evidence –and apparently and according to Lees the offender had to search for her with a light torch and his dog... But then, she never saw him again; (Remember?).
- Knowing and according to Lees, she escaped and while in hiding, the offender shifted the Kombi...**Wow!**
- Again, according to Lees, **after she escaped, she never saw him again**, which contradict her saying that he searched for her and that she hid for around five hours.

The Vanishing of Peter Falconio

- We know also that the offender had departed the alleged crime scene at **9.00pm** aiming for Alice Springs <u>because he had to be seen entering the truck stop at 0.30am</u> on the 15th of July 2001
- Because according to Lees and the Prosecution including our dear Mr Hepi, the CCTV man is the alleged killer – the accused – and Murdoch.
- Again, and according to Lees, she came out of her hiding place around five hours after the alleged killing and her alleged abduction to be rescued by a passing truck, BUT in fact,
- If Lees' story is/was true she would only have been hiding from 9.00pm on the 14th to 0.15am on the 15th because the alleged offender left the alleged crime scene at 9.00pm. <u>That is three hours and 15minutes not five hours. (she would still be very cold not warm)</u>
- Yes, she must have thought that saying five hours in hiding would support her claim that while hiding, she could see the alleged killer searching for her. The only issue here is the timing doesn't fit.
- <u>Why would she be hiding an extra say two hours on a pitch black and very cold night?</u>
- Would you be hiding in the bush all that time on a very cold winter night wearing only a light T-shirt and shorts and knowing the killer had gone, a killer who couldn't care less about you after killing your boyfriend?
- Would you be hiding all that extra time on a cold and pitch- black winter night and be found clean, nice and warm? NO, because it would not fit with the unknown Cruiser arriving at the Shell truck-stop at 0.30am. The time then should be 2.30 am on the 15th But we know why, the alleged killer had to drop his trailer somewhere.
- Furthermore, having the alleged killer, saying to Joanne Lees *"No I won't kill you"* knowing that [**SHE**] is his death sentence, I don't think she would last long. She would get the same treatment indeed…What do you think?

The Vanishing of Peter Falconio

I CAN CONCLUDE THAT:
- The alleged killing never took place,
- Joanne Lees has never been hiding for five hours or even for three hours and 30 minutes

This is one of the reasons why Joanne Lees was found nice and warm and clean when rescued…Rescued from what we still don't know [?] She must have been sitting in a car or the Kombi, with partners involved with the plot…Sorry conspiracy!

Going back in time, knowing that Lees was seen watching the sunset at Ti Tree alone at 6.10pm means that, Falconio was dropped somewhere or left Aileron, not with Lees, but with someone else [?] Perhaps with the Aileron man –Nick the lover –or someone else driving also a Land Cruiser before Barrow Creek because as you will see, there is a discrepancy of one hour.

That will be the subject for another chapter….

The Vanishing of Peter Falconio

29 - Did Joanne Lees Really Drive Slowly from Alice To Ti Tree?

According to the transcript below: 2007 NTCCA1 –MURDOCH vs THE QUEEN 10 JAN 2007

31) Falconio and Lees were positively identified at Aileron roadhouse. "Several witnesses gave evidence that two persons answering the general description of Peter Falconio and Joanne Lees came to Aileron roadhouse about 132kilometres north of Alice Springs and were served sandwiches between 3.30pm and 4.30pm on July 2001. (Please notice that here the date 14th is not mentioned where before it is always mentioned).

An orange colour Kombi van was seen to be parked outside. At trial an issue arose as to whether the persons seen were in fact Peter Falconio and Joanne Lees or whether they had stopped at Aileron"

An issue? Unbelievable!

Well, this already tells you that any excuse will do. What was the issue? Oh! We can't tell you, this is confidential dear, don't ask stupid question hey!

***

Aileron is a welcome rest stop along the Stuart Highway offering meals, accommodation and fuel. It is located close to Ryan Well Historical Reserve.

Aileron Hotel and Roadhouse is owned by Gregory Dick who testified at the trial in 2005 is located 132km north of Alice Springs and 370km south of Tennant Creek. A giant sculpture of an Aboriginal warrior (Anmatjere Man) guards over the roadhouse.

The roadhouse offers a convenience store, meals, free guest laundry, children's playground and visitor information. There is a collection of original Albert Namatjira water colour paintings in the dining room. The accommodation ranges from powered and unpowered campsites, backpacker dormitory and self-contained motel rooms.

In the art gallery there is a display of old photographs in black and white and sepia taken in the "old days" One in particular drew my attention: the Northern Territory $250,000 reward notice regarding the

The Vanishing of Peter Falconio

disappearance of Peter Falconio on 14th July 2001 (Bastille Day …synchronicity for a French man driving through?)

That is where I spent one day and one night driving back from Darwin after my road trip following the iconic train the Ghan from Adelaide to Darwin not on the Stuart highway but on the service track that runs along the railway line through a country unknown to me and most of the people.

In the afternoon on the 14th at the Aileron roadhouse on the Stuart Hwy 181km from Barrow Creek, (Aileron to Ti tree 62 km + Ti Tree to Barrow Creek 119km = 181km) Falconio and Lees were positively identified spending some time looking at some photos and brochures and served food by the owner Gregory Dick who testified at trial and three members of his staff, including Michael Otley the manager. However, even after being positively identified at Aileron, Lees kept denying the fact completely changing the timeline of events.

This is the best part of the lot.

Yes, Gregory and his staff including the manager remember Joanne Lees and Peter Falconio very well. One of the reasons being that Lees is a very good looking **"Sheila".**

They were served sandwiches. They had been looking at photographs displayed in that room at the exception of the reward poster for the disappearance of Peter Falconio (laughter in the background).

They also had been looking at some brochures as if they were planning a holiday trip.

According to Gregory and his staff, while they were there, Lees went outside to speak to a man. They spoke for a short time next to the fuel pump. According to members of the staff, they both knew each other. Of course, <u>no mention of this at the trial.</u>

- Then she came back in and the man went. <u>Apparently from the staff the man didn't bear any resemblance to Murdoch but more like Chris Malouf</u> (interesting).
- Also, the fact that Lees went outside to talk to the man means they knew each other. <u>There is no other acceptable explanation</u> and it's not mentioned in the transcript.

The Vanishing of Peter Falconio

Perhaps that is why Chris Malouf got arrested on the early hours the day after the alleged crime? But still the question remains: How did police get to him so quickly and released him so fast?

Nobody saw Lees and Falconio leave the premises together. I suppose they paid the bill and went. Nobody saw them both getting into the kombi.

- I am now wondering if Lees got in the kombi and drove off on her own and Falconio went with the man who spoke with her.

The man who spoke with Lees was definitely not Murdoch according to the staff.

The reason for me saying this is:

- The witness watching **Lees alone watching** the sunset at 6.10pm at Ti Tree (62 km away), is not a coincidence but rather some **synchronicity.**

Time is very important but no mention of this in her book nor in the transcript. I wonder why?

- The fact that Falconio and Lees were at Aileron between 3.30pm and 4.30pm on that 14 July 2001 could be interesting

Below is what Grant Algie the Defence lawyer said from Dean Mildren's book:

Algie to the jury: If the people from Aileron are right two issues arise...Peter F & J Lees were apparently at Aileron sometime between about 3.30 pm & 4.30 pm on that afternoon [14 July 2001]. ...They sat down...had something to eat, a cup of coffee or whatever. So how does that fit with the time for leaving Alice Springs...?

- *Even if they left Aileron at 4.30 pm, they don't get to Ti Tree until 6.30 pm or thereabouts. Where's the time in the middle gone if you find there is a time in the middle? So, Aileron could be very important to you...for assessing timeline and whether there is time missing or whether the estimate of the time leaving Alice Springs can be relied upon...If they were at Aileron, why didn't Ms Lees tell you about it? [Mildren p. 29]*

The Vanishing of Peter Falconio

Well, I don't know what Grant Algie means by "time in the middle", all I can say is that the time of departure from Alice Springs is only important because Lees claimed that they drove slowly from Alice to Ti Tree (195km) because they were not in a hurry but according to Sue Williams, they had to depart Alice around 5.00pm on the 14th to be at Ti Tree at 6.10pm for the sunset. <u>The average speed would have to be around 165/173kmh</u>… food for thought.

I don't know if Joanne Lees is telling the truth saying they drove slowly, BUT I am even more suspicious about Sue Williams claiming that they left Alice at 5.00pm. How did she arrive to such conclusion? Where did she get this information from? I find this very suspicious.

***

*Note; please all calculations done in this book relevant to the speed of the dying Kombi are based on 60 or 80kmh meaning at 60kmh the travelled distance is 1 kilometre per minute and at 80kmh the distance is 80km ÷ 60 = 1.33km/minute

***

Looking into Joanne Lees and Sue Williams claims we need somehow to calculate the time of departure from Alice Springs assuming Lees is telling the truth. To do that we have two facts and five witnesses. They are:
1 –the person who watch Lees watching the sun set at Ti Tree at 6.10pm – two the owner of Aileron Roadhouse who testify at the trial and three staff members including the manager.

- So, leaving Aileron at 4.30pm indicates that Lees and Falconio arrived between 40 and 55 minutes before watching the sunset at 6.10pm.
- <u>Both arrived at Ti Tree at **5.30pm** or **5.15pm**</u> (see calculation further down<u>).</u>
- In the meantime, between 5.30pm or 5.15pm and 6.10pm, Falconio vanished before Lees watching the sunset alone. What happen during those 40/55 minutes? (This must be what the Defence was wondering about [?])

The Vanishing of Peter Falconio

- Where was Falconio then?
- What is important whatever took place after Aileron is the arrival time at Ti Tree –the departure time from Ti Tree – the arrival time at Barrow Creek –the killing time – the abduction time –the killer departing time from the alleged crime scene –and the arrival of the CCTV man and his Cruiser in Alice at 0.30am on the 15th etc.

and

- What took place at Barrow Creek (the killing field) between the arrival of Joanne Lees and Falconio (back in the picture) until the time when Lees was rescued by Vince Millar the road train driver or five hours according to her claim

Nothing else for the moment.

HOWEVER, we must keep in mind and remember that Joanne Lees said that they drove slowly from Alice to Ti Tree (195km) in two (2) hours which is an average speed of 100kmh which contradict Sue Williams' claim (173kmh), and the speed capability of the Kombi.

Now please read the calculation slowly.

- Leaving Aileron at 4.30pm driving at 60kmh the arrival time at Ti Tree 62 km away is **5.30pm**
- Leaving Aileron at 4.30pm driving at 80kmh, the arrival time at Ti Tree 62 km away is **5.15pm**
- Between 5.30pm or 5.15pm, there is a difference of time of **40** or **55 minutes** to 6.10pm (watching the sunset).
- Or Lees must have dropped him somewhere before 6.10pm [?]
- Or Falconio didn't leave Aileron with Lees but with someone, he must have been somewhere else but where [?]Given the time spent at Aileron was from 3.30pm to 4.30pm may not indicate that Falconio and Lees left together at 4.30pm, we just don't know [/]
- Lees may have left on her own driving the Kombi [?]

The Vanishing of Peter Falconio

- Falconio leaving with the man seen talking to Lees near the fuel pump may have been driving to an unknown destination. The best option would be the alleged crime scene for [rehearsal]?
- You can also assume that Falconio left Aileron in a red Japanese car or in a Land Cruiser [?]

Could this be the issue mentioned in the transcript? "At trial an issue arose as to whether the persons seen were in fact Peter Falconio and Joanne Lees or whether they had stopped at Aileron". Is this the issue that must be put under the carpet according to the agenda like Murdoch's alibi which is now classified? Come back in fifty years, if you need the answer!

You must be joking…Remember "She was a: Good Looking Sheila.

There is definitely an issue somewhere and that is why we need to calculate the time of departure from Alice.

- **The calculated time of arrival at Ti Tree 5.30pm or 5.15pm**

So, without stopping at Aileron knowing that Ti Tree is 195km from Alice Springs,

- Driving at 60kmh or 1 km/minute it would take three hours and 15 minutes **(3.15)**
- Driving at 80kmh or 1.33km/minute would take 195 ÷ 1.33 = 146 minutes = 2 hours and 26 minutes say 2 hours and 30 minutes **(2.30)**
- Which means that driving at 60kmh the departure time from Alice to arrive at Ti Tree at 5.30pm is: **5.30pm - 3.15 hours = 2.15pm**

(Remember the arriving time at Ti Tree is not 6.10pm but 5.30pm. We must deduct three hours and 15 minutes from 5.30…<u>6.10pm. is the time Lees was seen by the witness not the arrival time</u>)

- Driving at 80kmh the departure time from Alice to arrive at Ti Tree at 5.15pm is
5.15pm – 2.30 hours = 2.45pm

***

The Vanishing of Peter Falconio

So, we have departing time from Alice 2.15pm or 2.45pm without stopping at Aileron. BUT Peter Falconio and Joanne Lees did stop at Aileron. Therefore, we need to calculate the time of departure from Alice arriving at Aileron at 3.30pm after travelling at 60/80kmh.

For that we need first to calculate the driving time, travelling at 60/80kmh.

***

Calculation of the driving time travelling at 60 and 80kmh to reach Aileron 134km away from Alice.
- Travelling at 60kmh it takes 134 minutes = 2hours and 14 minutes (say **2hours and 15 minutes**) or **135 minutes.**
- Travelling at 80kmh it takes 134km ÷ 1.33 per minute = 100.75 minutes say **100** or **1hour and 40 minutes**

Now we have to deduct the travelling time from the arrival time at Aileron

If travelling at 60kmh takes two hours and 15 minutes or 135 minutes from Alice arriving at Aileron 134km away at 3.30pm, the departure time from Alice is:
- 3.30pm – 2hours and 15 minutes or 135 minutes = **1.15pm**

If travelling at 80kmh takes 1hour and 40 minutes from Alice arriving at Aileron 134km away at 3.30pm the departure time from Alice is;
3.30pm – 1 hour and 40 minutes or 100 minutes = 1.40pm

Now the question is: Did Falconio and Lees drive slowly from Alice Springs to Ti Tree?

The correct departing times from Alice are 1.15pm and 1.40pm because we assume that they did not stop at Aileron according to Lees and that we also believe her story for the purpose of the exercise.

Departing Alice at 1.15pm arriving at Ti Tree at 5.30pm the total time travelling is:

- **1.15pm to 5.30pm = 4 hours and 15 minutes or 255 minutes.**
  That is an average speed of 195km ÷ 255 minutes = 0.76km/minute x 60 = **46kmh**

Departing Alice at 1.40pm arriving at Ti Tree at 5.15pm the total travelling time is;
- **1.40pm to 5.15pm = three hours and 50 minutes or 230minutes.**
  That is an average speed of 195km ÷ 230 minutes = 0.84 km/minute x 60 = **51kmh**

***

We can now conclude that Joanne Lees saying "we drove slowly" is correct and we must admit that Sue Williams is far from the truth. However, it certainly does tell us something: It tells us that;

There is/was always a discrepancy of 1 hour in the calculation. The discrepancy is nothing else than the time Falconio and Lees spent at the roadhouse.

Yes, obviously they drove at a speed compatible for the old Kombi the only thing being: She lied about stopping at Aileron

The fact that Vince Millar the road train driver saw at the alleged crime scene two men pushing a third one (the jelly man) into a red Japanese car, minutes before Joanne Lees flagged him down to be rescued is definitely food for thought.

- In his first declaration to police, Vince Millar mentioned the fact but for unknown reasons two pages went missing.
- Police drafted a new declaration to be signed by Millar who refused to do so as it was not what he had said.
- <u>All of this has never been mentioned –debated –or revealed to the Jury at the trial</u>. At the trial the red Japanese car was mentioned but not the three men. The Jury was totally oblivious of the three men which I believed would have raised strong questions and the main question would have been: Was the jelly man Falconio? And if so,

- How is it possible for the jelly man be alive at around midnight, when he is supposed to have been killed at 8.45pm, if we assume that the jelly man is/was Falconio?

- That is why I believe Joanne Lees kept denying the fact all along.

ANYBODY in their right mind would automatically assume that the third man (the jelly man) could only be Falconio. Was the event a decoy?

Lees was definitely seen watching the sunset. She lied about stopping at Aileron. We don't know the time of arrival at the alleged crime scene. She could well have arrived at 10.00pm or close to midnight [?]. I believe Joanne Lees should be recalled. Many questions deserve answers.

The Vanishing of Peter Falconio

30 - 6.10pm At Ti Tree [1]

This is all about Lees watching the sun set alone, because if she was alone meant that Falconio was not with her making the time line totally out of perspective and as a result discrediting her alibi and claim. As we know she is the only witness, a very unreliable witness. The same applies to the Prosecution (unreliable) acting as a witness when the job is to prosecute, not to act as a witness!

From Lees 'book page 49, Lees wrote and I read:

"I was driving and Pete was asleep in the back when I saw a petrol station up a head on the right……It was the perfect place to stop and wake Pete. I had to brake heavily to swing in and the sudden movement roused Pete without me even trying" Then, *the sun was beginning to set and the scene was golden and languid…Pete leaned up to the passenger seat and I told him I'd pulled up to watch the sunset before I got petrol across the road.*

Then page 116:

"Detective Kerr moved on. She started questioning me about the camel cup, about leaving Alice Springs, about watching the sunset at Ti Tree and what Pete and I had bought at the service station…The whole interview was traumatic and the detectives sitting in front of me were completely unperturbed by the obvious drama I was experiencing."

KERR: Sorry, you are going to have to actually speak……

KERR: You said to one of the, um, I'm not sure who it was that was with you that, you had to get to your email and delete it because there was some sensitive stuff on there…

(Here it is difficult to understand the way they speak; I found it painful, sorry for saying it).

KERR: Joanne we are not trying to upset you, we really just want to clarify some of this information to focus our enquiries.

LEES: Jeanette, honestly, you can't upset me, I'm just upset enough, okay

KERR: Okay, also um, we've got a statement from a person who was at Ti Tree at the same time as you and they saw you they overtook you actually on the road.
LEES: Right.
KERR: And they saw you pull up at Ti Tree and they said that it was only you in the vehicle.
LEES: No, no. That might be because Pete …was lying down in the back when we pulled up, that did happen. He was reading his book and I woke him up
He was reading his book and I woke him up (Um)…
KERR: And that this person said that they arrived at Ti Tree Roadhouse and he had a cigarette and watch the sunset and watched you watch the sunset for about five minutes
LEES: The person did and I was on my own? Is that it?
KERR: Yeah.
LEES: Well, no… Pete was there.
So, what happen between Aileron and the arrival at Ti Tree?

- From 5.30pm arrival time at Ti Tree to 6.10pm is **40 minutes** having driven at 60kmh from Aileron.
- From 5.15pm arrival time at Ti Tree to 6.10pm is **55minutes** having driven at 80kmh from Aileron.
- Plenty of time to drop Falconio as I said, but then, if Falconio left Aileron with a man (the Aileron man) we certainly have an issue indicating a plot, for people disliking the word conspiracy!

Denying stopping at Aileron must have been "The Excuse", but the excuse for what? The story is more than significant because Aileron is where Gregory Dick –his staff –including the manager fed them. Remember Lees was a "good looking sheila" (that is from a man's point of view). Seen and remembered by the witnesses, is as good as a photograph hey!

Lees and Falconio stopping at Aileron is definitely a true fact, but what is/was the motive behind for denying it constantly (up until the trial) and also been dismissed by the Court.... Corruption –something to hide – relevant to drugs or drug lords?

According to Gregory with whom I kept contact, this evidence was presented at the trial. By not mentioning Aileron, it seems Lees hoped her readers would not start thinking about the veracity of her faked story. Also, her failure to mention Aileron 62 km south of Ti Tree is compounded by the fact that Lees also failed to mention passing through Barrow Creek later on... Which I find extremely remarkable knowing there was a big party at that time (according to Robin Bowles). As you can see Joanne Lees cannot be trusted and the same applies to the Prosecution and others of course!

Lees has claimed that she couldn't remember passing at Aileron during the day and Barrow Creek later on, is even more than significant.

- If Lees was at Ti Tree at 6.10pm watching the sunset having left Aileron at 4.30pm it was still day light.

So, saying that she couldn't remember passing Aileron when in fact they stopped there –ate –and drunk is a big "Bloody lie" but what was the real motive for denying it up until the trial?

Even if you are driving on the Hwy when you get to Aileron going north during the day, there is one thing you can't miss: That is the statues of the man and the woman of Aileron. The height of the statues is at least five metres...Could be more. They are a focus point in the landscape. I am sorry but Lees is again a very unreliable witness. Her story is faked, it is/was a scam.... Not to be trusted.

- "So, at 6.10pm at Ti Tree Lees says she watched the sunset with Falconio.
- What counts is the departure time from Ti Tree at 6.30pm.
- The witness said five minutes. Then, say five to ten minutes to refuel at the service station,
- Then departing Ti Tree at 6.30pm, after using the bathroom which must have been a most and perhaps anxious moment passing those strange bush men (according to her book page 51). Well, that's the price you have to pay for being a "good looking sheila"

The Vanishing of Peter Falconio

Do you really believe Joanne Lees' story?

Now, this is about the trip from Alice Springs to Barrow Creek where Lees denied stopping at Aileron.

- She denied the fact that she was watching the sunset <u>alone</u> but we know she did.
- The statement from the witness did prevail according to police.
- That is why I am asking the question again:
- Did Falconio went with the man who spoke to Lees at Aileron? Who was the man?
- Could the man be her lover Nick who was in Australia at that time?
- If Falconio was not at Ti Tree with Lees watching the sunset, could it be that both (Falconio and the man) went to the alleged crime scene earlier to meet with Lees later to discuss, rehearse their strategy and check the site? Which would implicate staging.
- <u>And would also indicate that nobody can tell at what time she arrived at Barrow Creek.</u>
- Lees may well have arrived much later as said, then sit in the car, the car that Vince Millar saw with three men on board or in the kombi with the others (she would be warm) or even in an unknown Land Cruiser, then moving the Kombi before the arrival of a truck or any truck, or even sitting in the Kombi which was moved; **when, by whom, we don't know [?]**
- I believe Falconio was at the alleged crime scene…You with me!
- Not because his footprints had not been identified (<u>we shall discuss the footprints later</u> on)
- But because we need to challenge all her lies to get to the truth.
- One of the four unidentified footprints must be his. Therefore, she was there, but didn't get killed.
- Then we have Vince Millar claiming he saw two men pushing a third one into a Japanese car at the alleged crime scene minutes before rescuing Lees between midnight and 0.30am on the 15th …

- Which fits perfectly the number of people in the Japanese car: **1** Falconio -**2** the Aileron man/Nick the lover as one –**3** the driver of the car + Lees because being warm when rescued she had to be sitting in a car whatever the make of the car.

The only controversial issue about this is:
- If Falconio is one of the three men in the Japanese car, it means that he is alive just before or around midnight on the 14th (repeat I know)
- <u>Meaning that he could not have been shot at 8.45 pm</u>
- One of the reasons why we do not have a Dead Body.
- And the reasons, why the people who testified having seen him days after his death must be right. Why lying regarding something so important?
- This proves one thing: The unreliability of Lees supported by the Prosecution.

Further down, Lees really makes a mistake. So many incredible unproven facts but still Murdoch was guilty! Nothing complies with the rule of law: Beyond reasonable doubt.

Going back to the beginning of this chapter, this is what Lees said about her arrival at Ti Tree:
- *"I was driving and Pete was asleep in the back when I saw a petrol station up ahead on the right....*
- *I saw a layby on the left just before the petrol station....*
- <u>*I had to brake heavily to swing in and the sudden movement roused Pete*</u> *without me even trying....*
- *During the interview, Lees said* <u>*she "woke him up."*</u>
- *But in her book, she changed her story to* <u>*"the sudden movement roused Pete without me even trying."*</u>

Then, she said that Falconio "got out of the Kombi." According to Lees, Falconio did not go back to sleep. She wrote;
- *She braked the vehicle and* <u>*that is what awoke Falconio*</u>*.*

The Vanishing of Peter Falconio

- She wrote *that the vehicle stopped and almost immediately Falconio stepped out of the Kombi and stretched.*

In the statement Kerr had, the witness watched Lees, on her own, "watch the sunset for about five minutes."

- So where was Peter Falconio? The only possible solution is: Peter Falconio is/was The Invisible Man!

However, no mention also of Murdoch following them from Alice to Aileron then from Aileron to Ti Tree then again from Ti Tree to Barrow Creek hey! They should have let him pass…They were driving slowly (clapping in the background).

The other explanation being: Lees and Falconio did not leave Alice at 5.00pm as we know we just did the calculation. This not "The Philadelphia Experiment" (The movie 1984).

There are discrepancies in relation to time claimed by Lees and distances. She claimed she drove with Falconio (asleep in the back where no one could see him?).

- Even more remarkable that at one stage the Prosecution claimed that Murdoch thought Lees was travelling alone. Hard to believe hey! I think that the Prosecution needs a new Crystal Ball…Definitely!

But don't worry, soon Joanne Lees will make a bigger error.

31 - Footprints –Shooting

*[*3a] A footprint expert has confirmed that the four [4] unidentified footprints at the alleged offence scene didn't match Murdoch's footprints but belong to someone else

- According to the experts, the only footprints found and identified at the alleged crime scene **seems or is a probability that it belongs to Joanne Lees.** That is extraordinary (read from FFDA further down).

I can't get my head around. I am debating the issue starting with the above four unidentified footprints and asking: What about Falconio?

After all, if we have Lees' prints, we should have obviously Falconio's footprints also.

- I like to mention that you will find on the internet claims that because of rain, evidence was destroyed like wheel marks, footprints etc. Nonetheless, five footprints were found (Lees + four unidentified) regardless cyclone or not (if you know my meaning).
- So, please how do you explain Joanne Lees 'footprints and the four unidentified footprints found by the experts including some Aboriginal trackers?
- We should have then: Lees + Falconio + three unidentified footprints.
- But no footprints from Falconio creates a problem.
- The experts said four unidentified footprints: that is a fact. Who then owns the four unidentified footprints?
- **1** Falconio –**2** the driver of the Japanese car –**3** the Aileron man –**4** Nick Lees' lover?

OR

- **1** Falconio -**2** the driver of the Japanese car –**3** the Aileron man/Nick the lover as one – **4** and another man who drives a Land Cruiser?

The Vanishing of Peter Falconio

- We know that the road train driver saw two men pushing a third one into the red Japanese car, that is three people + Lees = four people but it says four unidentified therefore should be **[5]**
- Which means in the Japanese car we could have: **1** Falconio –**2** the driver of the car – **3** the Aileron man (as I said before)

OR

- **1** Falconio –**2** the driver of the car –**3** Nick the lover Nick or a Land Cruiser man?
- Which means the Aileron man and Nick the lover could be the same person [?]
- The Aileron man being the one who spoke to Lees near the fuel pump [?]
- Or Nick Lees' lover who was in Australia at the time [?]
- In the Japanese car we would have then: **1** Falconio –**2** the driver of the car – **3** Nick the lover or the Aileron man as one.

But that is only three unidentified footprints not four if the Aileron man and Nick the lover is the same person [?]

Who could own the fourth unidentified footprints?

- Could it be a man driving a Land Cruiser? **The CCTV man** (who was never identified regardless what Lees –the Prosecution –or Mr Hepi claimed) or **Chris Malouf** who allegedly camped 55 metres from the alleged crime scene, then was arrested on the same morning the day after the alleged crime but who then was released by police?

Well, the CCTV man may or may not be eliminated because he has to be seen at 0.30am being the CCTV man or Murdoch according to Lees and the Prosecution and Mr Hepi.

We need to prove that the CCTV man is not Murdoch or vice versa. But we need both for the exercise.

By the way everybody I spoke to believe that the man pushed by the two men into the red Japanese car could be Falconio.

The Vanishing of Peter Falconio

Now let me say this: When the alleged crime and the abduction took place, both men (Murdoch and Falconio) were not walking on their hands but more likely with their feet firmly on the ground; are you ok with that? And please remember this story truly belongs to Joanne Lees.

*NOTE: We need to understand that to identify a footprint, what you need is a shoe of the person of interest, so you can compare it with any unidentified prints. If you don't have a shoe, it is mission impossible… This must apply to Murdoch, Lees, Falconio or any unidentified person of [interest] or [not]. They had Murdoch and Lees' shoes. Lees' footprints were identified <u>but not Murdoch</u>.

That is why Falconio's shoeprints could not be identified, no shoes for comparison.

This on its own is a real puzzle. Somehow it is the proof beyond reasonable doubt that:

- Murdoch was not at the alleged crime scene, therefore incapable to have killed Falconio. I hope that you will agree with me.
Everything expresses doubt and only doubt, nothing else.
Everything is based according and related to Lees' claim, because she is the only witness.
- Lees was definitely at the alleged crime scene her footprints were identified and she was so to speak rescued there…From what we don't know [?]

One could claim that Murdoch may have disposed of his shoes on the day of the alleged offence or before being arrested but nothing else belonging to him was identified. It includes dog –car –trailer –blood – cigarettes butts etc.

SO,

Getting back to our footprints it is quite logical that Falconio's footprints could not be identified because the lack of a Dead Body, meaning that the experts do not have his shoes for comparison. The same applies to the time of death. It is the same story for the three unidentified footprints…. Bob's your uncle!

The Vanishing of Peter Falconio

Now to resume this chapter we should have: Lees + Falconio + three unidentified footprints all walking on their feet on the ground (Murdoch is out because the experts are positive, the footprints didn't match Murdoch's shoes).

SO, WE HAVE...

- Peter Falconio was there.
- The driver of the Japanese car was there.
- Lees' lover (Nick) or the Aileron man (if they are one) were there
- The driver of a Land Cruiser (Chris Malouf) was in the area.
- Someone else who also owns a Land Cruiser like the CCTV man must have been there according to Lees –the Prosecution –and Monsieur James Hepi.

In the Japanese car we may have:

- 1 Falconio –2 the Aileron man/Nick the lover -3 the driver of the car.

We have then: 1 Lees identified –2 Falconio not identified –3 the driver of the Japanese car not identified – 4 Nick the lover not identified –5 the Aileron man not identified. That is excluding any man who owns a Land Cruiser for the moment. But definitely excluding Murdoch for sure.

OK, what is this? Well, it is a big bag of lies. It appears to be the product of Lees' imagination and the creation of a crime that did not happen.

Extra reading from FFDA

According to FFDA [Media Release Extracts p228/229/230:] below

Analysis of a footprint found at the scene shows that, in all probability, it matches the shoes belonging to Joanne Lees. No time; 19 July 2001

The word probability was used to deceive. A probability is a maybe, BUT definitely not a certainty"

The Vanishing of Peter Falconio

This indicates "not a certainty". What is the prosecution trying to say? That Lees was there but no, Lees was no there…Does anyone comprehend this?

My deduction and my preferred option at this stage is: If Murdoch was not there, why a Guilty Verdict? Yes, I know; The DNA TRUMP CARD, but wait the book is not finished!

And to make things a bit more complicated……If Murdoch and Falconio were not at the alleged scene (only Lees) please explain the fact:

That Murdoch (who was not there) killed Peter Falconio (who was not there) ah! ah! ah!

Nobody can answer by yes or no. Doubt is constantly present. (Clapping in the background). This is a puzzle for Monsieur Poirot (He's better than the police!).

The Vanishing of Peter Falconio

32 - Most Of What the Jury Knows ...

…Including myself

What the jury knows I assume is mostly from Joanne Lees –the Prosecution and the Defence and of course from witnesses good or bad – experts good or bad, but they are also definitely influenced by the media.

Also (I only assume) knowing that the Judge's daughter Joanna Martin was in the relationship with a juror who sat on Murdoch's trial, that juror may have considerably and most certainly influenced the other jurors. Like in the movie "The Juror 1996 with Demi Moore and Alec Baldwin.

Anybody else get information from TV, newspapers, the media of course, radio, friends etc.

- The Prosecution gets information (didn't say facts) primarily from Joanne Lees, in this case being the only witness but also from other witnesses -experts and also from the media –television – newspapers etc. We learnt and know that, if the Prosecution doesn't like the testimony of a witness, (not fitting the agenda) the testimony will be rejected and dismissed… (Like the testimony of **Gregory Dick,** the owner of the Aileron Roadhouse.). Anything about the case not in accordance with their narrative and agenda will be ignored –dismissed and sometime ridiculed.

From what we have learnt and what we have established, we can see that this trial is/was by definition: NOT a fair trial!

I have transcripts of the appeals (downloaded from the internet) not the actual trial.

Actually, it is interesting that one can download the transcripts of the appeals from the net, but you must request the authorisation to obtain the transcript from of the trial which may be refused depending on: Who you are –what you do –and the reason why you need the document.

If the Department thinks it's OK, you may obtain the transcript for a very inflated price.

The jurors I assume only get the information from the Officials.

The Vanishing of Peter Falconio

What I hear or read is mostly from books –the internet –newspapers – witnesses like Gregory dick –Andrew Fraser when he was alive –Victor Susman and their televised show – from people helping me in my research etc. Not much from the Defence unless mentioned in books like the book by Judge Mildren, and of course unfortunately from some unfounded bias misinformation found on the internet. BUT I have also some good readings from the internet which have not been picked up by too many people (someone has to be lucky sometimes). I realised also that some people definitely love blood.

As I said the Prosecution runs the trial according to their narrative and agenda and so does the Defence, but I think the Defence could have done much better…The Defence had four years to prepare for the trial.

I suppose the Defence tried to do its best but I believe it could have done better to challenged claims by Joanne Lees –the Prosecution –the police –some experts –some witnesses like James Hepi etc. The DNA trump card was not properly challenged.

The most liable participants in the case are Joanne Lees –the Judge – the Prosecution –police – our dear Mr Hepi –and some people calling themselves experts.

The only true source of information about this alleged crime is deeply buried into Joanne Lees 'head. It is all about her. She knows what has taken place, she was at the alleged crime scene where nothing took place.

No wonder the Prosecution won the case. Just stick to what Joanne Lees says and the bloodstain of unknown source and we'll be right…Murdoch is guilty unless I say otherwise…Amazing!

- The fact that the Dead Body of Falconio has never been found;
- And that there are no proofs whatsoever that Murdoch was at the alleged crime scene knowing his footprints were never identified,
- As well as the wheel marks of his car and trailer.
- <u>There is no evidence of his dog being at the scene,</u>
- No evidence that a big gun was used, no emptied cartridges found and more.

The Vanishing of Peter Falconio

This alone I believe would have been sufficient for the case to receive a not guilty verdict if the Judge had been honest and if the jury hadn't been influenced.

- He definitely was not an honest and impartial judge.
- He hid the truth from the Jury about the majority verdict
- He wanted the verdict to be unanimous at all cost.
- A majority verdict would have saved and freed Murdoch.
- …And he certainly did not advertise about his daughter having a relationship with one of the Juror who sat on Murdoch's trial.

It was definitely a miscarriage of justice, a big farce, a total disgrace…. That was the agenda. But why? What is the reason behind all this? Big profits from drugs? Something secret, classified? Who are the beneficiaries –who profited from the verdict?

33 - How Did Joanne Lees Escape? Did She Really Escape?

- Yes, how did she escape from the back of the Cruiser? Murdoch's Ute has never been shown to the public eyes, Murdoch's Ute yes had an opening at the back, but a cage is/was blocking the exit. The Ute which should have been pulling a camper van.
- How did she escape with her hand tied up in the back on that <u>pitch black and freezing</u> outback winter night? <u>The temperature that night was between ten and 13 degrees.</u>
- Knowing that Lees was only wearing a very light T-shirt and shorts including the home-made cuffs being part of the outfit?

Well, we don't know even if we think we know. But there is a little problem. ….

On the photograph from the internet showing the unknown Land Cruiser owned by the unknown CCTV Man (not Murdoch's Cruiser) which has never been identified (for good or bad reasons), the canvas top has opening on all sides (there must be one on the other side but we can't see it on the photograph).

- Each opening is a large rectangle with a zip going all the way from top left to top right or vice versa like a suitcase.
- That is why the bottom of the corners are rounded. That is the design.
- So instead of having three zips for each opening, you only have one, as I said like a suitcase. Usually, this type of zip is very strong because canvas is a strong fabric and cannot be unzipped from the inside…Why?
- Because there is no need for it <u>as there is no communication between the cabin and</u> <u>the back tray.</u>

It's not like your sleeping bag which you may unzip from the outside or from the inside. In this instance, with the canvas top you can't from the inside only from the outside because it is not necessary – it is designed that way.

The Vanishing of Peter Falconio

Even judging by the poor photograph there is only one zip per opening to confirm what I just said. You can only unzip each opening from outside the car, not from the inside.

Now the reason for me saying this is:

- The alleged killer pushed Lees in the back of his car via the cabin, but this is according to her story. Imagine the killer lifting Lees putting her in the back when she is desperately fighting this alleged killer who couldn't even restrain her feet. So, imaging the killer lifting Lees who must be at least 50/60kg trying to push her onto the tray from the left or right side without dropping the sides He has to lift her to the height of 1.20m from the ground. Well, good luck to him.
- Her hands were restrained behind her back with the handmade cuffs made of cable ties (plastic) and tape (plastic).

Please understand before I continue that I am speaking here referring to the Land Cruiser seen on the CCTV film from the Shell Station in Alice Springs which has never been identified. The Cruiser on the film has three openings. BUT Murdoch's Cruiser has also three openings, (left –right – and back), but the back opening is blocked, because of a cage.

- Knowing that Lees claimed she escaped from the back, is a big lie. At what stage could she have brought back her hands to her front? She had only 15 minutes to organise her escape, from 8.45 pm to 9.00pm.
- Also, the person who made the cuffs made sure that each wrist was well apart easier to get your legs through. Even if it was easy to bring her hand to the front, she only had 15 minutes and she had to do it in pitch dark environment when the alleged killer was shifting the Kombi (remember?)
- Do you think Murdoch would have left any opening of the canvas unzipped?

My question is: Why would he leave it unzipped?

- My answer is: **NO.** He would not have left both sides of the canvas open meaning, Lees would have found herself in an even darker or pitch- black environment than the outside.
- Having said that, she said she escape from the back. Ok let us assume she did. We have not one opening unzipped, how is she going to escape? Her hands are tied up and she has no tools like a knife to cut the canvas.
- Mind you she claimed that it was pitch black we know, BUT on the morning after the alleged crime, she saw a similar parked four-wheel drive Ute.

Below is from the transcript: Please read slowly what she said;
Even more suspicious when reading the transcript 2007NTCCA1 – Murdoch vs The Queen **10 January 2007**

(32) After the police had arrived Ms Lees identified a standard white Toyota Land Cruiser utility with a green canvas cover as being somewhat similar to the vehicle driven by her assailant. However, she said that there were some differences. For example, in the vehicle looked at by her it was not possible to go through from cab to the tray at the rear. The canopy also seemed to be a different colour on the inside

Please understand, this was on the morning of the day after the alleged crime. She saw the Toyota Land Cruiser and I believe she tried to outsmart the officers with her comments, especially with her comment about the colour of the canopy on the inside.

If the alleged crime had really taken place, being inside in the back of the Cruiser in total darkness, how could she notice the difference of the shade of the canopy's colour on the inside?

If I had been the officer, her comment would have been "the alarm bell Perhaps it did.

The Vanishing of Peter Falconio

Remember police was called for a murder and abduction case. Lees was the victim (serious business) But I also believe that when questioned by police. Police was somehow telling her or giving her too many information or hints.

Looking at the vehicle Lees said there was some differences.

- Firstly, it was not possible to go through from the cab to the tray at rear (we all know that). Therefore, wrong vehicle not matching the alleged killer's vehicle (similar but not the same…interesting)
- But she didn't. She must have thought that some Cruisers had a communication cab/tray. Well, she didn't do her homework (first lie, not a mistake but lie).

Remember she is our only witness. She claimed someone killed Falconio, but there is no Dead Body and she is alive meaning that if a man has the audacity to kill her boyfriend at point blank but has the kindness to let her go (remember when she claimed the killer said to her: No I won't kill you), well I am sorry but I find this very remarkable indeed. Anyhow her comment is/was a LIE.

- Saying *"The canopy seemed to be a different colour on the inside"*, is truly laughable! and so is her belief about the communication cabin/tray

From the moment she flagged down the road train her mind must have been working overtime. She knew she had been seen at Ti Tree at 6.10pm watching the sunset ALONE (unforeseen). She must have been stressed. But in the morning after police had arrived when she pointed out the Land Cruiser. It must have been some kind of instantaneous self-defence or self-preservation mechanism "<u>I am telling the truth, look here, there is a similar car there</u>" I am a good girl". The problem is that later on, when questioned she still had no idea that no Land Cruiser has a communication between the cab and the tray.

Then mentioning the different colour of the canopy could have been probably the urge pretending to be a good observer for further reference making sure people will trust the voracity of her story.

The Vanishing of Peter Falconio

There are facts she definitely had forgotten like the fact that you cannot spend five hours in the open wearing a light T-shirt when the temperature is/was between ten and 13 degrees on a cold and black winter night and being warm when rescued.

Also, you cannot pretend having being pushed in the back of a Land Cruiser when there is no communication between the cabin and the back and when it is pitch black outside and even darker inside totally enclosed by the canopy and nevertheless being able to differentiate the different shade of green of the canopy. BUT her answer was; I need to look for other opportunities.

I am sorry, but no one can. We cannot trust Lees

So, OK the vehicle she observed in the presence of police was similar in look. Now let us go back to the Land Cruiser seen on the CCTV film.

- She wouldn't have been able to unzip the canvas top from inside, in the dark or pitch black with her hands restrained in her back.
- The only way for her to get out of the Cruiser is/was from either the right or the left side.
- Firstly, she would have needed a knife to cut the canvas if she could but having her hands tied up and no knife <u>I have serious doubts.</u>

If you have a different idea about how she got out, I am willing to listen.

So, Joanne Lees claimed that with her hands tied up behind her back, she managed to get out   not even noticing the trailer or any jerry cans (Um!). Also, I would have loved to witness the FALL!

As far as I am concerned it's all a big bag of lies and mission impossible.

, Now please tell me: How did she get out of Murdoch's Land Cruiser which has: YES, an exit at the back, BUT THAT EXIST IS BLOCKED BY A CAGE or even from the back of the Cruiser seen on the CCTV film which is NOT blocked by a cage? If she did, the fall would have been horrible. It could even have killed her. Also, even if the canvas had some slack, it would not have been possible for her to put her body feet and legs first through the slack…Impossible! Even if a miracle had taken place the fall would have been deadly as I said.

The three openings and the system of zips is relevant only to the photo of the Cruiser seen on the CCTV film, the Cruiser which the Prosecution wants you to believe is Murdoch's Cruiser. The fact is that Murdoch's Cruiser did not have three openings at that time (14th of July) only two because of A CAGE.

- Claiming she escaped from the back of the Cruiser is a LIE
- Even in the useless re-enactment you can see her getting out, [NOT] from back, but from the right side of the tray (driver side) <u>with the flaps of the canopy up and the sides dropped</u>…**AMAZING,** and they call this re-enactment!
- That is false information, a lie. But it's OK, she could claim whatever she likes.

Obviously, the Officials never had the intention of showing Murdoch's Cruiser on the Internet. If they did it would have been: Spot the difference hey!

Joanne Lees' claiming her escape is a LIE. NO CRIME WAS COMMITTED, PURE FICTION

- That is why she never saw the trailer nor the jerry cans (if any).
- Another false claim, but don't worry she found <u>*"other opportunities"*</u>.

Actually, a question remains;

- When the re-enactment took place, did the officials hired a Land Cruiser and asked Joanne Lees to show how she got out of the Cruiser. Murder in the outback series shows a bit of the re-enactment which is truly a big farce, nothing to do with real re-enactment at all.
- I hope they got a Cruiser with the right canvas and compatible green colour on the inside

The Vanishing of Peter Falconio

- If they did, I hope that there was an ambulance on standby! The fall would have been interesting to see.
- And by the way after her showing how she got out from the back, did police ask her to hide in the bush for five hours (as she claimed), just to prove the point: Her being warm and fresh after five hours. On the night of the alleged crime the temperature was ten to 13 degrees (repeat I know).

To use the language of the Prosecution; if you are satisfied with my comments, well I believe pitch black means very dark and escaping means escaping.

So, how did Joanne Lees escape?

Using the words "pitch black" in her mind was meant to emphasise the weather conditions on the night hoping to give more credibility to her story, but she had forgotten that she had pointed out a similar Cruiser on the morning the day after the alleged crime scene to police saying:

"The canopy also seemed to be a different colour on the inside", meaning one minute she is blind but the next minute she's OK!

Being in the back of the Cruiser with her hands restrained in the back with the cuffs, her environment must have certainly been pitch black and very cold.

But as you know she came out OK nice and warm and clean…Outstanding, extraordinaire!

Her answers reflect perfectly the way her mind operates and, why so many lies. It is very compatible with the old proverb which comes from Ancient Greece and is quoted in French from the 16th century by Erasmus: "Au royaume des aveugles les borgne sont rois" which translate "In the kingdom of the blind the one-eyed are king" It is a perfect match.

The Vanishing of Peter Falconio

34 - Re-Enactment

In chapter [28] I spoke briefly about the reason [why Joanne Lees was found nice and warm when rescued?]

Here, we are speaking of re-enactment. The definition is easy to comprehend: The acting out or repetition of a past event or situation.

- A re-enactment should prove or disprove claims made by witnesses in relation to:
- Any evidences and/or alibis, physical or otherwise.

In our case, it is to find out beyond any reasonable doubt if Joanne Lees our prime witness to this alleged crime is/has been telling the truth and nothing but the truth and I mean by that:

- Did Falconio really get shot... how and when?
- Did her abduction really take place... how and when?
- Did she really escape and how did she do it?
- Did she truly spend five hours hiding in the bush on a very cold and pitch-black winter night wearing only a light T-shirt and short, but found nice and warm when rescued according to Vince Millar th truck driver?

Out of these four questions, only the first cannot submitted to a re-enactment. If successful in proving beyond reasonable doubt that she is telling the truth, she must pass, not fail the re-enactment, like in the army. Then we'll known where we stand but not until then.

One must admit that for Joanne Lees staying in the bush for five hours dressed the way she was in an environment where the temperature is/was between 10 and 13 degrees is remarkable coming out nice and warm and clean as per Vince Millar's claim. Any other re-enactment would be fruitless.

Only what did happen to her own person can be re-enacted nothing else. How would she feel been locked up in a fridge for five hours where the temperature was 10/13 degrees? I will accept any answers excluding hers, but let's see how she comes out if we repeat the experiment ie locking her in a fridge for five hours without a cup of coffee and biscuits. Remember she is the only witness and a Dead Body has never been found.

The situation here is the location –the weather condition – the time and duration of isolation –the way the person is dressed and why would a killer let the only witness to his premeditated crime go free?

In Murder in the Outback, you may watch few video clips taken during the re-enactment. It is a joke. At one stage you can see how Joanne Lees (pretending) got out from the right side of a Land Cruiser where all the canvas flaps are up and the side gate down …A real joke!

Firstly, she comes out to from the right- hand side (driver side) where the canopy flap is up (unzipped) and she's not wearying any cuffs.

Well, a true re-enactment should be:

[1] Lees 'movement should be restricted (she should be cuffed) – **[2]** then someone participating in the re-enactment, someone should lift Lees onto the back of the Cruiser (because no communication between the cabin and the back meaning the alleged killer had to lift her up…you with me!) – **[3]** then all sides should be secured (zipped) – **[4]** then watch and witness how Lees gets out and how long it takes, **[5]** and finally check the performance after five hours. That would have been a real re-enactment….

Was the re-enactment done following the rules of engagement? **NOT AT ALL**.

Truly, the whole thing is/was a joke!

35 - Cable Ties

[4a] Lees admitted to having cable ties in the back of the Kombi (but denied that she used the ties to bind herself)

Here, we are speaking of **cable ties**. However, in the documentary on ATN 7 what is shown is not only cable ties but some kind of handmade cuffs which seemed to be easy to put on or off if someone is in a hurry. They (the cuffs) are made of tape and cable ties. We are not speaking here of simple cable ties which would be quite painful because they would have the wrists touching each other which would really cut into the skin, therefore leaving substantial painful marks. They are completely different than the one you may see in a movie or in real life. However, if you had been the alleged killer, you would not have made the cuffs. You could have gone to any sex shop and get the real one. That would have saved you some issues, like finding the black tape three months later ah ah! It would also have simplified the work for the DNA experts…Just like to mention it in case you are a real premeditated killer understanding such situation.

But, oh yes, I got it, someone made the cuffs indicating the alleged crime was meticulously planned, therefore premeditated. Of course, the alleged killer must have made the cuffs… Why? Well Murdoch is a meticulous killer, the Prosecution said so, even the Judge in his sentencing. Murdoch even wrap the head of the dead body in Lees 'jacket, then put the body onto the back of his vehicle. YES, the alleged crime was premeditated. WHY?

Because, it must have taken him some time to make the cuffs. He could not have made it at the alleged crime scene. <u>Murdoch must have premeditated his crime</u>…Clever bad boy –meticulous killer–very resourceful and full of empathy for his victim. Having made the cuffs in such a way that it would less painful for Joanne to wear (clapping in the background)

Murdoch could not have made the cuffs before but after he feared that Falconio and Lees were spying on him. So, he must have bought some lip gloss and tape and made the cuffs on the side of the road (laughter in the back) then disposing of the item at the alleged crime scene (the leftover of the tape and the lip gloss), so it can be found three months later…Clever boy our Murdoch!

- Also, among all this, a police officer took the handmade cuffs in a paper bag to Murdoch who was in jail accused of rape but found not guilty on all charges.
- He is/was definitely a target being a drug dealer and a bad boy.
- So, three months after the alleged offence at Barrow Creek a police officer takes the cuffs in a paper bag to Murdoch (still in jail awaiting trial for the rape case) as if the officer was bringing Murdoch's lunch.
- Definitely a real professional cop interviewing a man accused of murder! God help us.

Evidence in a murder case taken in a paper bag like a burger wow! Perhaps both were in the bag (the cuffs and the burger that is) making sure that Murdoch finger prints would be all over the restraints, with the compliments from the police force…Why not?

By doing so, contamination was more than possible. May be the officer simply gave the cuffs to Murdoch asking:

"Did you make these? ".... and Murdoch grabbing the cuffs replying:" Mate, I just can't re-call, what are they? Wow, what a farce, unbelievable!

Was the intention to frame Murdoch or to show him that the burgers are better at Hungry Jack! My instincts are telling me that it was to frame him because I don't think that the patch of bloodstain found (or put there) only on the back of Lees' T-Shirt could be sufficient evidence and that they were most probably setting up more evidence regarding the DNA, hoping that Murdoch would grab the cuffs wanting to look at them. (Possible, but only assuming, we know that police was desperate to get Murdoch's DNA). They really believed that Murdoch or the alleged killer was a real idiot! However, and interesting is to find, in the transcript that **Acting Deputy Commissioner of Northern Territory John Dalby** saying: "Police would not rely on DNA evidence"

- Knowing that the burgers are better at Hungry Jack and the cuffs were stored with all other items regarding the case, known as evidence in a room which according to the Defence was not well secured and could be accessed by anyone.
- I am asking is this truly a reliable evidence in a trial involving a murder case beyond reasonable doubt where a man is accused of killing a man in cold blood but let his girlfriend go free when she is the only witness?

Regarding the DNA testing done on the cuffs and the final results, I am asking:

- Was Murdoch's DNA found on the cuffs beyond reasonable doubt?
- Was Joanne Lees' DNA found on the cuffs beyond reasonable doubt?
- Was someone else's DNA found on the cuffs beyond reasonable doubt?
- Was the officer who put the cuffs in the paper bag wearing gloves?
- Was the officer who delivered the cuffs in the paper bag to Murdoch (in jail) wearing gloves?
- Was Vince Millar and his co-driver's DNA on the cuffs? Both had been helping to get rid of the cuffs when Lees was rescued.
- Vince Millar claimed that when he rescued Lees, she was still wearing the cuff. Interesting because in the previous chapter, we don't know when Lees freed herself from the cuffs. <u>Therefore, going back to what I said, the fall must have been much worse than what I first thought.</u>
- Three people then at the alleged rescued scene did touch the cuffs as they were trying to free Lees' hands and they were:
- The road train driver –his co-driver – Joanne Lees
- Trying to free herself before her rescue Lees must have left plenty of her DNA on the cuffs…I assume [?]

The Vanishing of Peter Falconio

Please, NO, NO don't come forward, I know the answer. It was done with extreme and utmost professionalism by police…of course! The taking of the cuffs to show Murdoch… that is.

The Vanishing of Peter Falconio

36 - One Fact That Nobody Can Deny

[5a] Murdoch was positively identified by four separate people as being in Fitzroy Crossing in Western Australia around 8.00pm WA time on the 15th July 2001, 1,412km away.

This has been proven.

The refuelling was confirmed.

Murdoch said and claimed that at the time of the alleged abduction he was nearly or close enough to Yuendumu 335km from Alice Springs (190km + 145km = 335km). (Court of Criminal Appeal Murdoch vs The Queen [2007] NTCCA 1 No CA 2/06 [20215807])

- Murdoch claimed that around the alleged time of the crime he was near Yuendumu. It doesn't mean that he arrived at Yuendumu at the time of the alleged crime. He could have left Alice Springs at any time and arrived at Yuendumu as per his claim (You will find out the time further on)
- As far as being near or at Yuendumu we don't know (but I will sort it out).
- The transcript also said that Murdoch claimed that between midnight and 1.00am on the 15th of July 2001 he was near the Granite gold mine, (I will sort it out also).

We know from chapter 31 (footprints/shooting) that four unidentified footprints have created a problem if the CCTV man is not included. Including him could fit the plot.

- **1** Falconio – **2** the Aileron man/ Nick the lover –**3** the driver of the Japanese car –**4** perhaps the CCTV man or another man who owns a Land Cruiser.

The Vanishing of Peter Falconio

37 - Toyota Land Cruiser

[6a] Murdoch's vehicle doesn't have a second compartment where Lees said she was pushed into; nor would it be possible, had the vehicle been of the variety implied, for a person to be pushed from the front section in to the rear.

We have already discussed this.

Now read this from FFDA p.299

"Yes, the police told me there was no such vehicle with front-to rear access, and that has put doubt in my mind. I looked for [sic] other possibilities." (Joanne Lees- blood on the track -naptn.org 26 October 2005)

I looked for other possibilities, ah, not bad, is this a joke? It made me sick when I read it.

If you have been watching the show on Channel Seven, she even added during the recorded police video:

"it was easy the seats were somehow folded down" ...Folding seats on a Land Cruiser Ute? That's a good one, the best I've heard for a long time!

Because saying "I looked for other possibilities" means that she is definitely doesn't care one iota. She is some kind of unreliable and untouchable witness, she does not give a damn about facts, she is free to change any claims she wants or need to be updated her way, she can create any lies she wants. The police and the officials will accept anything she says. Well, this is sickening!

Murdoch's car is a Land Cruiser (same as mine 75 Series), yes it may have bucket seats. Many Land Cruisers have bucket seats. BUT you will not find a Land Cruiser with a communication between the cabin and the tray (back of the Ute). I am myself a Land Cruiser man, and I know how a Land Cruiser is built, Toyota has never produced one. Originally the models we have here in Australia were conceived for Saudi Arabia and South Africa. The engine 1 HZ 4.2 diesel no turbo which I have was apparently made for South Africa. There is no way one can load an item from the cabin onto the back of the Ute. There is no communication between the cabin and the back. To load anything, it must be done from the back or from the sides. One must be outside not in the cabin. Furthermore, the seats are not folding seats. The back wall of the cabin makes it impossible to fold any seats. It is not a camping car. This is totally wrong coming from Lees, but it was accepted by the Prosecution –police –and all the officials including the Jury. I said police, because police checked over 16,000 Toyota Land Cruisers then gave up. Wow, that's what I call good police work hey!

Saying "I look for other possibilities" is the proof that she cannot and must not be trusted.

Here we are again, even more suspicious when reading the transcript 2007NTCCA1 –Murdoch vs The Queen 10 January 2007 (already discussed).

(32) After the police had arrived Ms Lees identified a standard white Toyota Land Cruiser utility with a green canvas cover as being somewhat similar to the vehicle driven by her assailant. However, she said that there were some differences. For example, in the vehicle looked at by her it was not possible to go through from cab to the tray at the rear. The canopy also seemed to be a different colour on the inside

What is the meaning of this? It means that when police arrived Lees identified a parked vehicle similar to the one owned by the alleged offender confirming that (already spoken, but I like to remind everyone again and again).

- She claimed she had been pushed from the cabin to the back of the Ute which is false. No Land Cruiser has connection between the cabin and the back of the Ute.

Lees also claimed that, when pushed into the back of the Ute:

- It was "pitch black"
- So, how is it possible for Lees being in the back of the Ute when it is "pitch black" to differentiate the inside colour of the canopy?

The Vanishing of Peter Falconio

This is another big mistake but as you know, she is free to change anything she wants.

She just needs time to think so she can find a different answer to fit the circumstances.

Beyond reasonable doubt if I may ask?
- Now, the police searching for a car described by Lees…What a joke, all they had to do was to ring Toyota and ask.

Furthermore, according FFDA p 360 Keith is referring to page 53 of Lees book *No turning back*, (which I have) she describes Murdoch's car in 2001, then giving a different description to the police then later on again in 2006 after the trial (again and again)

2001	*2006*
Chrome bull-bar	not stated
Bucket seats in front	not stated
Clear open space at rear	not stated
End open allowing exit	not stated
Lees pushed between bucket seats	not stated

(Declared in later Statement to police)

Further on according to FFDA referring to what Lees said:

"For Lees to say "from the beginning I am unsure how this happened is a blatant attempt to deceive her readers. And there should be no doubt that many, if not most, readers of her book are deceived. Lees told a precise and different story in the beginning to the one she told later to the jury". All reports related to the alleged vehicle of the man are based on statements made by Lees in 2001 and 2002, and this is how her statements about the front seats in that vehicle have been reported in the literature."

The Vanishing of Peter Falconio

And on 25 March 2002, this is what Lees herself told the British interviewer Martin Bashir, as noted by Richard Shears in his book:

"[H]e pushed me through a passenger door of his car.... [H]e grabbed me and pushed me through the seats into the back."57 (added emphasis.) That is what Lees was saying eight months after the alleged incident north of Barrow Creek.

Plenty of grabbing and pushing but no DNA on her or her clothing at the exception of the small bloodstain on the back of her T-shirt…Food for thought.

- <u>Plenty of time for Lees to come up with the right answer hey!</u>

"Serious questions were raised about her claims, and after searching over 16,000 vehicles throughout Australia the cops could not find a vehicle like the one Lees referred to. So, Lees changed her story in No Turning Back; 2006. In the beginning – 2001 and 2002 – Lees was sure she was pushed "through the seats" to the rear of the vehicle belonging to the man. But in 2006, Lees tells her readers she is "unsure" how she got to the rear. So, has Lees told us the truth, the whole truth, and nothing but the truth about everything since 2001?

Well, as I said before, <u>THEY</u> should have called Toyota.

Notice the two words not stated, sounds like similar or I changed my mind.
- Among other things…Well Murdoch's car doesn't have or didn't have a chrome bulbar.
- Second important fact about Murdock's car is a trailer which seems to have vanished like Falconio. Lees never mentioned the trailer: Why? This information will need some explanation later. It is important.

Lees should have seen the trailer when she escaped from the back of course as we know! which was blocked because of the cage as per Murdoch's claim (Laughter). After all, when Murdoch supposedly stopped them, she should have seen the trailer even before the killing and from the time he was following them from Alice…But who cares!

The Vanishing of Peter Falconio

Remember, she was pushed into the back of the Ute through the cabin (Clapping in the background). She should have noticed the trailer. This is definitely [not] beyond reasonable doubt (again and again).

According to FFDA on page 367 [63]

"63 One of the things Lees did not mention and was not resolved satisfactorily during the trial is the matter of the trailer which Murdoch was towing behind his Toyota.

Lees did not say the vehicle which she alleged the man drove was towing a trailer. Lees did not mention seeing a trailer when she lied about escaping out the back of the vehicle belonging to the man. There was no distinctive tyre impressions left by a trailer being turned at the site of the alleged incident. There was no trailer attached to the vehicle which was filmed by a CCTV camera at the Shell truck stop at Alice Springs.

Officials ignored Murdoch's trailer. When the subject arose, the convenient reply was that Murdoch must have unhitched his trailer and left it somewhere then drove off to attack

Falconio and Lees. Of course, there is no proof Murdoch did that –but the legal requirement of proof beyond a reasonable doubt does not apply in a kangaroo court. "

To put it blatantly, they picked up a guy on the CCTV who may have been involved or not with the scam, who has a car similar to Murdoch's one, but has no trailer, and they have the audacity to say that it is Murdoch's car, Murdoch having dropped the trailer somewhere, perhaps for an oil change…Real slander…But I will prove otherwise …Just wait.

Murdoch said that he had modified his vehicle before the alleged offence. It was done in May 2001 (many people who knew Murdoch did confirm.)

Being a Land Cruiser man, I also like to fiddle around like many people, adding things, changing the colour of the bulbar for example. Men like to play around with their toys. Nothing unusual about that!

The Vanishing of Peter Falconio

Several witnesses said that Murdoch regularly changed his vehicle appearances in an obsessive way, being a mechanic and, that this had started over a decade before the alleged offence.

I do the same and I am not the only one. Since I bought my Land Cruiser I have changed the colour of the front grill four times.

This doesn't prove that Murdock committed the alleged crime for God's sake!

38 – OH, La La! ……The Front Teeth

[7a] **ONE** most important feature about Lees alleged attacker, is the lack of missing front teeth –his huge size – his very short hair cut

That is something in a man…wouldn't you say?

Every person who knew Murdoch describe this as UNMISTAKABLE and that any description of Murdoch would focus on it.

However, according to FFDA p360 Keith is referring of Lees book (which I also have) "No turning back" where she gives description of her attacker

"On p. 54, she says she saw the man: "He was tall, taller than Pete."

Here we must stop so we can reflect on this. The Northern Territory police later interviewed Lees at the Barrow Creek pub about the alleged incident. Media releases were written based on what she said.

The cops did not make up the information in those releases. So based on what Lees reported, the following is how the man is described in NT police media releases at 07:45 and 10:45 on 15 July 2001

>The alleged offender is described as:
>40-45 year, possibly older
>Dark, straight hair to the shoulder, with grey streaks
>Long thin face
>Droopy grey moustache with corners tapering down below mouth
>Heavy bags under his eyes
>Medium build
>Deep voice, Australian accent"
>………She forgot the cap!

However, in Lees' 2001 description of her attacker (not in 2005) she didn't mention anything about Murdoch's teeth or short hair, or huge size, [NO], she said medium build. It should have been fresh in her memory. She didn't mention this to the artist chosen by police…Strange! Is she trustworthy? However, in her book she said: HE WAS HUGE

The Vanishing of Peter Falconio

The Defence claimed that this meant that Murdoch could not have been her attacker. Again, beyond reasonable doubt doesn't seem to apply according to Lees.

The Prosecution argued that Murdoch could have worn false teeth [sic] or capped teeth [oh yes] or that Lees merely didn't notice the absence of front teeth! (Laughter!)

Yes OK, but nobody will buy it.

Now I ask anyone: Would you have noticed a man built like a wardrobe, with very short hair, no moustache, with some front teeth missing with a deep voice and wearing a cap?

The Vanishing of Peter Falconio

39 - Cigarettes

There is a French song with the title: "*L'amour c'est comme une cigarette*", Love is like a cigarette. The song was written by Michel Mallory and Florrie Palmer and was first released by Sylvie Vartan in 1981…. Goes something like this….

"Love is like a cigarette,

It burns and it goes to your head.

When you can't do without it,

All that goes up in smoke.

Love is like a cigarette,

It blazes like a match,

It stings your eyes it makes you cry

And it goes up in smoke!" (Good song, beautiful melody)

https://lyricstranslate.com

[8a] Defence lawyer Algie claimed that James Hepi took cigarette butts smoked by Murdoch to give to police so as to extract DNA to frame Murdoch

Speaking of cigarettes, James Hepi, is also a drug user and dealer and ex- partner who has been doing business with Murdoch. Why would he do that? Payback time, something to do with drugs, a deal gone sour or hoping to be in the police good books or a cut of the $250,000 reward or hoping Murdoch will be found Guilty which in the process will eliminate his opposition in the drug cartel killing two birds with one stone.

- Where did the butts come from?

Well, according to FFDA p361 referring to Lees book No turning back (which I also have, just a reminder).

The Vanishing of Peter Falconio

"On p. 54, Lees says Falconio got out, then he went to the rear of the Kombi where he spoke with the man. Then he returned to the front of the Kombi where he reached in and "picked up his cigarettes from the shelf below the dash." But not one cigarette butt was found at the alleged crime site. And if the man was Murdoch which is doubly strange because he is/was a heavy smoker."

Interesting don't you think…So no footprints and [NO] cigarette butts found at the alleged crime scene neither from Murdoch or Falconio knowing that both were smokers…Fascinating, I smell another rat… It is a plague.

Actually, I just thought of something:

- May be none of them were at the alleged crime scene at 9.00pm on that night. All of them sitting in the Kombi somewhere not too far away from inquisitive eyes and ears, having the intention to return to the alleged crime scene around midnight for the decoy using the red Japanese car, and the arrival of a road train.
- **In the car: 1** Lees –**2** Falconio – three the Aileron/Nick the lover – **4** the driver of the Japanese car –and **5** the driver of a Land cruiser.
- Meaning the alleged killer driving the Land Cruiser would be leaving his waiting position at a time calculated for him to arrive at the Shell track stop at 0.30am on the 15th.
- In the meantime, the four partners in crime (**1** Lees –**2** Falconio –**3** the Aileron man/Nick the lover –**4** the driver of the Japanese car) all waiting for [A] road train to arrive.
- Meaning from 9.00pm no one was or could be seen at the alleged crime scene. As I said: **1** Lees –**2** Falconio –**3** the Aileron man/Nick the lover –**4** and the driver of the Japanese car, all waiting in the warmth of the car (the Kombi having been moved on due time

What do you think? Do you like my little theory?

The Vanishing of Peter Falconio

[9a] A police officer admitted receiving butts from Murdoch's former co-drug dealer James Hepi, but declined that he gave it to police in order to frame Murdoch.

So, a police officer is accepting cigarette butts from a drug dealer and ex-partner in an alleged murder case? …Just like that! Um! That's interesting…Only cigarette butts, nothing else? Why giving cigarette butts to police? Denying that he gave it to police to frame Murdoch (Um!) WELL…Monsieur Hepi nobody believes you!

The Officer (no Gentleman here) doesn't deny having accepted the butts! So why did the Gentleman (sorry the officer) accept the butts then? Shortage of tobacco somewhere along the line? People do smoke butts you know! (Laughter!)

The Vanishing of Peter Falconio

40 - Murdoch Interviewed....

[10a] Murdoch was interviewed by police three months after the alleged offence in relation to James's Hepi drug smuggling. When police asked him about his car, police did not connect the car's appearance to the description given by Lees to police.

AMAZING, not connecting the car appearance to the description given by Lees to police!

For anyone investigating an alleged crime, I find incredible that: Murdoch was interviewed three months after the alleged crime. How did police get to him, why three months, what were the evidence for his arrest?

- Murdoch was locked up in jail accused of rape but found not guilty on all charges?

Well, it's only when Lees saw the photograph (when in Sicily) of Murdoch accused of rape that things started to get hot for Murdoch because Lees had finally found her scapegoat … (But this is me thinking.)

Then, not connecting the car appearance to the description given by Lees to police! It can only prove two things: poor police work and Lees' description of her attacker's car was lack of knowledge and observation. Therefore, she did not describe Murdoch's car BUT someone else's car…What else can I say, what else can be said?

Three months after the alleged killing of Falconio, Murdoch (as seen on the documentary by CJZ) was arrested and questioned regarding the rape case in South Australia. The arrest and the questioning had nothing to do with the disappearance of Peter Falconio, but was well advertised, the media had a ball and **LEES HAD FINALLY FOUND HER SCAPEGOAT.**

How can a fair trial take place four years later after all this? It is definitely a trial by media and an incredible farce!

Lucky for Murdoch the Jury found him not guilty of the rape. He was then released, but wait…As soon as he got out of the Courthouse, he was arrested by the Northern Territory Police, in South Australia mind you, handcuffed…You know the rest if you saw the program. He didn't have long hair but very short hair (crew cut, I know he may have had a hair cut in the meantime) but as far as his size, he didn't shrink, he didn't look like a medium build man but more like huge gorilla.

So, three months after the alleged crime we have a newcomer James Hepi a drug dealer/ smuggler and also Murdoch ex-partner. If three months after the alleged offence at Barrow Creek Monsieur Hepi took cigarette butts smoked by Murdoch to give police to frame Murdoch, it could be only for one purpose: Extracting DNA and may be hoping to get a piece of the $250,000 reward as I said [he wished!] or getting a deal with police for some unknown reason (he did get a deal after all, but please don't mention it!) certainly not for checking the cigarette brand, meaning that Murdoch was already the prime chosen scapegoat and perhaps Monsieur Hepi had become or was already a police informer [?]…A the little worm eating on two fronts?

By the way, any DNA test results on the butts?

The report would have probably indicated that: Yes, Murdoch's DNA was found on the butts, but we are sorry the brand of the cigarettes could not be determined with sufficient accuracy!

- Why did the Prosecution closing argument win the case?
- Why can anybody see that Monsieur Hepi could be a police informer and, the man on the CCTV is not Murdoch…Size –very short hair –no moustaches –no trailer –different dog –no motive etc.
- I know why: Joanne Lees got confused recognizing the man,
- Confused recognizing the car without trailer,
- Confused recognizing the dog because I forgot to say that her description of Murdoch's dog was a Kelpie or cattle dog where Murdoch's dog is a Dalmatian, with black and white spots.
- Maybe Lees is colour blind. She would be perfect for Specks Saver's advertising program (Laughter) but definitely not to be trusted as a witness.
- On second thought, no, she is not colour blind because I just remember that when it was pitch-black she said: **The colour of the canopy seemed different on the inside….**

The Vanishing of Peter Falconio

It is strange that Joanne Lees identified Murdoch for the third time as her attacker four years after the alleged killing at Barrow Creek. You would think that Lees would have recognised Murdoch or at least giving some good and precise information on the morning of the day after the alleged crime regarding his appearance at Barrow Creek or even some days after knowing that the three of them were seen at the same restaurant (at different time) Well...she did however change her claim again as we know in 2005 at the trial.

Nevertheless, she gave a good description to police on the morning of the day after the alleged attack; long hair to shoulder, moustache etc. but it was the opposite of Murdoch, it was the very, very similar description of Chris Malouf!

- Is that why police arrested Malouf on the early hours of the morning after the alleged offence? Do we really know the real reasons for his arrest? How did they get to him so fast??? Oh yes, he did camp nearby. Any reasons for that?
- Where is Chris Malouf now hiding and who is he?

What happen in between with the published photograph of Murdoch regarding: Lees –Police –the media –the journalists –newspapers –the Northern Territory officials and all the public servants?

When Murdoch was arrested after three months for the alleged murder of Falconio, after being found not guilty of the rape, as far as the media is concerned, after all that publicity, he was already guilty for having killed Falconio in cold blood at arm's length with a big silver gun which has never been found...I wonder why?

People wanted blood, Falconio was pronounced dead (but no dead body) and Murdoch guilty, all this and no proofs. Looking at the welcome reception he received outside the courthouse the day he was found not guilty of the rape. Police was waiting outside the Courthouse ready to arrest him and they certainly did. He became the star of the year...He had been stamped with the word "Guilty" on his forehead, which I think is not a nice tattoo!

The Vanishing of Peter Falconio

I must admit that such publicity would have influenced the case. For Lees, his photo must have influenced not only her choice for the identification of Murdoch, she had also found her scapegoat. She knew his name and saw his photograph. Finding the photograph on the net had been a blessing and it was then in her favour. They now had a scapegoat and the scapegoat had a name: Bradley John Murdoch.

Everything was stagged, everything was going well according to [their] plan.

She and Falconio (don't forget he vanished, no murder took place) and partners were now more confident that the scam would work. It must also have given her the perfect opportunity to work out answers to any difficult and tricky questions and situation.

That scapegoat was going to be Bradley John Murdoch. He was going to be the perfect man for the job. He was not any man but the man suited to play the role of the man on the CCTV film which I don't understand because he didn't look like Murdoch but drove a similar Land Cruiser... The Bad Boy had long hair to the shoulder –moustaches etc.

Even the description of his car and dog was wrong. It shows that she didn't know much about car and dog, and by the way she had forgotten about the trailer. (Laughter in the background!)

It all means that, there is something very murky about her regarding the disappearance of her boyfriend, the man she loved so much but don't give a damn about because with all the money she made from the case and the story. According to FFDA, she didn't spend a cent looking for...The love of her life!

SHE knew that a crime didn't take place. She has constantly changed things around mind you accepted by the police –the experts –the Officials –the Prosecution –even the Judge... Remember: your verdict must be unanimous. That was an order, it must be unanimous...Like it or not.

I don't think (actually I am sure) we will never know unless someone bumps into Falconio by luck and has the chance and the courage to take his photograph. Then, believe you me: She will be crucified…They will be all crucified. What goes up must come down according to Murphy's Law.

But don't forget, time will come, especially with the new facial recognition technology or some unexpected whistle blower deciding to come out of the woodwork. Wherever you are in the world, if a camera picks you up, there will be no escape and no forgiveness!

***

***Note**: Don't forget also that the aim of my book is not to find the killer, but to clear the innocent.

***

Anyhow, I am still amazed that Lees changed her first description of Murdoch, his car, even his dog four years later. I find amazing that no one from the jury asked questions during the trial (perhaps someone did) when the life of a man is in the balance. Actually, speaking of the Jury, you already know the explosive fact. I am also amazed about the Defence. They had four years to get ready for the counter attack.

I think the jury was ignorant of many things and bullied by the judge and the Prosecution. Were the jurors scared to ask questions?

Yes, Murdoch may have been looking rough at that time, but he is a man so much bigger and taller (1.98m), has some missing front teeth, has short hair, doesn't wear a moustache (don't know about the deep voice). But he may have been wearing a similar cap! (Clapping in the background).

The Vanishing of Peter Falconio

41 - The Kombi –CCTV Man –DNA

[11a] Police took notes saying that Lees' kombi had shelves and show Lees's signature. Lees denied making the statement and said she cannot remember saying it to police.

Police is saying one thing, but Lees cannot remember and denies it, but no worries, her answer is accepted as fact? Wow! Food for thought! Again, Lees is contradicting herself. Lees always says, whenever she can: I cannot remember or similar or I don't know.... It always sounds like: No comment, it is never a certainty, it always indicates doubts.

Nevertheless, there is something much more important about the Kombi than the shelves and that is THE WINDOWS. The photo of the Kombi has been published in many books and on the Internet. The best one is in Roger Maynard's book inserted between page 90 and 91 (Where's Peter?). Sitting behind the wheel the driver has a 360 degrees view because of all the windows

What is so important about the windows? Well even with the 360 degrees view, being meters away from the two men, Joanne Lees didn't see the alleged killing of her boyfriend which is remarkable and a big lie.

- Well, it is because when Joanne Lees was revving the engine, where was she?
- She was sitting behind the steering wheel, she even said in her book page 53:

"The vehicle was white…then I felt afraid. The driver was gesturing…I felt uneasy and didn't want to stop…Then she said: "Pete stopped me and told me to wait inside where it was warm. I positioned myself in the driver's seat and left the door slightly ajar so I could try and see and hear what was happening". Then she said: "I began to think there must be something wrong with our vehicle. Pete walked towards the back of the Kombi and the other driver met him there".

This is very precise, Peter and the man met there, meaning at the rear of the kombi okay. Then she said or wrote if you prefer: "I heard Pete say cheers mate. Thanks for stopping us." (this was a repeat I know).

The Vanishing of Peter Falconio

Then further on, she wrote: "the man stood on the right of Pete and I could see him fully. He looked directly at me, he was taller than Pete, and his posture was stooped. He seemed to have his hands in his shirt and pockets" Meaning she could see both men because the man was taller than Pete…Do you agree? Yes, you must. Then further on she said: "Pete came back to the driver's side and told me everything was okay…he picked up his cigarettes from the shelf below the dash and asked me to rev the engine…I did this a few times…There was a big bang……then the man filled the window and stare back at me" (back at me is important).

The Kombi has windows all around. In any Kombi even with the engine's door up, the rear window would not be blocked. Joanne Lees would have seen the scene of events from A to Z. She saw the two men. She saw the man was taller than Pete etc.

Knowing the men were very close –she could hear them –she could see them.

BUT SHE DID NOT SEE THE MAN KILLING PETER FALCONIO AT POINT BLANK IN THE HEAD WITH A BIG GUN KNOWING THAT SITTING BEHIND THE WHEEL WITH ALL THE WINDOWS SHE HAD THE TOTAL VIEW AND CONTROL OF THE SCENE

Why That?

Is it because of what she said further on? "There was a big bang and my first thought was that it was the exhaust backfiring. It had done this before. I sat there with head in my hands, elbows resting against the steering wheel, hoping that we hadn't broken down in the middle of nowhere."

I sat up straight and looked out the driver's side window to my right?" Then she said: "the man filled up the window and stared back at me."

What would be the time laps be between the bang and the man filling up the window? Ten [10] seconds, [BUT] she didn't see the killing nor Falconio dropping dead on the ground?

What was the time laps between the moment she heard the bang –the man filling up the window – her restrain of her hands behind her back and

The Vanishing of Peter Falconio

the moment the man told her to get out of the Kombi? I assume not very long indeed. But NO, she did see the body of Falconio nor the mysterious trailer, which should have been attached to the Cruiser when the man pushed her out of the Kombi. Do you think that this is too farfetched?

You must understand one thing: If Falconio had truly been shot, it can only be between the back of the kombi (where they met) and the front of the Cruiser (the cruiser being parked behind the Kombi...Is that okay?

Do you know why she didn't see any of this? Because nothing took place on the 14th of July 2001, that's why.

[12a] A forensic expert has said that Murdoch was not the man in the CCTV video at Alice Springs truck stop, as Murdoch's build was far larger

So, one forensic expert says he is not the man, and the other says the opposite...People have to make up their mind. It is one or the other ...But which one? Remember: Beyond reasonable doubt. Nevertheless, the one fitting the agenda prevailed.

Absolutely true, Murdoch is 1.98 metres, he is a big man, Lees herself said he was huge. The claim by Joanne Lees and the Prosecution won the case making sure the jury would buy it: Murdock is the man on the CCTV at the truck stop, that all there is to it...Please don't argue! Well, it would have been easy to confront both.

It would have been simple to take Murdoch to the truck stop, (maybe they did) make him park his car with the trailer (Laughter in the back!) at the same pump, take him inside the shop and then checking what he looks like on the video when he comes out of the shop, of course wearing a cap with a small logo that nobody can read at the exception of Monsieur Hepi and walking slowly as if he wanted to be seen. All you had to do then was to compare the two ...But it must have been too complicated. It would have saved the taxpayers thousands! Do you think the Prosecution then could have won the case? Regardless of the exercise when watching the show on TV, anybody can see that the man on the CCTV is not as huge as Murdoch. Furthermore, the man from the CCTV is seen walking quite slowly as I said as if he wanted to be seen. Has the man been investigated?

The Vanishing of Peter Falconio

Yes, he was but could not be identified. Only three people could identify the man and his Cruiser and they are:

- **Joanne Lees –the Prosecution second witness– and our dear Mr Hepi third witness…and later on the Judge….**

For God's sake, this was an alleged murder case not a shoplifting case! But don't worry, I will prove otherwise soon

[13a] A forensic expert has said that the methods used to extract DNA from the hand ties was incorrect, and clearly showed that it was not Murdoch's DNA.

As I am definitely not an expert on DNA, I cannot make any comment but knowing the police took the handmade cuffs in a paper bag like a burger to question Murdoch in jail is very suspicious. It seems the police cannot be trusted. They say police are their own worst enemies, I am starting to believe this maxim. Remember the Azaria Chamberlain case? We are in Northern Territory in 2001where nothing seems to have changed.

Anyhow regarding DNA, for the one who believe the small patch bloodstain found only on the back of Lees T-Shirt [Um!] came from Murdoch is a lot of nonsense, it was rigged…Try proving me wrong when even if myself have no fact to prove it.

How and who can prove or disprove that the patch of bloodstain came from Murdoch? Who was in the lab when they did the analysis, who can verify the data?

What happen between July 17 2001 and October 24 2003…When it took 28 months for the carried DNA tests to reach the lab.

DNA testing had just been explored, nothing was certain, there has been more uncertainties than true proven facts. Many criminal cases received a guilty verdict based purely on the belief that DNA testing was full proof. Well, it was not and as a result many innocent people were wrongly accused and convicted and many true criminals walked free. That is a fact. You will understand if you research the internet.

The Vanishing of Peter Falconio

I can positively say that: THE BIGGER THE LIE THE MORE PEOPLE BELIEVE IT.

But in Bradley John Murdoch's case it didn't matter, he was guilty before the start because I believe the officials didn't want a repeat of the Azaria Chamberlain case and perhaps something we don't know about involving drugs and "drug lords"? A guilty verdict had to prevail and it was based only on that bloodstain of unknown source and the (alleged) DNA result which cannot be challenged unless an investigation takes place and even so. There are no proofs because no one can positively argue the result. Murdoch was guilty from day one.

Speaking of blood and DNA, what about the small pool of blood (animal/human/aliens?) found on the road, on the tar not on the dirt?

And what about police taking blood samples from Gary Murdoch's brother for the purpose of getting his DNA even before James Hepi dobbed Murdoch? (This will be discussed in more details further on).

The transcript of the appeal says no blood from Murdoch was found.

What is this Monsieur the Prosecutor? Did you ever thought that you could be wrong? Are you always right, did you see the blood coming out of Falconio's head after being shot at point blank because apparently and allegedly according to Lees; he got shot! Did you see Falconio dropping on the ground? Lees was there but didn't see Falconio falling on the ground when she must have been metres away (perhaps no more than three metres). He was shot she claimed, with a big silver gun, a gun which has never been found and a gun which later on was downgraded to a slingshot so to speak by the officials just to prove that if a smaller calibre had been used, the bullet would still be in his head…WOW!

But don't worry Monsieur the Prosecutor, I know that you don't believe Joanne Lees' story you said it yourself! (That's for later on).

What a joke. Anyhow the gun, that big silver gun Clint Eastwood type was never found, same for the smaller gun, same for emptied cartridges – footprints (Murdoch and Falconio) –wheel marks –trailer marks –dog poo or else etc.

The Vanishing of Peter Falconio

- Who was there to witness Falconio dropping dead on the ground? Please give me some answers....

A small amount of blood was found on the road under a pile of dirt for anybody to see, seems like a decoy, purposely done to attract attention because the killer's Cruiser must have had the four wheels on the tar so that no wheel marks could be found/traced on the dirt, could have been immediately interpreted as being a proof or "THE PROOF" of a human injury and fowl- play having occurred there. Knowing that there is not one evidence proving beyond reasonable doubt that Falconio bled. It is nothing less than a fantasy claim. What can be said, what do we do, who do we trust?

This, combined with the sound of what Lees first claimed as an engine backfiring or Falconio being shot by the exhaust pipe (Laughter) which later according to her was a gunshot which later again became the sound of a gun being fired (very funny) it became good enough evidence for the corrupt Northern Territory officials...Of course beyond any reasonable doubt.

Now, who could tell me the difference between the sound of a gunshot and the sound of a gun being fired? Please take your time before answering....

- There is no evidence at all that a firearm had been discharged,
    - No emptied cartridges found...Nothinnnnng!
    - No Dead Body,
    - No fresh blood from Falconio or anything else for that matter.

Please try proving the bullet is still in his head.

This is like the French movie Micmacs à tire larigot II (2009). If that is not a miscarriage of justice: What is? –Do you sleep at night Monsieur the Prosecutor –Monsieur Le Judge –Mademoiselle Joanne Lees –Monsieur Hepi?

- The only possible explication and proof is that Falconio never got shot,
- But simply vanished in thin air for reasons that nobody will never know.

- He will be found not dead but alive (according to Gregory Dick from Aileron).

According to FFDA, "The Northern Territory laboratory involved with the Falconio-case evidence contaminated some of that evidence, allowed evidence to be taken from the laboratory by the police, and allowed evidence to be destroyed which meant Murdoch's lawyers could not have an independent laboratory conduct any test to determine the validity of the findings of that Northern Territory laboratory – that is how kangaroo courts work"

Allowing evidence to be destroyed…Do you believe that –who gave the order –who was in charge? I am flabbergasted, I just can't believe it. The guillotine must be reset. We need a new trial –a new Appeal –a Royal Commission Inquiry and more.

From FFDA Part E Evidence p 71

All the DNA-related tests in the case are suspect. There were years of opportunity to have DNA evidence concocted or corrupted.

Yes indeed, it took 28 months from July 17 2001 to October 2003 to be precise for the alleged tests to be sent to the lab for analysis or if you prefer to arrive at the lab…. What took place in between along the journey? Don't you find this extremely suspicious?

"The issue that should have been addressed legally, but which was deliberately ignored, is that of evidence integrity, not how big the DNA numbers are. If the evidence was concocted or corrupted before the DNA tests were conducted, those tests are worthless. And the prosecution did not prove all the DNA-related evidence was unquestionable. But as it happened throughout the entire case, the benefit of the doubt was given to Lees not to Murdoch. For him, it was not a matter of being innocent until he was proved guilty. It was a matter of him having been declared guilty behind the scene before the trial. After that, officials needed to get big DNA numbers to the media and into the public's mind. (FFDA)

SO TRUE!

Who profited from the guilty verdict knowing there is no evidence to corroborate Joanne Lees' claims past –present –and future if I may ask?

Murdoch was a "nobody of worth", he was set up. He has never been "Innocent until proven guilty"

"We [Australians] now have a system of law in which the citizen can't defeat the government, in which the system has been rigged to assure that the citizen can't beat the government." FFDA page 271

Before closing this chapter and getting back to the alleged and mysterious patch of blood allegedly from Murdoch found only on the back of Lees' T-shirt, I can definitely say that:

IT WAS A PLOT AIMED AT MURDOCH TO PROTECT SOMEONE

Things are happening now in the state of Queensland regarding all the corruption involving the DNA labs which could have also taken place in 2001 in Northern Territory? Truly 28 months for the collected supposedly evidences arrival at the lab is beyond comprehension.

A patch of blood/DNA only found in the back of Lees' T-shirt only is remarkable indeed.

- Has anybody found a solution to this puzzle? **NO,** I don't think so. We are speaking of a patch found where nobody would expect one to be found! I know I said it again and again, but it is necessary. One needs to truly live the story to understand all that rubbish.

This on its own is an incredible mystery. I smell a "Huge Rat! "

Not only about the patch but also about the police –the company/lab who was responsible for the investigation. Again and again, why would a patch of bloodstain with Murdoch's DNA, if his. After all, why did police so keen to take a blood sample from his brother Garry?

Please stop and think. Not one reason or explanation can be satisfactory.

Whatever answer people may come up with, it will not be adequate – acceptable –satisfactory –or sufficient beyond reasonable doubt, but more likely to be suspicious about the lab who conducted the investigation. I think the company involvement is extremely suspicious and needs to be challenged.

***

The Vanishing of Peter Falconio

There is an extraordinary relation between Murdoch's case and Shandee's case –the DNA results –and the company/the lab who conducted the investigation

In Murdoch's case the experts on DNA found a sample of Murdoch's DNA on one only sample (on Lees' T-shirt, on the back, shoulder high). The experts (the company/lab) would be extremely lucky to find such patch where it would be near impossible to find unless it has been put there purposely.

Please remember what is written in the transcript below about the kombi –steering wheel –and gear stick means that it has to be equally relevant to the T-shirt.

[48] The Kombi van was removed by police from the scrub and transported to Alice Springs. In essence, counsel submitted that a jury could not conclude beyond reasonable doubt that there was no contamination at some stage in the process between removing the van from the scrub on 17 July 2001 and the handing of samples to Dr Whitaker on 24 October 2003.

- It took 28 months between the removal of the Kombi and the handling of samples to Dr Whitaker.

- Did this happen also with Lees' T-shirt? Did it take 28 months?

- Don't you think that anything could have happened in 28 months?

All items or evidence were store in a room which could be accessed by anyone. Well, if someone with bad intention wanted to pervert the course of justice using Lees' T-shirt, there was certainly enough time (28 months) to do so and leave the country without any worries.

BUT in Shandee's case it is quite the opposite; The experts (the company –the lab) have not found any evidence of DNA on samples or material belonging to her boyfriend which should have had his DNA all over the place …Like his car –clothing etc.……Well, the company/lab said: No, no DNA found … Again, who do you trust?

The Vanishing of Peter Falconio

42 Important –Interesting –Truly Funny

[14a] Forensics were unable to find any bullets or evidence of any bullets being fired at the alleged scene, either in the van or on the ground nearby.

Interesting because according to the Prosecution closing argument: "After stopping them the killer panicked and kill Falconio with a big gun (bang) making sure there was no blood anywhere by making a shot directly to his head. This is according to our second witness: The Prosecution!

If Murdoch was making sure, being a meticulous killer that no blood would be found anywhere, he would also make sure that no cartridges could be found on the ground, no cigarette butts etc. Also, where does the patch of blood found on the side of the road, on the tar, not on the dirt come from?

- Was it truly Falconio's blood? The transcript said no blood was found. Do you call this true evidence when according to the experts, no trace of blood was found, no bullets, no emptied cartridges and no big silver gun? Well, I believe it is but didn't work on Murdoch's favour.
- ...Then abducting Lees, binding her with *"The Cuffs"* and putting her in the back of his four- wheel drive, through the compartment between the cabin and the back of the Ute (Laughter).
- These were Lees' words? But then, where is the gun, the big silver gun Clint Eastwood type she claimed?
- Where is the Dead Body –the mess after shooting Falconio in the head –the emptied cartridges? The dragging marks of a dead body etc.

Ok, no Murdoch's footprints –no emptied shell –no wheel marks from his car and trailer –no cigarette butts –No excrement from Murdoch's dog –No dog's hair on Lees –no Falconio's footprints and so on.... Most importantly if we refer to the story of the footprints, it is a puzzle on its own. The fact that both of them were not there (may have or may have not) is remarkable to say the least. This is like a play on Broadway! What comes next? Can you imagine the scene?

- Do you think Murdoch under stress having just shot Falconio would have time in the dark to clean and clear up all that alleged mess knowing he has to be seen at the truck-stop in Alice at 0.30am on the 15th as claimed by the Prosecution?
- Making sure Lees is well secured in the back of the Ute,
- Especially knowing that if he is/was the CCTV Man departing the alleged crime scene on the 14th of July at 9.00pm, he certainly would be pressed for time to do the cleaning task….and the disposal of the Dead Body…Anyway, we know what he did with the body. You will find out in the sentencing of Murdoch.
- Then perhaps having a smoke, throwing the butt or butts on the ground for Mr Hepi as I said before to collect them,
- Then moving the Kombi (after Lees escaped?) to a different spot making sure it is parked neatly,
- Then looking for Lees (as per her claim) who escaped from the back of the Cruiser which is blocked by the cage. (Back means back –side means side.)
- Not even noticing the invisible trailer when escaping **(Clapping in the background).**
- Then giving up the search with his flash light and his borrowed dog (which didn't take place because the offender left the site at 9.00pm on the 14th) knowing that, it definitely contradict Lees' claim that she never saw him again after her Great Escape!
- Murdoch has time to modify his look just to look like the man on the CCTV
- Not forgetting that he has and must hurry to bury the Dead Body before reaching Fitzroy Crossing to be seen around 8.00pm NT time on the 15th.

Does this sound right?

The Vanishing of Peter Falconio

Obviously, the Officials never had the intention of showing Murdoch's Cruiser on the Internet. If they did it would have been: Spot the difference hey! (Repeat I know).

Then again in so much hurry after shooting Falconio he needs to be seen on the CCTV film at 0.30am on the 15th of July 2001.

- BUT, where is the Dead Body? Around Barrow Creek or on its way to Alice…Or after Alice (everything is possible).
- Because when he was picked up as the man on the CCTV (who doesn't look like him), I don't believe the Dead Body was resting in the Land Cruiser, BUT I could be wrong according the Judge. (This will be relevant to the words spoken by Martin Briand our Chief Justice during his televised sentencing of Bradley John Murdoch).
- Then again in so much hurry after taking drugs (ok for him, he sells the stuff),
- He drove like a maniac at 160km/h **for 19 hours** (1.00am to noon = 11hours + noon to 8.00pm = 19 hours on the 15th of July).
- Towards Fitzroy Crossing, **1,412km** on the Tanami **where there is no fuel for 580km** and no fuel at night or elsewhere.
- Pulling a trailer with all the corrugations up to 6/7 inches high (I just can see the trailer behind going up and down or even losing it).

Hey! What is this, Mr Bean touring Australia in a Land Cruiser or the Paris Dakar Race? (Weeping in the background).

Now, from FFDA p10/20 we read:

"Ms Lees said that contrary to reports, at no stage on Saturday night did she believe that the loud bang she heard was a gunshot. Instead, she described the bang she heard as sounding like a gun going off."

WOW! Another good one. Please explain the difference between the sound of a gunshot being fired and the sound of a gun going off when using the same gun? Lees believes that we are all stupid?

The Vanishing of Peter Falconio

Then:
"We stopped and refuelled at Ti Tree and watched the sunset.

And after we had been driving again for some time, a vehicle drove up alongside us, and Pete slowed down at first thinking it was going to overtake us. But he drove alongside us, his interior light was on and it was a four-wheel drive with a dog, the man pointed to the back of our vehicle and motioned for us to stop." [added emphasis]

Well, I thought they knew that; HE] WAS FOLLOWING THEM.

She claimed the man had a gun with which he threatened her. In her book, Lees says that weapon was a big "silver revolver." (p. 54) In the literature, it is also described as a western-style revolver. A drawing of this alleged weapon, which the artist prepared based entirely on Lees' description, shows something like a classic .45-calibre revolver. (see Part G) But like everything else in the case, this raised questions which are still unanswered.

Given the circumstances Lees described, Falconio had to have been shot on that highway in an execution-style killing – right up close. But, no projectile (bullet) was found, no evidence of any type of gun having been discharged was found, no evidence of blood spatter."

Before going any further, from what I just read, it definitely looks like FALCONIO GOT SHOT BY THE EXHAUST PIPE.... "BANG" ...I must be getting warmer!

From FFDA....no brain matter, bone fragments, hair, etc., were found. So, what did officials say about this? Well, to keep Lees' story alive, the weapon was downsized to a much smaller calibre, thus less powerful, weapon. That big-bore 45 was downsized to a 22-calibre. Officials did this because, to them, that dismissed the fact there was no evidence of a projectile exiting the body – thus no evidence of blood spatter, bone fragments, hair, etc. Just a little bit of blood on the road that flowed out of the head from an entry wound of a small calibre projectile." FFDA

It is truly amazing how much the Officials know about all the small details. Yes, the Officials did this. Downsizing the big gun to a 22 calibre. Can you believe that?

So, dismissing the fact there was no evidence of a projectile exiting the body does that mean that [THEY] have examined the Dead Body or what? So, there was a dead body found? Well, they must also think that we are definitely all stupid.

DOWNSIZING THE BIG GUN to a slingshot…. Ah! That's funny, referring to the gun. That's a real Clint Eastwood type movie.

Officials did this to dismiss the fact there was no evidence of a projectile exiting the body

- Thus, no evidence of blood.
- Why then pointing the very small patch of blood on the side of the road which apparently a mystery mixture of two bloods animal and human or perhaps Aliens [?],
- Who knows –Who cares! BUT actually, it was found to be from a road kill.
- **Is there anyone in the world who could tell me if the bullet which killed Falconio came out on the other side or is still in his head when you don't have a Dead Body?**

Anyhow, if Falconio had been shot it would have been next or in between the Kombi and the Cruiser.

- Did the kombi have two wheels on the dirt or four wheels on the tar?
- Falconio would have dropped dead right where he was standing,
- Did Falconio and the alleged killer moved around, walked with their feet on the dirt or on the tar while having a fag during their brief conversation? Because Falconio came back to the Kombi to get his cigarettes according to Lees in her book…Remember?
- Lees would have seen it all, but she claimed she didn't.

The Vanishing of Peter Falconio

- So, no spatters, no bone fragments, no hair, etc. Just a little bit of blood on the road (if blood of course) not on the dirt but on the tar.

But the officials downsized the big silver gun to a kind of "slingshot, so we shall never know.

- So, what can be said if there was no splatter of blood in the Kombi or anywhere else,
- All this according to the movie script making sure the bullet stayed in his head instead of hitting a tree behind or beyond. The Clint Eastwood type gun had definitely to be downgraded to what sound like a slingshot …Do you agree?
- As a result, leaving only a small entry wound.
- Indicating a small projectile or perhaps **an imaginary big one** as per Lees' description hey (big gun she claimed, big gun means big bullet).
- You do understand or believe that the bullet according to [our second] witness the Prosecution is still in Falconio's head?
- Therefore, it cannot be found on the ground using a metal detector. I was going to recommend Minelab detectors made in South Australia, expensive –the best, but no need for it now, the bullet is still inside his head.

Wow, that is all very well, the only problem…You need a Dead Body to prove it (clapping in the background).

I can tell that Murdoch was definitely a very meticulous killer, very resourceful and that Joanne Lees had a great imagination …Good on you "Babe", but nobody believes you dear!

What's going on? Was all this accepted as true facts and evidence beyond reasonable doubt?

OK, the officials did this to prove that no projectile came out of the head of the dead body. As a result, the projectile must be still in his head.

WOW! This is like I said before a copy of the French movie – comedy/crime: Micmacs à tire larigot where:

"Bazil (Dany Boon) has been a victim of weapons manufacturers his entire life…. His father was killed by a land mine, and Bazil lost his job

The Vanishing of Peter Falconio

after he was shot by an errant bullet -- which is still lodged in his skull. Now Bazil lives on the streets of Paris, where he encounters Slammer (Jean-Pierre Marielle). Slammer takes him under his wing, introducing him to other outcasts. With the help of his new entourage, Bazil devises a plan to exact revenge on the companies that took so much from him" Release date: 1 April 2010 (Australia) Wikipédia…[A funny movie, highly recommended, very entertaining].

…No Dead Body to prove it? This is the best of the lot! Well, when and if they find the body, they need to make sure to extract the projectile so it can be sent to a museum in Northern Territory, unless there is none (bullet that is).

Or if Falconio reappears he will need to get a CT scan (computerized tomography) because his life may be in danger…Like Bazil.

What do you think, was this funny?

From FFDA "NO worries, mate. Just change the evidence to suit the story you want people to believe. So, take your pick: no exit wound so no big blood spill, or, there was no big blood spill so there was no exit wound. Forget about someone pouring a mixture of animal and human blood on the road to make it look like Falconio met his maker on the Stuart Highway. Forget about all those ants and flies that were not there. And, certainly forget the missing bullet, the lack of gunshot residue evidence, and a strange contaminated blood stain/sample.

But in plain simple English, no one involved with the trial knows what the liquid was and who dropped it on the road. Nobody knows.

The Vanishing of Peter Falconio

43 - Murdoch Looking Different Depending and According To Lees

[15a] Murdoch did not closely match the description initially given to police by Lees in July 2001

That is very strange because she should have given the true description of Murdoch the man who was seen at the restaurant in Alice Springs, the man who "feared that they were spying on him".

Going through this puzzle is not an easy task. Your mind goes from left to right non- stop like watching a tennis game.

The first description of Murdoch given by Lees to police is the one below (FFDA)

"The cops did not make up the information in those releases. So based on what Lees reported, the following is how the man is described in NT police media releases at 07:45 and 10:45 on 15 July 2001

The alleged offender is described as:

40-45 year, possibly older

Dark, straight hair to the shoulder, with grey streaks

Long thin face

Droopy grey moustache with corners tapering down below mouth

Heavy bags under his eyes "

That is the description of the man who stopped them –allegedly killed Falconio –and then allegedly abused her.

This was the description of the killer by Joanne Lees on the morning the day after the alleged crime.

- Does the description fit her description of Murdoch? **NO**, it does not.
- Does the description fit her description of the CCTV man seen on the film in 2005? **NO,** it does not.

Long hair to the shoulder means long hair, droopy moustache means droopy moustache, but, NO mention of the size of the man (1.98m). No, the description doesn't fit Murdoch.

173

44 - Up Until Now, What Have We Got?

You must have realised by now that there are things we know and some we don't. What is acceptable and what is not? What facts do we have that could have contributed to a guilty verdict? …Well: None up until now. Only that patch of bloodstain if it truly belongs to Murdoch. [?]

But who is going to believe in the DNA experiment (not the Philadelphia Experiment the movie 1984 IMDb).

Knowing and according to FFDA files from the analysis were allegedly removed or destroyed prohibiting the Defence team from challenging the DNA test results. This on its own is scandalous.

- What happen in the Shandee Blackburn's case regarding the full-proof of any DNA testing?
- The definition of full-proof is: *"Incapable of going wrong or being misused."*

Everything in this case is doubtful, nothing but doubts, most of them upon Joanne Lees' claims and descriptions, lack of transparency from the Prosecution, the police and some supposedly experts.

For the Defence, nothing much to report from the Western front which is incredible. All we can see and feel is that the alleged crime was staged and the whole trial rigged.

- According to the Prosecution an alleged crime was committed, all based on Lees' claims and the miraculous DNA Trump Card.
- Murdoch found guilty of an alleged murder with no proofs.
- No Dead Body found.
- Time of death of our vanishing Falconio unknown [?]
- But we have a witness who confirmed that Lees was watching the sunset at Ti Tree at 6.10pm alone on the 14th of July.
- Assumed/calculated alleged **time of death 8.45pm** on the 14th of July 2001
- The Judge ordered the jury to come up with the unanimous verdict, not a suggestion but rather an order of prime consequences. Why?

The Vanishing of Peter Falconio

Well, I think I know why and you will find out further on during the course of this book…Be patient.

- Jury not informed of the Majority verdict (purposely without any doubt).
- Murdoch is a drug dealer (we all know that).
- Joanne Lees and Peter Falconio are drug users (we know that).
- Alleged crime scene Barrow Creek 303km from Alice Spring.
- Time of the alleged crime same as time of alleged death (above)
- Was Murdoch at the alleged crime scene? NO…(beyond reasonable doubt).
- Was Peter Falconio at the alleged crime scene? NO –YES? (**Not** beyond reasonable doubt).
- Was Joanne Lees at the alleged crime scene YES
- Did Joanne Lees witness the killing of Faconio? NO
- Kombi found on Hwy after being moved YES
- Who moved the Kombi? UNKNOWN
- Road train Driver rescued Joanne Lees. YES
- Weapon a big silver gun (Clint Eastwood style) WE DON'T KNOW - NOT FOUND
- Big silver gun downgraded to a small 22 calibre YES
- Emptied cartridges NOT FOUND
- Splatters of bones –Falconio's blood etc. NOT FOUND
- DNA reliability SUSPICIOUS. Some sample or files destroyed - removed YES/NO? Purposely? MOST PROBABLY [?]
- Cuffs taken to Murdoch while in jail in a paper bag YES
- Cigarettes butts given to police YES – By an ex- criminal YES –to frame Murdoch YES (without any doubt);
- Cigarette butts tested for DNA? WE DON'T KNOW –DNA test result on butts NOT available –samples destroyed. WE DON'T KNOW [?]
- Witnesses who saw Falconio days after his alleged death ignored and dismissed ridiculed YES

The Vanishing of Peter Falconio

- Reported to the police   YES
- Joanne Lees admitting having cable ties but denied using it   YES BUT NO PROOFS
- Questionable restraints ALL UNKNOWN/ DOUBTFUL Refer to **FFDA.**
- Murdoch –Peter Falconio –Joanne Lees seen at the same restaurant in Alice   YES ALLEGEDLY (some hours apart)
- Bloodstain on Lees' T-shirt tested for DNA   YES/ NO or UNCHALLENGED…. files removed or destroyed [?]
- Sketch artist inexperienced –YES –reliable   YES
- Identified footprints at the alleged crime scene   ONLY ONE (LEES)
- Unidentified footprints   FOUR
- Murdoch footprints identified?   NO
- Murdoch seen refuelling on the **15th of July around 8.00pm 1,412km** from Alice Springs, in Fitzroy Crossing Western Australia   YES
- Murdoch claiming he was near Yuendumu at the time of the alleged crime and 335km away from the alleged crime scene YES (transcript).
- Murdoch claiming that between midnight and 1.00am on the 15th of July he was near the Granites   YES (transcript).
- Joanne Lees claiming Land Cruiser had communication between seats and back of the Ute YES but FALSE
- In reference to Murdoch's car all claims made by Joanne Lees PROVEN WRONG but later not stated. Definition of not stated; unknown ACCORDING TO LEES
- Murdoch did not closely match the initial description given to police by Lees in 2001 but Lees changes her claims four years after YES
- Murdoch's trailer wheel marks –car –dog's footprints or else identified at the alleged crime scene   NO FOUND

The Vanishing of Peter Falconio

- Murdoch's dog wrongly identified by Lees, different type   YES
- Murdoch identified by Lees in 2001 YES/ NO MATCH. Lees changing her claim later in 2005   YES
- Lees unaware of Murdoch missing front teeth   YES
- Joanne Lees denying statement to police about Kombi shelves YES
- Forensic expert claiming the man on CCTV was not Murdoch YES [dismissed]
- Different forensic expert claiming the man on the CCTV was Murdoch   YES [accepted]
- Joanne Lees denying stopping at Aileron   YES According to transcript
- Claim by Gregory Dick that Lees and Falconio stopped at his roadhouse from 3.30pm to 4.30pm on the 14th of July DISMISSED.
- Joanne Lees giving a telephone call to New Zealand changing the timeline by two hours   YES

Well, that is quite a lot in both directions but not looking good for the Prosecution. Further on we will try to re-examine again anything relevant to time of assumed alleged death/killing of Falconio.

- The examination should indicate if the alleged crime is a pure fabrication by Joanne Lees –Falconio –and their accomplices.
- The time of the alleged crime can't be proven **NO DEAD BODY**. Very doubtful if no crime took place and no Dead Body found. But it can be calculated
- Everything only based and according to Lees' claims the only witness.

It is not possible to believe that a real crime took place because of the timeline, the absence of evidence and no Dead Body. It will also give some light on who may own the four unidentified footprints. So, let us take a break but keep on reading.

The Vanishing of Peter Falconio

*Note: If you follow my way of thinking, the hour of departure from Alice Spring regarding the speed at which they drove from Alice to Barrow Creek or Aileron to Barrow Creek is totally irrelevant.

What is relevant and I say it again: Is the time of departure from Aileron and Ti Tree and the time of arrival at Barrow Creek nothing else.

But knowing they stopped at Aileron by four witnesses, served food and drinks is also extremely significant. What happen at Aileron is paramount and very relevant indeed.

To me it indicates that Joanne Lees didn't expect to be seen at Ti Tree alone.

From the start we have [5] people involved as I said before:

- One identified footprint: Lees and four unidentified footprints
- Meaning [1] Falconio – [2] the Aileron man/Nick the lover –[3] the driver of the Japanese car –[4] and perhaps a man who owns a Land Cruiser [?]. Anyhow there is/was a man with a Land Cruiser because he is the one who allegedly shot Falconio.
- Lees spoke to a man at Aileron and according to the staff of the roadhouse they knew each other.
- Nobody saw the man leaving –nobody saw Lees and Falconio leaving together in the Kombi, we don't know if Falconio left with the man or by himself on foot (Laughter) because Falconio was not with Lees at Ti Tree watching the sunset.

Lees and the four conspirators in crime must have planned to meet somewhere. I am assuming, but I feel the most suited location would be the alleged crime scene.

There, they could discuss, rehearse the scam and check the site.

- Please, bear in mind that we don't know if the Aileron man is Nick the lover and if the man on the CCTV is involved. This is not farfetched but the most suitable location for them to meet had to be the alleged crime scene.
- We know that Vince Millar the truck driver saw two men carrying what looked like a drunk man (the jelly man) who was pushed into

a small red Japanese car (at the trial, Jury was told about the car, but <u>nothing about the three men)</u>.

- It would fit: three men in the car or: **[1]** Falconio **[2]** the Aileron man or Nick the Lover **[3]** the driver of the Japanese car.
- **[4]** The CCTV man driving the Land Cruiser already on his way to Alice to be seen at the truck stop. (That is four people if Nick the lover and the Aileron man are the same people).
- We do not know unless the Prosecution could tell us more about it being a witness (Laughter). Obviously if the Prosecution said: *This is what happen*, it must be correct (It means what it means, the Prosecution was a witness beyond reasonable doubt (clapping in the background).

My little finger tells me that I could be on the right track….

There is always a discrepancy whatever Lees said. Denying stopping at Aileron was a mistake and a true error of judgment from Lees.

Doesn't matter how you look at it, nothing much fits.

But knowing they were seen at Aileron by four witnesses, served food and drinks is hard to swallow after being constantly denied by Joanne Lees. Nonetheless at the trial Lees finally admitted having stopped there, but the Prosecution cleverly moved the goal posts. It was accepted by the Court…Obviously!

I feel that Lees committed suicide not knowing she had been seen alone watching the sunset claiming Falconio was with her.

Unfortunately for her she gave two wrong answers to police regarding the matter.

Who came up with the scam is another question, what was the MOTIVE is another thing. Was Falconio and Lees really in debt? They both had to be, she played her part didn't she. Is there a relation with some drug lords?

It is an alleged crime created by Lees and her partners in the scam, based on only four things:

- **Time of the alleged crime**
- **Time the killer left the alleged crime scene**.

The Vanishing of Peter Falconio

- **Time of Joanne Lees 'rescue.**
- **Time the CCTV man arriving at the truck stop.**

Of course, Murdoch was found guilty because of the DNA trump card, but that will be challenged...

It would be logical to assume that, if the killer left the alleged crime scene at midnight after searching for Lees five hours, the offence had to have taken place at midnight minus five hours = 7.00pm on the 14th. But it doesn't fit because if the alleged crime took place at 7.00pm knowing that Lees left Ti Tree at 6.30pm after refuelling the Kombi would mean that she drove from Ti Tree to Barrow Creek 119km in 30 minutes...You with me?

- The assumed calculated alleged time of death/abduction of **8.45pm** on the 14th make sense but not full proof as I said before because we don't know the whereabouts of Lees and Falconio between departing Ti Tree at 6.30 and Midnight time of Lees rescued.
- Yes, the rescue time is correct according to Vince Millar and the transcript.
- **But the time spent by Lees hiding in the scrub on that cold pitch- black winter night is absolutely not correct and false.**
- Then man on the CCTV (the killer or Murdoch according to Lees –Prosecution – James Hepi) was seen at the truck stop in Alice at 0.30am on the 15th of July 2001 (transcript) is to be challenged and it will be, trust my words.

Furthermore, as you will read in a next chapter Joanne Lees made a phone call to a friend in New Zealand modifying the timeline by two hours, another proof that the whole thing was staged, but was the telephone call investigated?

- That is why Murdoch's footprints were not identified, because he was not at the scene, but according to Lees he was. In fact, I believe both of them, Lees and Falconio were there rehearsing. Remember we don't have Falconio's shoes to prove it.

- That is why Falconio's footprints were not identified, but I believe that he was there, it's all about his shoes.

The Vanishing of Peter Falconio

- That is why Murdoch's dog footprints –his car –trailer's wheel marks were not identified.
- That is why the big gun was not found (and so is the small one ah ah!). Remember? The big gun was downgraded, (Clapping in the back ground).
- The emptied shells and any other evidences were never found.
- This is somehow concrete proofs that the whole story was staged
- And that is why there is no Dead Body and there shall never be one
- Unless Falconio is/was killed later on by someone else without Joanne Lees' 'knowledge [?], which is a possibility that we cannot dismissed.
- But don't forget he was seen alive in Bourke days after his death.

There are also more indications that can discredit claims made by Joanne Lees. Please read on, the book is not finished.

You must also keep on reading Dean Mildren –FFDA –and Robin Bowles.

I can definitely assume and conclude up to this stage that: Murdoch is innocent, he was setup from the start because he was not at the alleged crime scene and that no crime could have been committed, everybody hated his gust he was guilty before the trial. It was a big farce, it was staged, Lees saw his photograph when in Sicily and everyone fell for it.

***

Before the next chapter I need to say that up until now I have not yet disclosed the obvious fact or the proof beyond reasonable doubt that Murdoch could not have committed the alleged crime. Up until now, in theory everything is suspicious especially coming from Lees and the Prosecution. Everything needs to be challenged and proven …Keep on reading please.

The Vanishing of Peter Falconio

45 - Plan And Strategy

Well, Falconio must have been there. In fact, I believe that he was there: Why?

- Simply because both Lees and Falconio stopped at Aileron. There are four witnesses and Vince Millar saw three men in that Japanese car, and the most obvious she claimed that her boyfriend had been shot.
- At Barrow Creek Lees was rescued, rescued from what we don't know [?]
- Everything has been fabricated by Joanne Lees + Falconio + three other people.
- And according to the experts, we have four unidentified footprints.

But we don't know the motive and there are no witnesses (only Lees).

Could the motive be relevant to money and debts –drugs –drug lords, whatever you can think, even to get rid of Murdoch by his business competitors (Hepi and police). But I am only assuming. Nobody knows because it is impossible to prove something that did not happen.

How can you prove something which doesn't exist or didn't exist or never took place? You just can't, no one can.

The smarter in the case and trial was the Prosecution. The prosecutor knew that the big lie about the DNA trump card would work. The Prosecution knew that no one can/could prove something that doesn't exist or did not happen including all claims put forward by Lees.

Regarding the DNA, the Prosecution knew that the DNA theory would work magic…They had 28 months to fake it…Even longer… up to the trial (you will find out later).

The Prosecution knew that people are like sheep, the Prosecution knew that [a] patch of bloodstain would solve the problem even if it was not Murdoch's blood, even if it was not blood. Try proving it, try proving me wrong.

Monsieur the Prosecutor knew that DNA technology was in its infancy. He knew that nobody could with 100% certainty confirm something which couldn't be proven. Even nowadays it's impossible to predict with accuracy. It is not full proof far from it. Even the High Court agreed saying: "You cannot convict on DNA evidence alone –it not safe enough…" (Murder in the outback series).

The only thing which can be proven nowadays is the weather: Tomorrow the weather will be fine in between showers!

All the Prosecution had to do was to stick to Joanne Lees 'claims (with reservation as you will see further on) and the DNA theory. Nothing else would work. The proof was in the pudding.

That is why the Defence was not at all up to the task even after having four long years to prepare for the trial. The Defence should have done much better. Sorry to say that, but that's how I feel.

Also don't forget that some files of the DNA analysis/results had been allegedly removed or destroyed making it impossible somehow for the Defence team to challenge the DNA evidences presented by the Prosecution. …It is a sad story, but I must keep on speaking my mind.

The scam created and fabricated by Lees, Falconio and three other individuals had one purpose only: To benefit them. HOW, well I don't know? All I know is that it did benefit Joanne Lees financially. Nobody has any idea about the MOTIVE. All we can see is that the whole story was fabricated, and everybody fell for it.

It also means that, the Dead Body may reappear at a later date, not dead but alive and doing well. It will be then The Armageddon Day.

***

*Note: I am not excluding that Falconio may have been killed later on, but again try proving it. Don't forget I am not looking for the killer. I made it my mission to clear the innocent.

***

The vanishing of Falconio supports the theory that the Dead Body may have been buried somewhere, but it cannot be proven beyond reasonable doubt. The alleged crime had to look and feel real. To achieve that, more than one participant needed to be involved. I can confirm that five people seem to be the correct number:

- Lees –Falconio -+ three unknown footprints. The issue here is; we don't know who owns the four unidentified footprints. We don't have Falconio's footprints (remember).

Of course, along the way we have Murdoch found guilty on all charges. No one can prove the identity of the four unidentified footprints (1 Falconio –2 Aileron man – 3 Nick the lover – 4 the driver of the Japanese car and perhaps also –and/or five one man who owns a Land Cruiser (supposition).

- Regarding the unidentified footprints, there has to be a man who owns a Land Cruiser to fit the plot
- That is the one who according to Lees –the Prosecution –and Mr Hepi has been captured on the CCTV film. **That's the THEORY!**
- We cannot put a name on any of them because we don't have their shoes for the identification. It is so simple that sometime I wonder [?]

I have not included the CCTV man because mathematically the odds favours Murdoch because he was not there and we don't know if Murdoch is the CCTV man or not (but I will prove otherwise further on). Yes we know that he also owns a similar Land Cruiser (similar doesn't mean the same). But wait a new comer will be appearing shortly!

- **So' we have: 1** Lees –**2** Falconio –**3** the man from Aileron – **4** Nick the lover –**5** the driver of the Japanese car must have planned to meet at the alleged crime scene. We still have four unidentified footprints.

Right now, many questions need to be answered:
- Is/was the man from Aileron and Nick the lover the same person?
- If they are the same person, it would still work,
- We would still have three people in the car **[1]** Falconio – **[2]** Aileron man/Nick the lover as one – **[3]** the driver of the car.

The Vanishing of Peter Falconio

- I said a newcomer is on its way, and the CCTV man needs to be seen in Alice at 0.30am (15th) according to the transcript of the appeal.

The scam must have been planned well before, the timing had to be right and it would have worked well but, for the average mortal, and others, the main influencing fact was Lees' many claims supported by many unproven facts and the lack of a Dead Body. Nothing took place at the alleged crime scene. Nothing to do with beyond reasonable doubt!

- Yes, Vince Millar the road train driver, saw three men getting in a small car then he saw the car passing him at high- speed going north.
- It can't be a coincidence, who were the three men and where were they going …Bourke?
- Did the CCTV man drive to Alice purposely to be seen at 0.30am on the 15th of July?
- Yes, I think that he had to be part of their plan.

Also, was the CCTV man truly investigated? We know that police did try, but everything failed (no number plates, no credit card with a name on it etc.)

- **But Joanne Lees did hey**! (Repeat I know). She identified the man at the trial, so did the Prosecution and Monsieur Hepi.
- Then everybody believed that it was Murdoch's Land Cruiser…Remarkable!
- Nobody could identify the man or the car, **BUT** it is/was Murdoch and his car, because of the word "similar" meaning the "same" (Clapping in the background).

It is a real joke especially knowing that the back of Murdoch's Land Cruiser was blocked by a cage, which cannot be seen on the CCTV man's car, (refer to photo on the Internet).

- So why was Joanne Lees claiming that she escaped from the back of the Ute when Murdoch's Cruiser has no opening at the back?

The Vanishing of Peter Falconio

And why is that if you watch some of the re-enactment she come out from the side?

- But, oh yes, I know, Lees escaped from the Cruiser seen on the CCTV film but didn't or couldn't escape from Murdoch's Cruiser. That is why a choice had to be made, it's one or the other hey!
- Why would Vince Millar be lying about the small Japanese car he saw around 0.15am on the 14th of July with the three men on board living the site?
- Was it a decoy? But then, what about the declaration by people who saw Falconio days after his alleged death [?]Given that Vince Millar the road train driver saw the car minutes before rescuing Lees with three men on board is really food for thought! But, two pages of Vince Millar first declaration to police went missing. Another declaration was drafted and presented to him to be signed but he refused to sign it …Good man. But he had to comply by force at the end just to avoid great repercussions. That's what happens when the system is openly corrupt.

I said a newcomer is on his way.

The Vanishing of Peter Falconio

46 – Newcomer... New Suspect

At this present time only Bradley John Murdoch and the CCTV man own a Land Cruiser, but this is about to change making things even more of a headache and difficult to understand, why Murdoch was found guilty when nothing beyond reasonable doubt could have supported a guilty verdict...Only the suspicious and miraculous DNA trump card used by the Prosecution and the Officials did the trick.

Yes, there is now a new Toyota Land Cruiser owned by Monsieur Chris Malouf.

Who is this Monsieur Malouf?

According to Richard Shears in his book Bloodstain, "Chris Malouf had nowhere he could really call home "page 25

He was a drifter, his Toyota being his home so to speak according to Richard Shears.

Now according to FFDA page263 Part S staging

Everything Lees and Falconio were involved with, could have involved staging. If that seems extreme, note the following. In her book on the case, Robin Bowles reveals this disturbing fact: "**Chris Malouf** had passed through Barrow Creek and camped 55 metres from where the [alleged] incident took place – on the same night." (original italics; added emphasis)"

Then in FFDA on page 266, part S staging:

"So, on the same night (14-15 July 2001) the whole alleged incident at Barrow Creek took place, **Chris Malouf** from Western Australia is said to have camped just 55 metres from the killing zone. [15] Yet, this **Malouf** never heard anything, never saw anything, never suspected anything, etc. in relation to: the braking and stopping and the lights of two vehicles near where he was camped; the opening of two vehicle doors then talking, allegedly between the man and Falconio; the revving of the Kombi engine; the backfire of the Kombi engine or a single shot from a pistol (Lees said the man had a big silver revolver); the screaming of Lees as she fought with the man; the talking between Lees and the man when she was in the rear of his vehicle; the chase in the bush as the man pursued the only witness, allegedly of Falconio's killing; the starting of the Kombi engine then the driving of that vehicle

[16] from the scene (Why?); the starting of the vehicle belonging to the man then the driving of it away from the scene; then about five hours later the sudden air-braking

[17] and stopping of a road train; the unhitching of the trailers from the prime mover, then a three-point 180-degree turn of the prime mover; the prime mover crawling in a low gear as the drivers and Lees looked for the Kombi; the returning of that prime mover back to the trailers; the hissing air-brakes again, then the reversing of it to re-hitch the trailers; then a full-pull away of that midnight monster – throttle open wide, double-clutch gear after gear, exhausts roaring bright lights blazing. All that on a clear and cold Territory night would have been heard and seen kilometres away. So, was Malouf profoundly deaf? Was he really there? Or, was this claim of Lees about her being out there running around and hiding in the dark part of the staging and stalling to give Falconio five good hours to get far away from that place in a speeding Japanese-type sedan that was seen heading north by a driver of that road train? (see Insert) There is absolutely nothing about Lees' claims, and there are many of them, that has the ring of truth. Until the arrival of the road train (with its two drivers/witnesses), everything Lees said could have been concocted, contrived, and/or corrupted. Never forget, she was the only person who spoke about what (allegedly) happened north of Barrow Creek before that road train arrived. And if there is no indisputable evidence to corroborate her many claims – and there isn't – then the word of an identified liar must never be accepted as the truth, the whole truth, and nothing but the truth. "

Do you find this interesting? Will this solve the issue: Beyond reasonable doubt?

So, we have three Land Cruisers now. If I ask:
- Who is the CCTV man?
- Is he: Murdoch –the CCTV man himself –or Malouf?
- What would you answer? The three of them or none? Would your answer comply with the rule of law beyond reasonable doubt?

The Vanishing of Peter Falconio

There is also a possibility for the story to involve not two dogs but three [?], according to Roger Maynard in his book Where's Peter?

According to Roger Maynard, page 102 "…More intriguingly they did see his dog –a blue or red Healer, but definitely not a Dalmatian, as later stressed to police."

Interesting indeed! Then:

"There was the dead dog found at Neutral Junction Station north of Barrow Creek and east of the Stuart Highway…But the discovery of the large brown mixed-breed animal which had been shot, naturally aroused police interest, given Joanne Lees account of the dog in the Ute. "

- Could Malouf be involved with drugs or working undercover also related to drugs?
- I am asking again because: How did police get onto Malouf so fast knowing that he was arrested in the early hours of the morning the day after the alleged offence.
- To me, this is very suspicious [?]

Whatever you may think about the Officials –the Government of Northern Territory –the police –the experts –the Prosecution – the dear Monsieur Hepi –Joanne Lees, none of them were looking for the truth, the latter never told the truth. The agenda and the narrative had nothing to do with beyond reasonable doubt. It should not have contributed to a guilty verdict on all charges. The trial of John Bradley Murdoch was a trial by Media. It was a miscarriage of justice. Truly it was a Kangaroo trial in a Kangaroo Court.

The Vanishing of Peter Falconio

47 - Turbulent Waters

We have certainly established few things of prime interest, mostly a list of questions that needed to be answered only by YES or NO and my conclusions are not in favour of Joanne Lees –the Judge –the Prosecution – even the Defence –the police –the experts –the journalists –and obviously the media.

As I said, one important relevance in the case is that:

- Joanne Les is the only witness she can claim anything.
- Murdoch was not near the alleged crime scene (to be proven).
- We don't know where Falconio was, but he had to be there to fit with Lees 'story
- There is no Dead Body.
- Nothing belonging to Murdoch or his dog or else has been identified.
- We don't know who moved the Kombi [?]
- Joanne Lees and Falconio were identified at Aileron.
- Lees was seen at 6.10pm watching the sunset at Ti Tree alone but it seems that she arrived 40 or 55 minutes earlier [?]
- Her abduction took place between 8.45/9.00pm on the 14th of July (still assuming not knowing at what time she/they arrived at the alleged crime scene).
- She was rescued not long after midnight…Around 0.15am on the 15th
- A man who doesn't look like Murdoch was picked up on a CCTV video at 0.30am on the 15th in Alice Springs on the morning the day after the abduction.
- The CCTV man is/was Murdoch according to Lees and the Prosecution and others…
- We now have a third Land Cruiser
- Important claims from witness who saw Falconio Alive after his death dismissed, ignored and ridiculed
- Vince Millar first declaration tampered for unknown reason [?]

- We don't know who the Aileron man is/was [?]
- We don't know what took place at Aileron roadhouse between her and the man she spoke to near the fuel pump [?]

We are now going to examine what can be deducted from Falconio's alleged calculated time of death and Lees' calculated time of abduction, but before we do that, below are some good reads from FFDA to cheer you up

All from FFDA page 271, part T trial

"The problem with all this scientific evidence is that once it gets caught up in the frenzy of a chase, even evidence that is fundamentally flawed has a good chance of being accepted." Malcolm Brown2 The usual suspects smh.com.au 13 September 2007

"[A]fter a big case there was hardly any evidence that was the truth." 3 Bruce Day Hey Cop! 2008: p. 138

"Australian courts are little concerned with democracy or justice." G.E. (Tony) Fitzgerald the Australian 4 November 2005

"One of the key things about any law, as Geoffrey Robertson (5) puts it, is that it's got to have a system of law with some inherence in it that the citizen can defeat the government if necessary. We [Australians] now have a system of law in which the citizen can't defeat the government, in which the system has been rigged to assure that the citizen can't beat the government." (added emphasis)

From Keith Noble himself FFDA page 272

"Judges who do not insist on credible chains of custody for all physical evidence, conduct kangaroo courts." (original italics; original emphasis)

angaroo court sham proceeding denying Truth & Justice by: having no jurisdiction; using unqualified judge(s); hearing false charge(s); having predetermined outcome(s); refusing jury empanelment; curtailing jury considerations; disallowing proper defence; rejecting/ignoring evidence; accepting corrupt evidence; imposing inappropriate sentence(s); etc." (sic; original & added emphasis)

Keith Allan Noble CORRUPT TO THE CORE 2010: pp. 269, 584

The Vanishing of Peter Falconio

This should bring some lights NOT on the alleged murder of Falconio but on his volunteering disappearance! Where did he go and why? Where is he now and who was involved?

For some reason driving slowly the distance (Alice to Ti Tree 195km) must have been anchored in Lees' mind, but forgetting or being confused with all the changes she keeps on making, she gave the wrong answer. Usually that's how people get caught. A wrong answer to a simple question will destroy any alibi.

Do you remember the movie The Great Escape with Steve Mc Queen, when the two English escapees are boarding the bus surrounded by the Gestapo? As they are stepping onto the bus, one Gestapo guy standing next to the door say to one of them in English, not in German: "have a good trip" and the escapee replying "thank you very much".

Lees made make the same mistake when she said: We drove slowly from Alice to Ti Tree... Yes, they did drive slowly just to confuse people, however hiding the fact that they did stop at Aileron...It will cost her!

They definitely stopped at Aileron. But she kept on denying it. That is something she had to block at all cost, unfortunately she fell for it. That is/was a costly mistake. She got caught in her own little web. Being preoccupied about the time [6.10pm] time of the sunset at Ti Tree, claiming Falconio was with her (sleeping).

Unfortunately for Lees a witness claimed she was alone and that she didn't see anybody in the Kombi. Falconio with her or not would be hard to prove and easy to deny but the witness claimed otherwise by truly confirming that she was alone. (Murphy's Law).

Whether been concerned or not about the time [6.10pm] Lees could have just been killing time, perhaps waiting to meet someone not expecting to be seen...We shall never know.

- **Don't forget she/they [?] arrived at Ti Tree earlier.**
- For Lees to be seen at Ti Tree I don't think it was part of their staging plan.
- However, and repeat; between 5.30pm or 5.15pm time of arrival at Ti Tree and 6.10pm the laps of time is 40 or 55 minutes.

The Vanishing of Peter Falconio

- I believe Falconio didn't leave Aileron with Lees, but with the Aileron man.
- But I can't be sure.
- But contrary to the witness's claim, and her two different answers,
- Falconio being with her is/was not in her favour.

I think she didn't know that she had been seen. I feel that she didn't have the slightest idea.

What must have been important was to act according to the staging plan, but what was the plan, the motive?

- Meeting: **1** Falconio –**2** the Aileron man/ Nick the lover [?] –**3** the driver of the Japanese car –**4** and/or one of the two men who own also own a Land Cruisers (the CCTV man or Chris Malouf) at the alleged crime scene for rehearsal. Of course, excluding Murdoch.

If it was not for the suspicious DNA Trump card and if a majority verdict had been accepted in good faith, there is no doubt in my mind that Murdoch would be free today and Lees would be locked up.

Judging by the Prosecution and the Judge comments, anybody can see that Murdoch was guilty long before the start of this abominable and corrupt trial. It was definitely a premeditated execution of an innocent man. But as they said: "What goes up must come down." and I believe it will.

"[T]he European investigative system, which seeks the truth and is controlled by trained judges is necessarily better than a system which does not seek truth and is controlled by trained liars." Evan Whitton. Serial Liars. 2005: pp. 76, 77-78   FFDA p283

Having said that, Lees and Falconio have definitely stopped at Aileron. Why would Gregory Dick and his staff be lying? What would they hope to gain?

Falconio was definitely not with Lees at Ti Tree watching the sunset, therefore he must have gone with the man who spoke with Lees at Aileron…They knew each other. Staging is/was part of their plan, I put my money and life on it. Unfortunately, it can't be proven!

The Vanishing of Peter Falconio

You must admit that, all along the story beyond reasonable doubt, has never being first on the agenda.

The Vanishing of Peter Falconio

48 - The Road Train Driver Vince Millar

[16a] Claim by the truck driver from the new documentary on ATN 7
(Sunday 12th July 2020)

From The documentary by CJZ aired on ATN 7 on Sunday 19th July 2020; Vince Millar, the truck driver and his co- driver Rodney Adams travelling southbound (towards Alice Springs) who rescued Lees at the time, claimed… (Repeat I know)

- That minutes before arriving at the alleged crime scene he saw the headlights of a car making strange manoeuvres.
- Then a short distance before arriving at the alleged crime scene, he saw two men pushing a third man (jelly man) into a small red Japanese car.
- Then he saw the Japanese car passing him with three people on board driving fast going north (towards Darwin) minutes before rescuing Lees who flagged him down. <u>Minutes before is important</u> because even if one knew nothing about the case, anyone else would realise that Lees and the car being there at the same time, is not a coincidence.

The importance about this is: If the Japanese car was had been a normal car travelling north towards Darwin having no intention to stop where Vince Millar stopped to rescue Lees Vince Millar would have seen the headlights well before arriving at the crime scene. The road is nearly flat yes, few hills but hardly any, no mountains only few bends.

- But he saw the headlights of the car only minutes before arriving at the alleged crime scene.
- Seeing the three men getting on board in great hurry was for a reason. The driver must have been waiting for [a] truck to approach the scene, reason why he must have been waiting to turn his lights on one or two minutes prior to the road train getting to the location.
- The car was waiting for a big truck or a road train. Obviously when they saw the headlights of the truck and heard the sound, they were

ready for action meaning jumping into the car and taking off at high speed.

Remembering the words used by the owner of the Aileron roadhouse ..." Drug Lords" I feel is most interesting.

Then From FFDA p93/317 Part W Whereabouts

Road train driver Vince Millar said that as he drove south and approached the site of the alleged incident there was, "a small Japanese-type sedan driving fast [north] towards me, and passin' me before I reached Joanne." (see Part S, Insert) The logical questions to ask is, was Falconio in that sedan? And, was he dead or alive? This writer suspects the person who drove that Japanese type sedan was Darryl Cragan (aka Dags).41

"Ya know, I've done a lot of thinkin' about that car since then, because she wasn't cold, like you'd expect. What if that car took off with the evidence – the body three even – and she stalled me by gettin' me to look for her Kombi?" (added emphasis) (Vince Millar. in Dead Centre. 2005: p. 191)

Vince Millar's experience with Joanne Lees on that winter night is highly suggestive. The "small Japanese-type sedan driving fast" is not how this incident is presented in the official narrative. Lees claimed she had been outside for several hours, but Millar said Lees was warm – not cold. He also said and implied that she and her clothing did not appear as if they had been out in the bush for several hours, Millar said Lees was not dirty. And the stalling that Millar thought Lees was doing was repeated when she stalled the media at Alice Springs. (Lees' crying and failing to speak in full to the two detectives at Alice Springs, and at the committal hearing in Darwin, can also be considered stalling tactics.) It certainly seems that the jury was not told everything about Millar's experience with Joanne Lees on the night of 14-15 July 2001.

"Also forgot to mention to the cops that when I put my arms around her, she was warm. I remember thinkin' that was a bit strange her in a skimpy little T-shirt. I even thought for a minute that she might have just got out of the car I'd seen. The other thing was, she wasn't dirty. Her clothing all looked pretty intact, and there were only a few little blood smears on her shirt, like they might have come from her elbows. Ya know, I've done a lot of thinkin' about that car since then, because she wasn't cold, like you'd expect. What if that car took off with the evidence the body even – and she stalled me by gettin' me to look for her Kombi'."

***

Below, is what Keith Noble writes about Darryl Cragan (FFDA Part F Falconio page 93)

PAGE 3 19. "He looked quite evil" Who is this person? In the literature there are several references to a person that seems to fits this description. What type of vehicle was he driving? Roadtrain driver Vince Millar said that as he drove south and approached the site of the alleged incident there was, "a small Japanese-type sedan driving fast [north] towards me, and passin' me before I reached Joanne." (see Part S, Insert) The logical questions to ask is, was Falconio in that sedan? And, was he dead or alive? This writer suspects the person who drove that Japanese type sedan was Darryl Cragan (aka Dags).41 20

Nobody knows what really happen before Vincent Millar rescued Lees. When Millar rescued Lees the first thing he noticed as mentioned above was: She was warm, not cold after spending five hours hiding in the bush on a winter night (which we know is a big lie)
- Well, this has to be related to the time the CCTV man enters the truck stop. But here I need to be more precise; you need to understand that when she was rescued around 0.15am on the 15th at the same time (+ or minus ten minutes) the CCTV man enters the truck stop meaning; both are connected or seemed to be connected.
- Millar didn't know at that time that she had been or pretending to have been hiding in the bush around five hours.
- Then he found that her clothing was intact, she was not dirty. Mentally it would be easy for Lees to pretend she was traumatized.

The Vanishing of Peter Falconio

- She claimed that they were stopped by a man driving a Land Cruiser in company of his dog, and that her boyfriend had been shot by the man with a big gun and she was abducted by the man minutes after he shot Falconio etc.

Was Lees involved in the staged disappearance of her boyfriend irrelevant if his footprints were identified or not. All we know for real fact is that Murdoch was not at the alleged crime scene.

If all of this was staged, up until now, everything seems to work. She is rescued –she tells her story –makes her claim and Bob's your uncle!

However, when a staged criminal action takes place, for the scam to be successful there must be some solid alibis prior to the time of the alleged event. Everything from past actions will come and haunt anyone involved. Call it Murphy's Law. "You have the right to remain silent. Anything you may say can and will be used against you in a court of law".

If staging was involved, if Falconio reappears or is seen by someone taking his photograph then the time for the crucifixion is inevitable. Just imagine the consequences!

What could happen if the plan failed? Could the life of Falconio and Lees be then in jeopardy when drugs and drug lords could be involved? It could well be part of the equation.

- My answer is: Not maybe, but certainly.

When Millar rescued her, he was under the impression that she was stalling him…Why was she stalling him?

At the alleged crime scene, we have four unidentified footprints + Lees. Her prints were identified, she can't deny that, being rescued there.

Again, who owns the four footprints and again who could it be?

- **1** Falconio –**2** Aileron man/ Nick the lover –**3** the driver of the Japanese car – **4** and perhaps the man from the CCTV film or Chris Malouf? …Has to be a Land Cruiser involved because of the Land Cruiser on the CCTV film <u>which also might be a simple coincidence.</u>

The Vanishing of Peter Falconio

- Five people including Lees, and four unidentified…Turbulent Waters for sure!
- I firmly assume that the Aileron man is Nick the lover or vice versa. …[?]

Falconio could have been there if he didn't get out of a car or not. Nobody had his shoes to prove it or could he have been wearing some decoy shoes which I feel would be a bit farfetched. My suggestion of the decoy shoes is ridiculous, irrelevant, because we wouldn't have the shoes anyway having no Dead Body and we are not in possession of any other shoes.

- Was Falconio in that small Japanese car?
- Could he have gone south instead of going north with someone else? Pretty unlikely because if Falconio was seen in Bourke some days later and alive, the best way from Barrow Creek to Bourke would be to head north first.

This only tells you one thing;
- Doubt is present all along. Every words –sentences – facts that are not facts are very suspicious.
- Suggestions from the Prosecution are made to deceive and influence the jury who was definitely kept in the dark –everything is doubtful.
- Witness testimonies rejected, dismissed or ridiculed.
- Again, what does that tells you? It tells you that the whole trial a farce. It tells you that the alleged crime was fabricated by Lees, Falconio and partners in crime?

Please ask yourself about the three men in the Japanese car:
- It would be unbelievable for the "jelly" man to be Falconio (meaning that he was alive then),
- To think that Joanne Lees had forgotten about her claim that: HE (Falconio) had been shot five hours earlier.
- It would destroy any alibi and I believe again that she is the biggest liar.

The Vanishing of Peter Falconio

I know I said it too many times and I like to repeat it, but the only true fact regarding the alleged crime scene is:
- Lee was the only witness.
- No one saw Falconio being shot even Lees, BUT HE WAS THERE. She was there but she didn't witness the actual killing.
- So, <u>why was she there</u>? Don't you think this is very suspicious and mysterious?

She was the only person there.
- Murdoch was somewhere else,
- But we still have four unidentified footprints and none of them belonging to Murdoch.
- No footprints –no wheel - marks of his car or trailer –no footprints from his dog, excrements or else –no emptied cartridges –no blood – no cigarette butts knowing that Murdoch and Falconio were smokers– no hair from the dog found on Lees– no mess –no blood.

Don't you think that it would have been enough for the Defence and the jury to say "Hey wait a minute…". Do you reckon Murdoch could be a free man today as we speak?

But wait there is more!
- So, we can assume that in the small Japanese car we have:
- **1** Falconio + two the driver of the car who could be one of the two men as suggested in ***FFDA*** (Darryl Cragan (Aka Dags see above) also mentioned in the transcript of the appeal + three the Aileron man or Nick the secret lover.

I recommend to anyone to read Keith Noble Find Falconio Dead or Alive. Referring to the above, it's in section [F] FALCONIO from page 73 to 96 (Lots of reading, his book is amazing.)

Please notice that I have not included the CCTV man and Malouf, both own a SIMILAR Land Cruiser …Why?

The Vanishing of Peter Falconio

Well, regarding Falconio unidentified footprints there is definitely something not correct. Please read this slowly. It is about Falconio being killed at the location.

- Lees said: The man, the killer with long hair –moustache –deep Australian voice –medium size (which she changed later on using the word huge), bigger than Peter –who owns a blue healer (Murdoch owns a Dalmatian) stopped them.

What happen next?

Well, we know from her claims what took place if we trust her story, but her story doesn't fit.

- She didn't see the killing but she claimed her boyfriend was shot there because she heard a "BANG". Very impressive but not convincing!
- Not having found his Dead Body, his shoes could not be checked,
- But the road train driver Vince Millar saw three people in the small Japanese car. Again, the rule beyond reasonable doubt did not apply.

We are soaking in a sea of doubts. A guilty verdict must be pronounced beyond any reasonable doubt, there must not be any doubt. In this case every single argument is doubtful …Constant doubt. Not surprising that we can't get our head around it.

It is pure fiction. Judge Brian Ross Martin fail twice in his duty as a Judge.

- **Firstly,** for not having purposely instructed the jury regarding majority verdict. ***"Your verdict must be unanimous"*** he said. It was not an option nor a suggestion but an order. *"Your verdict must be unanimous"* (otherwise it's your job!).
- **Secondly** for not telling that a juror who sat on Murdoch's trial was in a relationship with his daughter Joanna Martin. (You will find out later).

The Vanishing of Peter Falconio

So, because this is pure fiction whatever we're trying to prove or disprove makes no difference and no sense at all, I can positively say that we definitely need Inspector Poirot.

Anyway, irrelevant of all this, if all this had been debated during the trial, if the Jury had known about all this nonsense, Murdoch would now be a free man…… This is an absolute miscarriage of justice and I am giving you the proper definition again and one of many from the internet:

"A miscarriage of justice is a failure of a court or judicial system to attain the ends of justice, especially one which results in the conviction of an innocent person".

The scenario unfortunately must have been staged for unknown reason: Falconio must disappear/vanish for good reasons and Murdoch must be the scapegoat…Good plan…But remember: Be nice to the ones on the way up as you may meet them again on the way down, and … You will.

The truth will always prevail. The truth and the reason for such staging will be revealed at the end of the movie when someone will bump into Falconio and take his photo…This will happen, the judge said so about the body… "it will be found but it will take some time!" These were the words referring to the Dead Body. All we need is a facial recognition, you only need one camera anywhere in the world or someone who can prove that Murdoch is/was not the killer…You're with me?

I pray for it to happen.

The Vanishing of Peter Falconio

49 - The First Obvious Fact

We spoke about it before but more needs to be said.

Like in the X-Files the truth is out there …But where?

Up until now everything I wrote was indicative of my views regarding the case and the big bag of lies.

Now let's have a solid and constructive conversation and analysis.

***

The crunch of the story starts at Ti Tree at 6.10pm on the 14th of July ending up with the crucifixion of Murdoch. It involves: Lees –Murdoch– the Prosecution –the Defence –the alleged crime scene –the time of the alleged offence –the CCTV man who according to Lees and the Prosecution in 2005 is/was Murdoch the killer – the killing time –the time spent by Lees hiding in the bush –the real time and exact time when the alleged killer left the alleged crime scene –the time when Lees came out of her hiding place – and how long after the killer left was Joanne Lees rescued etc.

This will put some light on why Joanne Lees was found warm and clean when rescued by Vince Millar after spending so many hours as per her claims, in the bush on a cold and pitch back winter night (I know it is a repeat but necessary).

According to the legend

- Joanne Lees was seen watching the sunset alone at Ti Tree 119 km from Barrow Creek at 6.10pm on the 14th of July.
- This was confirmed by a witness.
- Lees left Ti Tree at 6.30pm normally alone after refuelling and using the toilets aiming for Barrow Creek.
- Knowing that the engine of the Kombi was on its last leg the maximum speed that could be achieve with great risks was 80km/h.
- In previous chapters I did the calculation using an average speed of 60km/h and 80km/h (at 60km/h the life of the engine was saved)
- At 60km/h the drive took two hours to reach Barrow Creek.
- Arrival time at Barrow Creek 8.30pm on the 14th

The Vanishing of Peter Falconio

- That is when the killer stopped Lees and Falconio who was then back in the picture but only according to her story …Remember she was alone at Ti Tree.

Where did Lees pick up Falconio after leaving Ti Tree alone? We don't know but Falconio did return. Probably meeting at the alleged crime scene [?]

Now this is very serious business. However, at this stage everything is still science-fiction because the lack of fact but, the wind is turning!

- The alleged killer stopped them.
- That is when the two men got out of their car (Falconio and the killer)
- The Land Cruiser parked behind, close to the kombi both with no wheels on the dirt but on the tar meaning no trace of wheel marks on the dirt if you saw the re-enactment on TV (confirmed by the investigators and the Aboriginal trackers no wheel marks from Murdoch Land Cruiser and his campervan trailer and Kombi)
- A short conversation followed, Lees could hear the two men talking, Falconio came back to the Kombi to pick up his cigarettes, the conversation continued for a very short time,
- Minutes after Lees heard a bang
- Later on during the investigation, this, combined with the sound of what Lees first claimed as an engine backfiring or Falconio being shot by the exhaust pipe which later according to her claim was a gunshot (changing her claim again) it became good enough evidence for the corrupt Northern Territory officials, that a firearm had been discharged, but no emptied cartridges found, no Dead Body, no fresh blood from Falconio or anything else for that matter, and **NO GUN!**

Now, from FFDA p10/20 we read: Ms Lees said that contrary to reports, at no stage on Saturday night did she believe that the loud bang she heard was a gunshot. Instead, she described the bang she heard as sounding like a gun going off

WOW! Another good one. Please explain the difference between the sound of a gunshot and the sound of a gun going off when using the same gun? She believes that we are all stupid? (Repeat I know).

So, Falconio got shot apparently in the head at point blank (the Judge will confirm this in his sentencing of Murdoch, which was televised…If you believe him) drops to the ground metres away from both cars and Lees, but Lees sees nothing [?]

- Falconio allegedly and according to my calculation got shot at **8.45pm** after a short conversation.
- That is the killing time, the time when he fell dead, the time of death?
- Now that Falconio is dead on the ground not bleeding as not trace of his blood was found according to the experts (only the suspicious patch found on the tar (animal mixed we don't know with what: human or aliens?).
- The killer must then deal with Lees (by now, you know what I mean).

- Then he has to bury the body – then search for Lees who escaped – then the alleged killer not worrying a bit about her escape,
- Moves the Kombi, then leaves the alleged crime scene aiming for Alice Springs
- But the transcript says that he couldn't find her –as a result gives up the search – and leaves the scene aiming for Alice Springs just before midnight. All this as per Lees' claims. To me, *"couldn't find her"* contradict *she never saw him again*…Remember?
BUT NO, THAT'S NOT WHAT HE DOES.
- He leaves the alleged crime scene at 9.00pm arriving in Alice 303km away or three and half hours driving arriving at the truck stop at 0.30am…WHY?

- Because Murdoch is the CCTV man... **why?** <u>Because Lees and the prosecution said so</u>.
- Does a bit of shopping –however walking out slowly –gets in his Cruiser and leaves again quick smart being in great hurry after committing an alleged murder in company of his dog the Dalmatian, after taking drugs (easy for him he sells the stuff) but not before and according to the Prosecution reconnecting the trailer which was parked who knows where?
- Then full blast at 160km/h, could be more, takes off **<u>without saying good bye</u>** leaving his death sentence behind (meaning Lees) towards Fitzroy Crossing in Western Australia **1,412km** away to be seen by witness refuelling around 8.00pm (NT time) on the 15th of July 2001.
- How do you like that?

Now according to the transcript 2005 NTSC R v Murdoch-N0-1-15 Dec 2005 pdf

Below is what Lees and the prosecution claimed and wants you to believe.

I was shocked reading the words: "...the following is a convenient overview..." Definitely the correct technic to promote the culpability of the alleged offender (if you know what I mean). Definitely very convenient indeed hey!

"Opportunity to observe offender (I know this is a repeat but it is needed.)

[8] Ms Lees said in evidence at the preliminary hearing that at the time of the events it was "pitch black". As to what occurred after Ms Lees saw the male person pointing the gun at her, the following is a convenient overview taken from a Crown summary of facts provided to the court by way of assistance for the purposes of the pre-trial objections: "The offender told LEES to switch the engine off and moved inside the vehicle, pushing LEES to the passenger seat

The Vanishing of Peter Falconio

The offender directed LEES to put her head down and arms behind her back. LEES screamed and struggled with the offender and put her feet up on the dash board. The offender placed the gun at LEES' temple. LEES acquiesced removing her feet from the dash and placing her hands behind her back. ...

The offender placed cable ties (hand made from cable ties and electrical tape) around LEES' wrists and forced her out of the vehicle. LEES fell onto the gravel injuring her knees. The offender got out of the vehicle and lifted LEES' legs up by the ankles and attempted to put electrical tape around her ankles.

I am sorry but I need to stop here for a minute: Am reading correctly? Legs up! ...Wow, imagine the scene...Please continue reading, but ask yourself the question:

- Was the re-enactment following the same rules of engagement meaning; did someone lift Joanne Lees just to put her in the back of the Cruiser? A re-enactment means what it means.

LEES struggled and the offender was unable to securely tighten her ankles. The offender then punched LEES to the right side of the temple. The offender lifted LEES to her feet and placed

tape around her mouth and head. LEES struggled with the offender which loosened the effect of the tape. The offender forced LEES over towards the passenger side of his vehicle and removed a canvas sack from under the canopy over the tray in the utility. He then placed the sack over LEES' head and pushed her into the front passenger side of the vehicle. During this process the sack was dislodged from LEES' head. At this time LEES observed the dog in the front driver's seat. LEES described the dog as being a medium sized, shorthaired, brown and white, blue heeler. LEES attempted to get out of the driver's side door but was blocked by the dog. The offender forced LEES over the seats into the back of the utility.

Here I need to stop again: The offender forcing Lees over the seats into the back of the utility. Wow!... When was this written? What you are reading is from the transcript.

Now, what is a transcript?

- **A transcript is a written record of what was said during a case heard in court or tribunal.** Usually hand typed but voice recorder may also be used
- **When was the transcript written?** It was written in **DECEMBER 2005** the month of the trial.

The transcript was written in December 2005 that is four years after the alleged offence.

- So, for four years THEY (when I say "they" it always means the officials) keep/kept on telling you that Joanne Lees got pushed from the cabin onto the back of the Cruiser.
- When we all know that Toyota has never manufactured a Land Cruiser with a communication between the cabin and the back of any Cruiser.
- WHY IS THAT? Brain washing the Australian way?
- THEY still using the written fact from the transcript as proof of what the alleged offender did during the abduction of Joanne Lees, and how he did it.
- So, THEY are still using false information knowing that no Land Cruisers have a communication from cabin to back when speaking of a Ute. **This was meant to deceive**…And THEY have the audacity to want a unanimous guilty verdict.
- Do you find this a fair trial? If you do, I must be dreaming.

Whilst LEES was in the back of the utility she screamed out to the offender, "What do you want? Is it money? Is it the van? Just take it. Are you going to rape me?" 4 The offender came to an opening in the back of the utility (here again THEY really want everybody to believe that there is/was an opening at the back simply by dismissing the cage) and stated, "Shut up and I won't shoot you." The offender then walked away. LEES screamed out, "Have you shot my boyfriend? Have you shot Pete?

Again, the offender came to the back of the utility and said, "NO." LEES heard the offender walk down the side of the vehicle on the gravel."

The Vanishing of Peter Falconio

[9] In evidence Ms Lees said a light was on in the offender's vehicle when she was forced into that vehicle. Subsequent Events

[10] On the Crown case, Ms Lees then escaped from the back of the utility (here again) and hid in the surrounding scrub. She did not see the offender again.

Please remember she also claimed that she saw the alleged killer looking for her with his torch and his dog. She also claimed she heard the sound of a dead body being dragged…Food for thought hey!

Note* Please remember the words "Pitch- Black and, she did not see the offender again…

…For future reference.

[11] Approximately five hours later Ms Lees left her hiding spot and waved down a passing truck. The driver of the truck observed that Ms Lees was fearful and upset. Her wrists were bound by ties and she had tape around her neck and left ankle.

Well, according to [10] above, On the Crown case, Ms Lees then escaped from the back of the utility (here again it's false) and hid in the surrounding scrub. She did not see the offender again.

I may be stupid but she did not see the offender again means what it means.
- Firstly, we don't know [the time], it's all calculated assumptions…
- Secondly if her story is true, her escape must have taken place <u>only before</u> the departure of the offender (9.00pm on the 14th)
- Which means that, the offender had to move the Kombi <u>before</u> departing towards Alice Springs or someone else did because:
- The assumed calculated time of death being **8.45pm** is/was when Falconio may have dropped dead after getting the bullet in his head –then the killer showed up at the window of the Kombi with a big gun –then that's when the offender with great difficulty started to abduct Lees –then pushing her into the back of the Cruiser from the passage between the cabin and the back of course (laughter),
ALL THIS IN 15 MINUTES? WOW!

The Vanishing of Peter Falconio

Well, she could not have seen him searching for her with a torch and the help of his dog.

- Because: Her escape must have taken place <u>before</u> the alleged killer's return from having moved the Kombi, NOT AFTER …You with me?
- Because when the offender left the site, she would still be in the back of the utility (clapping in the background).
- I don't believe that he would have left without checking up on her meaning…
- He would have realised that she had escaped but no, he was not worried about her escape because he left anyway and as a result, <u>she didn't see the offender again</u>…
- Why? because he needed to leave at 9.00pm to be seen entering the truck stop in Alice at 0.30am …
- That's why I can tell that Lees's claim is a big -big bag of lies.

Also, because I believe that after pushing her in the back of the Ute, I don't believe for one minute that the offender would have left the opening open.

- For Lees to get out of the Ute with her hands tied up behind her back she needed a knife to cut the canvas if she could but her hands were still restrained when Vince Millar rescued her.

So, when she escaped "It was pitch black and …SHE did not see the offender again"

Mind you the dog would have found her within minutes. The area is flat and the bush trees are not very high. So please Ms Lees, don't think for one minute that we are all a bunch of morons. We do believe that our planet is spherical and revolves around the sun not the other way round.

[12] Ms Lees was taken to Barrow Creek. At about 6am police officers arrived at Barrow Creek and took a statement from Ms Lees. She gave a description of the offender which, speaking very generally, was not inconsistent with a description of the accused. 5 Identification

- Of course, the description of the offender which, *"speaking very generally"*, was not inconsistent with a description of the accused...What is the meaning of this?
- The description of the accused is the description of Murdoch "au naturel"
- I am sorry, but it is inconsistent with the description of the accused Lees gave to police the morning the day after the alleged crime;
- And that is: Long hair to shoulder –great set of moustaches – Kelpie for dog –invisible campervan trailer –not forgetting the big silver gun –some front teeth missing because the offender spoke to her (shut up and I won't shoot you) etc.

*[*13] It is the Crown case that after the events described by Ms Lees the accused etc...."

What you have just read took place of course after the accused shot Falconio leaving the body on the ground while moving the Kombi then leaving the alleged crime scene at 9.00pm

BECAUSE THE OFFENDER

- Had to be seen at the truck stop in Alice Springs at 0.30am on the 15th of July 2001
- But Lees was rescued after spending as per her claim 5hours in the bush after escaping. She escaped say **8.45pm + 10/15 minutes + five hours = 2.00am on the 15th.**
- Well, the man seen on the CCTV film entered the truck-stop at 0.30am **NOT 2.00am and left at 1.00am** on the 15th of July 2001 ...Do you know what I mean?
- Well, it doesn't fit, she was rescued before at around 0.15am on the 15th NOT **2.00am** (please ask Vince Miller).

She said it (underlined*)*
- *[10] On the Crown case, Ms Lees then escaped from the back of the utility and hid in the surrounding scrub. <u>She did not see the offender again.</u>*

- Not seeing the offender again means the offender had left.
- It also means that the offender didn't seem to search for her after she escaped with his wrongly described dog *(LEES described the dog as being a medium sized, shorthaired, brown and white, blue heeler)*.

Do you really believe all that nonsense? Lees stayed in hiding on that freezing (10/13 degrees) and pitch dark wearing only a light T-shirt not forgetting she was in shorts but found nice and warm –and clean when rescued.

- Do you really believe that 9.00pm on the 14th + five hours = 0.30pm on the 15th of July?
- **NO: 9 + 5 =14 where 14 means 2.00am on the 15th**. God, I just can't believe all this!
- The real rescue time is between midnight and 0.30am and do you also believe…
- That not one truck or a car drove by the alleged crime scene, on a busy highway at the exception of the truck driven by Vince Miller?
- When on busy night there is on average one truck every two minutes, if not more even being a Saturday night?

What else does that tells you? Well, it tells you that:

- Joanne Lees did not hide **for five hours nor three and a half hours** in the bush on a freezing and pitch- black winter night,
  It is a big lie, irrelevant what Lees and the Prosecution said.

(Personally, I believe Joanne Lees should be recalled – extradited to face the music)

- Even so, Lees has never been hiding in the scrub.
- Found warm when rescued, she had to be sitting in a car, most probably the Kombi with her associates.
- This is according to Vince Miller who is not an idiot and knows at what time he picked her up. When he said that she was warm and clean must have meant something…Don't you think?

The Vanishing of Peter Falconio

- <u>Is that why two pages from his signed declaration were purposely lost or misplaced or destroyed by police?</u>
- From 8.30pm time when <u>the killer stopped them</u> to 9.00pm time when he left the crime scene, the time laps is 30 minutes. Time involving the shooting and her abduction excluding the cleaning – burying of the Dead Body etc. I thought I mention it.
- Lees did not spend any time in the open. She –Falconio –and partners in crime must have been sitting in a car as I said above, or in the Kombi which had probably been moved by Falconio or her [?]

Now, who is/was the man who allegedly shot Falconio and abused Lees according to her talented imagination on the 14th of July leaving the crime scene at 9.00pm?

Murdoch or the CCTV man? Chis Maloof, someone else, perhaps Monsieur Hepi?

- Well, we don't know? But according to Lees and the Prosecution and Mr Hepi, it was the man that nobody including police could identified. But Lees and the Prosecution our second witness and Mr Hepi; it was the CCTV man. Always according to our **"*Trio*"** it was Murdoch.

All I need to prove now is; [IF] Murdoch is/was the CCTV man or [IF] the CCTV man is/was Murdoch. If I can prove that Murdoch is/was not the CCTV man and vice versa, it will be: Bob's your uncle, the solution and the mystery is partly solved…I know we still have to challenge…The DNA trump card!... Also, and last one from the transcript

[12] Ms Lees was taken to Barrow Creek. At about 6am police officers arrived at Barrow Creek and took a statement from Ms Lees. She gave a description of the offender which, speaking very generally, was not inconsistent with a description of the accused. 5 Identification (already mentioned above, just adding few comments).

- It says; police officers arrived at Barrow Creek and took a statement from Ms Lees.

- Officers (plural form meaning more than one)
- Then it says: …and took statement from Ms Lees
- So, I am asking: How many officers took a statement?

Because I can visualize more than one, each with their little note books writing.

- In reality what was the name of the officers who took Lees's declaration? The name should be in some file unless police is not in the habit of keeping files [?]
- When Lees was describing the offender, was she describing Chris Malouf? Because and again…
- Why and how did police find Malouf so fast –so early in time –but then released him so quickly? And by the way, what happen to him?

Do you really believe that not one vehicle, truck or car drove by the alleged crime scene during the five hours Lees claimed?... At the exception of the road train driven by Vince Miller and his co-driver?

- Do you remember what Falconio said to her from her book page 54?
- She wrote; *"Peter stopped me and told me to wait inside, where it was warm!"*

Before ending this chapter, I must mention something funny…

Please remember that the accused is a very bad boy and a cold-blooded killer, who has already according to Lees, the Prosecution and Hepi shot her boyfriend in cold blood with a big Clint Eastwood silver gun and who says to Lees in the fire of the action after pushing her in the back of the Cruiser: "SHUT UP AND I WON'T SHOOT YOU"

Do you find this funny and realistic? That's what the transcript says below:

4 "The offender came to an opening in the back of the utility and stated, "Shut up and I won't shoot you." The offender then walked away…She never saw him again…Do you believe the story, her story?

The Vanishing of Peter Falconio

So, now I am waiting for anyone…. TO PROVE THAT MURDOCH WAS THE CCTV MAN.

The Vanishing of Peter Falconio

50 - Three Men in a Red Japanese Car

This reminds me of a French crime drama film: Le Glaive et la balance 1962 (The Sword and the Balance).

Le glaive et la balance (English: The Sword and the Balance and Two Are Guilty)[1]) is a 1962 French-Italian crime drama film directed by André Cayatte. It was written by Cayatte, Henri Jeanson and Charles Spaak and stars American actor Anthony Perkins as the protagonist.

Plot[edit]

On the French Riviera, after the son of a wealthy local woman is kidnapped for ransom, the police begin an investigation. The two kidnappers manage to escape the police in a speed boat pursuit aiming for a lighthouse where police finally catch them. But at the lighthouse police found three men.

Most likely two of them are really involved, but one is not. Neither the police nor the court can decide how to solve that puzzle. (The internet).

***

In any great heist or crime involving a group of people. There are two paramount rules that robbers or scammers must comply to: The synchronisation of their watches and their alibi. Their defence story must be full proof. They all must give the same answers if and when questioned by police.

This is relevant to the three men in the red Japanese car.

- Joanne Lees the only witness claimed that her boyfriend was shot by a killer with a big silver gun on the 14th of July 2001

- We know that the alleged calculated time of the killing is **8.45pm on the 14th.**

- We know Joanne Lees claimed spending five **hours hiding in the scrub**. We know that it was pitch black and very cold and we deducted that it is/was pure fabrication.

- We know that she was rescued by Vince Miller around 0.15am on the 15th (between midnight and 0.30 am)

We know according to a witness that she was alone at Ti Tree watching the sunset at 6.10pm and we know that she left Ti Tree alone at 6.30pm arriving at Barrow Creek at 8.30pm (also calculated time but no proofs. She may have arrived much later)

This tells you that:

If Falconio was allegedly shot by Murdoch at 8.45pmon the 14th

The most remarkable thing about this is that, Vince Millar saw two men pushing a third man "The Jelly man" into that red Japanese car just before rescuing Joanne Lees

- Could the third man be Falconio?

- So, if it was, Falconio according to Lees, he got shot at 8.45pm on the 14th,

- How can it be possible that, if the third man is/was Falconio that he was still alive after midnight on the 15th?

- Because I think if Falconio according to more than one witness was seen alive in Bourke days after his death, the two must be strongly related.

Could it be possible that Joanne Lees –Falconio –Nick the lover –the Aileron –and a man driving a Land Cruiser (assuming the CCTV man) being so sure of themselves assuming that everybody or most of us are stupid, could it be possible [?] that they may have not synchronized their watches and could it be possible [?] that they never bothered to rehearse the answers that Lees would or should give police depending on questions she was going to be asked? Simply because:

- When Lees was questioned by police on the morning of the day after the alleged crime scene, the two men pushing the third man into that Japanese car must have been well on their way to some unknown destination, oblivious and totally unaware after fleeing the alleged crime scene that Lees had been seen by a witness watching the sunset alone.

- Then unable to communicate they are now facing this issue.

- Falconio the "jelly man" couldn't be alive nearly five hours after his death.

- Another logical reason is perhaps why Lees always kept denying that both stopped at Aileron Roadhouse, and the fact that four people saw her speaking to someone she knew.

- And that Falconio didn't go to Ti Tree with Lees, but with the Aileron man to some unknown destination but definitely not to Ti Tree.

As soon as the plot was activated (Lees 'rescue), the three men in the red Japanese wanting to be seen at the alleged crime scene (decoy [?]) were then ready and well on their way to who knows where [?]… From that time, there was no turning back.

The jury was told of the red Japanese car, but not about the three men, why that? It was never discussed nor mentioned nor debated at the trial. This raises some serious questions…Food for thought.

The Vanishing of Peter Falconio

51 - The Land Cruiser Man

The alleged murder of Peter Falconio now involves eight people and they are:

1 - Murdoch first Land Cruiser; **2** - Peter Falconio; **3** - Joanne Lees; **4** - the Aileron man; **5** - Nick the lover; **6** - the man from the CCTV who drives a Land cruiser (second Land Cruiser); **7** - Chris Malouf (third Land Cruiser); **8** - and of course the driver of the Japanese car.

*Note: Murdoch of course is out …NO footprints nor anything belonging to him.

Also involved are three types of vehicles: one kombi –one small Japanese car and three Land Cruisers

Some pages ago I wrote:

- So, we can assume that in the small Japanese car we have:
- **1** Falconio –**2** the driver of the car –**3** Nick the lover/the Aileron man/ Darry Cragan a man we know nothing about and we don't even know if he owns a Land Cruiser [?]
- Knowing that Lees was watching the sunset alone, Falconio not with her means that from the Aileron Roadhouse, someone drove him to the alleged crime scene OR somewhere else. [?]

Well, we have a theory but no proofs which I believe needs to be investigated, but how do you do that when the system is corrupt and knowing that nothing took place at the alleged crime scene? I know I am assuming but I trust it could give a new direction to the story.

Before I must say this: The Defence had four long years to think about how to proceed in preparation for the trial. It was not a real success but knowing of the corruption involved, it is not surprising. One can hardly blame the Defence.

I thought the case was going to be complicated, being an alleged crime with:

- No Dead Body –only one witness (the accuser) –no footprints of the killer –no footprints of the victim – time of death unknown,

The Vanishing of Peter Falconio

- Time of the victim's girlfriend spent hiding in the bush in winter but still nice and warm and clean when rescued.
- unidentified footprints but none of the killer or victim –
- First identification of the killer different four years later at the trial.
- Same for the killer's car – same for his dog etc.

Well, I was wrong, it was not complicated; it was and has been a nightmare because Murdoch was found guilty on all charges. That is not right!

- However, the case now could involve two Land Cruisers (excluding Murdoch) and they are: **1** Chris Malouf – **2** the CCTV man.
- Joanne Lees' first description of Murdoch to police was very similar to Chris Malouf. (I am starting to speak like Lees, I must refrain from doing it…Sorry).
- I know I've asked this question so many times but I need to ask again: Why was Malouf arrested by police so fast on the early hours of the morning at Barrow Creek when refuelling and then released even faster?
- How did police know about Malouf? Where did they get the information from?
- Is this information relevant to my questions mentioned in the TRANSCRIPT OF THE TRIAL?
- How did police get to him in such very short time? What is it that we don't know or that we should know?
- Was Chris Malouf arrested because of his long hair and his Land Cruiser or because of something else that we don't know? Perhaps it was a faked arrest (arresting an undercover player?)
- Could it be a decoy?
- Joanne Lees' first identification of Murdoch was a NO MATCH, in fact it was the opposite. The description she gave at the trial four years on didn't match Murdoch as well as his car –trailer –dog etc.

The Vanishing of Peter Falconio

- I know many Land Cruisers may have chrome bull bars and some may not? Finding the right one would be an expensive exercise.
- No Land Cruiser have a mean of communication between the cabin and the back. Definitely NO COMMUNICATION. Joanne Lees' claim was false and unreliable, a lie if you prefer.
- Joanne Lees cannot be trusted, she is extremely suspicious.
- Joanne Lees should have studied Land Cruisers and <u>the Officials should have rung Toyota Australia</u> (repeat I know, maybe I should use the word rehearsal instead).

This brings me back to the second Land Cruiser involved in this case (Malouf).

First and yes, it had to be a Land Cruiser. I haven't seen a photograph of his Cruiser but there are many to choose from. The Land Cruiser has been the most produced and sold vehicle in Australia. The named Land Cruiser is a registered Trademark. The vehicle can be identified from a long distance. Nearly every farmer owns one because they are good –tough and reliable, many have a green canvas canopy.

I believe the owner of the Land Cruiser (The CCTV man) and Malouf could be involved in the scam and the staging of this alleged murder. Why?

- As far as Malouf is concerned, I have no idea. He apparently according to Keith Noble *[FFDA]* and others:

Was camping at the alleged crime scene, 55 metres from it but not hearing any movement of cars –gun shots –screams for help by Joanne Lees etc.

Before I go any further, one fact is very INCREDIBLE, ACTUALLY I have no word for it.

Apparently from Murder in the outback, at one time Chris Maloof was showed the CCTV film. Do you know what he said? [HE] said: But…but…., THAT'S ME ON THE FILM… THAT'S MY CRUISER! Do you understand that?

- <u>He definitely should be recalled.</u>

The Vanishing of Peter Falconio

- This seems very suspicious but we don't know for sure beyond reasonable doubt about his involvement (I am not the only one admitting that it is very suspicious), so please don't think for one minute that my crystal ball is better).

The scam had to be based on three things as I said before:

- **Abduction time:** around 8.45 on the 14th of July (that is shooting then abducting) according to Lees. The assumed time we know is correct, BUT…It is only correct because Joanne Lees said so.
- **Time hiding in the bush:** around five hours according to the transcript and Lees (which is false). It is always according to her and as she is the only witness, try proving her wrong!
- **Time of her rescue,** between midnight and 0.30 am (0.15am).

If the case was real, when Lees escaped from the killer, it would be reasonable and obvious for the killer to search for her with his dog…

But we don't know if the CCTV man had a dog as it can't be seen or heard on the CCTV film.

So, we have the alleged killer giving up the search, then heading straight to Alice Springs to be seen at 0.30am on the CCTV film…. We know the time is correct (video clip –staff from the truck-stop –transcript).

But and I say BUT,

- **Why did the transcript say five hours when it is false?**
- What are the chances for a man who own a Land Cruiser
- Who has just shot someone in cold blood 303km away,
- Who then decides to do a run to escape police,
- Who choose Alice Springs for destination,
- Knowing very well it is a highly populated city,
- Knowing that it will take him around three hours and a bit more to drive away from the crime scene,
- Who stop at a truck stop where he could be picked up by a CCTV camera when refuelling and doing some shopping at the same time,

- Then walking out slowly, gets into his car with no worries at all, probably still transporting the dead body as the Judge **SAID,** which was not a suggestion but an affirmation.
- Then heading to Fitzroy Crossing **1,412km** at 160kmh hoping to be safe,

WHAT ARE HIS CHANCES TO BE PICKED UP BY A CCTV CAMERA?

- Well, he has all the chances in the world to be picked up….
- So why doing it?

WHAT ARE HIS CHANCES NOT TO BE PICKED UP?

- They are NIL.
- So why doing it?

He has all the chances to be seen and picked up by a CCTV camera. He has perhaps one chance in a billion or trillion NOT to be picked up. He would have more chance of winning the Powerball lottery…So place your bets now. It would be like parking your car in front of a bank in a NO Stopping zone,

- Then robbing the bank,
- Then walking out slowly,
- Getting into your car,
- Then stopping around the corner to get a take away coffee –full cream milk, two sugars in a café next to a police station

Hey, do you think the alleged killer or Murdoch would be crazy or what? Would you do that, would you be that stupid?

However, there is another scenario:

If the whole case is a scam and I definitely believe that it is, we have:

- Murdoch is nowhere near the alleged crime scene at and around 8.00/8.45pm (according to him in the transcript of the appeal)
- But near Yuendumu on the Tanami 300km from Alice
- Joanne Lees –Falconio –the Aileron man –Nick the lover – The driver of the Japanese car –the CCTV man who needs to leave

early–Malouf (who owns Cruiser 2), all of them at the alleged crime scene, perhaps rehearsing, making sure everything will go according to plan waiting for a truck to come around close to midnight, not because it is the right time for big trucks <u>but because it has to fit her alibi having spent five hours in</u> hiding.
- All sitting in the Kombi where it is nice and warm.
- Even more intriguing, why so many people involved? What could be the reward? Money, how much money –drugs? Gosh I just can't think of anything, whatever the reward is. The reward will have to be split according to the number of participants. I just can't get my head around it. If you think of anything I beg you please let me know.

*Note: The CCTV man may be a total stranger unaware of what's cooking at the alleged crime scene, we don't know. I cannot incriminate someone without proofs, but it cannot be dismissed…. Because the CCTV man can be replaced by Chris Malouf. What do you think?
- Before the arrival of the road train, the CCTV man or Malouf or someone else have already gone towards Alice because one of them must be seen at the truck stop at 0.30am <u>not before not after.</u>
- Now I will assume that the Aileron man and Nick the lover is the same person.
- At the alleged crime scene, we have:
- **1** Lees –**2** Falconio – **3** the Aileron man/ Nick the lover –**4** the driver of the Japanese car –**5** the driver of one Cruiser. All are at the alleged crime scene (repeat)
- Knowing that the five of them are at the alleged crime scene rehearsing the number is correct. five people, one identified foot prints [Lees] and four unidentified. So far so good. Tell me your thoughts on that please.
- If we eliminate Nick the lover who could be the Aileron man or vice versa?

- We could have the CCTV man or Malouf replacing the Aileron man or vice versa
- The driver of the Japanese car cannot be ignored nor removed, nor replaced.

We truly don't know which of two owners of the two Land Cruisers is involved?... If, they are involved.

This tells you that whichever way you look at it, you will never find the correct and satisfying answer…Mission impossible and no facts proving otherwise. One may spend a century writing about the story, nothing will ever be beyond reasonable doubt. Nothing but doubts.

I am more inclined to believe that Nick the lover is part of the scam but I am only assuming. Having no answer regarding this issue, indicate doubt and when doubt is involved, the sentence" beyond reasonable doubt "doesn't stand a chance. So why a guilty verdict?

- Who drove Falconio from Aileron to the alleged crime scene not to Ti Tree but to Barrow Creek?
- I strongly believe that one of the Land Cruiser must have been at Aileron.
- The logical time of the alleged offence according to my calculation is **8.45pm.**
- We know this is allegedly correct, because we know the departing time from Ti Tree. <u>We however don't know the arrival time of Lees at Barrow Creek.</u>
- Nothing took place at the alleged crime scene at **8.45pm** on the 14th.
- The only thing that took place at the alleged crime scene (witnessed by Vince Miller) was a man pushed by two men into a red Japanese car at a time close to midnight minutes before Joanne Lees was rescued.
- I see that as a decoy.

The Vanishing of Peter Falconio

Lees claimed she escaped spending around five hours (which is a lie) in the bush on a cold and pitch- black winter night but she was found warm – clean when rescued. Do you believe that?

- After the alleged killer leaves the alleged crime scene (The CCTV man/Murdoch/Malouf) she comes out coincidentally or suspiciously just on time to be rescued after spending five hours as per her claim in a cold surrounding but no worries!
- Meaning they were waiting for the correct time to act and a "big bloody" truck to appear, because:

When Vince Millar saw the two men pushing the third one into the car, and when he saw the car passing him by at high speed with three men on board, what were his thoughts?

I truly would love to know…Simply, I think they were waiting for a road train or any big truck, not a car.

Whilst waiting and rehearsing the CCTV man or Malouf or someone else could have been with them until time for one of them to leave so he could be seen at Alice Springs at 0.30am.

All this or most of it is what we know. I am simply trying to make anyone understand that,

The Vanishing of Peter Falconio

52 - Monsieur Malouf and His Cruiser

In the previous chapter I included monsieur Chris Malouf in the scenario because he needs to be included. He drives a Land Cruiser. We don't know for fact if the Cruiser had a chrome bull bar –if he was towing a trailer –if his dog was a Dalmatian –if he owns a big silver gun –and we don't know what type of shoes he was wearing. Nothing is known about him. All is unknown, but we know from two authors the following…

Yes, we have now a new entrant. Things are getting very murky…Who said that life was meant to be easy?

From the book of Richard Shears Bloodstain page 25/26 published 2005

Please remember also we don't know where all these information are coming from [?]

(Copied): "He (Chris Malouf) drove into Alice Springs on the morning of Saturday 14 July 2001 and decided to spend that night further north of town.

When Chris Malouf drove into Barrow Creek Hotel at first light the following morning for fuel, he suddenly found himself surrounded by police with gun trained on him. They grabbed his arms and cuffed him.

First thought: Knowing Malouf needed refuelling why not refuelling before finding a campsite. No, he didn't refuel on the 14th but the day after meaning he had to get fuel at Barrow Creek. We don't know why Maloof choose to camp near Barrow Creek? We don't know also if he camped before or after Barrow Creek, which is important if the intention to refuel was on the agenda

This took place only couple of hours after the alleged crime. So how did police get on to Malouf so quickly? (I think anybody would ask the same question). But I believe there has never been some debate on the topic at the trial, even before and during the investigation

"Hey; what's going on" he yelled. "What have I done?" Then he saw a woman being led out of the bar her eyes closed tight.

Not blindfolded why?

"Okay Joanne" he heard one of the officers say to her. Do it, Feel his head first…

The Vanishing of Peter Falconio

Lees eyes closed was scanning Malouf head –hair –face neck with her hands all this taking place in a pub …Unbelievable.

Then police took her to his van. She was asked to run her hands over the front seats and around the interior of the cab. His whole world was in there… Shit

After feeling around the back of the vehicle …she was led back inside. Her eyes were still shut.

This is a laugh! Truly did it really happen?

They kept Malouf 15 minutes or so before unlocking his handcuffs and telling him he could go. As he filled up with fuel, his hand shaking from the ordeal, he asked what all that had been about. The best he could find out was that the girl had been held up at gunpoint during the night and the police were still looking for the assailant –and Chris Malouf answered the man's description. Her head had been covered for a time as she'd struggled with him, so they asked her to feel him out with her eyes shut. "

What are they trying to say?

- If her head had been covered with a bag, she couldn't really know what he looks like...
- But she did see him, she knew what the alleged offender looked like, she even knew his deep Australian voice (Remember the offender saying: Shut up -NO I won't kill you).
- So why pretending that the offender put a bag on her head. It simply means that the scanning of Malouf's face served no purpose.

Apparently, that's what happened on the morning of the day after the alleged offence, which is not a good reference for police. Her eyes closed, not blindfolding her. One thing is certain, letting Joanne Lees scanning (the word police used) the interior and the exterior of Malouf's car was not a good thing to do.

Was police thinking straight on that early morning just few hours after the alleged crime and abduction? How did they find out about Malouf so quickly?

The Vanishing of Peter Falconio

The scanning of Malouf by Joanne Lees who said she was abducted having a bag over her head (which could somehow be displaced from her head at random to suit her declaration so she could judge the proper time to mention it, like noticing the breed of dog sitting behind the wheel when she was abducted by the offender in the cabin of his Cruiser), would serve no purpose at all. Having her going around in his van is astonishing, for what reasons?

The scanning of the interior/exterior of the van (wrong word speaking of a Cruiser)) must have left her fingerprints and DNA all over serving again no purpose. The police deserve a real medal …WELL DONE!

However, a few things seem to be a bit suspicious. It is about what Roger Maynard wrote in his book: Where's Peter on page 101/102 published 2005

1. It reads speaking of Chris Malouf" "*He even had and almost identical Ute with canvas canopy and had been camping near the Stuart Highway a few days previously*

2. *But after he was shown to Joanne and DNA tests were carried out, police eliminated him from their enquiries*"

- Again, using the words almost identical Ute is not correct. This is a murder case for God's sake! If anyone needs to describe a vehicle give me the favour to use the correct word. There are many vans of different makers, same with Utes. If it is Land Cruiser Ute, please use the correct words. Only then we may have a discussion.
- It sounds like Joanne Lees speaking *"almost identical, similar Ute"*
- Nothing is almost identical. Identical means identical
- **Would you be using the words: similar –almost Identical in a DNA investigation?**
- People probably would and I bet that they would believe that they are correct.
- Please don't always believe that we are all stupid. This is a murder case. An innocent man has been in jail already for 20 years, he deserves a bit of respect especially when innocent.

The Vanishing of Peter Falconio

- The purpose of the word Ute here is not indicative but meaningless.
- In a murder case this is crucial, there can't be any doubt.
- A man has been already in jail for a very long time because some people are definitely using the wrong words sometimes purposely…Not good enough!
- The word Ute doesn't differentiate between Land Cruiser –Hilux – Nissan etc.
  Again, I thought I like to mention it.
- Beside what I just said, I find the very fast arrest of Chris Malouf, the scanning by Lees on his person and car, followed by his quick release extremely suspicious.
- How did they get to him so fast in the first place? I know I keep on asking but that's me.
- What was the main reasons for his quick release?
- Please don't tell me that it is because Lees didn't recognise him as Murdoch (knowing that she didn't know what real Murdoch look like, but most importantly don't tell me that he was released after DNA test were carried out when it is perfectly known that no DNA investigation was activated on the morning after the alleged offence unless DNA test were carried out means: Taking a swab [?]

THIS IS IMPORTANT:

What was police thinking on that early morning on the 15th of July 2001?

I SMELL A RAT, I smell many, it is a real plague

In Bloodstain Richard Shears wrote: "When Chris Malouf drove into Barrow Creek Hotel at first light the following morning …"

First light the following morning means very early on the 15th July 2001.

So, after the scanning of Malouf by Lees took place, they released him. OK, what was the reason for his release?

Was the reason: …But after he was shown to Joanne and DNA tests were carried out, police eliminated him from their enquiries"?

What is the true meaning and interpretation of this sentence? To me we don't know if…DNA tests were carried out" means that YES. I believe they did.

Then police eliminated him from their enquiries…"

- Taking a swab for DNA testing is okay if the intention is to send the swab to a lab to find out the DNA profile of the person involve. Then what happen after that?
- After receiving the swab, the lab has to do the analysis. After the analysis is done, comes the result, meaning the DNA profile has been identified. Then, in possession of the identified DNA profile of that person ….
- Police and any investigators have the headache to match/compare the identified profile with a matching profile from the National Data base.

Originally and at the beginning of all investigation Police had around 2,000 people of interest according to the National data base, all because they owned a Land Cruiser similar to the one on the CCTV film from the Shell truck-stop.

SO, AND THIS IS THE MOST IMPORTANT…

"But after he was shown to Joanne and DNA tests were carried out, police eliminated him from their enquiries"? …

- Can only means that no match was found on the DNA National Data Base
- Or they have released Chris Malouf base on more than one LIE…
- Because on the early morning on the day after the alleged offence, as I said before;

NOBODY including police knew what the alleged killer looked like – NO DNA tests were carried out – nobody had Murdoch's DNA so that the profile could be compared /matched with all the DNA from the National Data Base. The arrest and release of Malouf is extremely suspicious as I said many times

It points to one direction: IGNORE –PLOT.

Again, DNA carried out on the early morning the day after the alleged abduction ...You've got to be joking? Too early in the peace!

The scanning by Lees on his person failed–on his car failed to produce any evidence. What evidence? What evidence were they looking for? ...A word from Lees saying, he is the man?

Is/was Malouf the Aileron man/the CCTV man?

Is that how police conduct investigation in a murder case in Australia? Wow, how interesting. Monsieur Poirot has a lot to learn. I hope that we are clear on that.

By the way, did police during the scanning asked Malouf to say few words? After all Lees claimed that Murdoch had a deep voice and was wearing a cap. (Laughter in the background)

No misinformation should be accepted here. Facts must be beyond reasonable doubt unless it is for a specific reason...If you know what I mean? (Clapping in the background).

One more thing according to FFDA page 312 vehicles [43]

[43] Lees said that man videoed at a Shell truck stop was "too old." He was not the man she encountered north of Barrow Creek. Strengthening this is the claim by Chris Malouf that the image is one of him. In Dead Centre; 2005: p. 116, Robin Bowles says: "Of medium height with a droopy moustache and long hair, Chris had passed through Barrow Creek and camped about 55 metres from where the incident took place – on the same night. The photo at the Shell truck-stop looked like him. 'It's me, I reckon – that's the same thongs, black hat and jacket as I wear,' he told **Genine Johnson of the Broome Advertiser**." (original italics)

One more thing; apparently when Malouf was shown the video clip from the truck stop, he said as you can read above.

"But, that's me on the video, that's my Cruiser!" Would you believe that???????

Very interesting also is Joanne Lees saying about the CCT man in the early stage that the man was too old but in 2005 at the trial he is the man.

The Vanishing of Peter Falconio

How interesting is that? Of course, it is logical why Malouf didn't hear anything or saw anything when camping 55 metres from the alleged crime, because nothing took place at the alleged crime scene or perhaps, he never camped at the alleged crime scene or both!

HOWEVER, not taking side, I don't understand why the experts and the aboriginal trackers found no evidence of someone having spent the night at the alleged crime scene even someone with a dog...When Malouf claimed he camped 55 metres from the alleged offence. Malouf had a dog. Sorry, I still smell a rat again and a big one. Was Malouf dancing with the police? Just coincidence or synchronicity?

It shows how many things were wrong. Murdoch was everybody's scapegoat. Can somehow confirm my thoughts and opinion? Please read from FFDA what follows. I found all this incomprehensible. Nothing complies with the rule of law: Beyond reasonable doubt.

From FFDA page 310 Part V vehicles

Corrupt Northern Territory officials wanted people (includes the 12 members of the jury) to believe it was Murdoch and his vehicle in the Shell truck stop image.35 But, even the cops said there was no evidence linking the never-identified person or the never-identified vehicle to the alleged disappearance of Falconio. And people who knew his vehicle confirmed it was not Murdoch's. In plain English, that CCTV image does not prove Murdoch and his Toyota were at the Shell truck stop in Alice Springs on 15 July 2001, or at any other time. That unclear image was only fit for presentation to a kangaroo court. It was and it was accepted. (It helped with the manipulation of the jury.)

...I totally agree

What a scam, what a miscarriage of justice, what an insult... Is this a true crime or a big farce? An innocent has been crucified because the Officials didn't want a repeat of the Azaria Chamberlain case or perhaps for some unknown classified reasons (especially when drugs and drug lords are involved too much to lose, plenty to gain as Gregory Dick said.

The Vanishing of Peter Falconio

So, we are back to square one, mission impossible. Impossible to prove anything beyond reasonable doubt. Why then a guilty verdict? See nothing hear nothing, but make sure Murdoch is guilty!

The CCTV man could be the man accused by Lees as being Murdoch – so could Malouf as long as they own a Land Cruiser. Nothing to do with beyond reasonable doubt, everything to do with Unanimous vs Majority verdict and more as we know as you will find out further on…Well done Monsieur le Judge, well done Monsieur le Prosecutor but time shall come, you shall all be judged. There is no escape!

The Vanishing of Peter Falconio

53 - Some Plan…

This is repetition but necessary.

Murdoch is nowhere near the alleged crime location (Barrow Creek), no wheel marks from his car or campervan trailer, no footprints including from his rented dog etc.

The plan

Murdoch was chosen as scapegoat…WHY? Probably because he is a drug dealer and he owns a Land Cruiser and that he may be a "real bad boy".

- Joanne Lees is the only witness
- Peter Falconio –Joanne Lees are drug users could also be dealers?
- Nick the lover could also be both, user or dealer.
- Could the man from the **CCTV** film or **Malouf** be connected? Both drive a Land Cruiser with an open passage between the cabin and the back of the Ute (laughter and clapping in the back)). Was any checking done on both?
- Lees definitely seen talking to a man at Aileron outside near the pump who could also be Malouf or the CCTV man or someone else [?]
- No one saw Lees and Falconio leaving Aileron together in the kombi. We don't know if they did but no one saw Lees driving on with Falconio being a passenger.
- No one saw the man who spoke to Lees leaving in a Cruiser, car, on a horse, bicycle or else.
- But when Lees was watching the sunset at 6.10pm at Ti Tree, a witness confirmed that Lees was alone.
- Lees denied she was alone, but gave two different answers to police related to Falconio being with her.

When she got to Ti Tree she said:

- [1] *Peter was sleeping – I woke him up*
- [2] *I had to brake hard going a bit too fast and the bump on the road woke him* up…

The Vanishing of Peter Falconio

Contradiction, meaning unreliable witness –the only one –not to be trusted. But, again accepted by the officials.

- Was the meeting between Lees and the Aileron man pre-organized (part of the plan)?
- Is it possible that Falconio and one of the three men (**1** Nick the lover – **2** the driver of the Japanese car –**3** the CCTV man/Malouf) left Aileron together in a car or a four- wheel drive? It would not have been noticed knowing many people drive Land Cruisers in the outback.
- Did Falconio leave Aileron with one of the men to a location where they would meet Joanne Lees? The most suitable would be the alleged crime scene.
- Could the man on the CCTV or Malouf be the owner of one of the four unidentified footprints? As a result, it could explain why Lees denied that she was alone at Ti Tree, Falconio being invisible?
- Could the CCTV man or Malouf be part of the plot for the following reason: Meeting with Lees at the alleged crime scene, re-checking the site, rehearsal?
- Was Lees killing time at Ti Tree?
- Did Joanne Lees -Falconio–Nick the lover –the Aileron man – the driver of the Japanese car –the man on the CCTV –or Malouf met at the alleged crime scene at night fall? If they did, we would still have four unidentified footprints.

BUT between the assumed and calculated time of death and her rescue, one would think that there were quite a number of cars or trucks on the road. I mean by that: When the killer left the alleged crime scene at 9.00pm, the most time Lees must have been waiting for the offender to leave the site was perhaps 15 to 30minutes. This can be deducted only from the transcript below because if the offender had to be seen at 0.30pm he had to depart at 9.00pm

- Leaving at 9.00pm means the offender had absolutely no time

The Vanishing of Peter Falconio

- To search for Lees and nothing else for that matter.

[10] On the Crown case, Ms Lees then escaped from the back of the utility and hid in the surrounding scrub. She did not see the offender again. (This is a reminder)

Meaning also that:

- The movement of vehicle she said she heard, the noise of someone walking on the gravel, the dragging pretending that it could be Falconio's body, the opening and closing of doors from a vehicle etc.
- All this is pure fabrication and lies from Joanne Lees
- The supposedly offender left the alleged crime scene within 15 minutes according to my calculation.

Then saying that she did not see the offender again means what it means. The best explanation is truly that:

- Nothing happened at the crime scene, no crime, no abduction no hiding in the scrub …Simply all lies

We don't even know that if departing Ti Tree at 6.30pm Lees got there at 8.30pm. She may have gone somewhere to meet Falconio and perhaps that they could all got there say 11.00pm or any time before her rescue, waiting for the decoy to serve its purpose (2 men pushing a third one into the Japanese car), waiting for a road train and waiting for the CCTV man to arrive in Alice Springs at 0.30am on the 15th. All this to support her alibi (having spent five hours in hiding), but all this is pure assumption. We shall never know therefore mission impossible.

It is a prefabricated story and everybody believed it.

Lees coming out of her hiding 15 minutes after the killer has gone would have had no problem flagging another truck. But it had to fit with her alibi as I said above.

- It had to be anytime around midnight. They also had to give time for the Japanese car to be faraway. Nearly six hours by the time police got to Barrow Creek (midnight to 6.00am) had to be sufficient.

The reason why Lees was warm –clean is because they all must have been waiting in the Kombi irrelevant having been moved. It was moved for a particular purpose for later on, an alibi for the alleged crime. It had to look real.

- In the Kombi **1** Lees –**2** Falconio – **3** the Aileron man/Nick the lover – **4** the driver of the Japanese car, and/or the CCTV man or Malouf or someone else [?]
- The participants would see the powerful lights of a truck at least five to ten km away (say 10km).
- A truck driving at 100kmh would travel 100kmh ÷ 60 = **1.6km each minute**.
- As a result, to travel ten km it would take 10km ÷1.6km/ minute = **6.25 minutes** for the truck to arrive at the alleged crime scene. Plenty of time to get ready.
- To travel 8km not 10, it would take 8km ÷1.6 km/minute = five minutes for the truck to arrive at the alleged crime scene. Plenty of time to get ready.
- Vince Millar said he saw the lights of a car acting strangely three to four minutes before arriving at the crime scene
- It would give enough time from the moment they saw the lights of the truck to get out of the Kombi –for Lees to position herself –for the driver of the red car and his two companions (the jelly man and the Aileron man) to be ready for blast off, say 1 minute and the trick is done. The truck driver sees the car taking off at high speed on their way aiming north with three men on board and then he sees Joanne Lees …All within five minutes…Bob's your uncle!

On the same day but much early in the peace (well after lunch) Murdoch is on his way to Yuendumu. Then later on driving to The Granite as per his claim in the transcript (will get to it soon)

The Vanishing of Peter Falconio

That is what I believe took place. What happen after that is unknown. I am convinced that people who saw Falconio alive after his alleged death in Bourke were definitely telling the truth. It makes sense.

Falconio was never going to be shot by the exhaust pipe, NOOO! It is pure fiction, an illusion. He was going to vanish and I believe that he has truly be seen by some witnesses after faking his death…Remarkable indeed.

Falconio couldn't care less about his footprints so are the others because once Lees makes her claims, they all vanished.

- **Try proving it**, try proving that he got shot when you don't have a Dead Body?
- Who is going to contest Lees' claim the only witness and the biggest liar.

How long can Falconio hide? Nobody can tell even Monsieur Poirot.

Beyond reasonable doubt means absolutely nothing anymore. We are living in constant doubt…No doubt about it!

This was not a crime case it was a plot –a stratagem –a machination –a ruse –a subterfuge etc. (For the one disliking the word conspiracy).

The Vanishing of Peter Falconio

54 - Short Chapter!

The purpose of this chapter is to make everybody think......

Please go back in time:

- Joanne Lees departing Ti Tree at 6.30pm arrives at the alleged crime scene at 8.30pm
- At 8.30pm the alleged killer stops her. Allegedly Falconio is back in the picture.
- At 8.45pm Falconio is allegedly killed with a big silver gun and the abduction of Lees starts.
- Lees escaped <u>while</u> the killer shifted the Kombi.
- At 9.00pm the alleged killer leaves the alleged crime scene
- She never saw him again (transcript).
- At 0.30am the alleged killer arrives at the truck stop in Alice.
- Between Midnight and 0.15am just before Lees flagged down the road train, the driver Vince Millar sees two men pushing a third one into a red Japanese car...Which could be interpreted as Falconio being the third man. The car takes off at high-speed heading north.

The jury was never told about the three men; why?

Between midnight and 0.30am on the 15th of July 2001 Lees is rescued. Deduction:

- If Falconio is the third man and alive
- Falconio could not have been shot at 8.45pm

Who are you going to believe?

This is I know a repeat. It is necessary for you the reader to understand what truly may have taken place and that is why you need to be told again so you can understand and visualise the full puzzle. However, bear in mind that I am only assuming.

55 - Still Debating…

[17a] An Aboriginal woman saw a car speed away from Barrow Creek shortly after the alleged time and attack.
- Shortly after the alleged time and attack? This is strange.
- **HOW DO THEY KNOW THAT? PLEASE EXPLAIN!**
- At what time did the woman see the car?
- Was it a car or a four- wheel drive?

Who is this aboriginal woman? What's her name –occupation? Where is she coming from? In which direction was the car going: North, south?... What a joke!

[18a] Blood was found at the scene. It appears that it was blood mixed with something else

Found at the scene. That is very precise without any doubt! Where at the scene? Under a small pile of dirt to attract attention?

That would be perfectly normal to find Falconio's blood at the site after being shot in the head point-blank with a big calibre. Blood mixed with something else! Yes, too easy…Mixed with what? Remember MURDOCH was not there.

[19a] Lees phoned a friend in New Zealand two hours after she had earlier claimed to have made the telephone call. Simply let say she rang her friend at 11.00 am but told the police that she made the call at 9.00Am or vice versa. Why? Thus, putting the time of Falconio's disappearance back by two hours.

AH! This is interesting and very important. Was the call investigated – mentioned –traced? Where was the call made from? <u>It would be amusing if the call was from Aileron</u>. Tampering the timeline to fit with their plan….

Anyhow, who cares Murdoch is guilty from day one, even before.

Tampering the timeline could be because she has always denied stopping at Aileron 134 km from Alice and 62 km to Ti Tree for good reasons and it could prove they stopped at Aileron. It would really be amusing if she rang from Aileron before the alleged crime rather than after at the scene as I said above. That would be the icing on the cake don't you think?

There at Aileron she spoke to a man she knew and Falconio must have gone NOT to Ti Tree with Lees but with the man, to some unknown destination which I believe could be the alleged crime scene.

Was the Jury explained all this in great details? I don't think so. Again, I am asking why?

So, the Judge and the Prosecution including Joanne Lees of course completely dismissed those reliable facts & witnesses: Why?

Anyhow, the Judge, nor the Prosecution, nor the police nor anybody else, has attempted to solve this problem, I don't know about the Defence, but Murdoch must be found guilty.

[20a] The Doctor who examined Lees after the incident found that she had no head wounds consistent with being punched repeatedly in the head, as she had claimed had happen.

This supports claim by Vince Miller the road train driver who rescued Lees that, she was in good shape physically. Mentally, we don't know. Stressed yes, because the stagging has to work therefore it must have been very stressful indeed.

According to the transcript of the Appeal [8] below:

"[8] The offender then punched LEES to the right side of the temple."

Lees was not abused by the killer or by the two men who could have taken Falconio away (assuming only) because we have deducted that Falconio and the two men are part of the scam. They are the major players (obviously) and that Falconio was at the scene of the alleged crime.

. The state of her clothes and physical appearance was good. She was warm, no apparent bruising, cuts, not a single dog hair on her clothes etc. SHE WAS CLEAN.

Extract from: Robin Bowles. Dead Centre; 2005: pp. 190-191. FFDA p266

"I also forgot to mention to the cops that when I put my arms around her, she was warm. I remember thinkin' that was a bit strange her in a skimpy little T-shirt. I even thought for a minute that she might have just got out of the car I'd seen. The other thing was, she wasn't dirty. Her clothing all looked pretty intact, and there were only a few little blood smears on her shirt, like they might have come from her elbows. Ya know, I've done a lot of thinkin' about that car since then, because she wasn't cold, like you'd expect. What if that car took off with the evidence the body even – and she stalled me by gettin' me to look for her Kombi'. (original italics; added emphasis)"

The Vanishing of Peter Falconio

56 - Four Years Later

[21a] Joanne Lees identified her attacker a second time four years after the alleged offence.

- As we know Lees was questioned by police the morning after the alleged crime, she gave the description of her attacker (Long hair – moustache etc.), roadblocks were installed. When Murdoch was questioned by Police three months after the alleged Barrow Creek abduction, he was already a prime suspect.
- It is after four years in 2005 that Lees identified her attacker; the CCTV man for the second time regardless what she said previously that the man was too old.
- Who's going to believe that after this change of direction?

When Murdoch was interviewed by police for the rape of a woman, where was Lee then? What was going through in her mind?

- Why is it that being in Sicily and being told by a friend (who is this friend what is the connection smell a rat again) to check the photo of Murdoch on the internet published in newspapers relating to the rape case, we have Lees saying; **He is the man** when questioned by police later on? **WHY?** Also, here the key word is **PHOTO**, not article …Very suspicious!
- We know her first description of the offender didn't match Murdoch.
- We know she can change her mind anytime, **(I will look for more opportunities…)**

Then, four years after in 2005 after seeing his photograph on the internet on the 10/11 October 2002 according to the transcript:

"[50] The learned Judge concluded that Ms Lees accessed the internet on10/11October 2002 at time not long after she had been advised by the police by telephone that they had a suspect…

So, why was police giving some information about the suspect to Lees and by telephone also? Is it just to make it easier for her to make a choice about her offender? Has she been influenced by police –and the media or also because of her relationship with the Judge's daughter Joanna Martin? She said no, do you believe her? (Please read Bowles book page 412).

Yes, he is the man pointing the finger at the man on the CCTV film who didn't look that Murdoch.

I let you be the judge, try to sort it out…Beyond reasonable doubt? You must be joking!

- When Murdoch was arrested by the NT police in South Australia mind you, Murdoch was already a scapegoat therefore the prime suspect.
- Lees had identified her alleged attacker on the morning of the alleged attack. Having done so she must have had a fair idea. The fact being that her claims are a huge fabrication.
- **Remember she didn't describe Murdoch as the man who feared they were following him.**

I am not surprised of the result. As far as the Defence team, what could they do when the system is rigged? They had however four years to study the case and I believe they could have done better.

To the driver of the road train Vince Miller, to the people at the pub in Barrow Creek after her rescue, to the police when she first was interrogated on the morning on the 15th of July, her description of Murdoch was nothing like Murdock, so was the car, so was the dog, no mention of a trailer or anything attached to it. That is not being presumptuous…

- SO, why did she positively identified her attacker four years later in 2005 after changing her story so many times? Would you call her a true witness or a big liar? Asking again: Was this a fair trial?

[22a] An expert forensic anatomist said; that Murdoch was almost certainly the man who was captured by video at Alice Springs at a truck stop in early hours of July 15th, just hours after the alleged offence, doing some shopping.

The Vanishing of Peter Falconio

"Was almost certainly the man". Wow, is this real fact or does it sound like oh yes it must be him, he is a drug dealer, I am not sure but it must be him...... Is this real fact?

Well, nowadays anybody and everybody is an expert, but who are the real experts here? Too many Chiefs not enough Indians wouldn't you say? The man from the CCTV doesn't look like Murdock. To make the matter more interesting the man coming out of the shop was walking very slowly as if he truly wanted to be seen on the film. And the icing on the cake is Chris Malouf recognising himself form the CCTV film...Unreal

Anyhow, the man and his Land Cruiser has never been identified by police, but he is Murdoch!

There is one man from the start who looked like the real Murdoch: Chris MALOUF.

I still don't know where he fits in?

- Was the similarity between him and the man first described by Lees the reason why he was arrested very early on the morning after the alleged crime? And, why so early in the peace? Was he already a police informer –a little spy?
- Police at that time had no idea what the real Murdoch looked like.
- Early morning after the alleged crime is another big issue. How is it possible for police to catch Malouf at such early stage, less than half a day (even less, say three to four hours) into the investigation?
- Could it be that police may even didn't have the visual drawing from the artist (chosen by police?)
- All police must have had is the verbal description given by Lees and nothing else.

What happen to Malouf after his release by police?

- Well, nothing happened of course because DNA tests were carried out (Clapping in the background).
- Did he become an informer or was he already? Anything is possible you know!

The Vanishing of Peter Falconio

After his release, no mention of Malouf, he vanished like Falconio…Do you smell a rat? Is everything clear? Has every single possibility or fact been investigated? Accepted –dismissed – ignored –or else?

Anyhow, one expert says YES, he is the man on the CCTV film but another expert say NO he is not the man…Who do you believe – who do you think was chosen?

Would you remember and agree that a man built like a wardrobe, a man who can hardly fit under a door frame, who has very short hair instead of long, who has no moustache and some missing front teeth is something out of the norm? Experts talk about the man as if he was an average size. For God's sake be fair!

[23a] A man was captured on CCTV at the truck stop in Alice Springs, left the truck stop minutes before police arrived

Wow, this is not mentioned in the transcript from the Criminal Court of the appeal (left before police arrived that is) …Why that? Did police truly arrive minutes before, if they did, perhaps they must or could remember the Land Cruiser [?]

I can't see the relation unless it's meant to deceive. Have you ever been refuelling your car when a cop car comes along and does the same, the police arriving at the truck stop doesn't mean they were chasing someone. They didn't arrive at the truck stop siren and blue lights on, if you know what I mean! I think this is going a bit too far. This is intentionally meant to influence and deceive…To deceive the Jury and others (no name mentioned)

From the documentary on ATN 7 on the 19th July 2020 everybody can witness a four- wheel drive and a man walking towards the shop. The angle of the camera was not really good, but the plates could have been readable.

- Who is the man, was he investigated, was this mentioned or deliberately kicked under the table? Then replaced by Murdoch? Murdoch also own a Land Cruiser you know!

[24] Lees admitting having an affair, without Falconio's knowledge with a man from Sydney named Nick

The Vanishing of Peter Falconio

Truly, who is the man, where is he? Is he also involved with drugs and the pre-fabricated crime and the faked abduction? According to ATN 7 he lives or lived in Germany. Is he a member of the group, is he a partner in crime? Do we know what he looks like? Yes, we know because I found his photo on the net. Is there a possibility that he could have been involved when he was working in a bookshop in Sydney at that time? Could he be the man who spoke to Lees at Aileron?

Cable ties contaminated

We spoke already about the ties, this is extra.

It doesn't look like cable ties it looks like handmade cuffs. Yes, the cuffs are handmade. The fabrication is a mixture of cable ties and black tape (no metal in it but I am not sure).

- It is alleged they have been contaminated? Contaminated with what, by what, by whom and when?
- Has Lees' T-shirt also been contaminated between the 17 July 2001 and 24 October 2003 (28 months) as previously discussed?

According to Keith Allan Noble FFDA p63

"Dr Katrin Both said she did not accept the [DNA-LCN] technique used to link Bradley Murdoch with the attack on Miss Lees and the alleged murder of her boyfriend Peter Falconio as a valid scientific method.

Sun Online Reporter. thesun.co.uk. 1 December

_ "The major DNA profile on the cuffs – a significant contribution – fitted Joanne, while [Vince] Millar was a minor contributor. But she [Carmen Eckhoff] found no other profile that pointed to a third person touching the handcuffs. It was not for her to conclude why, although there could only be two obvious reasons. The person who bound her had been wearing gloves; or only Miss Lees and Miller had touched the handcuffs that night.... Failure to find another person's profile bothered her so much that she searched the cable ties in various locations, subjecting them to various tests." (* third possible reason: Lees made the restraints; see Toohey below) Richard Shears. Bloodstain. 2005: p. 54

The Vanishing of Peter Falconio

That is what I call A GOOD ANSWER but NO, Murdoch made the cuffs! One thing is certain when Murdoch made the cuffs: First he used the cable ties and tape, secondly, he had enough time to make them nice and less painful having so much empathy for his victims. He didn't want Lees fragile wrists to be traumatised therefore the reason for using some soft plastic tapes. Murdoch is a very thoughtful man, he even thought about the distance at which her wrists would be placed, even hoping that she could escape. That is one of the reasons why the cuffs were not too tight (I assume).

[25a] Murdoch doesn't own a cattle dog, the dog said to have been with Lees' attacker.

That's another real funny one!

Murdoch own a Dalmatian Cross, not a cattle dog –or blue Heeler –or a bulldog –or else. Prosecution argued that either Lees confuse Murdoch Dalmatian with a cattle dog or that Murdoch borrowed a cattle dog for the alleged offence

- Ah ah ah! **borrowed a dog** wow! I don't believe it. This sounds like the Pink Panther movie! A rent a dog story! Or perhaps it was a sheep! Please, ask yourself: Is this real, is this a real trial?

[26a] Prosecution argued that Murdoch radically changed his physical appearance to conduct the alleged offence.

This is a statement, an affirmation from our second witness the Prosecution: He radically changed his appearance (past tense, supposition not a real fact, but meant to influence and deceive), it's not did he? BUT HE DID.

- So, he had to change his appearance twice, including the dog and his car…Wow!
- Was that before and after the alleged offence? <u>So, we assume he did it before and after.</u> Sorry we need facts this is not a fairy tale story, a man's life hung in the balance.

[27a] Alleged offence scene: Several pieces of evidence (?), including lip gloss and black tape were not found until three months after the alleged

The Vanishing of Peter Falconio

offence meaning the evidence was planted. The Prosecution argued that they may have simply been hard to find

Really? Too easy…Evidence, do you call this evidence? I can't believe it! It seems that it is also and always three months after! And the evidence had been hard to find…AMAZING!

So, three months after the alleged offence they have finally found some extremely important evidence to convict a man of murder; few pieces of tape and some lip gloss which were not found during the first search…Unbelievable! I hope they checked the evidence for DNA on both items. That was a good detective job, Monsieur Poirot is going to be very proud. The next piece of reading below is really AMUSING!

"From the outset, eyebrows had been raised about the standard of the police investigation and in particular the thoroughness in the undergrowth at Barrow Creek where Joanne [alleges she] had hidden for several hours. Superintendent Jeanette Kerr recounted how she stumbled across important evidence at the crime scene...three months after the area was supposed to have been examined." (Roger Maynard. How Joanne Lees' story has changed over five years. Crikey.com.au. 4 October 2006 FFDA p221.)

IMPORTANT EVIDENCE? Do you trust **Jeanette Kerr?** She apparently stumbled across important evidence. Again, three months after the alleged offence…Some tape and lip gloss? Are you for real? Yes, have you forgotten that Murdoch had so much empathy for Joanne that he used tape in the fabrication of the cuffs, preventing the cuffs to cut into Joanne's wrist, it was a very thoughtful idea. It was an important evidence and discovery. Murdoch cared for his victims, he was very meticulous, perhaps even using lip balm to grease the cuffs …Please be real!!

The alleged finding by Kerr is interpreted differently by this writer. For a trial, it was important to have certain evidence found at a certain place. It is believed that what Kerr found were planted items put there by her or some other cop. The items were "two pieces of black tape" that **Ian Spilsbury**, an official with Kerr, miraculously found as well as a "lip balm stick" allegedly left there by Lees several months earlier, bolsters this writer's belief. Both findings suggest **Kerr** and **Spilsbury** were involved with manipulating evidence. (FFDA p221.)

- Yes, I do believe the manipulation of the evidence definitely took place, but how can you prove it?

"You could take some of our police detectives up in an aeroplane and strip them bollock naked and drop them off at the fuckin' North Pole and they're that useless they couldn't catch a fuckin' cold never mind a fuckin' criminal. They are totally and utterly useless."[3]
(Paddy Joe Hill in Judge for yourself. 2004: p. 35 FFDA p221)
Wow! I must admit I love the language! It does compliment the actors! Below is also very interesting…To coach her what: LYING?
In chapter 17, Lees tells us her coach Phil Banton returned to Britain. Lees lied about his role in relation to the show trial, and her own words (pp. 197-198) confirm he was engaged to coach her. FFDA p416
No trace of a mess on the ground after a man has been shot in the head at arm's length! Hard to digest…Was this all the evidence proving that a crime took place?

57 - Ballistics

This is a real good one!

From Joanne Lees' book chapter 17, page 237/238 one can read:

"I waited until the ballistics expert had finished before re-entering the court room. **Carmen Eckhoff** was recalled to the witness stand to discuss the DNA match to Murdoch.

She said; until ballistics expert had finished…The word ballistic involves guns or any fire arms or any flying object, from flying saucer to cricket ball.

The definition of ballistic is:

- 1 -relating to projectiles or their flight
- 2 – moving under the force of gravity only

Question: What was the item necessitating a ballistic test?

- Ah! A gun, The Clint Eastwood type gun, the one which has never been found or the one which was downgraded to a smaller calibre?

BALLISTIC TESTING ON A GUN THEY DO NOT HAVE AND WHICH HAS NEVER BEEN FOUND…WOULD YOU BELIEVE IT!

IT IS LKE TAKING A DNA SWAB FROM THE DEAD BODY WHICH HAS NEVER BEEN FOUND

Then she writes about the discussion between Elliott and Eckhoff during the trial:

Mr ELLIOT: Was there a match between the Identifier results from 2004 and the results from the shirt taken in January 2003

Let us stop here for a moment;

We need to break the sentence in half;

Firstly: "Was there a match between the Identifier results from 2004"; meaning [some] results were received in 2004 (date no mentioned in the sentence)

The Vanishing of Peter Falconio

Secondly: "and the results from the shirt taken in 2003"; meaning the shirt landed on Dr Whitaker's desk on 24 October 2003 (see date further down and previously mentioned)

- So, the shirt was sent on the 17th July 2001 to Dr Whitaker and received on January 2003. That is 18 months. (The transcript says 24 October 2003), unless it went somewhere else in between [?]
- SO, from 17 July 2001 to October 2003 = **28 months** (6 +12 +10 =28)
- THEN, from October 2003 to 1st January 2024 or two months) = 28 + two months = 30 months + unknown in 2024 as no date for 2024 = we stick to 30 months
- That is in all a minimum of 30 months…You're with me!

Now, please check the date of the key events on page 498 of this book. Check 2 May 2024 –28 October 2024 –22 April 2025 referring to test results for the cuffs ok.

Does it mean that PERHAPS the test result for the T- shirt is surfing on the same TIME WAVE?

THINK ABOUT IT PLEASE.

It means that it took a very long time to get some results, very long time, extremely long time. Meaning plenty of time to plant a BOMB or a SMALL PATCH of blood from an alleged killer or someone else, perhaps from his brother Gary hey, (you will find out later) obviously if the intention was not honourable.

  Sorry for the interruption.

Now and below is what Lees writes in her book No Turning Back page 238

Mr ELLIOT: Was there a match between the Identifier results from 2004 and the results from the shirt taken in January 2003 (from this sentence I understand that there have been 2 tests [1] in 2023 and another identifier in 2024. Meaning two different labs made some different tests on the T-shirt…Am I correct?)

The Vanishing of Peter Falconio

MS ECKHOFF: Yes, there was.

MR ELLIOTT: At all loci? (I need to stop for a minute. Here the wording used is incomprehensible for most of us. I have no idea of the meaning, so I use the internet. The meaning is bellow which I still don't understand and I am not the only one. So, do you think the jurors would?

"Terminology. A specific position along a chromosome is called a locus. Each gene occupies a specific locus (so the terms locus and gene are often used interchangeably). Each locus will have an allelic form (allele). The complete set of alleles (at all loci of interest) in an individual is its genotype. 19 June 2023"

MS ECKHOFF: Yes

MR ELLIOTT: And when you calculate the matched statistic, what did it turn out to be?

MS ECKHOFF: 1.5 times 10 to 17th, which hopefully I've transcribed correctly

(I have no idea what 1.5 times 10 to 17th means [?]).

MR ELLIOTT: You've got there a matched statistic greater than, and then there's the number, 150 followed by 15 zero to 1

MS ECKHOFF: Yes, there's about 150 quadrillion

Next in the next phrase Lees wrote: I was spellbound …Then further down she wrote: "How was the Defence going to deal with this?"

On page 239, what she wrote is incomprehensible, she wants the reader to believe that police or any investigators should be looking an alleged Dead Body with the head wrapped in her denim jacket…Please read:

"After court finished, I walked over to the DPP with Sharon and we had a discussion with

Anthony Elliott about the day's evidence. Anthony became very engrossed in our conversation and began talking in great details about the possibility that my denim jacket, which was missing from the Kombi, had been used by Murdoch to wrap around Pete's head after he had shot Pete"

Now how is that for a surprise?...Do you get it? This more than A FARCE if you ask me…Murdoch wrapping the head of Falconio in Lees 'jacket! What else are we going to find out from Lees?

The Vanishing of Peter Falconio

I BELIEVE NOW THAT MURDOCH COULD BE A BUTCHER AND A DRUG DEALER.

I am now trying to understand why did Lees mention this in her book? Well, we know she somehow has a great imagination, but I realise then that as well as creating answers for future questioning, at the time her mind was also working overtime on the manuscript for her book for which she got paid a great amount of money. She didn't have to look for a publisher for her narrative non-fiction story, it is the publisher who paid that great amount for her to write her book, even before her writing it. You will find the amount further on…Keep on reading please.

Perhaps she also wanted to emphasise, make herself an important personality as well as using this as a distraction that could be used later on in time as a distraction for any readers…we don't know [?]

This was a revelation, this is remarkable. Have you ever heard of such witness?

Was it just to show her readers that yes of course Murdoch is guilty and yes of course I am telling the truth? Sorry, but I don't believe one word coming out of that woman's mouth. It is repulsive.

Also, I like to remind you that the transcript says it took 28 months to dispatch some samples to Dr Whitaker (….and the handing of samples to Dr Whitaker…), from the 17 of July 2001 (three days after the alleged crime) to 24 of October 2003. We are speaking here of all DNA test carried out on the steering wheel of the Kombi – the gear stick – the cuffs –and perhaps also Lees' T-shirt.

- We know from the transcript of the appeal that the tests on the steering wheel and gear stick had been tampered.
- The tests on the cuffs gave no positive results and the tests on the bloodstain found on the back of Lees' T-shirt where the source is unknown and very suspicious (tampering), because I like to know why police ask and took blood/DNA sample from Murdoch's brother (Gary) even before the dobbing of Murdoch by Monsieur Hepi (More about it further on, be patient).

The Vanishing of Peter Falconio

As I said, anyone with bad intentions had plenty of time to act according to the agenda and that is to make sure that Murdoch is found guilty.

In Lees 'book published in 2006 she doesn't hide her excitement at the thought that Murdoch was going to be found guilty…Her plan/their plan was working!

HOWEVER,

Mr Elliott first question again from Lees' book page 238: "Was there a match between the identifier results from 2004 and the results from the shirt taken in January 2003",

Tells you that:

>1- The date of the received results is 2004 but the day/month are unknown therefore difficult for anyone to understand/challenge
>
>2- The results regarding Lees' T-shirt were also received in 2004 and as above day/month unknown.
>
>3 – "…and the results from the shirt taken in January 2003 "means (the way I understand it) is that the carry out tests on the T- shirt (taking a swab) took place in 2003…WHY? You would think taking swab on the shirt would have taken place earlier. From 17th July 2001 to January 2003 that is nearly 18 months …<u>Very suspicious.</u>
>
>4 – So, why is the transcript saying that it took 28 months to dispatch the samples (plural) to Dr Whitaker (….*and the handing of samples to Dr Whitaker*…), from the **17 of July 2001** (3 days after the alleged crime) to **24 of October 2003**?
>
>5 – So, **Mr Elliott** says January 2003 but the transcript says 24th October 2003….
>
>6- And also, as you will discover later on regarding the cuffs. The manacles (for not using the word cuff) according to the Prosecution had to be re-tested. Do you know when? Well at the beginning of the trial. The trial had to be and was suspended for a number of weeks so that the cuffs could be sent to England <u>to be re-tested by Dr Whitaker</u>…ncredible in my books.

PLEASE EXPLAIN

If that is the case, we can read from the transcript about the DNA:

A)

[50] **Ms Eckhoff** gave evidence for the purposes of the objections to the DNA evidence. She understood that crime scene examiners had examined the Kombi van before it was moved from the scrub. In particular the outside of the vehicle had been dusted for fingerprints and examined for signs of blood

B)

*[*53] As to the steering wheel, **Ms Eckhoff** said that while she was waiting for the fingerprint examination to be completed, she saw a police officer touch the steering wheel. She could not say why he did so, but he did not appear to do it for the purposes of adjusting the steering wheel or driving the vehicle. The officer did not touch the gear stick. **Ms Eckhoff** advised the officer that the forensic examination had not been completed and he and his team were to have nothing further to do with the vehicle.

C)

20 Contamination

[48] The Kombi van was removed by police from the scrub and transported to Alice Springs. In essence, counsel submitted that a jury could not conclude beyond reasonable doubt that there was no contamination at some stage in the process between removing the van from the scrub on 17 July 2001 and the handing of samples to **Dr Whitaker** on 24 October 2003. In addition to the risks of contamination through handling by police officers, counsel contrasted the conditions that existed at that time in the laboratory in Darwin with the stringent conditions under which LCN is conducted at the Wetherby Laboratory. Counsel contended that in these circumstances the evidence cannot exclude the real possibility of contamination before the samples reached the Wetherby Laboratory.

Do you think this is a joke? It also tells you that,

The Vanishing of Peter Falconio

- DNA test on Lees' T-shirt were carried out (assuming swabs) on **January 2003** or nineteen months (16/18 months) after the alleged crime
- Remember that Lees was asked by police to surrender her T-shirt on the 15th /17th July 2001, the same day they tested Chris Malouf…(No comment!). **But I thought Malouf was tested tested on the 15th of July** (what are they talking about???)
- But the real dates according to the transcript are; from 17 July to 24 October 2003 or **28 months** after the alleged crime, a crime which was so much advertised of course to the benefit of Joanne Lees and the Officials, **but why 28 months?**

Also, regarding the killing, one would think for sure that, shooting a man in the head or any part of the body, metres away from his girlfriend would leave a big impression on her and leave quite a big mess especially using a big Clint Eastwood type gun which of course was

downgraded to a smaller calibre, because it didn't fit the agenda and ballistic. Gosh, doing "ballistic" tests on a gun that has never been found? …Amazing! Nevertheless, they had the choice of two guns

- A big Clint Eastwood type.
- Or a 22 calibre…Is this real, is this a joke?
- When no gun big or small had been found

For good reason the girlfriend would have seen her boyfriend dropping dead on the ground after the shooting and, I would not have given much for her safety…If you killed one, you need to kill the other. You can't leave such reliable witness and the only one alive… Anyhow, if you would fire a bullet in the head of someone at point-blank range, you wouldn't worry about the Dead Body, you would just leave it cold and done on the ground and if someone was nearby the person would get the same treatment for sure…But remember:

- **Falconio just vanished in thin air**

The Vanishing of Peter Falconio

- Falconio was not with Lees watching the sunset but, both were at Aileron having a late lunch, looking at brochures like two good happy holiday makers!
- Both were at the alleged crime scene where apparently, he was shot.
- Then around 4/5 hours later, alive he is pushed into a Japanese car [?]
- Then a week or so he re-appears alive and doing well…Remember what **Gregory Dick** told me? (he is alive and doing well!). WOW…

His alleged death is based only on the claims by Lees our Cinderella who stayed behind looking for her lost shoe…. (More clapping in the background).

The Vanishing of Peter Falconio

58 Bradley John Murdoch – Peter Falconio – Joanne Lees

They are all involved with drugs.

Murdoch is a drug dealer mostly marijuana and perhaps some other drugs. Not a good role model for sure.

Falconio and Lees are drug users, marijuana- ecstasy and perhaps some other drugs. Maybe they also sell…Not good role models as well!

[28a] Falconio owes money to the taxation office. According to **Maureen Laracy**, an accountant for **Deloittes** in Alice Springs, whom Falconio saw that morning, told the Northern territory Supreme Court, in Darwin, that she had informed him he owed the tax office money. Describing their 15 minutes meeting at 10 am on that day, she asked him if he wanted to continue and have a tax return completed, but he declined.

"She said his was a common reaction. When they find they owe money, they just want to get on the plane to get home."

Falconio is alleged also to have enquired on how he could fake his own death. Conspiring with Lees or not? Maybe she is unaware of his plan but I doubt it because they both were at Aileron…And THEY WERE SO MUCH IN LOVE!

Just to commit an insurance fraud difficult to understand, unless it is related to drugs and drug lords.

The life insurance theory (Radio Times documentary series "Murder in the outback).

The documentary also revealed that one of Falconio's colleagues had come forward to the Australian authorities anonymously, to suggest that he may have faked his own death.

"There is no doubt in my mind that Peter Falconio is capable of carrying out the scam," said

the unnamed friend. "I would not be in the least bit surprised if he attempted to defraud a life insurance policy just for the money. Before he went away, he told me he had taken out a policy."

Was this investigated? That would be easy to check.

"In the statement, he describes himself as a friend of Peter's and says he was called 'dodgy Peter' because "he was always scamming".

The Vanishing of Peter Falconio

Falconio's body has never been found, leaving some people believing there could be some truth in it and that he could be alive.

Former defence lawyer Andrew Fraser explained the 'friend' and colleague said Peter joked about people trying to scam the company he worked for. The Australian police have discounted the theory that Peter faked his own death. A former journalist who covered the case said: "There's no way a son could have faked his own death and maintained his absence for so long knowing that his family were so upset.

"That proves to me that the insurance scam allegation was perhaps unfounded."

- Murdoch remains in prison for Peter Falconio's alleged murder and the alleged assault on Joanne Lees in 2005. He plead not guilty and maintains his innocence.
- Falconio's body is still missing, with the Prosecution relying on a small bit of DNA on Joanne Lees' T-shirt which allegedly matched Murdoch's.
- Murdoch was diagnosed with cancer last year promoting the police attempt to get a confession in exchange for moving him to a prison closer to his family.

Murdoch can apply for parole from 2033 but if he doesn't reveal the location of Falconio's body his application will be denied.

Now, if true, why would Falconio faking his own death? Is there a connection with drugs and some drug Lords, question I keep on asking; is it for money owed, small or large amount? Could he have been kidnapped for money owed? Being involved with drugs is a very nasty business as we all know, but this is only supposition …We need facts! The only facts we have now is the lack of the Dead Body which in a sense points to the right direction: Disappearance, not murder.

As far as Lees is concerned, she keeps on denying (up until the trial) under oath against all evidence that she and Falconio DID NOT STOP at Aileron roadhouse when four people said that they did. It shows that there

The Vanishing of Peter Falconio

is something unclear but nothing to do with driving slowly from Alice to Ti Tree (just a reminder).

At Aileron she definitely spoke to a man she knew. Some arrangements must have had to be made before stopping at Aileron. The plan without any doubt was that she was going to Ti Tree after meeting the man at Aileron, then on her way to Barrow Creek the alleged crime scene.

She must have been very worried, even if the deal was going according to plan. If Falconio didn't go with her it could also mean that he was also conspiring (staging).

Was Lees playing on more than one front?

Admitting having an affair without Falconio's knowledge, the man she loves so much, meaning Falconio tells you they were keeping secrets from each other. She must have been well aware and well prepared for this type of scam.

She truly proved it by not being cold but warm after pretending having spent around five hours hiding in the bush on a very cold night and also coming out of the alleged ordeal nice and clean. Again, why was Murdoch found guilty, why?

The Vanishing of Peter Falconio

59 - From The Daily Mail Uk

This article is already a couple of years old…food for thought!

"Stepfather of British backpacker Joanne Lees says he now believes Australian killer Bradley John Murdoch is INNOCENT of murdering her boyfriend Peter Falconio in 2001 - after watching controversial C4 documentary"

- *"Stepfather <u>Vincent James</u> said he was 'convinced' of Murdoch's innocence*
- *Murdoch convicted of murdering Mr Falconio north of Alice Springs in 2001*
- *He pleaded not guilty to murder and has professed his innocence ever since*
- *Mr James said his opinion on case had been swayed by British documentary*
- *He said he was 'convinced Bradley Murdoch is innocent' but didn't at the time*
- *Series presented alternative theory Mr Falconio may have faked own death"*

By RYAN FAHEY FOR MAILONLINE and CHARLIE COË FOR DAILY MAIL AUSTRALIA

PUBLISHED: 02:02 AEST, 11 July 2020 | UPDATED: 16:00 AEST, 12 July 2020

"The stepfather of British backpacker Joanne Lees says he now believes Australian killer Bradley John Murdoch is innocent of murdering her boyfriend Peter Falconio in 2001 - after watching a controversial documentary on TV.

Mechanic Bradley John Murdoch, from Broome in north-west Australia, was convicted of murdering Mr Falconio, 28, and assaulting his partner Joanne Lees, then 27, on a remote stretch of highway near Barrow Creek in the Northern Territory in 2001.

He pleaded not guilty to the infamous outback murder and has maintained his innocence despite a court sentencing him to life in jail following a DNA match found on Ms Lees' T-shirt.

The Vanishing of Peter Falconio

Murdoch, now 62, is believed to have hidden Mr Falconio's body, which has never been found despite extensive searches.

Ms Lees hid in bushland for five hours while Murdoch hunted her with his dog, before she managed to flag down a truck driver.

Speaking from the town of Huddersfield, where the couple grew up, her stepfather Vincent James said his opinion on the case has been swayed by a British documentary series which aired last month.

I'm convinced Bradley Murdoch is innocent, I didn't at the time but I do now,' Mr James told News Corp.

'I watched the program and [from] all the forensic evidence it would appear that he's not guilty,' the stepfather said.

At the time when I was there, I thought he was guilty but now I don't.'

Though the conviction was largely based on Ms Lees' DNA being found on Murdoch's shirt, Mr James said the new evidence in the documentary swayed him.

The series entitled Murder in the Outback - broadcast on the UK's Channel 4 - is geared towards exploring alternative evidence, not provided at court during Murdoch's trial and point to other parties having been involved.

Roger Maynard, one of the first journalists on the scene, discussed the most convincing piece of new evidence with 7news.com.au.

Vince Miller, the truck-driver who picked up Joanne on the night after her assault, said that while on the same stretch of road just a few miles before he picked her up, he saw a red car at the roadside.

Three men were by the car, two of them holding up a third.

According to Maynard, the men didn't want to be interrupted by the trucker when he asked if they needed help. They bundled the third man 'like jelly' into the back seat and drove away.

The truck driver said he now believes the man being held up could have been Mr Falconio.

Ms Lees reportedly still owns property in Huddersfield but is rarely seen in the town - in West Yorkshire, 14 miles outside of Leeds.

The Vanishing of Peter Falconio

Mr Falconio's parents also still live there and have spent much of the past two decades dedicated to finding his body.

In June's episode of Murder in the Outback, a former defence lawyer made a shocking claim from one of Peter's friends who said the backpacker was 'capable of faking his own death and committing life insurance fraud'.

Police in Australia have discounted suggestions Mr Falconio faked his own death.

The lawyer, Andrew Fraser, said a person claiming to be a friend of Mr Falconio's suggested he had committed life insurance fraud.

He told the cameras: 'One such theory that came to our attention is that Peter Falconio may have faked his own disappearance.

'It's a statement that comes from somebody who describes himself as a mate of Peter's. And that statement paints a picture of Peter Falconio that many people may find surprising.'

The anonymous friend - who was working three nights a week for an insurance company - told Australian authorities that the backpacker was known as 'dodgy Pete' because he was always known for scamming.

He explained he'd chatted to Peter about how people were taking out life insurance policy cover for a couple of months before going to a foreign country and putting in a false claim.

In a statement, the unnamed friend said: 'There is no doubt in my mind that Peter Falconio is capable of carrying out the scam.

'I would not be in the least bit surprised if he attempted to defraud a life insurance policy just for the money. Before he went away, he told me he had taken out a policy.'

Last year, Murdoch was diagnosed with cancer, triggering a last-ditch attempt from police to elicit a confession in exchange for moving him to a prison closer to his family.

The murderer is being held in the Darwin Correctional Centre where he spends his days in the kitchen as a pastry chef and has become known for his desserts.

He was diagnosed with cancer in 2019, according to the NT News.

The Vanishing of Peter Falconio

Police hope the 'backpacker killer' will reveal where he buried the body in exchange for being transferred from his Northern Territory jail to a Western Australian prison to be closer to his family as he battles cancer.

Murdoch can apply for parole from 2033 but unless he reveals the location of Mr Falconio's body, the application will be denied. "

The Vanishing of Peter Falconio

60 - Did Lees Make Money from The Story and How Much?

Money, money, money...The ABBA great band...Must be funny...in the rich man's world

What follows is from FFDA an open window on Joanne Lees' financials ...Food for thought!

"So that monster Murdoch was sent to the slammer in Darwin, Lees went off and made heaps of money selling her stories after she told everyone that "I would never ever sell my story to anyone," and witness for the prosecution, and then went on to make big money from her stories about". Falconio going missing. FFDA p26

MONEY LEES MADE

FROM FALCONIO'S VANISHING

Would you believe in the suggestion that making money was a prime reason why Lees involved herself in the disappearance of her boyfriend Falconio the man she loved so much? Reading from FFDA p389/390/392 should be a surprise thanks to Keith Noble.

_ "Ms Lees from Huddersfield, recently returned to the scene of her ordeal with a Granada camera crew to film a documentary for Trevor McDonald's Tonight programme. She is believed to have been paid more than £30,000 for her story." (added emphasis)

(Patrick Barkham. guardian.co.uk. 25 February 2002)

"I heard...that she's been paid $250 000 advance. With the $120 000 from the Bashir interview, a potential $50 000 payout from the Northern Territory government as a victim of crime, (This is a real joke ...that's me speaking not FFDA) and royalties from her book, she would be doing well." (Robin Bowles. Rough Justice. 2007: p.204)

"Joanne began writing her autobiography, No Turning Back, for which she reportedly received £250,000." (Natalie Clarke. dailymail.co.uk. 2 May 2008).

The Vanishing of Peter Falconio

"[Martin] Bashir got the interview he was after, for the price of £50,000 ($AU126,000)." (added emphasis). (Ginny Dougary. ginnydougary.co.uk. 1 October 2006)

"I'd never do that! I would never ever sell my story to anyone" 85 (original italics; added emphasis) (Joanne Lees. Dead Centre. 2005: p. 57)

"A spokeswoman for...**Hachette Livre Australia** said it was exceeding all our expectations' in its first week. Lees was reportedly paid **$630,000** to write the book." (Garry Maddox. smh.com.au. 13 October 2006)

"Incredibly, after all her anti-media comments and her pledge never to sell her story [see above], Joanne agreed to appear in an ITV documentary about the case in exchange for a payment reported to be about £50,000 (then $135,000)." (Roger Maynard Where's Peter 2005 p139)

"[T]hat Lees...made a reported STG250,000 ($A631,792) from a book deal and serialisation rights, and another STG50,000 ($A126,358) from a television interview, has raised further questions with some." (Nine News. ninemsn.com.au. 8 October 2006)

"Mr Algie insisted the question was relevant 'because motive to perpetuate this story is relevant.' Joanne then confirmed she had been paid AUD$120 000 for an exclusive interview
[with ITV]." (Richard Shears. Bloodstain. 2005. p. 175)

After vowing never to take money to tell her story, in March she was talking to Britain's ITV for a reputed $80,000." (The Sun Herald. The public trial of Joanne Lees. 14 July 2002)

My story for The Weekend Australian was wrong in one respect– Lees had not returned to the precise [alleged] killing scene. The TV crew had taken her to some anonymous stretch of the Stuart Highway to do her re-enactment. It would later be revealed that Lees was paid A$82 000 for the story, which aired in Australia in March 2002 and went down very badly." (Paul Toohey. The Killer Within. 2007: pp. 79-80)

The Vanishing of Peter Falconio

"She'd agreed to appear on the British ITV current affairs show Tonight With Trevor McDonald, produced by Granada Television, for the Bashir interview aired on 18 March 2002, and for a payment of $120,000 (50,000 pounds)-(Sue Williams. And then the darkness. 2006: p.199).

How much more do you need?

It would be very interesting to witness the aftershock if Falconio resurfaced and doing well (the words of Gregory Dick at Aileron). It would be the ultimate proof of Lees' involvement with his disappearance. It is quite possible but difficult to visualize the long list of those taking legal action against her and him (What goes up must come down!).

To all Lees' apologists, here is a question – Given Joanne Lees has probably made about a million 86 Australian dollars on the disappearance, how much money has she put up as a reward for information leading to the finding of "Pete" – dead or alive? The answer is $0 (Zero)

If she really loved him as much as she said she did, she would have encouraged people to find him. This is what she said on p. 64:

"I was going to take him home to England and never let him out of my sight again, once I'd found him." But it seems Lees has not spent one minute looking for her Pete. Finally, do not look for any of the sums stated above in No Turning Back. Lees mentions no specific amounts of money she made from Falconio's disappearance. (FFDA p 390.)

87 In 2001, journalist Mark Wilton worked for the local newspaper at Alice Springs – Centralian Advocate. He interviewed Lees, but later Lees denied and retracted everything she told Wilton. Why did Lees do that? Well Wilton did not pay Lees anything, and it is said that she wanted to sell her stories contrary to what she claimed. And later, she did sell them for large sums of money. (FFDA p.392)

I BELIEVE WE HAVE ENOUGH EVIDENCE TO UNDERSTAND WHY LEES DIDN'T DO IT FOR THE MONEY....

The Vanishing of Peter Falconio

61 - Monsieur Murdoch and The Tanami

According to the Prosecution –the Judge –the Officials –some experts –and Joanne Lees: Who is Monsieur Murdoch?

Monsieur Murdoch is a very meticulous killer –he is the CCTV man – he has a dog –drives a Land Cruiser 75 series – and according to Lees he is the killer of her boyfriend (easy case!)

The killer of her boyfriend? Yes, that is what she claimed. Lees said: "Yes he is the killer, I was there, trust me" and everybody agreed.

Well, a lot of people did trust her. I didn't and still don't!

If according to the Prosecution the CCTV man is the alleged killer having shot Falconio in cold blood then leaving in a hurry towards Fitzroy Crossing. Let's see if he could reach Fitzroy Crossing without running out of fuel or time.

But before:

We need to do the exercise to see if the CCTV man leaving Barrow Creek at 9.00pm after killing Falconio at 8.45pm on the 14th after searching for Lees knowing that she has never been hiding

- Then giving up his search but departing the alleged crime scene, arriving in Alice at 0.30am on the 15th
- Then doing some shopping which probably took less than 1 hour (from 0.30am to 0.45am or even up to 1.00am)
- Finally departing the truck stop at 1.00am (According to the transcript of the appeal);
- Could make it to Fitzroy Crossing on time according to the deadline of 8.00 pm (NT time) on the 15th to be seen refuelling?

We know from the Court of Criminal Appeal, that the Land Cruiser enters the truck stop at 0.30 am on the 15th, so let's stick to it. The departure time being 1.00am (Transcript).

62 - The Key Assumptions Underpinning the Prosecution's Case

In his summing up to the jury, Defence Counsel Grant Algie challenged the two key assumptions underpinning the Prosecution's case (which we shall also discuss further on during the course of this book.)

There are two assumptions that have been made very early in the investigation of this matter, and indeed which continue to form the foundation of the Prosecution's case.

1- If there was a bad guy at Barrow Creek, he actually left his DNA or blood on Joanne Lees.

2- If there was a bad guy at Barrow Creek, that guy is the man in the Shell truck-stop Station.

Knowing that the man seen on the video footage entering the truck-stop at the wheel of his land Cruiser has never been identified by police or any other investigators, it is logical to assume that we have now TWO PRIME SUSPECTS, and they are:

3- The CCTV Man and his Land Cruiser (alleged killer)

4- ...and Bradley John Murdoch (also an alleged killer)

This is paramount, we must understand that we have two people here as prime suspects.

Therefore, we only need to prove who is the killer? The CCTV man or Murdoch?

How can we do that? Well, the CCTV man as we know according to the transcript ([160] Murdoch v The Queen [2007] NTCCA1- No CA 2/06 [20215807])

- The CCTV man is departing Alice at **1.00am** on the 15th of July 2001
- Murdoch as per his claim is departing Alice at **3.10pm** on the 14th of July 2001 because Murdoch claimed that at **3.30pm** on the 14th he was at the turn off of the Tanami or 20km north of Alice. That took 20 minutes.

The Vanishing of Peter Falconio

The CCTV man

The journey is as follow: Alice Springs –Tilmouth Well –Yuendumu – Rabbit Flat Road House – The Granites (Granite gold mine) – Billiluna – Halls Creek –Fitzroy Crossing –eventually Broome.

Leaving Alice at 1.00am (15th) therefore travelling at night via Tilmouth –Yuendumu

By passing Rabbit Flat (that was 22 years ago), we don't know if he refuelled there because there are no data available on the net because Rabbit Flat closed permanently in 2010).

Then from Rabbit Flat he still would need to drive another 453km via The Granites to Billiluna where fuel was available, then to Halls Creek, then from Halls Creek to Fitzroy Crossing where he was seen refuelling, 1,412km from Alice, then eventually onto Broome.

Murdoch (same journey)

- Leaving Alice at 3.10pm (14th). He will find Tilmouth Well and Yuendumu open for fuel.
- At Rabbit Flat same story, we don't know, no data available.
- By passing Rabbit Flat he still would need to drive another **453km via** The Granites
 to Billiluna where fuel is/was available, then to Halls Creek, then from Halls Creek to Fitzroy Crossing where he was seen refuelling, **1,412km** from Alice then onto Broome.

You understand that both men are doing exactly the same trip pulling a campervan, facing the same obstacles, but each having left at different time and each taking the same risk if I may say because only one of the two is the killer or truly; MAY BE NONE OF THE TWO ARE. The CCTV man could also be a total stranger to the alleged case, just to make things more complicated.

- According to the Prosecution –Joanne Lees –Monsieur Hepi, the CCTV man is Murdoch and the alleged killer. Knowing this, <u>I cannot name both the CCTV man.</u>
- Perhaps neither of the two is the killer as I said [?]

The Real mystery Killer

The alleged killer cannot be both. I am just saying the killer because according to Lees and the Prosecution and Monsieur Hepi and now the Judge, the CCTV man [is/was] the killer [and] Murdoch.

- The CCTV man may have a bigger risk of running out of fuel or time after having committed the alleged crime especially leaving Alice at 1.00am on the 15th
- Also, he is in great hurry therefore he must get fuel when needed and when available.

Also, we don't know if the CCTV man cruiser or Murdoch's cruiser are fitted with one or two fuel tanks?

- That is something we don't know. We need to do the calculation with two tanks first then with only one tank for each car (starting with two because I have some doubt if the cars are fitted with one tank only).

Anyhow you need to refer to the distances in the next chapter for better understanding (plus or minus 10km) to form an opinion.

I am saying it again; we have TWO PRIME SUSPECTS.

The Vanishing of Peter Falconio

63 - Distances (Internet –Hema Maps)

Alice Springs to Aileron = **134km**

Aileron to Ti Tree = **62km**

Ti Tree to Barrow Creek = **119km**

Alice Springs – Tilmouth Well = **190km**

Tilmouth Well –Yuendumu =**145km**

Yuendumu to the Granites = **254km**

The Granite to Rabbit Flat = **57km**

The Granite is very close to Quartz Ridge 57km south of Rabbit Flat Roadhouse. (311km – 57km = 254km)

Yuendumu to Rabbit Flat = **311km**

Rabbit Flat to Billiluna = **280km**

Billiluna to Halls Creek = **196km**

Halls Creek to Fitzroy Crossing = **290km**

Fitzroy Crossing to Broome = **400km**

Alice Springs to Yuendumu = **297km**

Alice Springs to the Granites = **551km**

Alice Springs to Rabbit Flat = **608km**

Alice Springs to Billiluna = **888km**

Alice Springs to Halls Creek = **1,084km**

Alice Springs to Fitzroy Crossing = **1,412km**

Alice Springs to Broome = **1,774km**

The Vanishing of Peter Falconio

Barrow Creek to Fitzroy Crossing = **1,710km** via Alice Springs

Barrow Creek – Yuendumu = **318km**   via Aileron, turning right via Pine Hill & Mount

Denison meeting the Tanami at Yuendumu.

Barrow Creek – Rabbit Flat Roadhouse = **629km** via Aileron

Barrow Creek – Halls Creek = **1,105km** via Aileron

Barrow Creek – Fitzroy Crossing via Aileron turning right = **1,395km**

***

Aileron to Ti Tree = **62km**

Ti Tree to Barrow Creek = **119km**

Aileron to Barrow Creek = **181km**

Ti Tree to Barrow Creek =   109km +10km = **119km**

Rabbit Flat Roadhouse to Billiluna **280km** (open Mon-Fri 8.00am to 11.00am and 2.00pm to 4.00pm Saturday open from 8.00am to 10.30am Sunday closed). This is important.

Halls Creek – Fitzroy Crossing = **290km**

Alice Springs – Halls Creek = **1,084km**

The Vanishing of Peter Falconio

64 Calculation and Choice

As from now the story truly grabs you until the end of the book because from this chapter, we are dealing with true facts that cannot be dismissed nor ridiculed. Also, I have never said or accused the CCTV man of being the killer. Knowing that [HE] and [HIS] Cruiser have never been identified it is impossible to tell what direction [HE] took after departing the truck-stop. Nobody can. However, the fact that he and his Land Cruiser was published on the internet, one would think that the man would have recognised himself. It would not be unreasonable for the man then to present himself at any police station asking questions. As a result, he also is suspicious. Therefore, he is also a Prime Suspect, even more *according to* Joanne Lees –the Prosecution –even the Judge. I like to make this very clear…Thank you for your understanding.

***

Wel,l we need to find out who will win the race. The race is between:

- **CCTV man** which according to the Prosecution –Joanne Lees is departing Alice at **1.00am on the 15th**
- **And Murdoch** himself claiming that at around **3.30pm on the 14th of July** he was at the turn off Alice/Tanami. Refer to transcript *[61].*

Which of the two will reach Fitzroy Crossing according to the Deadline 800pm on the 15th to be seen refuelling?

The CCTV man and Murdoch have only one choice to reach Fitzroy Crossing to be seen at 8.00pm refuelling. Both will do exactly the same trip, only the hour of departure is different.

1 – The CCTV man

- The CCTV man has only one choice and that is departing Alice Springs at 1.00am on the 15th of July. Don't forget he is in great hurry if he is the killer

2 –Murdoch

The Vanishing of Peter Falconio

Murdoch himself has also and only one choice according to his claim that is: Departing Alice Springs at 3.10pm on the 14th of July… It takes 20 minutes from Alice to the turn off where the Stuart Highway meets the Tanami. Murdoch said that at 3.30pm he was at the turn off. So, 3.30pm - 20minutes = 3.10pm on the 14th of July

***

In Alice departing at 1.00am (15th) after having his photo taken by the CCTV camera the CCTV man must now be heading towards Fitzroy Crossing 1,412km away. Please remember the CCTV man is also the assumed killer according to Joanne Lees and the Prosecution our second witness.

After refuelling we don't know if he has reconnected the trailer because on the CCTV footage there is no trailer, but we need to assume that a trailer; exist, even if Joanne Lees didn't see it. We don't know also if his car is fitted with one or two tanks and we don't know if he has changed his appearance before or after committing the alleged crime [?] (I will discuss this later on).

Also, both the CCTV man and Murdoch have been awake since the morning on the 14th, each didn't take a nap simply because: They ate or got some takeaway at the same restaurant where apparently a patch of his blood (not saying DNA) got on the back of Lees' T-shirt (don't know –where – when –and how?) then the alleged killer followed Lees and Falconio fearing they were spying on him (repeat).

[Repeat is needed, we must re-live the story] …The killer changing his appearance while keeping an eye on Joanne and Peter must have been fascinating if he did, because he couldn't afford losing them. Then he stopped them at Barrow Creek and shot Falconio as we know from Lees' claim …… BANG! With a big silver Magnum…Make my day!

All we can confirm up until now, is that they didn't get much sleep, simply because Murdoch of course was too busy and too preoccupied with Falconio and Lees feeling they were spying on him. That is why Murdoch the assumed killer was involuntarily pushed or forced to commit the crime and the abduction…Oh what a joke!

The Vanishing of Peter Falconio

No sleep after the killing because he had to make sure Lees was safe and secure, had to move the Kombi parking it neatly, then had to walk back to the alleged crime scene to clean up the mess, then had to search for Lees while his rented dog was playing with the ball. All that time from morning to midnight already with no sleep, just perhaps a pizza in the stomach…WOW, all this from 8.30/9.00pm on the 14th. The killer won't be getting any sleep soon.

This again proves one thing:

JOANNE LEES HAS NEVER BEEN HIDING FOR AROUND FIVE HOURS BEFORE BEING RESCUED. THAT IS A LIE OF HUGE PROPORTION.

The Vanishing of Peter Falconio

65 - We Definitely Have…

Two prime suspects - why?

We know from the Prosecution supported by the Judge that:

1- If there was a bad guy at Barrow Creek, he actually left his DNA or blood on Joanne Lees.

2- If there was a bad guy at Barrow Creek, that guy is the man in the Shell truck-stop Station.

[BUT] we know also something that nobody can deny, something that is full proof.

We know that the man seen on the CCTV camera as well as his cruiser has never been identified by police or anyone else at the exception of the Judge –Prosecution –Joanne Lees –monsieur James Hepi – monsieur Hall and all the others who testified against Murdoch without any proofs.

The only possible and logical deduction which is FULL PROOF, is that:

Not being identified means that NOBODY can tell what direction and route this unknown man and his Cruiser took when departing Alice Springs. He may have gone towards London –Paris –or New York. Nobody can tell that if he went on the Tanami towards Fitzroy then onto Broome. I trust this will be clearly understood by everyone. If it's not we are all doomed.

Therefore, we have two PRIME SUSPECTS: One going somewhere and Murdoch going to Fitzroy Crossing driving on the Tanami. This will tell you if Murdoch was at the alleged crime scene at the time of the alleged crime calculated by me at around 8.45 pm because we have no dead body and no proofs that a crime was committed. Please God (if there is one) make sure people understand.

One think that we don't know also and will never know is how many fuel tanks the CCTV man's Land Cruiser was fitted with but we will do the calculation assuming two fuel tanks are fitted then same calculation with only one tank.

What we know is that Murdoch's Cruiser was fitted with a long-range fuel tank but we will do the same calculations. We also know that he bought a fuel container in Alice Springs

The CCTV man with two tanks

The Vanishing of Peter Falconio

Refuelling in Alice departing **at 1.00am on the 15th of July 2001**

- Having 19 hours (1140 minutes) to do the drive from 1.00 am to 8.00pm on the 15th to cover the distance (1,412km) non-stop Alice –Fitzroy Crossing.
- The average speed on the overall 1412km ÷ 1140 = 1.23km/minute x 60 = **74.4kmh** and I mean non-stop from Alice to Fitzroy Crossing after reconnecting the trailer which was not seen on the CCTV film…Why? Nobody knows.
- You must understand this is an overall average speed over 1,412km. But sometimes due conditions of the road/track the average speed will change drastically indeed.
- We are only calculating the journey from Alice to Fitzroy (1,412km) not Broome because the CCTV man we assume was seen refuelling at 8.00pm on the 15th 2001with a car fitted with **two tanks**.

MURDOCH himself

Refuelling in Alice at a BP Station (NOT SHELL as claimed by the Prosecution and partners) during the day (time unknown) departing on the 14th of July 2001 around 3.10pm.

- Same calculation with **two tanks** after reconnecting the trailer according to the Prosecution our second witness who claimed it was dropped somewhere just to commit the alleged offence which of course, would indicate a premeditated crime if crime there is/was (laughter in the background).
- He has **28 hours and 50 minutes t**o do the trip from 3.10pm on the 14th to midnight = 8hour and 50 minutes to midnight + 12 hours to noon on the 15th + 8.00 hours to 8.00pm on the 15th = **28 hours and 50 minutes** or 1,730minutes).
- His average speed will be: 1,412km ÷ 1,730 = 0.81km per minute x 60 = **48.97km/h.**

Then we will do the same calculation with one tank.

The Vanishing of Peter Falconio

I need to say it again:

- **They have to drive** on the Tanami from Alice to Fitzroy with a vehicle which is not new,
- Pulling a trailer which was reconnected we don't know where and when.
- With all the obstacles that I mentioned at the beginning that is:
- Corrugations up to six to 7 inches deep – potholes – bull dust – wild life and a great chance to have more than one puncture when pulling a trailer.
  - **The CCTV man** has to sustain an average speed of 74 km/h for 19 hours (being in a hurry)
  - **Murdoch** has to sustain an average speed of 48.97km/h for 28 hours and 50 minutes (not in a hurry)

Sometimes their speed will drop to 20km per hour even less according to track conditions. If not, it could mean losing the trailer or break everything! Trust me, I did the drive twice. Wow, that is an achievement on its own.

To sustain any average speed, they need to drive at speed of [xyz] up to [XYZ].

It is a non-stop-drive, the Tanami is not a four-lane highway. They wouldn't even have time for a pee. Can anyone drive 1,412km pulling a camper van on the Tanami at that speed for 19 hours non-stop? (That is the CCTV man having ten hours less to achieve the drive therefore being terribly disadvantaged and in great hurry).

Ask any grey nomads towing their caravans or trailers or a road train driver. I can visualise the trailer bouncing like hell, even losing it for sure.

Let me give you an example: I drove from Alice Springs to Finke (Apatula) returned trips three times during the last five years.

Each year the Finke race is on. It is a two- day event. First day Apatula – Alice, second day Alice – Apatula. Distance each day 240 km.

For cars, quads, bikes the average time is under 2hours or 120 minutes (it is actually around 1.50 or 110 minutes) with average speed **of 131kmh.**

The Vanishing of Peter Falconio

The average speed on any highway would be greater obviously. Here they are not driving on the tar but on the dirt –sand –rocks etc. Please check out the geology for the Finke Race as well as the Tanami. Ask Tobi Price or watch his videos on You Tube but bear in mind that they are driving a totally different vehicle and they are not pulling a campervan trailer. Then come back and talk to me. Sometime it is more than 180km up to 200km for loss of speed in very hard terrain, sand etc. But that is for 2hours, NOT 19 hours non-stop to cover a distance of 1,412km…It is worse than the Dakar Race!

Also, as I said above, the CCTV man is in great hurry to reach Fitzroy Crossing contrary to Murdoch who is not.

The Vanishing of Peter Falconio

66 - For Your Perusal

This is a short paragraph to prove my point regarding the Tanami telling you about the speed you may need to drive especially towing a trailer. Obviously, it is from the Internet.

"Is the Tanami suitable for trailer and caravan? The rain can close parts of the road at short notice. In the desert when it rains it pours. The speeding vehicles can pick up blinding dust making driving conditions even more treacherous. Another inconvenient are storms. A desert storm can turn the dusty track to a muddy pool in minutes or even worse, wash it away. If you're actually stuck other people can't stop to help you because they'll get stuck themselves. Some parts of the road are prone to severe corrugations, making for an uncomfortable and slow drive at times. Take ample supplies of fuel, food and water as various roadhouses along the track can be unreliable. It's a remote-travel area with limited services and supplies: the longest stretch without fuel is 600km between Billiluna and Yuendumu. You should also carry enough drinking water to last two trips, as all dams and bores along the route are classified as undrinkable. Driving across the corrugations and the dirt needs patience and experience. The Tanami Road is just shocking – the corrugations can get six/seven inches high and it sounds like you're driving an express train. You're down to just 20kmh because the road is so savage. Beware loose surface and dust corrugations. It's a fight to survive. Careful driving: Techniques are advised. Experience counts. Prepare your car for the journey ahead. Expect 360 miles with no food and fuel with temperatures up to 45C. It is recommended that 4WD vehicles are used for the road and outlying areas, and you will need to be well-prepared and self-sufficient. It is not recommended for caravans or trailers."

The Vanishing of Peter Falconio

67 - The Fuel Factor

I think the fuel factor has been ignored or dismissed by most people and so was the time.

The fuel usage

Well, you may disagree with me, but fuel consumption for a man accused of a crime, who has to flee a crime scene in a hurry is a detail that people have forgotten. He cannot run out of fuel, then calling NRMA for assistance.

- With my 1996 Land Cruiser 4.2 diesel 75 series (no turbo) with already 600,000km if I drive at 80/90 km/h (2,000revs) stopping from time to time during long distances I use 12/13litres per 100 km.
- If I drive at 100km/h (2,300 revs per minute constant) it jumps to 13/14/15 litres per 100km (I never drove long distances over 90kmh).
- I always drive between 80 and 90kmh. Most of the time it's 80km/h I never drive over 2,000 revs per minutes). The minimal fuel usage is, between 12 and 14 litres.

Three years ago, on a trip from Canberra to Ivanhoe NSW driving along the railway line from Euabalong west I decided purposely to run out of fuel. My tank holds exactly 86 litres. I drove 635 km until I run out. I have a video to prove it. That is a fuel usage of 86 ÷ 635 x 100 = 13.5 litres.

That is a fact.

If the Land Cruiser is fitted with a two inch or three or even four-inch exhaust pipe, it could also increase or decrease the fuel usage depending on which one is fitted (mine is a two-inch pipe.) You must remember, that the **CCTV man** and **Murdoch** are pulling a campervan which increase the fuel usage and reduce the speed (that is another fact).

Also, one must take into account that a non-stop drive (I mean non-stop) of 1,412km will increase your oil usage… The engine will get hot, trust my word. Old car or new one makes no difference, watch out! If the *car is a* V8, it's up to 22 litres per 100km at 100kmh on highway. Toyota has increased the length of the cabin at one stage giving more legroom by five or six inches but, I can't remember when. This reminds me my French Military Service we had some trucks (GMC and Studebaker) with fuel usage of 1 litre per km (petrol was cheap then).

Estimation of their fuel usage

I reckon the CCTV man's cruiser or Murdoch's one when driving on the Tanami pulling the trailer (if they can) to keep the average speed of nearly 75km/h or 49km/h would use close to 12/14 litre per 100kmh (more for the CCTV man having only 19 hours to reach destination) Sometime he will be driving at 20km/h. sometime he will need drive at 110/140kmh if he can for the loss of time.

They are not driving on a highway pulling a trailer. This is real business! City people have no idea.

A Range rover just driving around the city uses nearly 20 litre/100 so is the Jeep Wrangler, some friends could support my claims…Reason why they got rid of the cars.

I will use an average of 14 litre for both Cruisers. Don't forget getting away from an alleged crime scene you cannot runout of fuel or time if you are the killer.

I think this is a fair estimation so I will stick to 14 litrs per 100km. An average tank on a cruiser is 90 litres. If a cruiser is equipped with a second tank, the capacity of the second tank is normally 80 litres (90 + 80 = 170)

The Vanishing of Peter Falconio

68 - The Court of Criminal Appeal

This is a long chapter and serious business not to be laughed at. We need this chapter before doing the calculations. Make yourself a cuppa, take a break then come back.

- It will be the race between the **CCTV man** leaving Alice at **1.00am** on the 15th
- And Murdoch himself leaving Alice at **3.10pm** the day before ...
- Who will win?

Be patient the calculation will be done but before we need to clarify certain things

Below in italic are copies of paragraphs from the Court of Criminal appeal. As you know anything can be VERBALY tampered with but not when it's in writing.

- This tells you the arrival time in Alice Springs of the unknown Land Cruiser at 0.30am on the 15th at the **Shell truck stop.**
- Time of the man walking after doing his shopping who doesn't seem to be in great hurry at 0.45am or close enough
- His departure from the Shell truck- stop at 1.00am on the 15th
- And of course, not being the true representation or description of Murdoch but only himself: The CCTV man
- That's all we know about him and his Cruiser contrary to what Lees and the Prosecution and Mr Hepi and the Judge may think.

Also, from the beginning of the book, there are a lot of repeats. They were and are necessary.

In this chapter you will realise and understand why sometimes in just say ten sentences, why the Prosecution made so many repeats usually referring to only one word and the relevant synonyms.

I call it brain washing. Usually the word involved is: LIE or synonyms having the same meaning as well as the same purpose...The jury must believe Murdoch has lied all the way.

I am not apologising for the numbers of repeat in my investigation. The word count for this work is over 131,000 words. It could be said 100 times depending on the topics. That is 1,310 words per repeat. Make sure you that you count the number of times you read the word LIE and appropriate synonyms. Please do, be curious.

Please read slowly.

"IN THE COURT OF CRIMINAL APPEAL OF THE NORTHERN TERRITORY OF AUSTRALIA AT DARWIN Murdoch v The Queen [2007] NTCCA 1 No. CA 2/06 (20215807) BETWEEN: BRADLEY JOHN MURDOCH Appellant AND: THE QUEEN Respondent CORAM: ANGEL ACJ, RILEY J & OLSSON AJ REASONS FOR JUDGMENT (Delivered 10 January 2007)"

Ground 5 - Lie as evidence of a consciousness of guilt (Applications for extension of time and leave)

[147] By this proposed ground the appellant seeks to challenge the learned trial Judge's instruction to the jury that if they found the appellant told a lie about whether he was present at the Truck Stop, as alleged by the Crown, the lie could be used by the jury as evidence of a consciousness of guilt of the offences charged.

- It means that Murdoch is challenging the trial judge accusing him to be the man on the CCTV film. The jury must believe that he is Murdoch… Remember the judge ordering the jury… <u>Your verdict must be unanimous, nevertheless forgetting to mention that his daughter was:</u>
- <u>In a relationship with a juror.</u>
- If the jury agree that Murdoch has lied; he is the man on the film. Well Murdoch did not lie referring to his claim further down. Proving that Murdoch is the man on the video is another story.
- As alleged by the Crown of course Murdoch is the man …But no proof beyond reasonable doubt.
- Of course, if the appellant is the man on the CCTV film Murdoch is guilty …But it has to be proven

***

[148] It was the appellant's assertion at trial that he was nowhere near Barrow Creek at the time of the events related by Ms Lees. In fact, he was well on his way across the Tanami Desert, en route to Broome.

- Of course, if Murdoch was not at the truck stop, he must have been somewhere else. This has to be proven by both sides.

***

]149] In the course of the trial the Crown led evidence designed to establish that the appellant had been present, with his Toyota Land Cruiser utility, at the Shell Truck Stop in Dalgety Road Alice Springs in the early hours of 15 July 2001. Two employees who were on duty at the Truck Stop at the time were called to give evidence.

- Called to give what evidence; evidence that the man on the CCTV film definitely looks like the man on the CCT film (clapping in the background)

...*The Crown led evidence designed to establish [that] the appellant had been present...The pronoun [that] is an affirmation designed to influence the jury. It would have been to the benefit of the appellant to use the conjunction [if]. It then would read; designed to establish [if] the appellant had been present...at the Shell truck stop.*

- This truly means that the two employees must have also been influenced by the crown (had been present).
- Yes, we know the man and the Cruiser were at the truck-stop –yes both have been present, BUT have they been identified by police? **NO –NO –NO**, both have never been identified...No number plates and no identity card...Is that clear?
- ...Gave evidence that [a] CCTV man and his Cruiser was at the truck stop (*has been present*). **And that was Murdoch of course.** BUT right now, the only real proof and meaning is; the CCTV man seen on the CCTV footage is the CCTV man.
- All those words without a single proof. If you are a clear minded person that's how you would understand it:

The Vanishing of Peter Falconio

- Both the Crown and the two witnesses confirmed that the Land Cruiser and the man seen on the CCTV film is truly the representation of a man and his Land Cruiser and nothing else.
- Sorry no one yet can prove beyond reasonable doubt that the man and the Land Cruiser seen on the CCTV film is/was Murdoch Land Cruiser and his Cruiser.
- First nobody even police or Monsieur Poirot could identify the vehicle (no registration number) no trailer. Only Joanne Lees –the Prosecution –and Monsieur James Hepi and the Judge can now agree and declare that yes, the CCTV man is Murdoch.
- Can't see any Dalmatian dog (the one looking like a cattle dog) with his head out of the window or sitting behind the wheel.
- As far as the man is concerned, he could not be identified, but he paid cash! (Clapping in the back ground).

***

[152] below Mr Head when describing the man's hair thought that it was black.

Was it black or was it not?

- Thirdly the man had to walk to the shop to pay and do small shopping which would indicate that the two employees and Mr Head saw the man (of course they did) This is in no way some real evidence beyond reasonable doubt that the man they saw was [a] killer or Murdoch.
- The man paid cash, impossible to prove that it was Murdoch or someone else or the killer.

***

[150] The witness Mr Head said that, at about 12:30 am, he observed, by means of a monitor at the console, a white Toyota Land Cruiser single cab tray top utility with a green canvas canopy at the diesel pump. He could not see its registration number.

- AH! He could not see the registration number but it was Murdoch (Laughter in the back).

The Vanishing of Peter Falconio

- There are many Land Cruisers in this country especially in the outback and nearly all of them have a green canvas if canvas top they have. I have never seen a pink canvas top!
- But unable to prove the identity of the vehicle "could not see the registration number" It is a good trump card for the Prosecutor, <u>he can say what he likes</u>: Believe what he believes… Don't believe what Murdoch says…Your verdict must be unanimous. Well Monsieur the Prosecutor, it's your word against his, but I shall prove otherwise beyond reasonable doubt.

***

[151]   A man subsequently came in and paid for the fuel and some other items such as iced coffee, water and ice, all of which were paid for in cash.

Finally, some real evidence: The man bought iced coffee –water and ice, and paid cash!

- Well, how do you prove the identity of someone getting fuel and buying few items if that someone paid with cash? If you have the answer, please let me know.
- Remembering what the man bought, you must certainly remember the colour of his hair or what he looks like (I know, it's on the receipt). You, would and should remember if he is 1.75 or 1.98 tall.
- You also must remember other things like: Murdoch is definitely not slim but big, **<u>HUGE</u>** if using Lees' word.
- You should certainly remember some of his missing front teeth unless he never spoke or open his mouth. <u>You wouldn't be telling a lie if I may ask?</u>

***

[152] This witness gave a description of the man as being slightly taller than himself (he being 175 centimetres in height), of slim build, wearing a cap with some sort of white motif and some sort of jacket and jeans. This

The Vanishing of Peter Falconio

man had a dark, messy moustache and his hair was down to his collar. The witness thought that his hair was black. He was wearing sneakers. His age appeared to be in the late thirties or 40.

Yes, this looks like the first description Lees gave police (looks very similar hey!)
- Slightly taller (wow!) and wearing a cap with some sort of white motif (déja vu).
- Anything about missing front teeth? I mean… He went to pay, someone saw him. His size 1.98m, the opposite of slim, his voice if he spoke (deep voice as claimed by Joanne Lee).
- The witness thought his hair was black. Was is black or was it not? Is this going to be like the dog, Kelpie –sheep dog –cattle dog –poodle –rented dog -Dalmatian with black and white patches or with brown or dark patches or may be light silver or cream patches –even a sheep why not, each have four legs and may look similar!...... Do you know what I mean?
- Yes, I understand the witness thoughts –didn't really know –was not sure –may be?
- Could it be Monsieur Malouf? <u>After all Malouf apparently said that it was him on the</u> <u>film which is remarkable…</u>Remember?

But police did eliminate Malouf from their suspect after being scanned by Joanne…Still asking why? Lees with her eyes closed however not blindfolded and after DNA tests were carried out (I still don't know when and how), but knowing it was much too early in the peace for the tests to be conducted…Food for thought! Unless you know the meaning of DNA were carried out [?] or unless you know more than I do.

[153] The cash record for the items purchased showed a time of 0045 hours and a cash total as $136.65.
- Is this true evidence or a joke? Yes, the cash record shows the hour and the total BUT does it show the name –address –phone number

The Vanishing of Peter Falconio

–religion of the man –the name of his wife or girlfriend –if he is a vegetarian – if he smokes, but most importantly the registration number etc.? They really think again that we are all stupid.

- Anybody paying cash cannot be traced but we know the man was driving a Land Cruiser with an unknown number plates and no trailer and…Wearing a cap with a small logo…But it was: MURDOCH because of the tiny logo on the cap that nobody can see.

***

[154] Mr Head identified the man as being the person depicted in the video exhibit P 251 (being the electronic record from the Truck Stop video security system).

- That is a good one. <u>Mr Head identifying the man on the video as being the man on the</u> <u>video</u>…That is exactly what it means. Really a reliable and intelligent witness.
- Mr Head identified the man as being …Be careful, if you need to say it…
- Mr Head has identified the man; which man? Murdoch or the man on the video or Nick the lover or the man of the Japanese car? Nasty trick Mr Head.
- Yes, **Mr Head**, all you are telling us is: that you have identified the man on the video as being the man on the video. Mr Head you deserve a medal.
- One needs to be clear headed when asked questions in a murder case.

***

[155] The witness Deborah Southerden said that she actually authorised the use of the fuel pump when the console first beeped, because Mr Head was temporarily absent from the console, restocking the fridge. She thought that she noted the number of the vehicle at the time, but could not subsequently 62 find any record of it. She had a memory of 333 in the number. (There does not appear to have been any direct Crown evidence

of the registration number of the appellant's Land Cruiser at the time of the Barrow Creek incident, although there is evidence of registration numbers of vehicles owned by him at

other times. None of the latter include a digit combination of 333).

...She thought that she noted the number of the vehicle... Meaning she was definitely sure –certain. To me it means she was not sure. Being not sure is a real fact, like cheese and chalk.

BUT NOW WE ARE ENTERING THE PARANORMAL WORLD, THE UNKNOWN...

- That's another good one: *"There does not appear to have been any direct Crown evidence of the registration number of the appellant's Land Cruiser"* Meaning the registration could not be seen on the film. But, *"although there is evidence...include a digit combination of 333* meaning the unknown previous vehicles owned by Murdoch didn't match the registration number of vehicle seen on the CCTV film. To me that's what it sounds like.
- Which means they could not match the previous registration numbers of Murdoch's past –present –and even future vehicle. Aren't you proud of our Justice system and the ones in charge?
- Beyond reproach for her memory. Definitely beyond reasonable doubt for losing a piece of paper she was not sure she wrote. No wonder she couldn't find it later.
- Just like Vince Millar first sign declaration when two pages went missing, BUT don't worry police drafted two modified new ones, then asking Vince Millar to sign, but he refused because it was not what he said on his first declaration.
- Perhaps **Ms Deborah Southerden** could have had a memory of number "666, The Antichrist or $333 \times 2 = 666$! that's why she got confused hey!
- Furthermore, why would she note the number? Was she suspicious that the man had the intention of leaving without paying or perhaps she knew already that he was a killer and that

he must be Murdoch? Was she taking note of number plates for every car the electronic system can't record? How long after the alleged offence, was she questioned?
- Anything to deceive. I think this is truly going a bit far. Has she been told what to say by the Prosecution –the Judge –the Police or else, like Lees who had someone to teach her what to say and what to answer
- *[156] This witness also identified the content of exhibit P 251 as being related to the incident.*
- Oh yes, and what is that? A big silver gun Clint Eastwood type with the barrel still smoking –the handmade cuffs made with the same tape to the one found three months after the alleged offence including the lip gloss belonging to Joanne Lees? What is exhibit 251?

***

[157] Other evidence was called by the Crown with the object of establishing that the person who is seen in the security video was, in fact, the appellant. The detail of that evidence will be canvassed in relation to other proposed grounds of appeal.
- Ah yes, and what is this other evidence?
- <u>Was in fact, the appellant</u>… So, Murdoch is already the man on the CCTV film –the killer without any proofs…Yes, the Prosecution definitely believes that we are all a bunch of idiots. Perhaps the jurors were a bunch of idiots also…They must have. They should all be facing a mirror at the exception of the one in relationship with Joanna the Judge's daughter hey! (clapping in the background).
- What is the meaning or definition of: To canvass?
- Example: solicit votes from (electors or members) –propose an idea or plan) for discussion.
- Transitive verb. To go through (a district) or go to (persons) in order to solicit orders or political support or to determine opinions

or sentiments canvass voters canvassed the neighborhood to solicit magazine subscriptions. (the Internet)
- Could it be soliciting votes from the jury? Remember the judge's daughter being in a relationship with a juror who sat on Murdoch's trial. Could it be also the need to be advertised? Could it be a proposed idea or plan, a solution acceptable by the jury? Like unanimous verdict?
- It is very specific to the word solicit …What do you think?

***

[158] The appellant elected to give evidence. He said that he left South Australia on Thursday 12 July 2001 in his 75 series Land Cruiser, towing a camper trailer. He had arrived at Port Augusta by about midnight. He said that he eventually arrived in Alice Springs at about 10:30 am on Saturday 14 July 2001. His evidence was to the effect that he first went to the Red Rooster store to purchase some chicken and then took his vehicle to Kittle's car wash and cleaned it with a high-pressure spray.

This should be recorded somewhere, there must have been some witnesses wouldn't you say so? Was this investigated?

Wow interesting, Murdoch's Land Cruiser is the same as mine 75 series the best ever made. I could have been in Alice in 2001 and arrested because I had a Land Cruiser 75 series hey! Gosh I must be lucky!
- Well, interesting story but what's interesting is not what Murdoch bought at the Red Rooster but what he did after.
- Was he at Barrow Creek? Did he manage to be seen at Fitzroy Crossing 1,412km away at 8.00pm on the 15th of July 2001? Yes, he did we know that.

***

[159] The appellant testified that, having gone to Barbecues Galore and Repco to make some purchases, he drove to a BP service station in Alice Springs and refuelled his vehicle. He told the jury that he thereafter drove north about 20 kilometres out of Alice Springs and turned off on the Tanami Track at about 3:30 pm.

The Vanishing of Peter Falconio

Do they sell big guns at Repco? Perhaps Murdoch went there hoping to buy a big gun with the intention to pay cash for it?

- Absolutely correct, the Tanami start about 20km north of Alice then turning left you are on the Tanami.
- At what time did Murdoch refuel at the BP Station, not Shell Station? Of course, no mention of the time. But according to the transcript using the words ...*thereafter drove north* means that if you deduct 20 minutes from 3.30pm and 3.10pm he must have refuelled around 2.50pm [?] Was this also investigated? Someone at BP –Barbecues Galore –and Repco must have few things to remember....
- WOW, he didn't refuel at the Shell truck stop at 0.30am the next day. Ah Ok, I understand why he is the CCTV man! Because what we are debating now is the relationship between The CCTV man and Murdoch. **"BOTH BEING"** the same person...How amazing!
- Refuelling at BP not at Shell is really the icing on the cake hey!
- Claiming Murdoch is the CCTV man who refuelled at the Shell Station when in fact Murdoch claim that he refuelled at BP...Would be funny if this had been checked perhaps no one checked hey...They probably didn't? Assuming of course!
- Now, I definitely believe that the average citizen wouldn't be challenging this.
- But how many people besides reading the headlines or small articles here and there would take time searching for the truth or at least trying to understand including the Defence.

The transcript says The CCTV man or Murdoch stopped at a Shell Stop when in fact Murdoch claimed having refuelled at a BP Service Station. But for the Prosecution Murdoch refuelled at BP, then drove to Shell just to buy Ice coffee –water and Ice and re-fuelling again...AMAZING

Was the BP Station equipped with a CCTV camera?

Has this information been checked? May be not, so what can we do? Even the BP Service Station may not be aware of it. What do you think?

***

[160] He asserted that, at about 8 pm on 14 July, he would have been almost to Yuendumu on the Tanami Track and nowhere near Barrow Creek. He denied that he was the person depicted in the Truck Stop security video. He further testified that, between midnight and 1 am on 15 July, he was somewhere near Granites Mine on the Tanami Track - about 500 kilometres from the Stuart Highway.

- This is what I am going to CALCULATE. <u>This is Crucial.</u>

[161] Against that background the learned trial Judge, inter alia, directed the jury in the following terms:

Here we are, that's where THE BRAIN WASHING STARTS with words related to lied –untruthful –satisfied –denied…you'll see…Happy reading.

Now with respect to the accused and being untruthful about being at the truck stop. If you are satisfied that the accused was untruthful when he denied to you and others that he was at the truck stop, there is additional use that you may make of that fact that the accused has been untruthful. If you are satisfied that the accused has deliberately lied about being at the truck stop, and if you are satisfied that <u>the accused told the lie</u> because he knew that the truth would implicate him in the murder of Peter Falconio<u>, you may use that lie</u> as some evidence of consciousness of guilt on the part of the accused. If you are satisfied that the accused <u>disclosed in this way a consciousness of guilt,</u> it is another piece of circumstantial evidence that on its own cannot prove guilt, but is to be considered in conjunction <u>with the rest of the</u> <u>proven facts.</u> In giving you this direction, I must emphasise some matters.

The Vanishing of Peter Falconio

First, you must be satisfied that the lie was deliberate. Secondly, you must be satisfied that the lie relates to a material issue in the case. You might think there is little doubt that a lie by the accused as to whether he was at the truck stop is material to the case. Thirdly, and importantly, it is only if the accused told the lie because he perceived the truth is inconsistent with his innocence that the telling of the lie may constitute evidence against him. It must be a lie which an innocent person would not tell. You will quickly appreciate that innocent people tell lies for a number of reasons, including panic, or perhaps because they think that even though they are innocent, the truth might wrongly implicate them in the offence. Before you can use the evidence of the lie about the truck stop as evidence of a consciousness of guilt on the part of the accused, you must reject all other possible reasons and be satisfied that the telling of the lie is explicable only on the basis that the accused knew the truth would implicate him in the offences. That is, that the accused was conscious that if he told the truth, the truth would convict him. This direction, ladies and gentlemen, only applies to a lie by the accused, if you find that he lied, about being at the truck stop. If you find the accused has lied to you or anyone else about other matters, those lies about other matters cannot be used as evidence of a consciousness of guilt. Other lies may, however, be used by you, if you see fit, as reflecting adversely upon the accused's credibility as a witness. I stress that you may only use a lie as reflecting adversely upon the accused's credibility if you are satisfied that he deliberately told a lie. Well, are you satisfied that the accused lied about being at the truck-stop. If you are so satisfied, are you satisfied to reject all innocent explanation.

Are you satisfied that the lie is explicable only on the basis that the accused knew the truth would implicate him in the crime that is that he lied because of a consciousness of guilt.
Well, ladies and gentlemen, for example, you must carefully consider whether it is reasonably possible that the accused lied because he was afraid that he would be falsely implicated. On the other hand, the Crown put to you that with the exception of Mr Helpi, right from the outset, before suspect and

before he might have had reason to lie if innocent, the accused displayed a consciousness of guilt by falsely denying that he was at the truck stop."

This small paragraph above [161] starts with the words: with respect to the accused and being untruthful about being at the truck stop" Wow, Murdoch is the CCTV man he lied!

***

[166] Attention was drawn to the fact that the effect of the directions given was to render it plain to the jury that they could not move direct from findings that it was the appellant at the Truck Stop and that he had lied about that situation, to a finding of guilt of murder.
…. directions given was to render it plain to the jury

Of course, Murdoch is the CCTV man! Please give me the favour to count how many times the word LIE and synonyms or any words indicating a LIE has been used in this small chapter, including the Prosecution favourite words if you are satisfied" You should be surprised! …Brain washing full on with one purpose only; to deceive a bench of morons called jurors who I think belong to a club named Jury (you need to be a member I believe) including the "others" and he ones with no brain.

- Could we use this paragraph [161] in relation to the Judge's daughter Joanna being in a relationship with the juror (name unknown yet) who sat on Murdoch's trial knowing that Joanna and Joanne Lees were inseparable friends all along the investigation and the trial and most probably even after the trial. All we would need to do is to change –exchange –or swap the names. We will then have a new movie …So book your seat right now!
- We could also use the same language: If you are satisfied or if you are [so] satisfied that Joanna Martin was in a relationship with a juror who sat on the accused trial…Bla bla bla!

The most fascinating about the CCTV man accused of being Murdoch is that he may be in some distance future the CCTV man could well be lodging a defamation case against Murdoch for stealing his identity… That could be another good movie hey!

- Here we have a guy who drives a Land Cruiser with no trailer, entering a Shell station in Alice Springs at 0.30am on Bastille Day which is the 14th of July in the French calendar in the year of 2001
- Is a total stranger (Perhaps not?) Nothing is known about him and his Cruiser which cannot be identified because the number plates cannot be read by the CCTV camera or not matching the ones on vehicles previously owned by Murdoch (deafening clapping in the back ground).
- **BUT HE IS DEFINITELY MURDOCH**

Never mind about that, because the man without any proofs is Murdoch. It is not a question of, is he? But he is.

- Did police ever check Murdoch's Cruiser?
- Did police ever uploaded the photo of his cruiser on the internet (front – left –right back –and centre?).
- Did they check the bull bar to see if it was chromed?

I bet they didn't, nothing of the kind which would not surprise me. …How can you trust the system?

- Paragraph 161/166 are truly a BIG BAG of words. What a language just to say he's guilty and please don't argue! But don't worry Monsieur "Le Prosecutor" some people can see through you… You will not escape Judgement Time …It will come. So, let's start the autopsy
- Please give me the favour of counting the word LIE and synonyms above [161] and let me know if that was enough.
- Would you believe below is the number of the word LIE and synonyms used in the small chapter (word count 680), represents 7%.
- If that is not promoting a guilty verdict: What is?

- Yes, they are all the key words and synonyms to proclaim Murdoch's guilt without any proofs beyond reasonable doubt. Well done Monsieur the Prosecutor!
- In these two paragraphs the jury is bombarded non-stop with allegations that Murdoch is guilty and lying beyond reasonable doubt. Key Words are included in every sentences. Each word is meant to induce into the jury's mind that Murdoch is guilty. This was the narrative and the agenda.
- For the Prosecution Murdoch is guilty, he must be found guilty.
- Your verdict must be unanimous but where did Murdoch get his fuel, Shell or BP. I am very curious about this.
- No wonder the judge wanted a unanimous verdict.
- Don't forget the judge mislead the jury by ordering a unanimous verdict, hiding the fact that a majority verdict would have been acceptable in Northern Territory.
- That is a miscarriage of justice.

Nothing positive about Murdoch. Yes, I know the Prosecution's job is to prosecute but the Prosecution was doing more than that…… Brain washing full on. Not surprising that Murdoch was found guilty. What a farce! Nothing positive about the Officials also!

***

[162] The learned trial Judge directed the jury that they should bear in mind that the appellant had a specific reason for not wanting to be involved with the police or with an investigation of any sort, because he was running drugs. He said that they also needed to consider whether it was reasonably possible that he lied to his friends and acquaintances in Broome about the matter for that reason. He reminded the jury that they should further consider whether it was reasonably possible that, having earlier told a lie, the reason that he might have subsequently lied was that he did not wish to admit having lied in the first place and had just continued with it.

- Gosh here we are again, LIE –LIE –LIE …… Murdoch is lying!

- But nobody minds Monsieur Helpi a drug runner and dealer, ex-partner who dobbed his partner, who gave cigarette butts to police and who knows what else?
- Murdoch ex-partner in the selling of drugs being a witness. Would you trust him?
- Or the accuser and the alleged victim also drug users/dealers …No, don't mention it please!
- Yes, Murdoch must be lying to his friends and acquaintances. I don't think that he has many …Friends that is!
- Yes, it was reasonably (but not beyond reasonable doubt) possible that, having earlier told a lie, the reason that he might have subsequently lied which means that of course Murdoch has lied and because he has lied, he must of course tell another lie.
- Of course, he will not admit having lied if he did not lie.
- Would you admit a lie if you didn't lie?
- I find this SO PATHETIC and WOEFUL.

***

[163] In the foregoing circumstances the appellant asserts that the directions concerning inferences as to guilt that the jury could draw if they were satisfied that he had lied concerning his presence at the Truck Stop were problematic in circumstances when presence at the truck stop simpliciter could not be shown to be linked forensically with the crime at Barrow Creek.

- Another good one: Yes, Monsieur the Prosecutor, it could not be shown to be linked forensically with the crime because…. Murdoch was not there.
- The vehicle cannot be identified (no number plates) but it is Murdoch's Cruiser
- The witness lost the piece of paper with the correct number plate, all she thought she could remember is 666 …sorry 333…which really does help!
- No camper trailer attached to the vehicle

- Murdoch is not slim but big or huge and tall…With some front tooth missing and he has a deep Australian voice hey!
- Impossible to trace the man because he paid with cash, but to support the case we know the man bough ice coffee –water –and ice. That was a big help indeed because we know now that it is/was Murdoch because <u>he lied</u> and bough ice coffee –water –and ice (laughter and clapping in the background).

***

[164] On the hearing of the appeal, Mr Barker QC intimated that the appellant was content to rely on that submission.

- No comment.

***

[165] Mr Wild QC stressed that the proposed ground of appeal, as formulated, had to be considered in the context that, during his summing up with regard to the evidence of Dr Sutisno and in reference to a series of captions such as "offender image" on documents and like oral references made by her, the learned trial Judge gave the following specific directions: "… *Now obviously it is you who needs to decide in this case who the offender was and if eventually <u>you are satisfied</u> <u>that it is the accused who is shown in this Truck</u> <u>Stop video</u>, then all that would prove that the accused was in Alice Springs at that time in the early hours of 15 July. That becomes a piece of circumstantial evidence, that is, evidence of one circumstance to be considered by you in conjunction with the rest of the evidence. 66 <u>The fact that the accused was in Alice Springs, if that's your finding</u>, eventually, in the early hours of 15 July, of course, by itself and I stress by itself could not prove that the accused was the offender. So please just ignore those sorts of captions if you like because they are there for the working purposes of Dr Sutisno and others. And just bear in mind that what we're talking about here are a series of circumstances which eventually you'll be asked to put together, make findings about, and put together. So, I will direct you further about that later on, but I emphasise the mere fact, if you find it to be a fact eventually, that the accused was in Alice Springs at this time cannot by itself*

prove that he was the person at Barrow Creek. It will become, if that's your view, one of the circumstances.".
<u>*The fact that the accused was in Alice Springs, if that's your findi*</u>

- What is this:*" if that's your finding"?* Of course he was in Alice. Murdoch never denied being in Alice Springs, he told where he was and what he did.
- What kind of rubbish is this?

Being in Alice doesn't mean Murdoch is/was the killer
- Monsieur the Prosecutor Murdoch was in Alice Springs on that day, he said it himself, he never denied the fact, but not at the time you want everybody to believe.
- Please we don't need another big bag of words.

"So please ignored those sorts of captions if you like because they are there for the working purposes of Dr Suttisno and others".
- Just like people who saw Falconio walking the street after his death! No comment! ...<u>But please ignore those sorts of caption!</u>
- Yes, being in Alice on that day and morning is not the proof beyond reasonable doubt that he was at Barrow Creek committing the alleged crime.
- But he lied –he is/was lying.
- BUT the funny thing is the only identified footprints belongs to Joanne Lees.
- And if you are satisfied that she has been lying…. which indicates that her boyfriend Peter Falconio must have been walking on his hand or being totally invisible.
- Are you sure that you are not confusing Murdoch and Chris Malouf or someone else? Who could be that someone else?

[166] Attention was drawn to the fact that the effect of the directions given was to render it plain to the jury that they could not move direct from

findings that it was the appellant at the Truck Stop and that he had lied about that situation, to a finding of guilt of murder.

- Again, *"that he had lied"* and few words and sentences meaning absolutely nothing in proving Murdoch's culpability
- And yes again *"that he had lied about the situation"* But who is lying?

***

[167] Mr Wild QC submitted that the Crown case was presented on the footing that the appellant's presence at the Truck Stop gave him an opportunity, in time and space, to have been at Barrow Creek when the relevant events occurred there.

- Gave him the opportunity in time and space to have been at Barrow Creek…Of course.
- My God what a world we are living in…<u>Frightening</u>!

[168] There is no substance in the proposed ground of appeal on the basis sought to be formulated by the appellant. To the extent that this proposed ground may have an inter-relationship with the proposed Ground. 14, that is an aspect that falls to be dealt with in that setting

- Of course, there is absolutely no substance in the proposed ground of appeal. Don't argue: Murdoch is guilty, you don't need any explanation!
- WE need proofs, tell us where the dead body is –tell us where the big silver gun is – tell us where the gun downgraded to a 22calibre revolver is –the emptied cartridges –the trailer –tell us why so many witnesses saw Peter Falconio after his alleged death by firing squad –tell us where his dog was etc.
- Tell us why a majority verdict was not accepted or even suggested. Tell us why the judge failed to instruct the jury about it?
- Tell us why the Judge daughter was in relationship with a Juror who sat on Murdoch's trial – tell us about what Joanna Martin's

boss said about that relationship which has never been advertised, tell us why...
- Thanks to Robin Bowles
- <u>Tell us more about the Judge</u>...That's for another chapter.
- We need proofs beyond reasonable doubt. This is definitely not proper

***

[169] No proper basis has been shown either for an extension of time or the granting of leave in respect of this proposed ground. The directions given by the learned trial Judge were beyond reproach and the ground sought to be promoted is plainly untenable. The relevant applications must therefore be dismissed"

- Oh yes, the directions given by the judge were beyond reproach and hiding the fact about a majority verdict is definitely beyond reproach in a murder case where there is no Dead Body and where the only witness is the biggest unchallenged liar.
- And where the accuser is the only witness who cannot confirm that she has actually see her boyfriend being shot,
- ...and whom when under stress when questioned by police said "**I HAD NOTHING TO DO WITH HIS DISAPPEARANCE AND SO IS NICK**" (actual police video of the interview mentioned further on).
- And the fact that nothing belonging to him was identified at the alleged crime scene including his dog –car and trailer and the rest and not even a single cigarette butt.
- And also, the fact that the only footprints belong to the accuser our only witness.
- Yes, the direction given by the judge were beyond reproach but far from beyond reasonable doubt.
- Do what I say don't do what I do!

The Vanishing of Peter Falconio

Gosh! That was definitely a scam. Unfortunately, Murdoch was found guilty. It was meant to confuse –deceive –and to induce it into the Jury's mind.

Forget what Murdoch says, he was in Alice therefore he is definitely: [1] the CCTV man [2] the killer beyond reasonable doubt.

Ok, let's see what the Prosecution is going to say about the following:
- The prosecution claims that Murdoch is the CCTV man…
- Therefore, the alleged killer, because being in Alice on the 14th he had the opportunity to commit the alleged crime, the reason why he must have been following them,
- Then stopping them –then shooting Falconio right in the head –then abducting his girlfriend.
- Then he had to bury the dead Body (not forgetting to wrap the head in Lees 'jacket which apparently was stolen from the Kombi) somewhere not knowing if he had a shovel –if he had time –then giving up the search for Lees –then driving back to Alice with the purpose to be seen on the CCTV film.
- All this in half hour…Even less…Wow!
- Then of course heading towards Broome at 160kmh after taking drugs.
- After having changed his appearance for the second time,
- Because the first time was to commit the alleged offence hey!

So according to the transcript of the appeal he is therefore the man on the CCTV film.

Well, let's see if departing Alice springs at say 1.00am on the 15th of July he will reach Fitzroy Crossing 1,412km away on time at 8.00pm without running out of fuel, on time to be seen by four witnesses refuelling his car in Fitzroy Crossing WA. But before closing this chapter:

Where was the Defence, what was the Defence doing?

The Vanishing of Peter Falconio

69 - Who Will?

Who will win, who will fail reaching Fitzroy Crossing around 8.00pm on time for the deadline on the 15th of July 2001: The CCTV man or Murdoch?

The CCTV man is in great hurry…Murdoch is not!
- **The CCTV man** will depart Alice at 1.00am on the 15th first with two full tanks. Then again same calculation with only one tank.
- **MURDOCH** will depart Alice at 3.10pm on the 14th
- This should prove beyond reasonable doubt if the man on the CCTV film is Murdoch.
- It could also somehow give an indication that perhaps the CCTV man is a total stranger to the case because we don't know [?]

For the CCTV man and Murdoch to drive to Fitzroy Crossing. It involves: Time –distances –fuel and knowing that each will be towing the campervan trailer.
- The prosecution said the man on the CCTV film is Murdoch.
- So, the CCTV man also hid the trailer somewhere, but where? **I also forgot all along to ask if the Land Cruiser seen on the CCTV film was fitted with a tow bar.**
- I like to remind you that Joanne Lees didn't see a trailer when pushed into the back of the Cruiser and no mention of it when she escaped.
- I just had a thought: Perhaps the trailer was parked at the BP Service Station?

***

Below is the link to the calculator regarding the distances relevant to the locations of interest from Alice Springs –Tilmouth Well –Yuendumu –the Granite –Rabbit Flat –Billiluna –Halls Creek –Fitzroy Crossing. It calculates the distance –driving time –and flying time (Not needed) for your perusal. It's all there on the net.

The Vanishing of Peter Falconio

The only driving time from Rabbit Flat to Fitzroy Crossing available on the internet is given by https://www.distancesfrom.com

Distancesfrom.com was first indexed by Google more than ten years ago."

We have:

- Alice to The Granite **551km** –driving time 12h36 minutes is given by link below (the Granite airport NT 0872 to Alice Springs NT 0870 driving time via Tanami Road/state route **5**
- Alice Springs to Tilmouth Well =**190km** –driving time =2h35 (155 minutes)
- Timouth Well to Yuendumu =**145km** –driving time =1h40 (100 minutes)
- Yuendumu to The Granite = **254km** –driving time 8h30 (510 minutes)
- Yuendumu to Rabbit Flat =**311km** –driving time =9h20 (560 minutes)–
- Yuendumu to Billiluna **591km** (Yuendumu Rabbit Flat 311 km + Rabbit Flat Billiluna 280km = 591km) –driving time =12h40 (760 minutes)

***

Note:

We do not need to calculate from Yuendumu to Rabbit Flat and from Rabbit Flat to Billiluna because that was 22 years ago. We don't know the hours of opening and closing at Rabbit Flat. Rabbit Flat closed permanently in 2010.We are in 2024. No data is available from the internet. We will therefore assume that both men will not refuel at Rabbit flat.

*Note: I started to investigate the case late 2017. We are now in 2024, that is the reason why I said [2024]

***

- Billiluna to Halls Creek 196km –driving time five hours (300 minutes)

- Halls Creek to Fitzroy Crossing 290km –driving time three hours (180minutes)

***

Also, HEMA maps show opening hours for fuel at certain locations.
- Tilmouth Well: 7.00am – 9.00pm seven days –phone 08 8956 877
- Yuendumu: Mon-Fri 6.00am -8.00pm –Sat 7.00am-8.00pm –Sun closed –phone 08 8956 4006
- Rabbit Flat closed since 2010 No data for opening and closing hours in 2001, you couldn't get fuel outside the hours –Closed Saturday and Sunday (I think?)
- Billiluna Mon-Fri 8.00am -11.00am and 2.00pm - 4.00pm – Sat 8.00am to 10.30am Sun closed but you can get fuel outside the hours for a fee of $10/$20
- Halls Creeks open 24/7

***

The trip took place 23 years ago where road conditions… Well, that was long time ago and during that time things do change drastically. To get on the bus in 1967 the minimum cost was five cents. My rent was $ 8.00, a lobster Mornay in a club was $2.50. Time has changed so did the roads and tracks. Murdoch did the trip 23 years ago…Imagine the road 23 years ago hey! I myself did it in 2017 and 2018 with no camper…It was very rough!

An average speed of 74kmh or 48kmh would require both men to drive faster than 74kmh and 48kmh if they can, because of roads or tracks condition and the UNPREDICTABLE!

Please understand this; it's not because they are going to drive at 150km/h that they are going to get there early. NO, the reason for both to drive faster is to compensate for the loss of speed/time in hard and dangerous conditions.

The CCTV man and Murdoch will lose time: They may have to stop for a pee –they may have a puncture with the car or trailer – they will have to refuel more than once –they may expect the unexpected or Murphy's Law etc. As a result, they need to take all this into account if one can. In reality Murdoch has more time. He does not have 19 hours but 28 hours **and 50 minutes** (from 3.10 pm to midnight + 12 to noon + to 8.00pm = 28h and 50 minutes to the deadline 8.00pm on the 15th of July)

This tells you of a possibility that the CCTV man won't make it.

For example, assume that you are driving for two hours a distance of 200km on a three- lane highway.

The first hour you travel at a speed of 100km/h meaning you have driven/covered a physical distance of 100km during the first hour.

For the next 100km the traffic is so bad that your speed drops to 50 meaning to cover the last 100km will take you two hours (100km ÷50km = two hours…basic maths)

In total to travel the 200km has taken you three hours meaning you average speed is

66.66 km or 200km ÷ 3 = 66.6 km/h, that is a big difference, just in three hours you lost 33 percent.

- Hey, looking at my example and the number 66.6 and if you have a good imagination, well it should remind you of Mrs Deborah Southernden and the registration number (333) she wrote on a piece of paper which disappeared and me suggesting number (666) the antichrist. Sorry but I find this amusing! I thought I mention it.

You understand now what could happen on a track like the Tanami over a distance of 1,412km. That is why sometimes they will need to drive at speed of XYZ [?]…Think about it and towing a trailer wow! A non- stop drive, no time for a pee and no sleep.

Having said that let's do the maths.

*Note:

Average speed: When the distance is known as well as well as the driving time, to calculate the average speed is basic maths: you divide the distance by the time in minutes which gives you the distance you have travelled for one minute. Then you multiply the result by 60 which gives

The Vanishing of Peter Falconio

you the average because there are 60 minutes in one hour (I know that you know, just helping the Prosecution).

Fuel: You'll know what to do.

The Vanishing of Peter Falconio

70 - The Obvious Fact – The Race Is On

Just like to remind you my favourite quote by Sir Arthur Conan Doyle: "There is nothing more deceptive than an obvious fact"

From page one (1) up until now, you must admit that it is/was a big bag of words giving no solution regarding certain issues. It's all about claims made by Joanne Lees and her story.

Most of the things claimed by the Prosecution and Lees are not making any sense. Nothing can be proven. One thousand books could be written and still having no answers. It will be better writing a fiction book. All I can say is: I don't know –we don't know –nobody knows.

BUT

I always believed that there has to be more than one obvious fact. Facts that could be proven correct beyond reasonable doubt. Yes, facts are present, the only thing is; what are they and where are they? In fact, the case has not one but many obvious facts.

They are:
- The fact that yes, Lees or Falconio did drove slowly from Alice to Ti Tree, but Lees avoiding telling the truth and that is: Having stopped at Aileron for 1 hour.
- The fact that Lees was watching the sunset alone at Ti Tree at 6.10pm alone
- The unknown time of her arrival at Barrow Creek –the time the offender stopped them –the time of the killing.

- The time of the offender's departure from the allege crime scene. We know the arrival time in Alice (0.30am) if offender there is [?], but knowing that there is no dead body creates a huge headache. Perhaps the CCTV man could even be a total stranger [?]
  - But because Lees and the Prosecution the Judge and Monsieur Hepi claimed the CCTV man is Murdoch. This has to be challenged and proven wrong.
- The fact that Joanne Lees never hid for five hours

The Vanishing of Peter Falconio

- The fact that she was found nice and warm and clean after spending so much time on a very cold winter night.
- The fact that in a pitch-black environment she was able to distinguish the different shades of green of the canopy on the inside.
- All the other facts like no communication between the cab and the tray – her claim she escaped from the back of the Cruiser not noticing a trailer – changing the description of the offender many times and his dog and denying she made a lot of money from her prefabricated story etc.

One question remains: Is/was the CCTV man seen on the film Murdoch?
- That is what I am going to calculate and prove.

Speaking like the Prosecution, if you are satisfied that in the absence of a Dead Body the vanishing of Peter Falconio could be an indication of foul play? Well, keep on reading.

- It is certainly very possible without any doubt that Peter Falconio may have been killed, **but not by Bradley John Murdoch**.
- The First calculation will be about the **CCTV man** departing Alice at 1.00am on the 15th of July 2001 with his car fitted with two tanks then with one tank.

- Then it will be Murdoch's turn leaving Alice at 3.10pm on the 14th of July 2001 with his car fitted with two tanks then with one tank.

So "mes amis" the race is on between the CCTV man and Murdoch.

Who will reach Fitzroy Crossing successfully – who will fail? Please place your bets now.

The Vanishing of Peter Falconio

71 - Second Choice of Route....

Again, one more thing before the calculation which I nearly forgot:
This is also logical and very important

The CCTV man and Murdoch have the choice of two routes to reach Fitzroy Crossing and it needs to be mentioned. One cannot hide the fact that there is/was a possible second route.

According to the transcript Murdoch claimed he drove on the Tanami from Alice Springs to Fitzroy Crossing, but the reason why he didn't take the alternative route is simply because:

- If Murdoch is the man on the CCTV film,
- It would be stupid of him to; kill Falconio at barrow Creek, then
- Having committed the alleged crime, it would stupid to go back to Alice Springs to refuel at the Shell Station [um!] at 0.30am on the 15th because he could go north on the Stuart Highway where he could refuel without having to go back to Alice.
- It would be stupid driving back to Barrow Creek where he would be seen again around 4.30am on the 15th (1.00am + three and a half hours = 4.30am) which is interesting because it is around the time where Chris Malouf makes his apparition at Barrow Creek or as per his claim having camped at the alleged crime scene. But nonetheless got arrested by police on the early hours of the morning. Food for thought.

Alternative route:

Aiming for **Fitzroy Crossing** via **the Buchanan Hwy –the Buntine Hwy** and the **Duncan Road** and finally **Fitzroy Crossing**. His itinerary would be:

- **Alice Springs to Aileron** 134km + **Aileron to Ti Tree** 62km + **Ti Tree to Barrow Creek** 199km + 10km =315km arriving at 4.30 am (driving at and around 100kmh when possible).
- Then he would drive to **Tennant Creek** 210km (2hours) - then **Tennant** Creek to **Dunmarra** 355km (3h45minutes) –then onto **the Buchanan Hwy** –from **Dunmarra** to **Top Springs** 235km (no

time available) –then onto the **Buntine Hwy** from **Top Springs** to **Wave Hill** (Kalkarindji) 175km 2hours and 30minutes –then still on the **Buntine Hwy** from **Wave Hill** to **Nicholson** 235km (no time available)–then onto the **Duncan Road** from **Nicholson** to **Halls Creek** 175km (no time available) –then from **Halls Creek** to **Fitzroy Crossing** 290km **(3 hours)…..** <u>**A total of 1990km**</u> an extra of nearly 600km

Now why would he drive back to Barrow Creek which would be far more risky having to drive through town again at 4.30am in the morning hours after committing a crime and where police could already be there wondering about the alleged killing.

Do you really think the CCTV man or Murdoch could be that stupid?
 Fuel should be available:
- On the Stuart Highway I would say 24/7 all hours from Ti Tree – Tennant Creek –up to Dunmarra
- Then Dunmmara to Top Springs –Wave Hill –Nicholson all dirt all the way to Halls Creek (no time for fuel availability).
- Halls creek 24/7 –Fitzroy Crossing (no time available, however he could refuel at 8.00pm, we know that) etc.

The CCTV man and Murdoch wouldn't be that stupid, they would not drive an extra 600km. Murdoch drove on the Tanami because he knows the way and I will prove it soon.

Now and most probably you may not be aware of it, but besides the transcript of the appeal, (not the full transcript of the trial) not excluding the media, there are a lot of files, papers and

books from different authors like: Defence lawyer Algie –Judge Dean Mildren –Keith Noble [FFDA] -Richard Shears (bloodstain) –Roger Maynard (where's Peter)– –Sue Williams (And then the darkness)–Robin Bowles (Dead Centre) –Anne Barker (North 's Australia correspondent for ABC) etc.

- Even from **Darryl Gragan** mentioned in Keith Noble book (which is quite astonishing knowing **FFDA** assumed that Darryl Cragan may be the driver of the Japanese car [?]).

From Judge Dean Mildren p.68 from Algie's summing up:

"Evidence...that it was not him at the truck stop...Mr Jamieson said he saw him at Fitzroy Crossing between 6.00 and 9.00pm the following evening [the 15th] (That is WA Time) ...So he left ...at 1.00am from the truck stop...that would leave somewhere between ...17- 20 hours to complete the trip. If you get in at 6.00pm you've only got 17 hours to do it and if you get in at 9.00pm you've got 20 hours to do it"

"...Murdoch doesn't think you could do it in that time and there is some support for that from other witnesses, not the least of which is Mr Cragan...[his] evidence of that topic was that on that trip, the Tanami track took in excess of 24 hours to do. And...if that's right then it makes it unlikely...that is if it was Brad Murdoch at the truck stop"

Commenting on the above:

Fitzroy Crossing is 1,412km from Alice Springs (Hema map)

- 17 hours = 1,020 minutes
- The average spend would be:1,412 ÷ 1,020 =1.38km/minute x 60 = **83.50kmh**
- To sustain and average speed which includes night and day driving you will need to drive at times over the average speed, more like 110/130kmh… That is a non-stop drive. Non-stop means non-stop, not even time for a pee and pulling a trailer.

- Pulling a campervan trailer is not feasible doesn't matter what anybody says.

Sergeant Hall gave evidence that it was possible to do these times. Algie argues that Murdoch's situation is completely different to Hall's situation driving a police car, for the following reasons:
- He is towing a camper trailer,

- He would be worried that he'd break something or damage his vehicle
- He's got pounds of cannabis on board to conceal and protect. What if he rolled the car, broke an axle or worse or police came along.]

Well with all respect to Sergeant Hall who is full of [BS] as we say in this country. This is not a trip behind the wheel of a V8 patrol car driving on a three or four lane highway having not even time to stop refuelling. A non-stop drive means non-stop drive…Are we clear on that?

The Vanishing of Peter Falconio

72 - R v Murdoch –The Falconio Case –A Study in Identification by Dean Mildren (Retired Judge)

Everything in italic is from **Judge Mildren's** book. It has to be told and read. It is a must. It is about the Route from Alice Springs to Fitzroy Crossing and time (page 204 to 215).

In the following section, the Chief Justice deals with the circumstantial evidence which goes to the question of whether Murdoch was the driver of the vehicle which cause Falconio to pull over, (top of page 204 section 4.14)

Page 207:

"Lady and gentlemen, a moment ago I mentioned that Mr Helpi believed that the accused had dobbed him into the police. I remind you in this context of the evidence of Mr Kotz, the conversation took place a couple of weeks after the registration of the re-built vehicle…According to Mr Kotz the accused was pretty distraught and said that he has done something wrong and that he had dobbed in his Kiwi mate. Mr Kotz understood this meant dobbing into the police and he knew who the accused was talking about

- You understand here, that Mr Kotz is saying that Murdoch had told him that [HE] Murdoch had dobbed his kiwi mate.
- Well, that is not how I understand it because Mr Kotz said that he knew who the accused was talking about…Of course not mentioning a name…Anything to deceive the jury…
- Well, did Mr Kotz truly knew who the accused was?
- NO, Mr Kotz did not know who Murdoch meant about that someone who had dobbed in his Kiwi mate.
- That was not Murdoch confession. It was Murdoch saying that a person (someone) had dobbed in his Kiwi mate and nothing else.

"In cross examination, it was put to Mr Kotz that rather than the accused saying he had dobbed his mate in the accused said my Kiwi mate's been "dobbed in". Mr Kotz denied that suggestion".

- Mr Kotz denies it of course!
- This means that Mr Kotz likes to pretend that, what he said was right but denies that Murdoch didn't say it.

The Vanishing of Peter Falconio

Murdoch denied that he said that [HE] had dobbed in his Kiwi mate. He described what he said in the following terms:

"I said to his mother who was sitting at the dining table –Ben Kotz sitting in the lounge room watching a video –and I said to Trudy: Someone –Helpi , had been busted in Broome. Obviously, someone had dobbed him in and I was probably going to get the blame for it."

Then further down still page 207:

"Obviously, when a person is charged with a crime, if it is unlikely that the person could have been at the scene of the crime at the time the crime was committed, that fact would be a piece of circumstantial evidence pointing in the direction of innocence.

"However, if the person charged could have been at the alleged of a crime and could have committed it, while that opportunity alone cannot prove guilt, it is a piece of circumstantial evidence to be taken into account with all the other proven facts in deciding whether the evidence, in its entirely, prove guilt.

- Sorry but using the words "could have" is definitely not a certainty but rather indicative of doubt.

*Note: I just like to remind the reader that, in this case only the DNA trump card contributed to the guilty verdict and obviously that Murdoch is/was the CCTV man. I will speak about "The DNA trump card" further on.

- When nothing belonging to Murdoch was found by the investigators/experts like footprints –campervan trailer –blood –dog -cigarette butts or anything else or anything associated with an alleged crime like gun –emptied cartridges –wheel marks from his car or campervan trailer –trace of a body being dragged –dog hair in the Kombi or on Lees –blood in the Cruiser – blood in the Kombi,
- And when equally nothing belonging to Falconio was found,

The only thing one can deduce is;

The Vanishing of Peter Falconio

- Nothing indicates that Murdoch was at the alleged crime scene,
- Murdoch is obviously a person who has been charged wrongly with a crime.
- And, if it is unlikely that the person (Murdoch) could have been at the scene of the alleged crime at the time <u>when no crime was committed,</u>
- That would be a piece of circumstantial evidence pointing in the direction …
- …Of innocence.
- The same should apply to Peter Falconio; no Dead Body –no footprints –no mark of a body been dragged –no blood etc. (<u>Just a little reminder hey!</u>)

Repeat from above: (Obviously, when a person is charged with a crime, if it is unlikely that the person could have been at the scene of the crime at the time the crime was committed, that fact would be a piece of circumstantial evidence pointing in the direction of innocence).

- Here…<u>If it is unlikely</u>" means what it means. That is the way the Prosecution operates, always creating doubt related to innocence. Murdoch cannot be innocent Murdoch must be guilty.
- We don't know, nobody knows, but it doesn't matter…Murdoch is guilty because he was wrongly identified at the truck stop, his Cruiser was similar…BUT,
- Police has been incapable to identify both: The Cruiser and the man BUT,
- Joanne Lees and the Prosecution and Monsieur Mr Helpi did. Hepi is a criminal, a drug dealer, a liar and most probably an informer, a man used as a witness (a real good choice if you ask me!).
- It is so ludicrous as to be amusing. Police couldn't identify the man and the Land Cruiser but it is/was Murdoch and his Toyota.
- Joanne Lees proved it, a woman who knows nothing about cars especially Land Cruiser!

- Knowing that all investigators/experts have found no evidence of Murdoch being at the alleged crime scene (no footprints etc.) as well as no evidence relating to a crime being committed (gun – emptied cartridges –Blood etc.),
- **It can be said that the word unlikely is a true synonym of "No it's not him"** just to be clear about it.
- What does this tell you about Joanne Lees being the only witness?
- What does this tell you about the Prosecution being our second reliable witness?

However, and miraculously the only evidence found three months after the alleged crime was some black tape –and a tube of lip gloss apparently belonging to Joanne Lees etc. It has been said that the evidence was hard to find (laughter and clapping in the back ground)

What is the meaning of all this, what can be deducted?

Still further p.207

"As you know the accused denied that he was anywhere near Barrow Creek at the time of the events. He was well on his way across the Tanami desert. in addition, the accused said he could not have made it from Barrow Creek to Fitzroy Crossing in the available time."

- Yes, we know that Murdoch was far away from the alleged crime scene.
- At the time of the alleged crime (8.45pm on the 14th) <u>he was near Yuendumu 297km</u> from the alleged crime scene.
- And again that, between midnight and 1.00am on the 15th Murdoch was near the Granites (Gold mine).
- But no mention of calculation done by the Prosecution –Mr Kotz – Mr Helpi –Mr Stanes – Mr –Ms McPhail –Mr Johnston – Mr Cragan –Mr Hall – Joanne Lees and anybody believing in Murdoch's guilt without any proofs.

Here is a typical example; In Judge Dean Mildren R v Murdoch: The Falconio Case (page 210 to 215 section 4.18). Section one can read:

(Section 4.18 is: Having discussed the possible speeds needed to travel the total distance in 28.5 hours, the next part of the exercise is to discuss factors which may have affected Murdoch's ability to have completed the journey in 28.5 hours or less, such as road conditions etc.)

"HIS HONOUR: Ladies and gentlemen, if you accept the exercise that I have just undertaken on the basis that the accused left Alice Springs at 1.00am on 15th July, he could have arrived at Fitzroy Crossing between 6.00 and 9.00pm Western Australia time, being 7.30 -10.30 Northern Territory time, if he had averaged 51.5 and just over 62kmh on the dirt and 100kmh on the bitumen.

If you accept that situation, what do you make of the accused's evidence that if he left Alice at 1.00am, he could not get to Fitzroy Crossing by 8.00pm. In that context you are entitled to bear in mind not only the evidence of Mr Stanes and Mr Hall, but the accused's own evidence that not being in a hurry he was travelling across the Tanami on his trip at between 50 and 65kmh possibly up to 70kmh"

Firstly, [THEY] always emphasize their facts that Murdoch left Alice at 1.00am on the 15th.

I need to say it again: MURDOCH LEFT ALICE AT 3.10PM ON THE 14TH

- **Secondly** *"Ladies and gentlemen, if you accept the exercise that I have just undertaken <u>on the basis that the accused left Alice Springs at 1.00am</u> on 15th July, <u>he could have</u> <u>arrived at Fitzroy....</u>"*
  <u>NO</u>, I do not accept the exercise.
- **Thirdly**: *"<u>If you accept that situation, what do you make of the accused's evidence that if he left Alice at 1.00am, he could not get to Fitzroy Crossing by 8.00pm.</u>*
- <u>**NO,**</u> I do not accept the exercise. It's always the same **[THEY]** want Murdoch to leave at 1.00am on the 15th

For the simple reason that the accused did not leave Alice Springs at 1.00am on the 15th July but at 3.10pm on the 14th July and that is ten hours earlier. The Prosecution never made an attempt to do any calculation according to Murdoch's claim that he left Alice at 3.10pm…He was guilty from day one. It was a cover up, why we will never know.

***

Again…**THIS MUST BE UNDERSTOOD; <u>MURDOCH LEFT ALICE AT 3.10 PM</u> ON THE 14TH OF JULY NOT AT 1.00AM ON THE 15TH**…Please.

***

It is definitely meant to deceive the Jury. Why?

The accused's evidence is: [HE] left Alice Springs at 3.10pm (3.30pm at the turn off to the Tanami) on the 14th of July 2001. Please read the transcript.

- <u>Not 1.00am on the 15th of July 2001</u>
- Meaning **[they]** are doing the exercise and the calculation based ONLY on the LIE that Murdoch is the CCTV man. <u>That is not the case</u>. This is not difficult to understand. It is not Murdoch who left Alice at 1.00am But the CCTV man. Please refer to the transcript. <u>Can this be clear for once and for all?</u>

The CCTV man is the CCTV man, Murdoch is Murdoch. The CCTV man and Murdoch are not one person, BUT TWO (2). We have TWO PRIME SUSPECTS.

- As you can see, no mention of Murdoch's claim (transcript),
- No mention that at the time of the alleged crime Murdoch was near Yuendumu
- No mention that between midnight and 1.00am on the 15th of July Murdoch was near the Granites
- No calculations done on that basis, totally ignoring Murdoch's claims that he departed Alice Springs at 3.10pm on the 14th of July 2001
- It is what I call being dishonest–deceiving –unscrupulous and misleading –and very corrupt.

The Vanishing of Peter Falconio

***

Now, speaking of average speed, it is important to understand the concept.

When travelling or planning to travel, the internet is a wonderful source of knowledge and information and so are the Hema maps.

Example: This is for people who do not have a personal computer or mobile phone (not everybody is up to the technology) and also for the people who seemed to know better like Mr Stanes, Mr Hall and Mr Helpi a con man and drug dealer.

I lived in Canberra for some times. The internet says; Canberra to Melbourne 663km –driving time six hours 54 minutes (414 minutes) on the M1 a three lane Highway.

- Your average speed is: $663 \div 414 = 1.6$km/minute $\times 60 = 96$kmh. That is correct and that is very accurate indeed. It fit within the speed limits and few speed cameras.

Once in a hurry, I drove the distance in five hours and 45 minutes (375minutes).

My average speed was then $663 \div 375 = 1.768$ km/minute $\times 60 = 106.08$kmh

Well let me tell you that, I was very lucky not having been caught for speeding, because each time when overtaking a car driving at 110kmh, my speed had to be 130/140kmh the car was the Lexus 2004 ES 300 very fast car. (For your perusal the world Lexus is interpreted as: Luxury Exports to the US)

I did the same again but from Canberra to Sydney 300km in three hours and 20 minutes (200 minutes)

- That was an average of: $300 \div 200 = 1.5$km/minute $\times 60 = 90$kmh
- Doing it in three hours and 20 minutes, when you reach the M 5 you really have to slow down as it gets really busy. Then the Harbour Bridge Tunnel, then Military Road one of the busiest Road in Sydney all the way to Manly. It is a challenge. Up until you

reach the M5 my speed varied between 120 and 140 and once more very lucky not to have been be booked for speeding.
- I needed to increase my speed from Canberra until reaching the M5 because when I got to the M 5 my speed dropped by half even more at time

By not driving over the speed limit, I would not have done it in three hours and 20 minutes.

This was a little exercise because I will be challenging **Mr Stanes** and **Mr Hall** shortly, not forgetting **Mr Helpi**

The Vanishing of Peter Falconio

73 - Monsieur Hall is Being Challenged

From Mildren's book: "…Asked to give an estimate of a reasonable time from Alice to the Great Northern Highway turn-off to Halls Creek Mr Hall said it could be done in 10-12 hours given the road conditions at that time. He added, what you might think is a very relevant and common-sense observation, that it also depends on the driver and the vehicle and whether the driver is experienced."

Monsieur Hall you don't have to tell us that, Murdoch is an experience driver; we know and so am I.

- Alice to turn-off to Halls Creek the distance is 1,084 km

The average speed for 10hours (600 minutes) non-stop driving is:
- 1,084km ÷ 600 = 1.80km/ minute x 60 =**108.40 km/h**

The average speed for 12 hours (720 minutes) non-stop driving is:
- 1,084 ÷ 720 =1.50km/minute x 60 = **90.33 km/h**

Do you believe this? When knowing that in bad conditions you will need to drop the speed by sometimes more than half when pulling a camper van…don't be ridiculous. Who is this Mr Hall? (The road is absolutely a nightmare from the turn off to Wolfe Creek crater to Halls Creek. I like to remind everybody that it is WOLFE Creek Crater and WOLF for the movie)

"…On Mr Hall estimation the trip from Alice to Broome would take just over 16 hours and a half to just 18 and a half hours plus stopping time"

- Alice to Broome 1,702km

The average speed for 16h and 30 minutes (990 minutes) non-stop drive is:
- 1,702 ÷ 990 = 1,702km/h x 60 = **104km/h** <u>**Non-Stop drive MEANS without stopping**</u>

The average speed for 18 and a half hours (1110 minutes) non-stop driving is:
- 1,702 ÷ 1110 = 1.53km/minute x 60 = **92km/h** <u>**Non-Stop drive without stopping**</u>

The Vanishing of Peter Falconio

Do you know the meaning of non-stop? For an average speed of 104kmh or 92kmh one cannot drive slower than 104 or 92 meaning for an average speed of 104kmh I believe you will need to push the car up to 140/150kmh and for 92 up to 120/130kmh and that is without pulling a campervan trailer.

Do you truly believe this Mr Hall? Who's paying you for saying such a thing? Are we here talking about the great Australian driver Toby Price already mentioned? Think about it, then call me back!

"…The accused told you he arrived at Fitzroy Crossing at about 8.00pm. Mister Jamieson said the accused arrived just on dark between 6.00 and 9.00pm. Mr Jamieson was unable to be any more precise. For the purposes of calculations, if you use the period 6.00pm to 9.00pm, that is Western Australian time. In Northern Territory time it means arrival at Fitzroy Crossing between 7.30pm and 10.30pm.

If a vehicle left Alice Springs at about 1.00am on 15th of July (here we are again, the CCTV man is not Murdoch. It is the CCTV man departing at 1.00am. Murdoch is departing Alice at 3.10pm on the 14th of July (10 hours earlier for God's sake). What is needed for everybody to understand the message? This is a disgrace Mr Hall)

….and arrived at Fitzroy Crossing between 7.30pm and 10.30pm Northern Territory time, that means a total of travelling time of between 18 and a half and 21 and a half hours.

How does that travelling time compare with other estimates? In particular, you will recall that Mr Hall estimated that travelling time between 80 and 90km/h, a vehicle could get from Alice to Fitzroy via the Tanami in 16 hours. Mr Hall said that estimate was based on someone experienced in a four- wheel drive and who would know the off-road conditions."

Yes, the average speed for 16 hours (960 minutes) is: 1412km ÷ 960 = 1.47km per minute x 60 = 88.25kmh (say 90) without stopping. That is minimum speed, one cannot drive under…

If you add 33% for loss of speed or (90 x 33% = 30 then 90km +30km = 120kmh But, all along the way you would lose more perhaps 50%

For 50% loss of speed (90 x 0.50 = 45 then 90km + 45km = 135kmh).

The Vanishing of Peter Falconio

Good luck pulling a campervan trailer. It would require speed of 120/130kmh could be more

- The problem is constant. [They] are trying their best making sure Murdoch will be found guilty by manipulating every single thing. Calculation done believing that the CCTV man and Murdoch are the same person departing Alice at 1.00am
- **AGAIN**, I like to remind everybody that Murdoch left Alice at 3.10pm the day before, on the 14th of July (Bastille Day) for God sake!

Now Mr Hall has a change of heart. Firstly, he said that it could be done in 10-12 hours to the junction at Halls Creek but now having modified the whole sentence it is 16 hours to Fitzroy Crossing.... (Dead silence in the background!).

- So, for ten hours the average speed is **108.4kmh** –for 12hours the average speed is **90.33kmh** as calculated before.

After the change of heart, it is now 16 hours (960 minutes) from Alice to Broome (1702km),

The average speed is: 1702 ÷ 960 =1.77km/minute x 60 = 1.84km/minute x 60 =106.37kmh

- This is truly laughable, still doing the calculation not assuming but telling the world that the CCTV man is Murdoch or vice versa who left Alice Springs at 1.00am on the 15th of July 2001 when nobody even police could identify the man on the CCTV film including his Cruiser....At the exception of Joanne Lees and the Prosecution and Monsieur Hepi the con man and drug dealer of course and now Monsieur Halls as well, not forgetting the Judge who believes the CCTV Man is Murdoch

Not a chance in the world for them to think otherwise. Has anyone read the transcript?

Then it says that he arrived just on dark between 6.00 and 9.00pm (WA time). What a farce.

The Vanishing of Peter Falconio

That is why I keep on saying that from day one Murdoch was guilty, even before the trial. Sometimes I even wonder why a trial took place and I am not the only one saying it (you will find out further on). If it had not been for the patch of blood on the T-shirt the case would have collapsed (that will be for a chapter on DNA). It is like watching Asterix and Obelix the movie.

"For the sake of this exercise, may I suggest that you put aside the truck stop video, just put aside the truck stop video for the moment, and ask the following questions; First, are you satisfied that leaving Barrow Creek at about 8.30pm, in a hurry to distance himself from the scene, are you satisfied the accused could have covered the 292km to Alice at about 110km/h? If so, that distance would take about just over two and half hours. That would put the accused in Alice Springs at about 11.45 pm...

Again, what's all this rubbish?

No, I am not satisfied. Joanne Lees according to my calculation if you believe her story, may have arrived at 8.30pm or around that time. To be certain we need proofs and some extra sensorial perception. Monsieur Halls says the killer left the alleged crime scene at 8.30pm. I calculated 9.00pm, but I am not worry about 30minutes difference, simply because we don't know and will never know at what time Lees got there. It's all science fiction.

The point here is, that finally someone here is ADMITTING that the alleged killer had to leave the alleged crime scene around that time (8.30/9.00pm), because "The Officials" want everybody to believe that Murdoch is/was the killer therefore he has to be the CCTV man and no one else. To do that, the alleged killer had to depart the crime scene using my calculation.

This is what [they] want you to believe. For the CCTV man being Murdoch of course he had to leave the alleged crime scene around that time (9.00pm) otherwise the five hours spent in the bush claimed by Joanne Lees wouldn't stand a chance to be accepted by all those idiots...You with me?

According to Monsieur Halls the alleged killer arrived earlier than 0.30am giving time to undo the trailer then get fuel at Shell, then he must

reconnect the trailer but the alleged killer is seen departing the Shell station at 1.00am, meaning:
- He had to reconnect the trailer after departing the Shell truck-stop.
- From 1.00am on the 14th the killer has 19 hours to reach Fitzroy Crossing by 8.00pm (1.00am to noon = 11hours + eight hours = 19 hours).

So, if that is the case admitting the killer left the alleged crime scene at 1.00am is because THEY want everybody especially the Jury to believe <u>that Murdoch is the CCTV man</u> for reason unknown to us, but it's all according to Lees –the Prosecution and Monsieur James Hepi and now we have Mr Halls barging in.

- It also still raises the question: At what time did Lees arrive at Barrow Creek with Falconio back in the picture, and did she spend five hours hiding in the bush? I know she didn't.
- That is in total contradiction that the alleged killer left just before midnight, because if Lees was waiting for the killer to leave after watching him searching for her with his rented dog which is total fiction, <u>would mean the killer would arrive at the Shell truck stop around 3.00/3.30 am on the 15th of July, which is not the case.</u>
- Suggesting the offender left the alleged crime scene just before midnight so she could claim the crime had taken place as well as her abduction. It was to embellish the veracity of her prefabricated story.
- As you can see Mr Halls said that Murdoch the killer left the alleged crime scene at 8.30pm on the 14th hey! He had to otherwise Lees 'story wouldn't be accepted.
Then the sentence: *"if it is your view, pick up the camper and drop it off, while getting then of course you have the accused –could the accused have been at about 0.30.045am?"*

This is a lot of rubbish again coming from Monsieur Hall's mouth. Mr Halls can't even form proper sentences. One needs to read at least three times each sentence to understand the meaning if you can. It is an absolute handmade disaster.

You cannot have the killer dropping the trailer before killing Falconio – then refuelling at the Shell stop –then reconnecting the trailer –then driving north till the turn off to the Tanami…It makes no sense.

The CCTV man is the CCTV man –Murdoch is Murdoch, that's all there is to it

THEY love using the formula: "If you are satisfied or I am satisfied".

It points to one direction; you must agree with them or yes you must believe what they say…Well, myself, I am definitely not satisfied.

"…. still leaving aside the truck stop video, are you satisfied given the distances, road conditions, accused's vehicle and driving experience and all the other factors, that if the accused was in a hurry to distance himself from the Northern Territory, he could have refuelled, left Alice somewhere around 1.00am and made it to Broome 28 and a half hours later. Could he have done that if he was towing the camper trailer? If you are not satisfied of those matters, the Crown would have failed to prove that the accused had the opportunity to commit the crime. If on the other hand, you are satisfied of these matters, then even if you put aside the truck stop video, the Crown would have proved that the accused had the opportunity to commit the crimes.

Well, I am not satisfied. The transcript says that the CCTV man departed the Shell stop at 1.00am, so why saying around 1.00am. The CCTV man does not have 28 hours and 50 minutes to drive from Alice to Fitzroy Crossing; he has 19 hours. What is relevant is the 19 hours he has to reach Fitzroy Crossing, nothing else. Will it be success or failure?

Murdoch did not leave Alice Springs at 1.00am on the 15th of July, the CCTV man did. Murdoch left Alice at 3.10pm the day before. You have waisted your time and you've got it all wrong!

For once and for all, is this clearly understood?

The Vanishing of Peter Falconio

74 - As I Said Previously....

As I said previously, we have to understand the case involves two [2] prime suspects: The CCTV man and Murdoch.

- **The CCTV man** leaving Alice at 1.00am on the 15th must reach Fitzroy Crossing by 8.00pm on the same day. He has therefore only 19 hours (1,140 minutes)
- **Murdoch** leaving Alice at 3.10pm on the 14th the day before must reach Fitzroy Crossing by 8.00pm the day after. He has therefore 28 hours and 50 minutes (1,730 minutes).

Alice Springs being 1,412 km away, the CCTV man minimum speed needs to be:

- 1412km ÷ 1,140 minutes = 1.23km per minute x 60 = 74.5km, say **74.31kmh**, say **75kmh** that is the minimum speed required. He cannot drive slower.
- **For Murdoch** the minimum speed needs to be:
- 1,412km ÷ 1,730 minutes = 0.82km per minute x 60 = 48.97 say **49kmh** which is also the minimum speed required. Again, he cannot drive slower

So, let us now do the calculation. You can see already who's going to be the winner!

The Vanishing of Peter Falconio

75 - First Proof Beyond Reasonable Doubt

The CCTV man first with two fuel tanks.

It's all about fuel and time; will the CCTV man have enough fuel and time to drive from Alice Springs, leaving the Shell truck-stop at 1.00am on the 15th of July and be seen refuelling at Fitzroy Crossing on the same evening day at 8.00pm?

In Judge Dean Mildren's book page 220 relating to section 4.20 of the previous page one can read:

- *"Ladies and gentlemen, first there is $124.50 worth of diesel. Well, you know the accused was driving a diesel vehicle. Toyotas are very common. The Crown put to you that the accused would be filling right up because he had been out of his way up to Barrow Creek and back.*

"On the other hand, it is not unusual, of course for people in the centre of Australia to be buying large quantities of diesel fuel."

What a joke!

Well dear reader, firstly for the Prosecution to address the jury saying that the accused would be filling right up because he had been out of his way up to Barrow Creek and back is very biased –unproven (nobody knows) – conniving and it makes no sense; why? Simply because of course the accused would be filling right up, he has to drive 1,412km and because there is no fuel available at night, if someone doesn't understand that; God help us!

- Also, he didn't drive to Barrow Creek following them to kill Falconio, then back to Alice (600km extra) to then departing Alice towards Fitzroy…NO –NO –NO, that's not what happen.

Up until now nobody can prove that the CCTV man is Murdoch and vice versa. That is what I am trying to do now, please be patient.

* Note; we will have an issue with Rabbit Flat Roadhouse because the roadhouse closed permanently in 2010, therefore we don't know the opening and closing time in 2001. As a result, the CCTV man and Murdoch may have to refuel before or after Rabbit Flat. They may lose time if they have to wait for the fuel depot to re-open. However, it makes no difference.

*Note; The capacity of two thanks being 170 litre (90 + 80). It is the equivalent to what people would call long range. Also, all calculations are done without counting stopping time for refuelling or even having a pee.

***

The CCTV man departing Alice at 1.00am with 170 litres

Driving to Tilmouth Well, then to Yuendumu –The Granites –bypassing Rabbit Flat roadhouse –Billiluna Station –Halls Creek –Fitzroy Crossing Fitzroy –and eventually Broome not calculated because there is no need for it.

***

ALICE TO TILMOUTH WELL 190km departing 1.00 am (on the 15th) with170 litres

Alice to Tilmouth Well 190km –driving time 2h35 (155 minutes)

Average speed = 190 ÷ 155 = 1.22 km/minute x 60 = **74kmh**

Fuel usage = 1.90 x 14 = **27 litres**

Left over fuel on arrival = 170 – 27 = **143 litres**

Arrival time =1.00am + 2h35 = **3.35 am** (15th) **TILMOUTH CLOSED** reopen 7.00am

---

TILMOUTH WELL TO YUENDUMU departing 3.35am (15th) with 143 litres

Tilmouth Well to Yuendumu 145km driving time 1h40 (100 minutes)

Average speed = 145 ÷ 100 =1.45km/minute x 60 = **87kmh**

Fuel usage = 1.45 x 14 = **20 litres**

Left over fuel on arrival = 143 – 20 = **123 litres**

The Vanishing of Peter Falconio

Arrival time = 3.35am +1h40 = **5.15 am** (15th) **YUENDUMU CLOSED** reopen 7.00am

He may or may not refuel because he has enough fuel to get to the Granites (254km) then onto Rabbit Flat another (57km) then to Billiluna (280km) = 591km away. We don't know if Rabbit Flat is open or closed having no data. That was 22 years ago!

The drive will require 5.91 x 14 = 82.75 litres (say 82). Having 123 litres. He has enough fuel to reach Billiluna.

He has the choice of refuelling at Yuendumu but he had to wait until 7.00am (Sat) or by-passing Rabbit Flat not getting fuel. He will choose not to refuel because of the waiting time and of course because he has enough fuel and he is in great hurry!

Now he has to drive from Yuendumu to Billiluna bypassing Rabbit Flat for fuel a distance of 591 km with two fuel tanks and 123 litres left in his tanks.

YUENDUMU TO BILLILUNA departing 5.15 am (15th) with 123litres

Yuendumu to Billiluna 591km –driving time 12h40 (760 minutes)
Average speed = 591 ÷ 760 = 0.77km/minute x 60 = **47km** (46.65)

Fuel usage = 5.91 x 14 = 82.75 litres **(say 82)**

Left over fuel on arrival = 123 - 82 = **41 litres**

Arrival time = 5.15am + 12h40 = **5.55pm** (15th) **BILLILUNA OPEN** if you pay the $10/20 fees

***

He needs to refuel at Billiluna because he has to drive another 486 km to Fitzroy Crossing but he needs (4.86 x 14 = 68 litres) when he has only 41 litres left. It is outside the hour ((Sat 8.30 am to 10.30 am) but he will get fuel by paying the fee charged for refuelling outside normal hours but, I don't think for one minute he would be stupid to make a fuss about it. Also knowing that in the outback, 5.55pm is not too late knocking on the door asking for fuel.

BUT WE HAVE ONE ISSUE (time).

To reach Fitzroy Crossing from Billiluna to be seen at 8.00pm (15th) in Fitzroy, The CCTV man after refuelling at Billiluna has now from 5.55pm to 8.00pm on the (15th) 2hours 05 minutes (125 minutes) to complete the drive a distance of: Billiluna to Halls Creek 196km + Halls Creek to Fitzroy Crossing 290km = 486km.

That is an average speed of 486 ÷ 125 = 3.88 x 60 =232.80 km/h pulling a trailer which was re-attached where and when: We don't know.

***

We don't need to do the calculation Billiluna to Halls Creek then from Halls Creek to Fitzroy Crossing a distance of 486km knowing he hasn't got enough time.

***

I doubt that the CCTV man will arrive on time unless he is driving Blue Bird. (The Bluebird-Proteus CN7 is a gas turbine-powered vehicle that was driven by Donald Campbell and achieved the world land speed record on Lake Eyre in Australia on 17 July 1964. The vehicle set the FIA world record for the flying mile at 403.1 mph (648.7 km/h…The internet).

THE CCTV MAN FAILED TO ARRIVE ON TIME at Fitzroy Crossing to be seen at 8.00pm on the 15th of July 2001……Not because of lack of fuel but because of the lack of time.

ALSO, I like to point out that the CCTV man may have had the option to stop at Balgo off the Tanami but has indicated on Hema's map (Sat –Sun Closed- card access only), but it wouldn't be to his benefit regarding the distance because Balgo is 33km off the Tanami an extra 66km because he has to get back to the Tanami. As far as time is concerned it will not make any difference: NOT ENOUGH TIME.

***

The Vanishing of Peter Falconio

I like to point out also that Yuendumu is 311km to Rabbit Flat. Assuming that he stopped at Rabbit Flat, the time of arrival should be calculated as if it was open. I have calculated that the CCTV man did not stop.

Here I will calculate the CCTV man stopping at Rabbit Flat using the same average speed of 47km/h for the total distance from Yuendumu to Billiluna. According to the internet, it takes 12h and 40 minutes to drive the 591km (page 344).

If it takes six hours and 30 minutes from Yuendumu to Rabbit Flat [311km] it will take six hours and ten minutes to drive from Rabbit Flat to Billiluna [280km] (12h 40 minutes – six hours 30 minutes = six hours and ten minutes

He departed Yuendumu at 5.15am on the (15th)

YUENDUMU TO RABBIT FLAT departing 5.15am (15th) with 123 litres

Yuendumu to Rabbit Flat **311km** – <u>driving time 6h30</u> (390 minutes)

Using average speed calculated for Yuendumu to Billiluna of 47kmh, we have; driving time 6h30 (390 minutes)

Average speed = 47km

Fuel usage = 3.11 x 14 = 43.54 say **44 litres**

Fuel left over on arrival = 123 - 44 = **79 litres**

Arrival time = 5.15 am + 6h30 = **11.45 am** (15th) **Opening /Closing UNKNOWN**

THEN

RABBIT FLAT TO BILLILUNA departing 11.45am (15th) with 79 litres

The Vanishing of Peter Falconio

(Using same average speed of 47kmh) the time is six hours and ten minutes.
Rabbit Flat to Billiluna 280km driving time six hours and ten minutes (12hours 40 minutes – six hours and 30 minutes = six hours and ten minutes = 370 minutes)

Average speed =   47km

Fuel usage = 2.80 x 14 = 39.2 **(say 40)**

Left over fuel on arrival = 79 – 40 = **39 litres**

Arrival time = 11.45am + six hours and ten minutes = **5.55pm** (15th)
BILLILUNA OPEN if you pay the $10/20 fees.

We have the same issue as before, irrelevant of Rabbit Flat being open or close. With two tanks of fuel, the CCTV man has enough fuel to reach Billiluna even if he doesn't stop at Rabbit Flat. It makes no difference whatsoever.

To reach Fitzroy Crossing from Billiluna to be seen at 8.00pm (15th), The CCTV man after refuelling at Billiluna has now from 5.55pm to 8.00pm on the (15th) or 2hours 05 minutes (125 minutes) to complete the drive a distance of: Billiluna to Halls Creek 196km + Halls Creek to Fitzroy Crossing 290km = 486km. That is an average speed of 486 ÷ 125 = 3.88 x 60 =232.80 km/h pulling a trailer which was re-attached where and when: We don't know.

You know the rest…

We can safely conclude that the CCTV man is not Murdoch because he failed to reach Fitzroy Crossing on time for the deadline in both calculations. Are you satisfied with that?

Please Monsieur the Prosecutor buy a calculator and a new crystal ball!

Departing Alice Springs at 1.00am on the 15th of July 2001 the CCTV man accused of being Murdoch the alleged killer of Peter Falconio, is a fabricated fact and a big farce and so was the miraculous DNA results that needs to be challenged. One cannot carry out DNA tests on the 17th of July 2001 and then sending the tests 28 months later on the 24th October 2003 to be analysed by a forensic laboratory without raising suspicion…Do you agree? The DNA will be debated further on. You will also find out who first gave blood for the first DNA test..But you know already hey.

As far as the calculation, it shows and we may conclude: the CCTV man is not Murdoch. The question remains: Was he involved in the disappearance of Peter Falconio. Is a member of the Falconio –Lees – Nick –Hepi –Malouf team or else?

Now please, ask yourself the question: Who is the owner of the Land Cruiser which has never been be identified?

The purpose here, was not to find the alleged killer but to clear the innocent, because truly I don't care about Falconio and Joanne Lees and their partners in crime but my heart bleeds thinking of an innocent man accused of an alleged crime without any solid proofs beyond reasonable doubt. The man has already been in jail for over 20 years.

It is a total disgrace, a miscarriage of justice by excellence. They should be all recalled to face the music. We need a Royal Commission Inquiry. The case needs to be re-open.

What a vicious world we live in! Please have a little prayer for the innocent.

Below is from the Internet just to support my cause and my work. How rough is the Tanami track?

"The Tanami Road is just shocking – the corrugations can get six to seven inches high and it sounds like you're driving an express train. You're down to just 20 to 30 kmh because the road is so savage. Beware loose surface and dust corrugations."

Tanami Road is one of Australia's great Outback Adventure trackshttps://www.dangerousroads.org › Australia › 1711-tanami.

*Note The owner of Rabbit Flat was renowned for being bad tempered, you got fuel there during normal hours but not outside the hours.

Armed to the teeth, he would shoot anyone getting close to his front door if the intention was to get fuel or else after hour. You had no chance getting fuel after hour. His property was like Fort Knox. The legend has it that, it was because of GOLD. It is alleged that some parts of Lasseter's Lost

The Vanishing of Peter Falconio

Gold Reef could be on the property …Um? I wonder if true? Could be possible…. Food for thought!

Below is also from the internet two examples copied from a forum about the owner of Rabbit Flat and the Tanami.

"I have worked out along the Tanami….run trucks out along it too and therefore I have a fairly low opinion of its state. It's a truck/trailer killer. Miles of endless corrugations and truth be known IMHO ordinary scenery. As for camping and places of interest? nah can't think of one. Rabbit Flat Roadhouse is closed now and the bloke who ran it was a mean old ornery cantankerous bastard anyway. By all means tick it off the bucket list of trips to do between Broome and Alice Springs (perhaps check out Wolf Creek at the WA end) but fair dinkum Yuendumu and Tilmouth Wells ain't really that high up on the 'must see' list".

"Tyre pressures lowered is essential on the corrugations of the Tanami <20psi cold makes the ride waaay better. I reckon the Gibb corrugations are a breeze compared to the Tanami. Also, 'tis better to travel light if possible...light 'n' lean means less things to rattle"

The Vanishing of Peter Falconio

76 - Second Proof Beyond Reasonable Doubt

The CCTV man with one fuel tank

We must continue the calculation to prove my point and to clear Bradley John Murdoch

The CCTV man leaving Alice at 1.00am on the 15th of July 2001 with only one tank or 90 litres.

We can see that with two tanks departing Alice Springs 1.00am (15th) heading to Fitzroy Crossing to be seen at 8.00pm on the 15th of July 2001 THE CCTV man FAILED.

ALICE SPRINGS TO TILMOUTH WELL 190km –departing 1.00am (15th) with 90 litres

Alice to Tilmouth Well 190km –driving time 2h35 (155 minutes)

Average speed = 190 ÷ 155 = 1.22 km/minute x 60 = **74kmh**

Fuel usage = 1.90 x 14 = **27 litres**

Left over fuel on arrival = 90 – 27 = **63 litres**

Arrival time =1.00am + 2h35 = **3.35 am** (15th) **TILMOUTH CLOSED** open 7.00am

---

TILMOUTH WELL TO YUENDUMU departing 3.35am (15th) with 63 litres

Tilmouth Well to Yuendumu 145km driving time 1h40 (100 minutes)

Average speed = 145 ÷ 100 =1.45km/minute x 60 = **87kmh**

Fuel usage = 1.45 x 14 =**20 litres**

Left over fuel on arrival = 63 – 20 = **43 litres**

Arrival time =3.35am +1h40 = **5.15 am** (15th) **YUENDUMU CLOSED** open 7.00am

The Vanishing of Peter Falconio

Again, like before the CCTV man has to drive from Yuendumu to the Granites then to Billiluna bypassing Rabbit Flat (where he wouldn't get fuel because outside the hour) for fuel a distance of 591 km He needs 82 litres but has only 43 litres therefore he needs to refuel at Yuendumu when it re-opens at 7.00am (loss time 7.00am – 5.15 am = 1h45 minutes after refuelling he will have again 90 litres

The CCTV man must refuel at Yuendumu at 7.00am

YUENDUMU TO BILLILUNA departing 7.00am (15th) with 90 litres after refuelling.

Yuendumu to Billiluna 591km –driving time 12h40 (760 minutes) departing time 7.00am (15th)

Average speed = 591 ÷ 760 = 0.77 x 60 = **46.65kmh**

Fuel usage = 5.91 x 14 = **82litres**

Left over fuel on arrival = 90 - 82 = **eight litres**…He just makes it!

Arrival time = 7.00am + 12h40 = **7.40pm** (15th) **BILLILUNA OPEN** if you pay the $10/20 fees (remember he had to wait 1 hour and 45 minutes at Yuendumu therefore the arrival time is different)

Same issue the CCTV man has only from 7.40pm to 8.00pm or 20 minutes…. Not enough time to reach Fitzroy Crossing. He FAILED departing at 1.00an on 15th July 2001

77 - THIRD PROOF BEYOND REASONABLE DOUBT

Murdoch's turn

Murdoch leaving Alice at 3.10pm (14th) with two fuel tanks (170 litres)

In chapter [159] of the transcript next page, Murdoch claimed that he turned left 20 km north of Alice Springs around 3.30pm on the 14th. Then with the time of departure we can do the calculation for the whole trip.

Alice Springs to Tilmouth Well 190 km takes 2h35 (155 minutes)

Average speed 190 ÷ 155 = 1.22 km per minute x 60 = 74 km

To drive 20km from Alice to the turn off should take approximately 20 ÷ 1.22 = 16.39 minutes, say 20 minutes

I have an assumed a figure of 20 minutes for Murdoch to drive to the turn off (claiming that he was at the turn off around 3.30pm)

- **The departing time should be 3.10pm** (3.30pm – 20minutes) =**3.10pm**, this we knew already. It is just a reminder. We don't know yet if Murdoch is the killer that is why we're doing the calculation.
- **He has no reasons to be in a hurry** or taking drugs. He is totally relaxed, not stressed but ignorant of the plan (didn't say conspiracy) created by Joanne Lees –Peter Falconio –and partners in crime, including the Prosecution who believes anything Lees says/said.
- Simply Murdoch is totally oblivious about what has taken place at the alleged crime scene that is if something has taken place. He is going to be hit by a ton of bricks in a few months so to speak.

We are now going to calculate the option with Murdoch being himself, not the CCTV man nor the alleged killer departing Alice Springs on the 14th at 3.10pm, after attending some small business like washing his car as claimed in the Court of Criminal Appeal chapter 159 and 160 of the transcript (below) and after refuelling at BP, not SHELL.

***

The Vanishing of Peter Falconio

[159] The appellant testified that, having gone to Barbecues Galore and Repco to make some purchases, he drove to a BP service station in Alice Springs and refuelled his vehicle. He told the jury that he thereafter drove north about 63 20 kilometres out of Alice Springs and turned off on the Tanami Track at about 3:30 pm.

***

[160] He asserted that, at about 8 pm on 14 July, he would have been almost to Yuendumu on the Tanami Track and nowhere near Barrow Creek. He denied that he was the person depicted in the Truck Stop security video. He further testified that, between midnight and 1 am on 15 July, he was somewhere near Granite Mine on the Tanami Track - about 500 kilometres from the Stuart Highway.

***

REMEMBER MURDOCH IS NOT DEPARTING ALICE AT 1.00AM ON THE 15TH, BUT 3.10PM ON THE 14TH (10 hours earlier)

ALICE TO TILMOUTH WELL 190km departing 3.10pm (14th July) with 170 litres

Alice to Tilmouth Well 190km driving time 2h35 (155minutes) departing 3.10pm (14th of July) 170 litres

Average speed = 190 ÷ 155 = 1.22 km/minute x 60 = **74kmh**

Fuel usage = 1.90 x 14 = **27 litres**

Left over fuel on arrival = 170 – 27 = **143 litres**

Arrival time = 3.10pm + 2h35 = **5.45pm** (14th of July) **TILMOUTH OPEN** closing 9.00pm

---

TILMOUTH WELL TO YUENDUMU 145km departing 5.45pm (14th July) with 143 litres

The Vanishing of Peter Falconio

Tilmouth Well 145km driving time to Yuendumu 1h40 (100 minutes)

Average speed = 145 ÷ 100 =1.45km/minutes x 60 = **87kmh**

Fuel usage = 1.45 x 14 =**20 litres**

Left over fuel on arrival = 143 – 20 =**123 litres**

Arrival time =5.45 pm + 1h40 = **7.25 pm** (14th July) **YUENDUMU OPEN** closing 9.00pm. Murdoch has two options which are: Refuelling at Yuendumu which is still open or at Billiluna. He chose not refuel at Yuendumu

---

Well –well –well this is not the story of the three holes in the ground, but close enough!

- In relation to chapter [160] above and Murdoch's claim, **WELL…. IT FITS LIKE A GLOVE**. (*He asserted that, at about 8 pm on 14 July, he would have been almost to Yuendumu).*

Well, he was at Yuendumu at 7.25pm…Pretty close! Food for thought! Murdoch told the truth. He cannot be the CCTV man nor the killer but we still don't know until the whole exercise is done.

YUENDUMU TO BILLILUNA departing 7.25pm (14th of July) Not having refuelled has still 123 litres left in his tanks.
Yuendumu to Billiluna 591km –driving time 12h40 (760 minutes)

Average speed = 591 ÷ 760 = 0.77 x 60 = **47.kmh** (46.65)

Fuel usage = 5.91 x 14 = **82litres** (82.74)

Left over fuel on arrival = 123 - 82 = **41 litres**

Arrival time = 7.25pm + 12h40 = **7.05am** (15^{tof} July) **BILLILUNA CLOSED** has to wait till 8.00am to open (no fees) **Lost time 55 minutes** but gained 1 hour sleep if needed.

The Vanishing of Peter Falconio

Murdoch refuelling at 8.00am (15th of July) **170 litres**

Now we must go back to Murdoch's claim (transcript)
- Murdoch claimed that around midnight and 1.00am on the 15th he was not far from The Granites. The Granite goldmine is **57km** before Rabbit Flat Roadhouse or **254km** from Yuendumu. So, let's go back for the time being at Yuendumu and calculate if he was close to the Granites between midnight and 1.00am on the 15th of July.
- Murdoch <u>not refuelling at Yuendumu</u> has to drive to the Granites **254km** with 123litres of fuel left in his tank.
- Then driving from the Granites to Rabbit Flat (**57km**) then to Billiluna (280km).
- That is a total of 254km +57km +280km =**591km**
- The fuel needed to drive 591km is 5.91 x 14 = **82 litres** (he has enough fuel to reach Billiluna. On arrival he still will have 123 – 82 = **41 litres**, but he will need to refuel at Billiluna obviously).

Knowing that;
- **The Granites is 254km from Yuendumu**. The average speed from Yuendumu to Billiluna being **47km/h** or 0.77km per minute.
- Departing Yuendumu at **7.25 pm** (14th of July) to be at the Granites between midnight on the 14th of July and 1.00am on the 15th of July requires three simple operations.
- **Firstly**, to calculate how long he needs to drive from Yuendumu departing at 7.25pm on the 14th <u>until the clock says midnight, then when the clock says 0.30am, then when the clock says 1.00am</u>

At midnight, he has driven: 7.25pm to 0.00 = 4hours 35 minutes = 275 minutes

At 0.30am, he has driven four hours 35 +30 minutes = five hours five minutes = 305 minutes

The Vanishing of Peter Falconio

At 1.00am he has driven five hours five minutes + 30 minutes = 335 minutes

---

Yuendumu is 254km from the Granite Gold Mine
The average speed to Blliluna is 0.77 km per minute, so we will have…

At midnight he has driven at 0.77km per minute = **275 x 0.77 = 211.75km**
Murdoch is **254km – 211.75 = 42.25km before the Granites**

At 0.30 am on the 15th he has driven at 0.77km per minute = **305 x 0.77 = 234.85km**

Murdoch is **254km – 238.85 = 19.15km before the Granite**

At 1.00am on the 15th he has driven at 0.77km per minute = **335 x 0.77 = 257.95km**

Murdoch is **257.95 – 254 = 3.95km after the Granites**

I will repeat:

At midnight Murdoch is 42.25 km before the Granites

At 0.30am on the 15th Murdoch is 19.15 before the Granites

At 1.00am on the 15th Murdoch is 3.95 after the Granites

TO PUT IT SIMPLY BULL'S EYE-BINGO
Murdoch could not have done better even if he wanted to. To me this is NEW EVIDENCE or perhaps I should call it OTHER EVIDENCE.

The Vanishing of Peter Falconio

MURDOCH IS/WAS TELLING THE TRUTH, so, is Murdoch the CCTV man?

Murdoch's claim that at the time of the alleged crime he was near Yuendumu and that between midnight and 1.00am on the 15th of July he was near the Granites is nothing but the truth. That is specifically what Murdoch claimed according to the transcript of the appeal, but it fell on deaf ears because everybody claimed that Murdoch was the CCTV man. They voluntary did all calculations with Murdoch departing Alice at 1.00am on the 15th. This has never been challenged, why? Food for thought? It is a disgrace.

It is/was definitely a miscarriage of Justice. Murdoch has never been assumed innocent until proven otherwise.

Now I am asking:

- Is Murdoch the CCTV man, is Murdoch the alleged killer of Peter Falconio?
- Please Joanne Lees, did you witness Murdoch the bad boy killing your boyfriend with a big silver gun?
- Many people are waiting for your answer dear, (Tears of joy in the background).
- YES, this is definitely a proof beyond reasonable doubt.
- Nobody ever took the time to do the calculation because the Officials truly wanted Murdoch to be guilty like in the Lindy Chamberlain case and they also believed that we are all stupid.

So, if Murdoch was not at the alleged crime scene at the time of alleged killing at 8.45pm on the 14th of July 2001 but 551km from Alice Springs please explain how he could manage to allegedly kill Peter Falconio?

As it is no Murdoch, who is the alleged killer". It is/was not a crime, it is/was AN ALLEGED CRIME.......

Good on you Sherlock Holmes! (1859 - 1930) good on you Monsieur Poirot!

***

The Vanishing of Peter Falconio

We know from the calculation page 385 the arrival time at Billiluna is 7.05am on the 15th but Murdoch has to wait until 8.00am to refuel (loosing 8.00am – 7.05 am = 55 minutes) –then to Halls Creek 196km then to Fitzroy Crossing 290km = 486km

- We know from the above his arrival time Yuendumu was **7.25pm** (14th)
- We know his arrival time at Billiluna was **7.05am** then departing at 8.00am
- Murdoch has from **8.00am** (15th) to **8.00pm** (15th) to be seen refuelling at Fitzroy Crossing. He has = **12 hours** to reach destination meaning Fitzroy Crossing.

Do you think he will make? Shall we put money on?

BILLILUNA TO HALLS CREEK 196km departing 8.00am (15th of July) 170 litres
Billiluna to Halls Creek 196km driving time five hours (300minutes)

Average speed $196 \div 300 = 0.65 \times 60 = 39.2$ **say 39km**

Fuel usage $1.96 \times 14 = 27.44$ say **27 litres**

Left over fuel on arrival $170 - 27 =$ **143 litres**

Arrival time 8.00am + five hours = **1.00pm** (15th of July) **Halls Creek open 24/7**

HALLS CREEK TO FITZROY CROSSING 290km departing 1.00pm (15th of July) with 143 litres (sealed road)
Halls Creek to Fitzroy 290km driving time three hours (180minutes) departing 1.00pm (15th of July)

Average speed $290 \div 180 = 1.61 \times 60 =$ **96.66kmh**

Fuel usage $2.90 \times 14 =$ **41litres**

The Vanishing of Peter Falconio

Left over fuel on arrival 143 - 41 = **102 litres**

Arrival time 1.00pm + three hours = **4.00pm** (15th of July)

SUCCESS MURDOCH REACHING DESTINATION FOUR HOURS EARLIER WITH NO ISSUES.

Murdoch arriving at Fitzroy Crossing at 4.00pm. That is four hours earlier on the 15th. This must indicate that he could have stopped somewhere to rest for a duration of at least 4hours unaware about his future to be.

It is difficult to comprehend what Murdoch must have felt during the trial, it is beyond imagination.

Nobody can imagine what Bradley John Murdoch must be feeling now after 20 years already spent in prison.

Again, Murdoch is/was not the CCTV man nor the killer! What do you think Gentlemen of the Jury?

Would you say Murdoch is guilty on all charges? Who is/was the CCTV man?

The Vanishing of Peter Falconio

78 - Fourth Proof Beyond Reasonable Doubt

Murdoch with only one fuel tank

According to Judge **Dean Mildren**, The Final Address by the Prosecutor page 125 one can read;

"**MR WILD**: *Now, your Honour, I've got one other matter I can deal with today, just quickly. The amount of diesel that was purchased by the man in the truck stop. You've got Exhibit p270 which is the receipt from the truck stop. It's in your book there. The man at the truck stop purchased diesel fuel, I think purchased 117.56 L, which is more than fits in most of cars, I suspect. So, it's somebody who's got an enlarged tank of some kind. Not surprising for a four-wheel drive, I accept that. But, nevertheless it's one of the factors you might bear in mind."*

"This is a man at the truck stop, if it is Mr Murdock, who has to travel 1,400km, which he can do, he's got that range with his long- range fuel tank and his petrol. So, he's filling up. The reason he's filling up you might think he's spent 600km worth of his diesel up to Barrow Creek and back, and he's up at BP in Alice Springs at 2.00pm, and he's driven the track up to Barrow Creek and thereabouts, and done a few little twists and turns, and back down to Alice Springs, he's got 600 km empty fuel he has to fill up."

"So, he fills up……and up to the road a bit and Jack no doubts out and has a walk."

"And you will see in the video –and my learned friend relies on this too –is that the man who deposits his purchases after them, put them in the right –hand side, back driver's side of the canvas, flicks it up, in it goes, no mesh in there of course. That's what my learned friend relies upon as well, because there was a mesh, therefore it couldn't be done. The Crown says there was no mesh in that vehicle and that's why it could be done, and that's Mr Murdoch's vehicle."

Who is my learned friend?

- What a lot rubbish from above.
- **Firstly,** because in the outback people keep their fuel tank full especially when planning a long trip.

- **Secondly,** he wants the jury to believe that the Killer of course being Murdoch has been using more fuel because he had to follow them from Alice to Barrow Creek to kill Falconio, then back again to Alice where he arrives at 0.30am in the morning filling up at Shell truck-stop then on his way to Fitzroy Creek driving at high speed on the Tanami …Sure we are a bunch of idiots!
- But further on, the transcript says that Murdoch refuelled at BP at 2.00pm (oh yes, I have forgotten about that 2.00pm<u>), but no mention of the Shell truck- stop at all.</u> So, did Murdoch stop at the Shell truck-stop? We know the CCTV man did, but Murdoch…YES –NO –NO –YES?
- Also, up until the CCTV man hit the news, did anybody including police checked Murdoch's Cruiser? I am referring here about the mesh/cage blocking the back of the Cruiser where…Joanne Lees claimed she escaped from the back. Truly voluntary distraction from the Prosecution our second witness as I call it.

The spoken and written words coming from that lawyer/ prosecutor are atrocious, very poor quality, bad and very unpleasant. One needs to read each sentence at least three to four times before grasping the meaning, especially if English is your second language. That is of course if you understand the meaning. Bad story telling. Not surprising that the jury may have been influenced and deceived, all the jury had to remember was; if you are satisfied the defendant has lied, he must be…Guilty! Simple don't you think?

Anyhow, what has the above to do with "the price of fish on a rainy day"? What language is this? What is the Prosecution trying to say?
- So, on the 14th of July Murdoch arrives at Alice Springs
- Does some business –goes to the red Rooster –had his car cleaned –<u>bough a fuel</u> <u>container before refuelling at BP Station</u>.
- Leave for Alice Springs towards Fitzroy Crossing at 3.10pm on the 14th

Now please let me say this;

The Vanishing of Peter Falconio

Murdoch claimed he refuelled at BP at 2.00pm. Now please assume Murdoch fearing Falconio and Lees spying on him he decides to follow them. So instead of taking the Tanami, he followed them to Barrow Creek so he can shoot Falconio with his big gun right!

Knowing that it takes around three hours driving to Barrow Creek or round about, [HE] therefore arrives at 5.00pm. That is three hours and 45 minutes earlier, just to kill Falconio.

- So, if I may ask, what would he do in the meantime?
- You don't know?
- Well, I know, he is making the home- made cuffs? Ah ah ah! I think this is quite amusing. Please spare a little thought for Murdoch.

Now, we have Murdoch departing Alice (<u>not at 1.00am</u>) but at 3.10pm (14th) with one tank or 90 litres…

ALICE TO TILMOUTH WELL 190km departing 3.10pm (14th July) with 90 litres

Alice to Tilmouth Well 190km driving time 2h35 (155minutes) departing 3.10pm **90 litres**

Average speed = 190 ÷ 155 = 1.22 km/minute x 60 = **74kmh**

Fuel usage = 1.90 x 14 = **27 litres**

Left over fuel on arrival = 90 – 27 = **63 litres**

Arrival time = 3.10pm + 2h35 = **5.45pm** (14th July) **TILMOUTH OPEN** closing 9.00pm

---

TILMOUTH WELL TO YUENDUMU 145km departing 5.45pm (14th July) with 63 litres

Tilmouth Well 145km driving time 1h40 (100 minutes)

Average speed = 145 ÷ 100 = 1.45km/minutes x 60 = **87kmh**

The Vanishing of Peter Falconio

Fuel usage = 1.45 x 14 = **20 litres**

Left over fuel on arrival = 63 – 20 = **43 litres**

Arrival time = 5.45 pm + 1h40 = **7.25 pm** (14th July) **YUENDUMU OPEN** closing 9.00pm

Murdoch is refuelling. In the tank 90 litres

YUENDUMU TO BILLILUNA departing 7.25pm (14th of July) with 90 litres
Yuendumu to Billiluna 591km –driving time 12h40 (760 minutes)

Average speed = 591 ÷ 760 = 0.77 x 60 = **47.kmh** (46.65)

Fuel usage = 5.91 x 14 = **82 litres**

Left over fuel on arrival = 90 - 82 = **eight litres**…He just makes it!

Arrival time = 7.25pm + 12h40 = **7.05am** (15th) **BILLILUNA CLOSED** open 8.00am

Refuel at 8.00pm Sat (15th) no fees. <u>Lost 1 hour</u>. In tank 90 litres.

Now, when Murdoch arrived at Billiluna the calculation shows that he had only eight litres left in the tank. Driving in the outback low on fuel is a very risky business. Trusting Murdoch logic and common sense when he arrived at Yuendumu, he had 43 litres of fuel left over (that is half tank). That is why he did refuel at Yuendumu at [8.00pm], but remember that in Alice it is alleged that Murdoch bought a fuel container which usually have a capacity of 20 litres. Also remember my Land Cruiser is also a 75 series. In chapter 67, I tested my fuel usage by purposely running out of fuel. I drove 635km with 86 litres. Yuendumu to Billiluna is 591 km, Murdoch had no problem with fuel. I thought I mention it.

THEN

BILLILUNA TO HALLS CREEK 196km departing 8.00am (15th of July) 90 litres

(If you haven't been driving on the Tanami as I did, between Billiluna and Halls Creek, the sharp rocks –bull dust and corrugations are more than a nightmare).

Billiluna to Halls Creek 196km driving time five hours (300minutes)

Average speed $196 \div 300 = 0.65 \times 60 =$ **39kmh**

Fuel usage $1.96 \times 14 =$ **28 litres** (27.54)

Left over on arrival $90 - 28 =$ **62 litres**

Arrival time 8.00am + five hours = **1.00pm** (15th of July) **Halls Creek OPEN 24/7**

Murdoch doesn't need to refuel but he will, departing **1.00pm with 90 litres in his tank.**

HALLS CREEK TO FITZROY CROSSING 290km departing 1.00pm (15th of July) with **90 litres** (sealed road)

Halls Creek to Fitzroy 290km driving time three hours (180minutes) departing **1.00pm** (15th of July) **with 90litres**

Average speed $290 \div 180 = 1.61 \times 60 =$ **96.kmh**

Fuel usage $2.90 \times 14 =$ **41litres**

Left over fuel on arrival $90 - 41 =$ **49 litres**

Arrival time 1.00pm + three hours = **4.00pm (15th of July)**

SUCCESS, MURDOCH MAKES IT WITH ONE TANK. HE IS NOT THE CCTV MAN NOR THE ALLEGED KILLER.

YES, SUCCESS Murdoch makes it to Fitzroy Crossing not because some issues regarding fuel but because departing Alice Springs at 3.10pm on the 14th of July and not being the CCTV man nor the alleged killer, he had enough time. We don't need to do the calculation further on (Fitzroy Crossing to Broome)

As we can see Murdoch has arrived at 4.00pm on the 15th four hours earlier, he must have had some time during the trip to have a rest and as we know from Alice to Fitzroy Crossing, he was not a man in a hurry. The Judge, the Prosecution and of course Joanne Lees claimed that Murdoch was the man on the CCTV film and that he was lying.

Remember the Prosecution's words: "If you are satisfied that HE is lying…If you are satisfied, I am asking now: Who was lying with no proofs beyond reasonable doubt? …Who was assuming, who was lying? Joanne Lees and Peter Falconio knew absolutely nothing about outback Australia – Land Cruisers –four-wheel drives –dogs and mostly about people. I think Joanne Lees and the Prosecution believed that we are all a bunch idiots and morons as I said many times, but wait; what goes up will come down.

The Vanishing of Peter Falconio

79 - I Am Sorry to Disappoint You

According to Joanne Lees –the Prosecution –Hepi –the Judge and many others, the CCTV man and his Land Cruiser who has never been identified left Alice Springs at 1.00am on the 15th of July 2001 running away from allegedly having killed Peter Falconio but voluntary sparing his girlfriend by letting her go free, that man I am sorry to disappoint you, failed to reach destination on time. Actually, he did more than that, he run out of full and made you feel like the absolute idiots. I would be guilt ridden if I had been in your shoes

THE PROOF IS IN THE PUDDING, MURDOCH WAS NOT THE CCTV MAN

Below are the details regarding departing and arriving time for each location and each suspect.

Calculation for the CCTV man departing Alice Springs **at 1.00am** on the 15th of July

ALICE –TILMOUTH WELL

Departing **1.00am** –arriving **3.35 am** (15th)

TILMOUTH WELL –YUENDUMU

Departing **3.35am** –arriving **5.15am** (15th)

YUENDUMU –BILLILUNA

Departing **5.15am** –arriving **5.55pm** (15th)

Time left to reach Fitzroy Crossing 486 km two hours and five minutes – required speed 232kmh to reach destination

The CCTV MAN FAILED. Not enough time to reach Halls Creek and Fitzroy Crossing.

Calculation for Murdoch departing Alice Springs **at 3.10pm** on the 14th of July

ALICE –TILMOUTH WELL

Departing **3.10pm** –arriving **5.45pm** (14th)

TILMOUTH WELL –YUENDUMU

Departing **5.45pm** –arriving **7.25pm** (14th)

YUENDUMU –BILLILUNA

Departing **7.25pm** –arriving **7.05am** (15th)

BILLILUNA –HALLS CREEK

Departing **8.00am** –arriving **1.00pm** (15th)

HALLS CREEK –FITZROY CROSSING

Departing **1.00pm** –arriving **4.00pm** (15th)

Also, regarding Murdoch's claim that at the time of the alleged crime he was near Yuendumu and that between midnight and 1.00am on the (15th) he was near The Granites we have:

Murdoch at Yuendumu at **7.25pm** (14th), then,

At midnight (14th) he was **43.25km** before The Granites.

At 0.30am (15th) he was **19.15km** before The Granites

At 1.00am (15th) he was **3.95km** after The Granites

SUCCESS for Murdoch. He is/was not the CCTV man and vice versa.

To me this NEW EVIDENCE has been purposely ignored because the Officials believed that we are all a bunch of idiots including the jurors and the Defence team.

The Vanishing of Peter Falconio

80 - About Bililuna

For your perusal Billiluna is 280km from Rabbit Flat and 176km from Halls Creek. (Hema map) Below are the opening hours for people travelling the Canning Stock Route –fuel availability.

Kururrungku Store - Bililuna Station

Store opening times are Mon – Fri 8 am to 11 am & 2 pm – 4 pm Sat 8 am – 10.30 am Not open Sunday. Fuel is available @ $2.60 p/l both Diesel & Opal. Out of hours fuel is available. A $20 opening fee may apply.

The store has a wide variety of fresh fruit & veg, a huge selection of frozen meat and also a large variety of general groceries, Clothing & Footwear. Ice creams, drinks & Ice etc. Basic automotive such as Oil, Power Steering & Brake Fluid, fuses & Tools are available. We also carry a selection of Phones, Cameras, Hard drives & USB Flash drives, Memory cards, Telstra Phone cards, Mobile top ups & SIM Cards.

We have both ATM & Internet banking facilities. **Fuel is reliably available** But, do Call beforehand on 08 9168 8076

The Vanishing of Peter Falconio

81 - Closing Argument

Everything in italic is from the Internet, authors or transcript of the appeal

Anything not in italic is how I felt reading it. It includes my comments.

It was allegedly stated that this is what really happened.

[29a]   Murdoch saw Lees and Falconio while in Alice Springs, and believed that they were following him. So, he drove behind them as they travelled on the Stuart Hwy, and then stopped as to get rid of them, because he feared that they may be spying on him and may contact police in relation to drug running.

This was already discussed

The question here is who was following who?

Before reading the following please remember that Lees claimed she was driving slowly from Alice to Ti Tree. Following someone for 200km at low speed is not an easy task if you need to be incognito especially in the outback... Claiming they drove slowly is true. It shows one thing; a discrepancy of one hour which is the time they spent at Aileron, but we still don't know the real the time of departure from Alice Springs and the whole motive for this alleged crime which never took place.

.... So, he drove behind them as they travelled on the Hwy...

Meaning the alleged killer must have waited for them at the restaurant or somewhere else so he could follow them. He may also leave before Lees and Falconio, stopping along the way, waiting for them to drive past and then following them but we don't know.

Or perhaps they were following him, then him slowing down, most probably putting his car window down, getting his arm out and making the gesture to overtake him ...nice and polite. Then, he drove behind them. ...Is this a joke?

Do you think that travelling in the outback is like driving in a city? Is this some evidence that Murdoch is the killer?

Anybody travelling in the outback knows and would be aware of someone following. This is totally absurd, unfounded and bias. A man is innocent until proven guilty.

The Vanishing of Peter Falconio

[30a] It has been argued that Murdoch radically changed his physical appearance to conduct the alleged because he feared they were spying on him.

No, this is not acceptable, this is a farce. However, this is also important.

We will need to do the exercise:

Where and when did he change his appearance and the one of his dog, car, and trailer? After buying some chicken in Alice, while they were in Aileron looking at some brochures, around Ti Tree or before Barrow Creek?

Murdoch was at the turn off to the Tanami at 3.30pm –Them at Aileron at

3.30pm…On the same day…interesting to say the least!
I know it's a repeat but it is definitely necessary.

- So, he followed them. Lees and Falconio are in front all the way to Aileron. Then he must have been waiting for them to depart Aileron at 4.30pm (14th) aiming for Ti Tree.
- OH YES, that's where he must have made the cuffs…plenty of time one hour exactly. Why didn't I think about it before?
- According to the witnesses working at the Aileron Roadhouse (transcript) the orange Kombi arrived at Aileron at 3.30pm and left at 4.30pm (from Gregory Dick and his staff).
- Then again still driving slowly to Ti Tree…Remember Lees claiming they were driving slowly from Alice to Ti Tree without stopping at Aileron, because Lees keeps on denying having stop there…
- … Anyhow this doesn't indicate nor explain where Murdoch could have changed his appearance and the one of his car and dog etc.
- <u>Murdoch of course having previously dropped his trailer somewhere.</u>
- All we know about Murdoch's description at this **stage** is the description given by Lees to police in 2001 (long hair –moustache)

The Vanishing of Peter Falconio

when first interrogated on the morning the day after the alleged abduction…
- …But changing it four years later in 2005.
- We don't know if it is before or after the scanning Monsieur Malouf with her eyes closed hey!

I will discuss Murdoch's possibility of having changed his appearance to commit the alleged offence soon.

We have now:
- OK, now it is time for Lees to depart Ti Tree (alone) heading towards Barrow Creek not realising driving through Barrow Creek (Um!)
- Falconio not with her.
- But Murdoch still following…Absolutely remarkable!

Then Lees (I didn't say they) because Falconio…. Well, we don't know where he is. He vanished before Lees watching the sunset at Ti Tree. When Lees was watching the sunset alone, he was "The Invisible Man".
- So, by the time Lees arrives at Barrow Creek (Falconio is back in the picture if you can get your head around it) Murdoch must have had the time to change his appearance before the alleged crime scene [?]
- The alleged killer stops Lees and Falconio looking like a different man altogether. The unidentified footprints, is to pretend they had been stopped by some alleged killer who is of course Murdoch. Falconio, then got shot and she got abducted.

Lees claimed that Murdoch, the man she first described long hair – moustaches accompanied by his borrowed or rented dog stopped them 10km north of at Barrow Creek (that is probably why she didn't notice driving through Barrow Creek (clapping in the background). Nobody was there, not one witness. Only Lees …Very interesting!!

Then later on during the investigation, no Murdoch's footprints, no Falconio's footprints. His footprints of course couldn't be identified

The Vanishing of Peter Falconio

because, nobody knows what shoes he was wearing and nobody knows where the DEAD BODY IS…Does that makes sense?

We don't need to go back hundred times to come to the conclusion that everything is a farce. It is staged, it is an illusion, the illusion of a crime that never took place but Murdoch was found guilty on all charges only because of the DNA trump card which is going to be challenged before the end of this book.

The Vanishing of Peter Falconio

82 - Closing Argument [2]

This is also a most important part of the whole case. It needs some strong reflection from the reader. It is about M1 and M2 where M1 relates to 2001 and M2 to 2005.

It is a long chapter

You will need to read each sentence more than once, read slowly and try to understand each sentence just to get your head around. You will have to go back to previous sentences many times. This will show you that the Jury and the public have been fed with facts that nobody in their own mind would believe. It was obviously meant to deceive and influence. In fact, it could have worked in favour of Murdoch, but the Defence was unable to read the small prints. Was the Defence sleeping all that time, totally oblivious and unwilling to react about what must have been said? I truly can't comprehend how the Defence was thinking.

The most devastating thing was, that it ended with a guilty verdict. Well, the Defence had four years to think about it… Poor homework if you ask me.

***

This chapter is very similar to a small problem called: The missing dollar.

It was put to us kids when we were around 14/15 years of age in math classes. I will tell you about it in my next chapter. It shows how misinformation can work miracles. Please pay attention this is very serious.

Firstly, and again, we need to read the small paragraph below:

"Murdoch saw Lees and Falconio while in Alice Springs, and believed that they were following him. So, he drove behind them as they travelled on the Stuart Hwy, and then stopped them as to get rid of them, because he feared that they may be spying on him and may contact police in relation to drug running"

This is what the jury must have been told beside "Your verdict must be unanimous". Using the words "he feared that they may be spying on him and may contact police in relation to drug running", the intention is to deceive and influence the jury or anyone else for that matter.

It tells you that Murdoch –Lees –and Falconio knew each other, and that is the reason why he feared that they were spying on him and perhaps one of the reasons why Murdoch shot Falconio (the plot!).

If they knew each other, it can only indicate that at some point they may have had some small business dealings but I am only assuming [?]. Anyhow the three of them are in the business of buying or selling or both.

- It definitely indicates that Falconio and Lees knew what Murdoch looked like and vice versa......Obviously or perhaps not [?]
- Well, perhaps it's not obvious knowing that nothing is real,
- Perhaps they didn't know each other, how can you prove that? It could simply be fiction all the way [?]
- I don't know but don't forget it appears that, it is what has been said and assumed. The words "Murdoch saw Lees and Falconio is an affirmation. It's not like saying: He may have seen Lees and Falconio. The Prosecution was not at the alleged crime scene as a witness.
- There was only one witness at the alleged crime scene: Joanne Lees witnessing some events which I truly believe never took place.

She was a witness at the location but not a witness to the actual alleged shooting at the scene even pretending being no more than three metres away from each man (incredible, if you believe her story). All she claimed was: she heard a BANG which I said before could have been Falconio being shot by the exhaust pipe, but no, because she said later that she heard a gunshot. People should make up their mind: Exhaust, gun?

- We need to understand that on the morning after the alleged attack when Joanne Lees claimed and first gave a precise description of her attacker to police,
- She didn't describe the man who stopped them as Murdoch, the man who was at the same restaurant on the day of the alleged

crime, a man they saw and probably knew. (She could also have said: Oh YES, we saw him at the restaurant.)
- But a man with long hair –moustache –huge according to the transcript etc.

That is one fact. The Prosecution knew it (otherwise why claiming it?)

What police knew on the early hours of the morning of the 14th was only what Lees told them (the first description of the attacker).

In fact, nobody knew who the attacker was and what the attacker looked like. So, we have:
- Nobody knew what the attacker looked like. (Until Lees gave a description)
- <u>Nobody knew if the attacker had modified his appearance to conduct the alleged attack.</u> Furthermore, even now and for the last 20 years nobody knows if Murdoch the assumed killer did change his appearance to commit the alleged murder and if he went back to his natural appearance after having committed the alleged crime.
- Nobody knew if the attacker had modified his appearance before or /and after the alleged offence.
- Nobody knew if he had changed his look before Barrow Creek and again after having committed the alleged offence or after Alice on his way to Western Australia.
- Nobody knew what the attacker looked like before Joanne Lees was questioned by police.
- The only thing police knew was that an alleged abduction and crime had apparently been committed at Barrow Creek where Monsieur Malouf spent the night but heard and saw absolutely nothing (Um!).
- <u>That's all police knew at that time.</u>
- The only thing police knew after Lees gave her first description was: A man with very long hair, long moustache and a deep voice –wearing a cap –driving a four-wheel drive with a chrome bulbar –

- with bucket seats –with a communication/passage between the cabin and the back –with no trailer –a man who had a sheep dog (not a Dalmatian dog) …No mention about the missing front teeth and the size of the man.
- That was the man described by Joanne Lees, the man who stopped them at Barrow Creek –the man who shot her boyfriend in cold blood near the Kombi and the four wheel drive – with a big silver gun Clint Eastwood type– the man who abducted her –the man who pushed her in the back of his four wheel drive through a passage between the seats and the back of the car–and the man she escaped from –then hiding five hours in the bushes on a pitch black and very cold winter night in Northern Territory on the 14th of July 2001…. **That was all!**
- Nobody knew that Lees was having an affair with a mysterious lover from Sydney, a man with whom she had in one day given or received 28 calls <u>before her boyfriend's</u> <u>disappearance.</u>
- It is only after police interviewed Lees that police knew what they were dealing with and the description is the one above and nothing else. That is all police knew on the morning of the day after the alleged attach in 2001.

That is why based on Lees' description police started to erect road blocks looking for that type of man. Are you ok with that?
- I trust that we are clear on that: Nothing was known about the man until Lees gave her first description to police on the morning the day after the alleged attack.
- If Lees –Falconio –Murdoch knew each other, her description to police should have been the true physical description of Murdoch, the one from the restaurant, the one they saw…<u>Couldn't be more basic!</u>

***

The Vanishing of Peter Falconio

The first description claimed by Joanne Lees in 2001 of her "attacker" is a man who didn't look like real Murdoch in 2001, who didn't look like the CCTV man in 2005 BUT more or similar (lovely word) to Chris Malouf.

- WHY?
- Because the Prosecution who was a witness (of course) claimed the man modified his appearance to commit the alleged crime.
- Also, he didn't look like the man on the CCTV because the man on the <u>CCTV was</u> <u>not in the picture then,</u>
- Nobody knew about him and nobody knew what he looked like. **He could not be identified and as a matter of fact he has never been identified including his Land Cruiser:** Are we clear on that?
- The road blocks were installed because police were only looking for a man fitting the first description given by Joanne Lees.
- Yes, I know it was the man according to the Prosecution. The man on the CCTV film was Murdoch, but as you have read it was wrong. The CCTV man couldn't reach Fitzroy Crossing on time...You with me?

I will call the man first described by Lees to police as [M1] for alleged Murdoch 1; long hair, moustaches etc. The attacker.

BUT

In 2005 at the trial Lees after changing her claim Lees decided that Murdoch was the CCTV man. He was no longer the man described by her as "too old" but nevertheless he became the man on the CCTV footage and the man who stopped them at Barrow Creek.

Given that she said the man was no longer too old; she identified the CCTV man as Murdoch.

I will call the man on the CCTV film [M2] for alleged Murdoch 2 (the CCTV man)

M1 and M2 are not Murdoch in his natural look. M1 is M1 and M2 is M2

- In 2001 the only thing known was:

The Vanishing of Peter Falconio

- **M1** was the attacker who looked like as per Joanne Lees' first statement and description to police: **The attacker.**
- Not long after, the drawing by the artist chosen by police was released.
- In 2001 even after Lees gave her first description of **M1** nobody knew what **M2 or Murdoch** looked like.
- In 2001 police only knew about **M1**, nothing else.

(repeat I know... sorry).

Just put yourself in the shoes of the first police officer who must have interviewed Joanne Lees and knew nothing about what really took place or didn't take place.

- All what police needed was a description.
- Lees gave **M1** as the man: long hair –moustache –drives a white four-wheel drive –owns a cattle dog – a big silver gun –wears a cap with a small logo – medium size –has a deep voice –never mentioned the campervan trailer etc.
- The man (**M1**) stopped Lees and Falconio –shot Falconio using a big Silver 44 Magnum or the equivalent– then he abducted Lees
- That is the type of gun Lees described, even the colour, a silver one.
- Then as we know, he pushed her in the back of his car through the space between the seats etc. However later on the officials admitted that the killer or Murdoch did have a lot of trouble shifting Lees onto the back of the Cruiser because if true it must have been a hard task to lift her by the legs (of course she must have been fighting ...imagine the scene hey!)
- When police questioned her about the space between the seats and the back of the car her answer was: *"I got through easily because the seats were folded or flat"*. (From the show on Channel 7 Plus – Murder in the outback 2022).
- Now please explain why in 2001 she said that it was **M1** and then in 2005 it was **M2?**

The Vanishing of Peter Falconio

- Knowing that **M1** and **M2** didn't look like each other.
- Because allegedly the Prosecution argued in 2005 (below)) that <u>**M2** had modified his look to become **M1** to commit the alleged offence.</u>
- So according to the above sentence and the Prosecution **M2** must be Murdoch in real life who had just committed the alleged offence, <u>who with the help of his makeup</u> artist went from **M2** to **M1** to kill Falconio
- Even if both of them didn't look like each other why choosing Murdoch who didn't look like **M1** or **M2**
- **M1** looked like **M1**
- **M2** looked like **M2**
- **Murdoch** looks like Murdoch

Do you understand all this? Do you smell a rat, a big one?

In 2005 at the trial, the Prosecution argued;

"The Prosecution allegedly argued that Murdoch radically changed his physical appearance to conduct the alleged offence because he feared they were spying on him"

So, if in 2005 Murdoch "au naturel "or M2 "radically changed his physical appearance ", to become M1 means that M1 is not the naturel physical looking M2 or Murdoch…Gosh!

- How did the Prosecution know that? Radically means what it means. How could the Prosecution be certain that the man who allegedly killed Falconio and abused Lees was Murdoch who had radically changed his physical appearance to conduct the alleged offence because he feared they were spying on him? Really, can you answer that?
- When no one knew what **M1** looked like in 2001 in the early hours of the morning or **M2** looked like in 2005 at the trial and even before that. **NOBODY** knew what the alleged killer look like until Lees gave her first description to police as **M1**

The Vanishing of Peter Falconio

- **M2** became **M1** because **M2** radically changed his appearance to commit the alleged crime. Of course, according to the prosecution our second witness hey! Do you follow?
- Was the Prosecution there? The Prosecution was not at the alleged crime scene, the Prosecution was not a witness. This was meant to deceive and influence the jury, and anybody else. Nothing more, nothing less.

- **M1** first described by Lees was not Murdoch in his natural look. **M1** was **M2 wearing a different makeup (not mentioning the car –the dog etc.**
- How did the Prosecution know that **M1** in 2001 was **M2** who had modified his appearance to commit the offence? What type of crystal ball was used to arrive at such conclusion? Are they for real?
- How did the Prosecution in 2005 could say that **M2** was Murdoch who changed his look becoming **M1** to commit the alleged offence?
- In 2001, the Prosecution didn't know what **M1 –M2 – Murdoch** looked like because nobody knew what was happening on the 14th of July (only Lees and her accomplices in crime).
- Nobody knew anything about **Murdoch –M1 – and M2** until Lees gave her first description to police as **M1**
- Allegedly the jury may have been told that the real Murdoch radically changed his physical appearance. Unless you have proofs beyond reasonable doubt this is not acceptable.
- This is no evidence unless you have proofs beyond reasonable doubt. The Prosecution's job it to prosecute, not to deceive and not to induce into the jury's mind something that even himself as prosecutor knows is wrong and meant to deceive and knowing that the jury will believe it without the notion that it must be beyond reasonable doubt.

The Vanishing of Peter Falconio

So, in 2001 if nobody knew about the real Murdoch or the alleged crime, it is only when police interviewed Lees on the morning after the alleged offence that police finally got some idea about what the culprit looked like … ie M1

- That's why most probably Chris Malouf was arrested and released within half hour, which is interesting because apparently Malouf said that the man on the CCTV looked like him or was him. He apparently even said *"But that me on the video"* (sorry it is definitely hard to get your head around this type of claim). Also, how did police find Malouf so quickly? As I said before the police arrested a disguised informer …A decoy [?]

Police only knew what M1 looked like (Lees description) and that is why they started establishing road blocks (not before).

- The road blocks were hoping to catch **M1** only (long hair – moustache –with a cattle dog –driving a four-wheel drive with no trailer (I didn't say Land Cruiser),
- **The road blocks were not intended to catch M2 or Murdoch; [only M1.]**

Are we clear on that? Police was looking for M1, not M2 and not for the real Murdoch

- Knowing that **M1** look like the man with long hair, Moustaches etc.
- And **M2** looks like the man on the CCTV film,
- How is it possible and admissible for the Prosecution and Joanne Lees and Mr Hepi to claim in 2005 that the real Murdoch in his natural look was **M2** who shot Falconio, looking like **M1**?
- Then claiming that **M1** after committing the offence went back to look like **M2**,
- Knowing that **M2** is not Murdoch because he doesn't look like Murdoch
- And knowing that **M1** the first description of the attacker by Joanne Lees was **M1** who doesn't look like **M2** nor **Murdoch**.

The Vanishing of Peter Falconio

Someone must have had a large wardrobe and a good makeup artist because all this take time.

This tells you that what Joanne Lees and the Prosecution claimed is a big bag of lies. This is what I call a conspiracy, at plot. The whole system is/was rigged. (Please go back to my chapter 15) regarding my views on the word conspiracy.

The trial was definitely a miscarriage of justice. Shame on anyone who thinks evil of it.

Murdoch must have been a prime suspect when being accused of rape because of the publicity and photographs published in newspapers.

Nobody knew what real Murdoch looked like in relation to the alleged attack on the night of the 14th of July…Nobody. It is a created fact. When they say radically changed his appearance, it is truly an incredible lie meant to deceive and influence the jury and everyone else, because in 2001 when the alleged offence took place, nobody knew the appearance of real Murdoch –M1 –or M2

This should have been debated at the trial.

The only witness (Lees) has been feeding people with false facts under oath, when a man's life was in the balance. That is/was an evil crime, punishable by law. She should now be the one on trial. She should be recalled to face the music.

In 2005 the Prosecution tried to induce into the jury's mind a FABRICATED fact. Fact created by Joanne Lees supported by the Prosecution and the Judge, and I am still wondering: Who is the man on the CCTV film?

I don't think we need to do the same exercise again for Murdoch's dog, car or trailer. We know it will be a waste of time. A dog doesn't go from Dalmatian to Blue Heeler without a good makeup artist, and the attacker was not renting a dog (clapping in the background)

Murdoch should not have been convicted. It was definitely a miscarriage of justice, a farce, a trial by media, a kangaroo court of the highest level…God help us.

The Vanishing of Peter Falconio

ANYHOW

We now have proofs that:
- Murdoch is/was not the man on the CCTV film because he was successful reaching Fitzroy Crossing on time <u>contrary to the CCTV man who failed</u>
- That Joanne Lees has never been hiding in the bush for the duration of her claim
- We know that she could not have escaped from the back of Murdoch's Cruiser because the Cruiser had no opening at the back because of the "cage" nor she could escape from the sides which were zipped and that her movement were restricted by the home-made cuffs and that she did have a knife to cut the canvas open.
- We know that the alleged fictitious killing could have taken place at **8.45pm** on the 14th of July because Lees left Ti Tree at 6.30pm. But the calculated time has been pure fiction and there are no proofs telling us at what time [she] arrived at Barrow Creek [?]…**I didn't say [THEY]**
- We can deduct that no crime took place on the 14th of July 2001 <u>because also there is</u> <u>no Dead Body.</u>
- **We only have Falconio's head wrapped in Joanne Lees' jacket according to her book** (laughter in the background)

Knowing all this, what is going to happen next with this can of worms? Well, the only thing we can do at this stage is to challenge the DNA trump card.

***

The alleged killing of Falconio is/was certainly a good plan which owes it success to the DNA card, which can still be challenged knowing that it took 28 months for the tests to be sent or arrived on the desk of the forensic lab and knowing that one expert on DNA disagreed regarding how the whole procedure regarding the analysis was conducted. Also and most importantly

The Vanishing of Peter Falconio

The High Court said: YOU CANNOT CONVICT ON DNA ALONE IT IS NOT SAFE ENOUGH.

How do you feel knowing what's happening now regarding the corruption within some companies involved in the business of DNA?

Some laboratories involved in DNA testing and analysis are now involved with corruption of the highest level… it's on the news nearly every day (2022). THEY can't hide forever.

It is a scam of major proportion. An innocent man has already been in jail for the last 20 years. It is evil.

The intentions of the Judge and Prosecution were definitely immoral. The jury was deceived and kept in the dark all along. Perhaps some of the jurors could be corrupt (you will find out my reason for saying this further on). You only need 1 or two jurors to be associated with the "Official" for the trial and the verdict to ends up in the "swamp".

The Juror (the movie 1996) is a typical and explicit example about what could take place in a Court House when the "Institution" is corrupt for reasons unknown to most of us.

From Wikipedia (very good movie)

"With his gangster boss (Tony Lo Bianco) on trial for murder, a mob thug known as "the Teacher" (Alec Baldwin) tells Annie Laird (Demi Moore) she must talk her fellow jurors into a not-guilty verdict, implying that he'll kill her son Oliver (Joseph Gordon-Levitt) if she fails. She manages to do this, but, when it becomes clear that the mobsters might want to silence her for good, she sends Oliver abroad and tries to gather evidence of the plot against her, setting up a final showdown".

You cannot prove something that never took place. The only solution is to have a Royal Commission Inquiry. I am truly serious about it, bring back Joanne Lees and the others into the witness box and start asking serious questions. The same needs to apply to the DNA testing. You may then catch, Falconio alive if he is and lock them all up for life and after life.

83 - Ah, The Missing Dollar!

This problem was put to us kids when we were 14 or 15years old in math class. We had only two minutes to answer. The answer had to be verbal, we were not allowed to use pencil and paper. When looking back, it was a revelation and a good lesson. It told us that in life, finding the solution to any problem one must think. One needs to make sure that any words spoken by the speaker must be understood fully. To put it simply ONE MUST THINK.

Here we go, but because you are much older you have only 30 seconds to come up with the answer like on the TV show: Letters and numbers with Richard Morecroft…Please don't cheat.

***

Three men dinning at a cheap restaurant in Alice Spring. Each of the man has only $10. After dinning they asked the waitress for the bill. She comes back with the bill. The cost for the three meals is $25.

They each give $10. She comes back with a $5 dollar note.

They say to her: "Sorry, we can't split $5 in three, could you give us five single dollar coin".

She comes back with the coins. Then each of the men takes $1 giving the remaining $2 to the waitress.

Now, giving $10 each and each getting back $1, we have:

$10 - $1 = $9

So, we have $9 x 3 = $27 + $2 to the waitress = $29

Where is the missing dollar?

If you haven't got the answer within 30 second, please use matches to find the answer…Try this with you children or friends!

If you failed within the time frame will mean that you are prone to propaganda –faked news –and created facts but, don't worry, you are not the only one!

84 - Closing Argument [3]

Long chapter....

[31]   After stopping them, he panicked and kill Falconio, making sure that there was no blood anywhere by making a shot directly to his head, then he abducted Lees, binding her with cable ties and putting her in the back of the four-wheel drive.

From here, we know of the prefabricated facts. Lees followed suit because she had created an image and a profile for the identification of Murdoch in 2001 accused of killing her boyfriend and her abduction which never took place because there is not one single evidence proving otherwise and because she is the only witness. It is all prefabrication by Lees mostly, Falconio and their accomplices. The alleged killer could have been M1 –M2 –M3 -or Zorro the avenger!

Ok, Murdoch flagged their car down, they stopped, he panicked then bang, bang, kills Falconio in cold blood directly to the head with no worries because he thought they were spying on him...Simple, the perfect premeditated crime has taken place. Do you really believe that? But he lets Lees go free...How nice! Definitely extremely premeditated.

This is not Love story but Lees 'story.

***

[32a] Once in the back of the car, Murdoch tried to dispose of the body. Then Lees escaped in the bushes nearby. Murdoch (the alleged killer) then search for her for five hours with a flashlight and his rented dog and gives up.

Oh definitely, what a joke. Please notice, it's never the alleged killer, ALWAYS Murdoch.

- Truly did the alleged killer try to dispose of the Dead Body? No, no, no that is not correct, because according to Lees and the transcript of the appeal, it must have taken place before the killer left the alleged crime scene. AND, the alleged killer had only 15 minutes at his disposal to accomplish the task...Food for thought.

The Vanishing of Peter Falconio

***

The details of subsequent events relied upon by the Crown for the purposes of the pre-trial objections are set out in my reasons for judgment in R v Murdoch (No 1) [2005] NTSC 75. In substance it is the Crown case that the accused forced Ms Lees into his vehicle from where she escaped into the scrub. While Ms Lees was hiding in the scrub the accused shifted the Kombi van and left it in the scrub on the western side of the Stuart Highway.

Definitely a Pink Panther style movie. Perhaps I should get in touch with Fox Studio.

Is this for real? I am asking you, is this truly what took place at Barrow Creek?

***

[33a] Murdoch then buried Falconio in a place unknown in Central Australia outback, wrapping Falconio's head with Lees denim jacket so as to prevent any blood getting in the vehicle.

Well, it gets better and better as we go along. We know he didn't bury the body; no shovel.

But we know now where the Dead Body is: Somewhere in Central Australia. Gosh someone has a good crystal ball!

However, we know something very important about the alleged killer and that is:

HE PANICKED but still had time to wrap Falconio's head in Lees' denim jacket. This is the icing on the cake. The author of the book is the accuser… Would you believe it?

Finding Peter Falconio is now a walk in the park:

- **Find Lees 'jacket" hey!**
- Again, it makes me think of the French movie: Les Visiteurs: It is a very funny movie, the whole world should watch it.

***

The Vanishing of Peter Falconio

From Wikipedia, the free encyclopedia

Les Visiteurs (French pronunciation: [le vizitœʁ]; English: The Visitors) is a French fantasy comedy film directed by Jean-Marie Poiré and released in 1993. In this comedy, a 12th-century knight and his squire travel in time to the end of the 20th century and find themselves adrift in modern society.

Les Visiteurs was the highest-grossing film in France in 1993 and remains the fourteenth highest grossing film in the country today. The publicity for the film used the tagline Ils ne sont pas nés d'hier ("They weren't born yesterday"). Reno and Clavier reprised their roles in a sequel in 1998, the American remake Just Visiting in 2001 and a second sequel in 2016. The Castle of Ermenonville, in Oise département, served as decoration for the castle of Montmirail in the current time and the Cité de Carcassonne for medieval period.

***

"Messieurs of the Jury" you have now the right to speak!

***

[34a] Then Murdoch panicked, and, rather than driving through the bush straight to Broome, he drove all the way back to Alice Spring, where he is spotted on close circuit television at the truck stop, getting supplies before heading to Broome, where he travelled non-stop at great speed, taking amphetamines to keep itself awake and alert.

So, from reading this, Faconio is dead and buried. Actually, Murdoch should have left the dead body in the Kombi just to make things easy for all the experts and me!

I think the Prosecution needs a new Crystal Ball!

[35a] Murdoch then altered his physical appearance does the same to his vehicle so to avoid detection, and immediately stopped running drugs because he feared that he might be linked to the murder.

So, the alleged killer changed his appearance after departing Alice Springs??? I am now very confused, I thought he did after the alleged shooting [?]

Also, I thought that he already stopped taking drugs! This is just ludicrous, when will this stop? We spoke about this already in details. Nothing fits! But Murdoch was found guilty.

***

[36a] Mr Wild has suggested that there was no evidence whatsoever of any police corruption, and urged jurors to dismiss any suggestions as an unfounded conspiracy theory that was plucked out of thin air. He has suggested that all of the evidence points to one obvious conclusion –that Murdoch killed Falconio. He stated that whilst no dead body has been found yet, it will be eventually, that it was only a matter of time, but it may take quite some time.

Here we are, Monsieur Wild doesn't like the word conspiracy. He had more than one synonym he could choose from, but he believes that we are all a bunch of idiots.

Monsieur Wild I believe that all along, you never believed Joanne Lees' story. Do you recall the time when you said:

- *"If Bradley Murdoch's DNA had not been on Joanne Lees's shirt I would have advise against bringing him to trial".* **YOU DO REMEMBER DO YOU?**

***

[37a] Mr Wild has stated that Joanne Lees should be expected to have mild discrepancies with Murdoch's appearance such as length and colour of his hair, not noticing his teeth, the description of his car and dog, and other inconsistencies, because Lees was under a lot of stress and pressure during the incident.

Yes, Mr Wild you must be right. Lees was under extreme stress and pressure. Who are you trying convert?

- **I should look for other opportunities she said.** (Just a reminder).

[38a] Mr Wild has asked the jury to ignore the evidence of the sightings of Peter Falconio and to dismiss them as not accurate, highlighting

discrepancies in the stories of the various people who said to have seen him alive in the days after the attack.

Here we are, of course…Ignore is the word, sounds like "mum's the word" why not, may as well! All witnesses are lying except Lees and Monsieur Hepi. Anybody and everybody is an expert, but Murdoch is guilty.

Peter Falconio was seen a week after is alleged death by very genuine and very reliable witness

DEAD MEN DO NOT WALK THE STREETS AFTER THEIR DEATHS

***

39a] Mr Wild has stated that the DNA does match, and that there is no chance that it is not Murdoch's DNA. Mr Wild has stated that this is why the jury must find him guilty

YES, that is why the jury must find him guilty …Of course, my word is my bond.

Well, the DNA does match. Don't argue…It does match…Is this how you solve a murder case? You don't even need to do any testing just proclaim that it is a match! Remove and destroy few files or samples is the way to solve the issue. It cannot be in contradiction to what the Prosecution wants you to believe.

And by the way, who's blood was used for the DNA testing? Gary's blood…Murdoch's brother?

Ignorance, stupidity, carelessness……or CORRUPTION?

Monsieur Wild I like to remind you that the CCTV man failed to reach Fitzroy crossing. Sorry to disappoint you again.

[40a] Mr Wild has said that Murdoch was a methodical killer, and that the crime was premeditated to "get rid of" someone, and suggested that he may have thought that Lees was travelling alone, since Falconio was asleep in the back when she was driving. He suggested that the methodical actions to get rid of any evidence suggesting he did it, as well as quickly getting away suggests the act of someone with extreme premeditation, and that it is the work of an obsessive methodical person, a man just like Murdoch.

The Vanishing of Peter Falconio

Fascinating… He thought that Lees was travelling alone…So why was he following them?

When did Murdoch start believing that Joanne Lees was travelling alone? Premeditation?

What is the meaning of this? Think about it: He thought that Lees was travelling alone because Lees and Falconio were spying on him is remarkable.

So, one minute it is SHE was alone but next minute Falconio is back in the picture wow! This is really a beautiful story where nothing fits.

Of course, Murdock knew that you were not alone dear. That is why according to you he allegedly murdered you boyfriend…Have you forgotten?

***

[41a] Mr Wild has asked the jury to ignore coincidental evidence that seemed to suggest that Murdoch didn't do it, stating that he had ample time to change the evidence to fit the story, to later suggest that he didn't do it.

Of course, ignore the coincidental evidence that seemed to suggest…The impossible.

So, the Prosecution wants you to believe that Murdoch had plenty of time to change the evidence…And what evidence needed to be changed?

That was the closing argument or part of it.

I shall spare you Chief Justice Brian Ross Martin's summation who seems to be surfing on the same or even bigger wave. (Chief Justice Brian Ross Martin, was the trial Judge.)

85 - Up To Here...

Up to here, I mostly wrote about what Joanne Lees did –said –pretended –lied –imagined etc. All of her answers are lies at the exception that she was seen at Ti Tree at 6.10pm on the 14th and that she truly was picked up by Vince Millar around 0.15am at the alleged crime scene on the 15th. This second part so to speak is more like an overview of the situation from the alleged time of events up until the trial. The same applies to the Prosecution – the Defence and witnesses. I didn't say much about the DNA trump card which has been the only tool used to incriminate Bradley John Murdoch. The proof was in the pudding……HE was found guilty on all charges.

I am here now to discuss the DNA and the program "Murder in the Outback" which was aired on Channel 7 (four episodes that can be viewed on 7Plus).

"Murder in the Outback is a TV Mini Series 2020. It is a major revealing depth re- examination of the Falconio and Lees mystery an infamous case from 2001 concerning a horror story of abduction and death on a lonely Australian highway…(From the Internet, I like to mention it again). I recommend the viewing to anyone interested in True Crime.

So, this is what I am going to talk about in this second part of my book. Trust me it is truly a "hell" of a challenge…It is fascinating to discover as you go along some truly bombshell information. Please keep on reading…

However, I like to remind everybody that anything uploaded on the Internet will be seen and read irrelevant of time. It is there to stay

86 - The Prosecution Never Believed Joanne Lees' Story

However, Rex Wild QC went for it! (Remember Rex Wild is the prosecutor, just making sure).

From here every piece of information is paramount –incredible –hard to believe –fascinating and sometime even funny. I can't get my head around about the received verdict: Guilty on all charges.

Every piece of information here and further on in italic is from the internet or from the TV Mini Series Murder in the Outback and from reputable authors including transcripts.

The verdict of Bradley John Murdoch is/was based uniquely on two things:

- Joanne Lees 'claims our only witness.
- The DNA provided by a tiny bloodstain of unknown source found on the back of her T-shirt which according to some forensics experts came from Murdoch but however (we don't know how because nobody knows) disputed by others. Those claims either true or false had the full support of Rex Wild QC and the Judge Martin Brian but/and however not shared by the Defence, and some forensics experts and by a large number of the public. It includes also Dean Mildren (retired Judge) in his book R vs Murdoch the Falconio Case a study in identification and circumstantial Evidence (mentioned previously) –Keith Noble – Robin Bowles etc.
- **Only the DNA result** was sufficient in incriminating the accused. The ending proved it: Guilty on all charges.

Below are two documents from the Internet.

- One from **Stuart Tipple the Defence Lawyer in the Azaria Chamberlain case,**
- The other from **Rex Wild QC the Prosecutor in Murdoch's case and trial.**

Both documents relate to very similar case and the lack regarding the Presumption of Innocence which shows that nobody was looking for justice.

Regarding the DNA (analysis and results), Dr Both disagreed with Dr Withaker.

Dr Both does not accept the scientific validity of LCN and identified a number of areas which are of concern to her. (LCN means low copy number which I do not understand and I am not the only one...So it's up to the forensic experts).

However, what is most remarkable in my view is; why on earth Rex Wild QC came up producing a play with a name like "THE INQUISITION" proclaiming their mistakes in the Chamberlain case but and however not feeling sorry about it.

I believe Lindy Chamberlain and Bradley John Murdoch could be both regarded as "Heretics"

"The heretics of the inquisition were the Cathars in the early organised prosecution of the non-Catholic Christians.

Catharism was a Christian or Gnostic movement between the 12th and 14th centuries which thrived in Southern Europe, particularly in northern Italy and the south of France (the internet)"

Torture was used only to get a confession. In Murdoch's case (2001) society has become more educated. We now don't torture people any longer but, we send a certain category in prison for life only if their claims don't fit the narrative and the agenda of the "Master". Here the Government (the officials). The whole concept I can say is very similar and has not changed since: If your views are not in accordance with the narrative and the agenda whatever you may claim will be ignored and dismissed unless you have more financial means to prove your point and innocence. You know what they say "Money talks bullshit walks" You will be locked up for life like Murdoch and like the witness testimony in Bourke who saw Falconio after his death, your claim will be ignored –dismissed –and even ridiculed.

Only one word is sufficient to dismiss a true fact: IGNORE

A typical disgraceful example now in July 2023 is the story of Nigel Farage a British broadcaster and former politician who was Leader of the UK Independence Party from 2006 to 2009 and 2010 to 2016 and Leader of the Brexit Party from 2019 to 2021. (Wikipedia)

The Vanishing of Peter Falconio

Well, the bank decided to close his account simply because some of his views didn't fit the bank's narrative and agenda. I found this to be a total disgrace.

The same situation applied in relation to the Covid vaccine, for example: If you don't get vaccinated, we will take your job away from you and send you broke. But for Bradley John Murdoch it is: If you don't tell us where the Dead Body is, there won't be any parole, you will die in prison!

"The failure of authorities (The Azaria Chamberlain case, Stuart Tipple was the Defence Lawyer).

In the book, Tipple explains how he believed the police fell into the trap of 'confirmation bias' - and had already made up their minds about Lindy's guilt in the initial investigation.

"They made their minds up that this was a murder. Any evidence to the contrary, they really weren't interested in," Tipple said.

"It was something we heard time and time again from the witnesses, that when they gave anything at all that was supportive of the Chamberlains, they would be told, we don't want to know about it. This was a murder."

A trial by media

In one of the letters Lindy wrote to Tipple from prison, she blamed the media for the guilty verdict.

"There's no doubt the media had a big part to play," Tipple said.

"I think the bigger part was the poor police investigation and poor science. And one of the things that astounds me is that it could still happen today, that you can be trialled on bad science.

"Scientists can go into court and be regarded as an expert, and give absolute nonsense science and convict you of murder. It's easier to have that evidence accepted than for that scientist to have a scientific paper published because there's no peer review."

Dingo attacks still happening

Just this year, there was an attack on Fraser Island where a small child was taken by a dingo from a camper trailer, in circumstances that were very similar to the Chamberlain case.

"The experts, regarded as the greatest pathologists in the world, said that there was no way in the world a dingo could grasp a 10-week-old baby," Tipple said.

"In April this year, they grabbed a 14-month-old toddler. So in 40 years, what have we learned? Not very much."

The Dingo Took Over My Life is released on December 4th"

***

"THE TERRITORY INQUISITION(S)

"A Play Reading produced by Rex Wild QC (The Prosecutor in the Murdoch case).
Tuesday 24 and Wednesday 25 May 2011.

Photography of the Alice Springs play Review by Bob Watt reading kindly supplied by Claire Ryan.

BOB WATT WAS THE COURT REPORTER ON THE NORTHERN TERRITORY NEWS FOR ABOUT 15 YEARS BEFORE HE RETIRED IN 2005. AT THE TIME OF THE FIRST TWO INQUESTS. HE WAS MANAGING EDITOR OF THE CENTRAL! AN ADVOCATE IN ALICE SPRINGS. THE FULL TITLE OF THE PLAY WAS: THE TERRITORY INQUISITION(S) INTO THE DEATH OF AZARIA CHANTELLE LOREN CHAMBERLAIN (AND THE PRESUMPTION OF INNOCENCE)

The choice of the "Azaria case" to feature as a play to celebrate the centenary of the Territory's Supreme Court was a good one, if perhaps predictable. No other case (which involved two inquests before the trial of Lindy and Michael Chamberlain and after eight years their acquittal) has attracted such widespread interest, publicity and strongly held opinions. Not even the more recent Falconio case", even though drugs, blood and a presentable young woman were in there.

The Vanishing of Peter Falconio

From a media point of view the Azaria case had everything – an exotic location, a baby, an animal, some blood ("if it bleeds it leads") pathos, black magic and a whiff of matricide on the desert air.

The choice to feature the early inquests was also appropriate, pointing to the injustices the Chamberlains suffered in these hearings which lacked the traditional protections given to suspected people, then being committed for trial by a coroner- a power taken away by a later change in Territory law.

The play's author, Rex Wild QC, quite cleverly cobbled together some interesting
pieces of evidence and procedure from the two inquests.
Much of it probably not sexy enough to be featured in the media at the time, the play gave a clear insight into the position the Chamberlains were put in television. The playing of that television footage on a screen behind the play's magistrate was effective.
The exchanges between counsel during the second inquest show that the Chamberlains' lawyers had little to work with, battling what amounted to a prosecution case with a "tell 'em nothing" attitude by counsel assisting the coroner. As a former DPP, Mr Wild was brave to highlight the questionable tactics of the counsel assisting the coroner in the second inquest.
The play concentrates more on the second inquest. After all, from the first inquest Denis Barritt SM did find the dingo guilty and might have been lauded for his decision, had he not upset the legal fraternity by announcing it on national.

Mr Wild says in the program acknowledgements he had access to the transcript of the second (Gerry Galvin CSM) inquest and that was why the play concentrates on that inquest, following quite closely the original exchanges 30 www.lawsocietynt.asn.au volunteers for the male roles, some being played by women both at Alice Springs and Darwin. I didn't attend the Alice Springs reading but in Darwin I wondered if some of the players were overcome by nerves. Perhaps the lack of "big red dresses with flour bags on their heads" on the bench left them uncertain as to who they should address. A notable exception was Ken Conway who took the part of Barritt SM and (importantly) that of Des Sturgess, assisting the coroner in the second inquest. It was a dramatic part and Mr Conway played it out fully, depicting Sturgess as a terrier who (pardon the reference) got his teeth into the business and wouldn't let go, playing his cards extremely close to the chest. He was eminently despicable. Actually, Mr Conway was the only non-practising lawyer in the cast. For many years he has been associated with Brown's Mart as producer, director and actor, so his theatrical flair was not unexpected. He showed a nice sense of the dramatic - and was obviously familiar with his lines.

Georgia McMaster, who read the part of Lindy Chamberlain at both venues, gave a masterly between counsel, the bench and the witnesses.

Some of these exchanges make quite gripping reading - but I can't say the same of the presentation by a number of the players. Some were as wooden as the Court furniture. Appealing for players in Balance last year, Mr Wild said: "Learning of lines is unnecessary. All that is required is a little dramatic flair (which we lawyers have in abundance) and some attitude to go with any poetic licence the script provides." He may have been disappointed. Much of the flair fizzled and there seemed to be a shortage of performance, imbuing Lindy with the apparent lack of emotion and occasional displays of defiance that convinced some people of her guilt long before the trial.

In Darwin, Jon Tippett QC, who has a great voice, made an excellent narrator. The narrations tie together the narrative and fill in the gaps necessary to keep the performance to a reasonable time. And John Lawrence SC was a suitably stern, no-nonsense Galvin CSM, although Galvin didn't take up counsel assisting's implied threat to the media to behave (I said Sturgess was despicable).

All in all, despite some lack of flair, the audience of 150 or so were treated to a very interesting and at times engaging evening. And there was a revealing postscript recounting Justice Dean Mildren's interview in 2009 with Ian Barker QC, the principal prosecutor at the Chamberlain trial, during the judge's research for his recently- published history of the Northern Territory Supreme Court.

Mr Barker told him: "If I had known at the time of the original trial what I now know, I would have advised the government not to proceed with the trial."

As Rex Wild commented, "IF BRADLEY MURDOCH'S DNA HAD NOT BEEN ON JOANNE LEES' T-SHIRT, I WOULD HAVE ADVISED AGAINST BRINGING HIM TO TRIAL.

Wow, wow, wow! What a revelation….

- So, Monsieur the Prosecutor, you knew but did absolutely nothing to prevent this miscarriage,
- You knew that the experts on ballistics were doing tests on a big gun which has never been found,
- You knew that this mysterious big gun was later on downgraded to a smaller calibre to fit the narrative and the agenda,
- You knew that there should have been **NOT ONE BUT TWO** Main Prime Suspects, but you all kept your mouths shut, thinking that we are all a bunch of idiots,
- You knew that our prime and only witness Joanne Lees could not have come out of her hiding place after five hours being warm – unbruised –and clean when the "black Dark Night" temperature was between ten and 13 degrees (Celsius not Kelvin),
- You knew that the CCTV man left Alice Springs at 1.00am on the 15th contrary to Murdoch who left at 3.10pm on the 14th, but you all kept your mouths shut.

- Is there anything that you would like to tell us about the DNA PLOT to make us believe that the bloodstain found on the back of Lees T-shirt, of unknown source belong to Murdoch,
- Is there anything you would like us to know about why it took so long (28 months) for some items of prime importance to arrive in the lab of those experts,
- Is there anything you like to tell why Murdoch alibi is now classified or top-secret,
- **BUT THE MOST REMARKABLE** is the fact that you knew, including your mates, that the man and his Cruiser seen on the CCTV film; was NOT Murdoch and his Land Cruiser.
- **HOWEVER,** without his trailer, the one <u>Joanne Lees never saw nor mentioned even when she escaped</u> and without his rented dog (tears of joy in the back ground), you knew people would start asking questions

YES, THAT IS TRULY REMARKABLE.

NOW dear readers, I am asking: What are your views on this amazing play, any comments? What do you think Rex Wild QC meant? Do you think the mysterious bloodstain could have been planted –could it be even Murdoch's blood? Even so, are you satisfy that Joanne Lees may have been sitting at the restaurant on the same chair (as suggested by some) where Murdoch sat previously at different time indicating or suggesting a transfer of Murdoch's blood and as a result onto the back of her T-shirt? Well, I think that it is a laughable suggestion.

To me it sounds like Rex Wild inner thoughts were: Well, Joanne Lees 'claims will not do the trick… So, let's use a bloodstain and pretend that it came from Murdoch…What do you think?

Well, enough of this. We know from all previous chapters that all claims made by Joanne Lees are "Big Bags" of lies supported by Rex Wild irrelevant of his deepest inner thoughts.

The Vanishing of Peter Falconio

87 - Murdoch's Brother Gary and His DNA

From The Guardian

"Getting a DNA sample from a person of interest is no easy task. You need to find someone who doesn't want to be found and then convince him or her to give you a sample. **Gwynne** knew if her team approached Murdoch directly, he would go to ground.

"If he disappeared, we wouldn't have found him," she says. "He was an expert in disguise. He was constantly changing the look of his car. He would swap the mudflaps, the plates, the hubcaps and the canvas."

So, they decided to approach Murdoch's brother, Gary. This was risky and they only had one shot at it, but Gwynne was confident after she learned there was a falling out between the siblings.

"I thought a lot about who could convince Gary to give us a DNA sample. In the end, I sent the young, quiet, female detective because I thought her approach would give us the best opportunity – and my intuition paid off."

The forensic expert advised that the DNA from Lees's T-shirt was 150 quadrillion times more likely to have come from Murdoch than someone else.

"I couldn't believe we had a match. We now know who touched Joanne Lees on her shirt. We now know who touched the gear stick in the Kombi. It was Bradley John Murdoch."

The press went crazy. Papers across the country homed in on Murdoch and Alice Springs was flooded with TV crews and British reporters.

"Bradley Murdoch knew we were on to him and he panicked. He started to escape and this man knows the bush like no other. We had a window of opportunity to find him and we knew that it was now a hunt."

Police all over Australia were on the lookout for Murdoch and he may have eluded them if he hadn't committed another crime.

On 28 August 2002 the South Australian police arrested him in the coastal town of Port Augusta, 300km north-west of Adelaide, for the suspected rape and abduction of a woman and her 12-year-old daughter. Gwynne listened in via speakerphone as they made the arrest.

"I felt a mixture of excitement and apprehension. We were now under enormous pressure. We had to be in a position where we could arrest him and transfer him to the Northern Territory should he be acquitted or bailed of the South Australian charges."

Interesting piece of reading don't you think? Because not only police ask Murdoch's brother Gary for blood sample, but **Gwynne said Murdoch was in hiding** making him hard to find. South Australian police didn't seem to have difficulty in finding him regarding the rape case? Are we facing ANOTHER BIG LIAR?

Questions: What items/samples/swabs were taken from the crime scene and when?

- Who tested the items/samples/swabs and when?
- What items/samples/swabs were taken to Professor Whitaker in the UK and when?
- What opportunities were there for items/samples/swabs to be contaminated either accidentally or deliberately?
- What happened to the DNA test taken from Murdoch's brother Gary?
- What were the legal reasons for taking it?
- What DNA evidence did the Defence challenge?

14 August 2002: Police take a blood sample from Murdoch's brother Gary in Perth. That is 13 months after the alleged crime…Why? Don't you think that in possession of Lees 'shirt for 13 months, THEY would have tested that small bloodstain?

- So why getting Murdoch's brother DNA?
- Initially WA cops didn't interview Murdoch as a suspect (Robin Bowles p. 175)
- Cops interview Murdoch and accept his alibi. They refuse to reveal what it was… (Richard Shears p.113) **why? What is so secret about it?**

The Vanishing of Peter Falconio

- Murdoch was on the NT's list of 'persons of interest' (around 2,000 people).
- The police needed Murdoch's DNA to do a comparison with the smudge on the T-shirt.
- Full non-identical siblings share about 50% of the same DNA with each other.

"When the national police alert failed to produce any sign of him (Murdoch), police visited his parents and his brother Gary. They all said they had no idea where he would be. Then, desperate to be sure they weren't wasting time chasing false leads, police asked if Gary would be prepared to give a blood sample to compare with the DNA result on Joanne's T-shirt. It is unclear whether Gary agree purely in order to rule himself out of inquiries, or because he was so convinced is brother was innocent it would help him too.

But on **14 August 2002** he had a swab taken. If the DNA on the T-shirt was Bradley Murdoch's, Gary's would show up as a close match. (Sue Williams p. 224)

"The sample revealed common alleles to the 'unknown male' police were seeking." ie Murdoch (Bowles p. 155)

- Allele are different versions of a gene which vary according to the Nucleotide base present at a particular genome location… For more information please, refer to the Internet

"In the end, Taskforce Regulus opted for a different way of testing Murdoch's link to the t-shirt smudge.

On **14 August 2002**, they travelled to Perth and approached Murdoch's older brother, Gary, for his DNA sample. The costs of this decision became clear when it later emerged that Gary promptly phoned Murdoch to warn him of the heightened interest of the Falconio investigators. However, the police's gambit yielded a partial DNA match after Gary consented to the sampling, perhaps because he didn't think his brother was the highway stranger. (Bowles 2005:151; Maynard 2005:159-160; Williams 2006:224). (Gans, Jeremy. 2007.)

The Vanishing of Peter Falconio

"The partial match - to be expected if a blood relative of Gary's was the source of the smudge was certainly enough, in combination with the other information gathered by Taskforce Regulus, to objectively narrow the investigators' suspicions to Murdoch himself. However, Taskforce Regulus eschewed (avoided) relying on this technique as a means of justifying the sampling of Murdoch. Instead, when Murdoch was located two weeks later [in SA], none of the information gathered by the investigators up to that date was used to justify either his arrest or the taking of his DNA sample." (Gans, Jeremy. 2007.)

Note that this is before they interviewed Hepi on ten September 2002. Now check this:

"Gary had also heard that one of the **Coffin Cheaters** had put out a contract on his brother." (Bowles p.155) Note that Murdoch belonged to the **Gypsey Jokers** for a while (Bowles p. 174) Also on page 156 in her book not to be dismissed:

- "Although some local police had been suspicious of Hepi' associates…He also said that Murdoch had a number two buzz cut, and was always clean shaven. But rumours flew that Murdoch had shaved off a Mexican style moustache, grown a full beard to disguise it, cut his long hair short and so on. His friends and colleagues insisted he'd never had long hair or any kind of moustache. Photos that might verify any of these claims seemed to be in short supply…(I thought I mention it!)
- What did they already know/suspect about Murdoch to warrant testing Gary's DNA? They didn't have Hepi's statement then.
- Did the fact that cops were selling hydro in Broome have anything to do with it? (Bowles p. 174)
- What was the other information gathered by the investigators up to that date and why was none of it used to justify either his arrest or the taking of his DNA sample?
- Was there a legal reason for this decision?
- Is the 'other information gathered by Taskforce Regulus' Hepi's statement?

The Vanishing of Peter Falconio

- Was **Eckhoff** testing Gary's sample against the T-shirt swab? As we are speaking Eckhoff, please read from:

From The Guardian

"Getting a DNA sample from a person of interest is no easy task. You need to find someone who doesn't want to be found and then convince him or her to give you a sample. **Gwynne** *knew if her team approached Murdoch directly, he would go to ground.*

"If he disappeared, we wouldn't have found him," she says. "He was an expert in disguise. He was constantly changing the look of his car. He would swap the mudflaps, the plates, the hubcaps and the canvas."

"So, they decided to approach Murdoch's brother, Gary. This was risky and they only had one shot at it, but Gwynne was confident after she learned there was a falling out between the siblings."

"I thought a lot about who could convince Gary to give us a DNA sample. In the end, I sent the young, quiet, female detective because I thought her approach would give us the best opportunity – and my intuition paid off."

"The forensic expert advised that the DNA from Lees's T-shirt was 150 quadrillion times more likely to have come from Murdoch than someone else."

I couldn't believe we had a match. We now know <u>who touched Joanne Lees on her shirt</u>. We now know who touched the gear stick in the Kombi. It was Bradley John Murdoch."

Do you believe that? Do you understand the narrative and the agenda? You don't need to be a mind reader! Then...

"The press went crazy. Papers across the country homed in on Murdoch and Alice Springs was flooded with TV crews and British reporters".

The Vanishing of Peter Falconio

"Bradley Murdoch knew we were on to him and he panicked. He started to escape and this man knows the bush like no other. We had a window of opportunity to find him and we knew that it was now a hunt."

"Police all over Australia were on the lookout for Murdoch and he may have eluded them if he hadn't committed another crime."

"On 28 August 2002 the South Australian police arrested him in the coastal town of Port Augusta, 300km north-west of Adelaide, for the suspected rape and abduction of a woman and her 12-year-old daughter. Gwynne listened in via speakerphone as they made the arrest.

"I felt a mixture of excitement and apprehension. We were now under enormous pressure. We had to be in a position where we could arrest him and transfer him to the Northern Territory should he be acquitted or bailed of the South Australian charges."

Now, do you understand colleen Gwynne? Do you trust her?

Do you believe that she is trustworthy when she speaks of Murdoch and when you read the follow up…

"On 28 August 2002 the South Australian police arrested him in the coastal town of Port Augusta, 300km north-west of Adelaide, for the suspected rape and abduction of a woman and her 12-year-old daughter. Gwynne listened in via speakerphone as they made the arrest.

"I felt a mixture of excitement and apprehension. We were now under enormous pressure. We had to be in a position where we could arrest him and transfer him to the Northern Territory should he be acquitted or bailed of the South Australian charges."

Now, do you know who is this Ms colleen Gwynne? Do you trust her?

But there is more…

Behind the scenes of THE Colleen Gwynne 'abuse of office' charge
by Christopher Walsh | Jul 19, 2020 | NT Politics, Opinion | 1 comment

ANALYSIS: *The serious abuse of office charge laid against NT Children's Commissioner Colleen Gwynne has exposed troubling integrity issues in the NT's public institutions and raised some uncomfortable* *questions for the Gunner Government ahead of the Territory election next month…….*

Reflecting on Colleen Gywnne's attitude and integrity in her job and her impartiality in **2020** must tell you what she must have been during the investigation from **2001** up to the trial in **2005**… even after… (no comments).

From the net obviously. Interesting internet piece of reading don't you think? Because not only police ask Murdoch's brother Gary for blood sample, but Gwynne said Murdoch was in hiding making him hard to find. <u>South Australian police didn't seem to have difficulty in finding him</u> as I said regarding the rape case. Are we facing **ANOTHER BIG LIAR**?

Questions: What items/samples/swabs were taken from the crime scene and when?

28 August 2002: Murdoch arrested for the SA rape
- Note that this is only 14 days after the NT police take a sample of Gary's DNA.
- NT police request samples of Murdoch's blood via a Forensic Procedures Application.

On 4 September 2002 SA Attorney General Michael Atkinson & NT Minister for Police, Fire and Emergency Services, Syd Sterling, signed an agreement saying that it was in the 'public interest' to transfer the DNA. (Media Release Office of the Chief Minister) (Maynard p. 170)
- Murdoch's Defence lawyers challenged the transfer but **on 6 September 2002** SA Magistrate **Gary Gumpi** issued a court order agreeing to the Forensic Procedures Application.
- "It is fundamentally obvious that the purpose of testing the blood one would cynically suspect, is not in respect to these South Australian allegations. It is for the purpose of sending these samples to the Northern Territory." (Grant Algie cited in Maynard p.170)
- "Privately the defendant [Murdoch] also feared that his DNA sample could be interfered with between the time it left Adelaide

and when it was eventually compared with the tiny spot on the back of Joanne's T-shirt now being kept in Darwin." (Maynard p.170)

2 October 2002 Justice Ted Mulligan in SA Supreme Court rejected an appeal from Murdoch's lawyers.

- **Mark Twigg's** immediately announced he would appeal that decision [Mulligan's] but **on 8 October 2002** decided not to take the matter further. (Williams p.234) **Why?**
- On Tuesday, Mr Murdoch abandoned his legal battle to prevent Northern Territory police testing his blood. Neither Mr Murdoch nor his lawyer gave any reason for the decision to drop the appeal." (BBC Online News 10 October 2002)

24 October 2003: The samples/swabs were sent to Dr Whitaker in the UK

The samples (swabs?) were sent to Dr Whitaker on 24 October 2003 for the more powerful LCN testing.

Dr Whitaker and others at the Wetherby laboratory had developed a technique for the testing of samples containing very small quantities of DNA. It was the availability of this technique at Wetherby which led to the request of Dr Whitaker to examine the DNA samples in question. The Queen v Murdoch [2005] NTSC 76

- Did Whitaker have the actual manacles or only swabs?
- Note that the NT did not have Murdoch's DNA' sample at this time but they did have his brother Gary's DNA.
- **Did Ekhart** send Gary's DNA sample **to Whitaker?**

Food for thought don't you think? And all this beyond any reasonable doubt.

Links to support the case:

Jeremy Gans 2007 Catching Bradley Murdoch: Tweezers, Pitchforks and the Limits of DNA Sampling

https://www.austlii.edu.au/cgibin/viewdoc/au/journals/ClCrimJust/2007/14.html?context=1;query=gans%20jeremy%20%20tweezers%20;mask_path=

DNA Breakthrough in Falconio case 10 October 2002 UK

The Vanishing of Peter Falconio

http://news.bbc.co.uk/2/hi/asia-pacific/2313333.stm

Falconio family's relief at DNA link BBC News World Edition, 10 October, 2002 UK

http://news.bbc.co.uk/2/hi/asia-pacific/2315379.stm

The Vanishing of Peter Falconio

88 - The High Court Said...

I would recommend anyone interested in the case to watch the four episodes produced by Channel seven (7 Plus) aired documentary "Murder in the outback". We know from fact that the Prosecution emphasised that the man at the truck-stop was Murdoch. In episode three Andrew Fraser speaking and I quote:

- ***"The High Court said: You cannot convict on DNA alone. It is not safe enough***. *So, there must be some corroboration. That corroboration the police said; is Murdoch at the truck-stop because of the time the footage was taken, places Murdoch in Alice Springs at a time when he could have committed the crime and been back in Alice Springs feeling the car up and shot off on his way along the Tanami track"*
- So obviously the time the CCTV man enters the truck-stop means without proofs that it is Murdoch and because it places the CCTV man in Alice again without proofs it is Murdoch! And as you will read further on, the Dead Body of Falconio is in the back of the Land Cruiser according to our dear **Judge Martin Brian**. Well, that is a real good one!
- So, we have a man and his Cruiser who has never been identified, who enters a truck-stop in Alice at a time when absolutely nobody knows about some alleged events at Barrow Creek, that man is the alleged killer. That man is Bradley Murdoch simply because that man enters the truck-stop in Alice. Well, I should feel myself very fortunate because it could have been me knowing that I drive the same Cruiser a 75 series.
- **This can only happen in Northern Territory nowhere else.**

Obtaining Murdoch DNA was not an easy task. When Murdoch was arrested and charged for rape of a woman and her daughter but released after being found not guilty, police working on the alleged murder of Peter Falconio had no solution on how they could obtain Murdoch's DNA.

In episode 4, there is the video footage of the interview with John Dalby Former Assistant Commissioner NT Police:

The Vanishing of Peter Falconio

(Actual recording of Andrew Fraser and John Dalby).

"Once police had Murdoch in their frame, they had to find DNA evidence from Murdoch to compare with the DNA found on the back of Joanne Lees 'T-shirt. Three months later Murdoch was arrested for the rape of the woman and her daughter, and that gave police the opportunity to obtain his DNA... (From John Dalby).

"On advice from South Australia that Murdoch had been arrested, was a significant breakthrough in the investigation and the exciting part about it was I believe at this point of time we could get DNA sample from Murdock. Getting a sample from Murdoch's DNA was incredibly important to the whole case."

- Yes, it was a significant breakthrough in the investigation; [**THEY**] finally found Murdoch who according to [**THEM**] was in hiding. So why did South Australia find him so quickly? Was Murdoch really hiding?
- According to **Gwynne** who is really promoting the fact that Murdoch had gone in hiding and the excuse so they could ask his brother for DNA sample.
- Well, it seems that Murdoch was not in hiding and that is why South Australia had no problem in finding Murdoch regarding the alleged rape case. **Gwynne** is another big liar not to be trusted. The whole story is/was definitely a plot and a conspiracy.
- So, you can tell that already Murdoch has already been chosen as prime suspect and I believe that it's all about drugs –drug lords – and more...

AGAIN, this is extremely important. It is related to Murdoch's brother Gary and his DNA (chapter 86 and 87). I am a strong believer that two + two = four...Not five!

(Episode 4 from the television news' recording)

"In the hearing the Prosecution thought permission to DNA test and blood samples taken from Murdoch, but his lawyer Grant Algie told the court the application in the case was only a small screen to get the DNA for the Falconio investigation"

89 - The Sentencing of Murdoch

The words coming out of the Judge's mouth made me very angry, it was very upsetting, I felt extremely distressed. I could not believe what I was hearing. I am still thinking about it, it makes my blood boil.

(Episode 4; sentencing by Martin Brian actual footage)

From television News including video footage)

Here the Judge is the real hero! His outstanding achievements and his noble qualities are the proofs beyond any reasonable doubt as seen on the video that...

- **HE CANNOT BE TRUSTED**

(From Murder in the outback)

"Because of public interest the judge allowed the cameras into court to record his blunt remarks: I must sentence you on the bases of facts that I found proven and that are consistent with the verdict of the jury (of course). In July 2001 Mr Falconio and Ms Lees were aged 28 and 27. On July 14th, you destroyed not only their plans but the life of Peter Falconio. I am satisfied that you pretended (here of course the judge is addressing Murdoch) that there were sparks from the rear of the Kombi. Whilst Mr Falconio was looking to see if sparks were admitted and Ms Lees was revving the engine, you shot Falconio in the head."

Very simple, why didn't I think of it?

Well, there is another way to look at things. The Judge said: "I must sentence you on the bases of facts that I found proven and that are consistent with the verdict of the jury....

BUT now is what I think:

How to prove an innocent guilty in an alleged crime

- Ignore everything and every fact during the investigation which contradict the narrative and the agenda.
- When that has been established, convince the jury to vote Guilty on all charges
- Then the sentencing becomes a walk in the park...

- Because the main sentence is already formed. Simply turn it around. It will then read: *I must sentence you on the bases* **of facts that are consistent with the verdict of the jury**, **that I found proven**...What do you think?

Sorry for the interruption, back to the sentencing:

That is very precise; in the head...

Did Joanne Lees herself mentioned this at any time during the investigation and at the trial? Did she actually saw Murdoch shooting her boyfriend in the head with the big gun? I am a bit confused, I thought that [HE] got shot by the exhaust [?]...Because I thought that she only heard a BANG.

Monsieur "The" Judge, did you really saw Murdoch being shot in the head, were you there at that precise time? So, according to you, he did get shot in the head. Well, I've learned something new today.

Do you believe that when nothing belonging to Murdoch was ever found, not even the mysterious gun or emptied cartridges? How can it be so corrupt?

So, here we have Judge Martin witnessing something that even Joanne Lees didn't AMAZING!

"...You then confronted Ms Lees with a gun, (must be the same gun) tied her hands behind her back with hand cuffs made of cable ties. Ms Lees was either feel or was pushed from the Kombi...onto the ground on the verge of the Stuart Highway. In that process, she sustained abrasion to knees and probably her elbows. I am satisfied that you put the body of Mr Falconio to the rear of your vehicle..."

This is definitely the best one. Really, how did the Judge come to such conclusion?

- Saying "**I am satisfied <u>that you pretended</u> is pure fabrication,** it means what it means. It means that Murdoch pretended that there were sparks from the rear of the Kombi which could be right here using the verb pretended relating to sparks, but,
- "*That you pretended*" also means that when Murdoch was pretending, <u>he must have</u> <u>been speaking to</u> himself –about himself

or –about someone else –to someone else if you know what I mean [?]. Who could be that someone else? Well, it could only be him, the bad boy. Can you imagine Murdoch saying and using the words **"I pretended…Killing or having killed FALCONIO"**?

- What surprises me even up until now is that nobody said anything, no reactions whatsoever from the Defence and the Jury.
- <u>Please check on the internet: How to use the verb PRETEND in a sentence, then get back to me please, I beg you.</u>
- **Then saying: …You shot Falconio in the head.** That is very precise indeed. We know where Lees was **[BUT]** where were you Monsieur the Judge? Were you there? Did you actually see Murdoch shooting Falconio in the head as I said above? Perhaps you could tell us what he did with the gun after that?

Are you a witness as well as a Judge? Who paid you for using such words? You should know better Monsieur the Judge!

- Do you believe all this nonsense dear readers? Do you believe that, when nothing belonging to Murdoch was ever found? Do you really and truly believe in our justice system after reading such a rubbish coming from a Judge's mouth?

WAS THE JUDGE A WITNESS?

I know this is a repeat, I need you to read it again and again.

Also how is it possible for Murdoch to kill Falconio when in fact he was 551km away at the time of the alleged crime? It is a total disgrace

"…you then confronted Ms Lees with a gun, tied her hands behind her back with hand cuffs made of cable ties. Ms Lees was either feel or was pushed from the Kombi…

…Onto the ground on the verge of the Stuart Highway. In that process, she sustained abrasion to knees and probably her elbows. I am satisfied that you put the body of Mr Falconio to the rear of your vehicle….

Wow, I am satisfied that you put the body of Mr Falconio to the rear of your vehicle.

Well coming from a Judge's mouth that takes a lot of courage to even get the words out.

Really, how did the Judge come to such conclusion? Do I have to go through the same rubbish again?

Such conclusion means that Murdoch shot Falconio –then abducted Joanne Lees – then he pushed her onto the back of his Cruiser –then he put the body of Falconio to the rear of his vehicle next to his girlfriend "bla bla bla" ...Can you imagine the scene. Not bad hey!

Then he departed the alleged crime scene at 9.00pm on the 14th with the dead body of Falconio... But sorry Lees had already escaped. Is this for real?

Well, no problem for Murdoch because after having moved the Kombi, he must have realized when pushing the dead body of Falconio onto the back of the Cruiser that Lees was no longer in the back of his vehicle and surprisingly he couldn't care less.

And then you travelled across the Tanami to Broome. Somewhere on that journey you buried the body of Mr Falconio. I am satisfied that there is complete lack of any remorse. I fixed a non-parole of a period of 28 years commencing on 10 November 2003. Could you please remove the prisoner...."

DID THE JUDGE REALLY SAID SUCH THING –DID THE JURY TRULY BELIEVE THAT? WAS THE DEFENCE AWAKE?

Now after reading the sentencing by Judge Martin, have you noticed something very intriguing, even suspicious?

Firstly, the Judge is openly sentencing Murdoch by accusing him of having killed Falconio and the abduction of his girlfriend (I think his speech has been written perhaps by Lees [?])

Secondly the Judge is openly accusing Murdoch of having put the dead body to the rear of the Cruiser meaning that:

- When the CCTV man entered the truck stop the body of Falconio was/had to be in the back of the Cruiser unless he disposed of it on the way, but having no shovel does pose a problem. Well, I find this extremely distressing but however funny becauseThey found

The Vanishing of Peter Falconio

out that the blood found on the road, on the tar is NOT Murdoch's or Falconio's blood but rather animal like a road kill or aliens (which ever you prefer, aliens is better) but strangely and interestingly no blood of Falconio as I said was found either at the alleged crime scene or on the Kombi **[on]** or **[in]**. (Laughter and clapping in the background).

But Wait I Just Had a Thought

The judge got confused, he forgot to mention that Murdoch did wrap the head of Falconio in Lees 'jacket being a meticulous killer (according to her book No Turning Back page 239)

- Which brings me back to Lees 'escape; was she pushed to the back of the Cruiser before or after the body of Falconio (bless his soul) was put to the rear of the unidentified Land Cruiser, the one on the CCTV footage. (Unanimous laughter in the background).

I am sorry but saying I am satisfied "that you pretended" means what it means. It means that Murdoch did pretend –pretended –has been pretending of being the killer. I just like this to be understood: Pretending does not mean admitting. Can you spot the difference?

- Here the judge is addressing Murdoch directly on television openly saying and using the words "that you pretended (past tense; a tense expressing an action that has happened or a state that previously existed). Well, please check the definition and meaning of the verb pretend. This is definitely meant to deceive.
- It is a disgrace coming from a Judge's mouth, but the worse part being that the sentencing was televised (the media had a ball), no comments were ever heard since, even from the Defence Team.

Do you really believe Murdoch did such thing when in fact he always claimed that he was in no way near the alleged crime scene at the time, claiming that at the time of the alleged crime he was near Yuendumu and that between midnight and 1.00am on the 15th of July 2001 he was near the Granites. Did I prove it? Oh yes, I did. (Now you understand why repeats are necessary).

The Vanishing of Peter Falconio

My calculation proved that Murdoch's claims are absolutely true. The judge here is definitely telling a "Big Lie" to fit the narrative and the agenda, or perhaps SOMETHING ELSE.

- Saying "I am satisfied *"that you pretended"* **is pure fabrication.** It means what it means. What surprises me even up until now is that nobody said anything, no reactions whatsoever. No comments were ever published.

No real killer would "pretend". A real killer would deny any accusation, but would not pretend having committed a crime…This is the world upside down. This is bad English.

Murdoch was not at the alleged crime scene at that time; it is the judge saying it. It is false accusation coming from the Judge's mouth. It is worse than the actual alleged crime. The Judge needs to be facing the music…Maybe he will? (Clapping and cheering in the background).

Now, let's go back to Murdoch and the Judge saying; I am satisfied that you put the body of Mr Falconio to the rear of your vehicle….

Did Lees witness Murdoch throwing the body of her boyfriend to the rear of the vehicle? Herself being already in the vehicle or after she escaped because remember she claimed she watched him searching for her with his torch and his rented dog? So, she must have seen him putting the body to the rear of the Land Cruiser. Well, I am waiting for answers!

As if three liars (Lees –the Prosecution –Monsieur Hepi) was not enough we have now a fourth one, our dear Judge. We have now a perfect quartet where the Judge will be the conductor, a man of authority who saw the killing (shot in the head) and saw Murdoch throwing the Dead Body to the back of his vehicle. This is truly "Music to My Ears"

As a Judge, his sentencing language and accusations are a disgrace to all of us.

Please can you visualise the scene of Murdoch entering the Shell truck-stop at the wheel of his Cruiser with the dead body of Falconio in the back with his head wrapped in Lees 'jacket

I truly hope they're going to make a fantastic movie out of it.

The Vanishing of Peter Falconio

90 - More From Murder in The Outback Documentary

Here, I firstly listen to all four episodes. Then the next day I listen to each episode. Then it's all hand written for most relevant parts. It's all play/pause –write –and again play/pause –write making sure I don't miss a word. It's a quite slow job, lots of rewinding if you ask me. It requires good ears –some understanding of the English language.

Episode 1

1 – Vince Millar reading the declaration drafted by police after two pages from his first declaration went missing –claiming that is not what happened –they're not my words –this here is not my statement."

Vince Millar saying; it was dark, very dark, there was no moon."

2 –Re-enactment an attempt to reconstruct the events. Showing Joanne Lees –investigators and Kombi…A real farce! A real re-enactment would have been choosing a night with an average temperature between ten and 13 degrees then keeping Joanne Lees five hours wearing a light T-shirt and shorts and see if she comes out warm (repeat I know).

3 –Professor Barry Boettcher Blood Specialist commenting about the pool of blood found on the verge of the road. Boettcher was approached by Legal Aid to look at the case.

Written image reading; "In Murdoch's 2007 Appeal Ruling, the court determined: Dependent on the nature of the wound…It was also possible that there would be no external extrusion of brain or other tissue and relatively limited blood loss then Boettcher saying: If blood is present you get a pale blue luminescence using Luminol (chemical reaction) if a body had been shot and, then dragged somewhere, you would expect a blood trail –there was no blood trail in this case –further than this, there were no blood splatter at the scene –in my opinion based on DNA and blood evidence, I would not expect today to have a guilty verdict recorded against anybody.

4 – Introduction of Robin Bowles (author of Dead Centre) who spent more than 60 hours visiting Murdoch in jail with her first question; Did you kill Peter Falconio? –

The Vanishing of Peter Falconio

MURDOCH: "well no, how did you know he was even dead? "

ROBIN: "Bradley Murdoch is a very careful man –he's obsessive about tidiness –neatness and all the precautions he used to run his drugs –he is not the kind of guy who would shoot someone on the side of the road where anyone passing –and then let the person escaping to the bush as if nothing had happened."

5 – Image of Murdoch and his dog. If the dog looks like a Kelpie or any cattle dog, I am the true image of president Xi Jinping. (Cheering in the background).

6 – Introduction of Brian McDonald Forensic Scientist.

Fraser speaking; In this case what police found was one small spot of Murdoch's DNA on the back of Joanne Lees 'T-shirt around the shoulder blade area. The thing that has bothered me the most is why is there so little of Murdoch's DNA on Joanne Lees?

- <u>NO, I am sorry, what police found was not a spot of Murdoch's DNA but a small bloodstain of unknown source.</u>
- Because, at that time police were desperate to get his DNA and that is why police asked his brother for his DNA …Please don't put the cart before the horses.

So, in the presence of Andrew Fraser and Victor Susman, Dr Brian McDonald is going to run a small experiment using two actors for everyone to understand about DNA on how it can be transferred (I myself went through the same experiment when working in restaurant, it was interesting).

Dr Brian McDonald was part of the Defence Team at the trial. He is considered one of the best DNA experts in Australia. He now speaks:

"We shed cells from our skin (shedding). One square cm of our skin sheds on average 100,000cells per hour. We are shedding these all over the place; onto our clothes, everything that we do handle, our cars etc.

- *If some DNA get transferred on one item after it has been ceased, it's classified as contamination.*
- *If it is transferred onto an item before the crime was ever committed then it's irrelevant.*

So, the only DNA that become relevant for the purpose of deciding if someone is guilty or innocent is DNA that is transferred during the commission of the crime…

- *Therefore, why so little DNA on Lees if Murdoch handle Lees so much; cuffing her pushing her –putting tape on her ankles lifting her etc.?*

Dr Brian McDonald comment was when he was starting looking at the DNA in the case, it became very obvious that there was very little clear evidence at all.

Further on he says; "it doesn't tell us that there was direct contact between Lees and Murdoch."

- Then **Brian McDonald** told *"that the DNA found in the Kombi is so weak wouldn't exclude a large proportion of the population. It is so weak that it is difficult to attribute to anyone."*

"It would be expected to be found on an item handled by the perpetrator. DNA if it's not in blood is invisible. This is a simulation to look at the transfer which can occur which you are not able to see up front. Once the transfer has occurred turn on the UV light and you can see where this has gone in much the same way.

"When DNA is found on an item it doesn't tell us that the DNA got from the person to the item by the person directly touching it or the person ever be any way near it because the DNA can be transferred without them being involved"

7 - Window on Andrew Fraser's life in the drug business being a lawyer

8 - Andrew Fraser speaking; People think they know the story but they probably don't.

9 - Vince Millar; I know what part I played in it –but you know the police didn't get there till day brake –there is so much more to the story than people can even imagine.

9 - Here Andrew Fraser speaking about Vince Millar: Reading Millar's statement again there is a bit that catches my eyes –only minutes before Joanne Lees jumped out on the front of his truck -Vince describes a very

odd behaviour on the road ahead while he was driving –Vince described head lights in the distance doing littles circles –lights going on and off –very odd behaviour – this aspect of Vince's story has never been followed up on or investigated.

10 - Andrew Frazer and Victor Susman wanting to know more about the lights Vince Millar saw before rescuing Joanne Lees. After many discussions Vince finally agreed to meet. This is in brief the interview at Vince's house recorded on Victor mobile phone;

11 - Vince Millar; *Yeah mate, chuck'in 'u-eys, doing all sorts, doin'all sorts of weird things, man*

FRASER One car doing or more than one?

VINCE MILLAR *One car, you know –you wouldn't have been, like, a lot of cars –it just looks like one car, one bloke chuckin' a u-ey or .... and what I did, I flicked me lights off 'coz you can do that when you're in, out there, you know?*

Had all my clearance lights on, but I flicked me lights off. and I'm like what the...there? you know? Checkin'it out and that and I thought, oh, you know....it so I turned the lights back on and I... I was driving and all the sudden there was this little red car that pulled up, and there was a couple of blokes, yeah right on the side of the road and then I pulled up and out of me truck thinking they are broken down or something...

.I said oh, um, I went to walk over and they were.... all shunting back in the car and that you know? I' seen this bloke like. jelly and that you know? and I thought,' what's....goin' on there? and then, um, vroom they took off.

Yeah he was sort of in the middle of the other two blokes...he was....movin' around, so.... yeah, yeah, like you know, couldn't see his arms, but he was like that, and....bloke got in and ....pushed him in and ....then they were off.

Once I pulled up, mate, they were....out of there the way they got in that car and took off. There was something that they didn't want me to see so, thinking back now, and putting all the dots together, I'm pretty sure that that bloke in the middle very well could've been Falconio

FRASER Why was none of that recorded anywhere?

The Vanishing of Peter Falconio

VINCE MILLAR *After we pickup Lees we went up to Barrow Creek – next morning police finally came –They proceeded to write our statement as we dictated too – the next time I saw that statement, was two weeks before the preliminary court case –I was notified that the first two pages of my statement were missing and I was then presented with two pages already written...Too easy!*

and they said you've got to sign these –this is what we are going to call with –after reading these I turn around and I said; look I believe these are not my statements and I said I don't really want to sign it – Then it started to get a bit thick and I was told that um, you know, do I want to open up a can of worms – Why would they take the red car out of my statement?

FRASER With the first statement we were told red car.

VINCE MILLAR *Oh! with any significance, yeah I've told .... few mates....and stuff like that no one, no one with any sort of significance, no.*

FRASER Who was the bloke in the red car, who was jelly man, and what were they doing there? Suddenly there're all these other people in the frame......What comes next changes the entire case (Ending 47'28).

The Vanishing of Peter Falconio

91 - The Meaning of the Word Disappearance, according to Joanne Lees

Episode 2 highlights

(Starting 16'14 Fraser speaking): *"In my view the most significant thing we found was a scan report –the report scientific content analysis notes. The scan report was based on an interview the police did with Joanne Lee on the night of the 15th of July –that is the night the day after the event. Scan are reports from experts, they look at the language, the used words for evidence of deception to see they could reach to conclusion as to whether Lees was telling the truth."*

(Police speaking to Lees video clip): *"Your statement, we had it, we sent it away to some experts, they look at the content and they look at the language. Practitioners from Victoria –Queensland –Northern Territory – and South Australia have had a look at that, a number of them."*

LEES Yeah

POLICE *And that's* done *to assist investigators as an investigative tool."*

LEES *Come on this is gonna be bad news, what do they say?*

POLICE *The consensus without exception is that there is vital information missing from this statement....(.*<u>Here I cannot describe Lees 'body language, please use your imagination.</u>)

LEES *Right what information is missing...I don't know, I don't know...*

FRASER *"I am reading in the scan report itself... The very first thing on page two strikes me, she said; I don't know how but the next thing I remember was like being pushed out of the door or just be, well I don't remember being pushed out of the door....*

Then, the scan report comes up on my computer screen that reads: *"These statements are all indicative of a false statement account –there is missing time –missing information and no commitment to an account. This part of the story is particularly sketchy, the subject swings into present tense strongly indicating deception. The unanimous conclusion of the scan practitioners: This account provide by the subject has strong indications of *being deceptive –the statement has many contradictions and lacks commitment from the subject...* **The scan report was never mentioned at the trial."**

***

(Starting 26'36) **How the offender pushed Lees in the back of his car**; she said: *"Somehow he pushes me over* (present tense) *the seats into the back of the Ute...I go through easily...it's soft like the seats in the back of my car, like the seats have been laid back."*

FRASER...*" but by the time the trial came around she was not sure how she had got from the front to the back."*

***

(37'31) **Fraser commenting about Joanne Lees 'lover Nick Reilly**: *"That's what we found about Steph in the police files...police had discovered that she had been sending emails to a person by the name of Steph which was a pseudo for Nick...information to hand is that Lees was in fact having an intense moments with a person by the name of Nick Reilly – email correspondence how they were planning to meet up in Berlin in November 2001..continued correspondence went as far to indicate the name Steph which Lees and....they had chosen the name for a baby girl if they had one...Lees has attempted to hide her email and became particularly with...*(next words not audible)*...had released the email content to British media...this was couple of days after the shooting of her boyfriend....it didn't add up. To some people it makes the story less reliable*

(Nobody likes using the word alleged as in alleged crime...Why? Nothing has been proven).

Now it is police officer interviewing Lees from the original video clip:

POLICE...You obviously know that we're aware of the email sent...

LEES...Yes

POLICE From you to Nick and the reply...and just so that we're clear the email we're referring to is the one which you and Nick are making arrangement to meet in Berlin and it's signed Steph...

LEES...Yes

The Vanishing of Peter Falconio

POLICE…And the significance of Steph? is… Who's Steph?

LEES… Yep Nick just write Steph

POLICE… Why was it that, um, you intended to hide that email from us?

LEES… Because it's personal, um, and it's just no relevant…I know you're getting lots of background information but I had nothing to do with Pete's DISAPPEARANCE and neither has Nick, um I just find that you're wasting resources on just interviewing my friends in Sydney, and things, when you should be finding this man …

BINGO!

I need to stop for a minute. I had to make a cup coffee, excitement at its best if you know what I mean.…

Here Lees is very upset, very "pissed off" and ready to jump at police. If you have the opportunity to watch the video check her body language. But what came out instantly out of her mouth is the word DISAPPEARANCE knowing very well that:

- When first rescued by Vince Millar, she told him that a man had shot her boyfriend and then abducted her.
- She didn't tell Vince Millar that her boyfriend had disappeared but shot.
- Lees said the same thing to police when first interviewed on the morning the day after the alleged crime/killing/shooting.
- It is extremely suspicious regarding the truth about her story. To me this is a real big mistake: A BIG LIE and the answers to all suspicions that: **NO CRIME WAS COMMITTED IT IS/WAS A SCAM.**

When questioned by police on the morning after the alleged event she claimed that the offender came up or appeared at the window of her car with a big gun. To me that was [her] "introduction" of [A] big gun because for her story to be real, the killing of her boyfriend and her abduction there had to be a gun involved whatever the size (Clint Eastwood type or a downgraded to a 22 calibre). For someone shooting her boyfriend with a big

The Vanishing of Peter Falconio

gun, you need a gun. Shooting means killing…DISAPPEARANCE means what it means, but why –how –when and where is another story.

So, when questioned about her love affair she was not thinking about what she had claimed from the start about the killing and the gun and the rest. All she was thinking was to protect herself and her lover when the question popped up and also hoping that police wouldn't find more details about her relationship with "Nick" or "Steph. However, it was too late, the word DISAPPEARANCE popped up. It was an instantaneous and automatic self- preservation reaction. If her boyfriend had really been killed, it would have been a truly dramatic event and the first and only word that should have come out of her mouth would have been a synonym of the words kill or shot. NOT "DISAPPEARANCE" She was unprepared, her mind was not reading her imaginary and created transcript (like in the movie "The Great Escape with Steve McQueen 1963).

Joanne Lees' uncontrollable reaction when questioned in 2001 about the man who stopped them and who also allegedly shot her boyfriend (in the head mind you according to Judge Martin not Doc Martin) and then came up to window of the Kombi with a big gun which has never be found because it didn't exist, was pure self-preservation. That was a costly LIE. Unfortunately, it has never been challenged. Looking at the video anyone can see that she is upset –fighting –and wishing police would stop asking questions about her relationship with Nick. She needs to show that she was upset with the questions, but failed for it beautifully just by using the word disappearance. Also speaking of the offender appearing at the window with a big gun she said:

- **[He]** appeared at the window with **[A]** gun.

Then during the re-enactment, she said; he appeared with [A] gun which is correct in this context, but then when interviewed by the investigators she said; [HE] appeared at the widow with [A] gun (which is correct again and normal), but then she said: He then put [A] gun to my head. Well, that is something unusual. Putting yourself in her shoes;

- It would have been correct saying; **[HE]** appeared at the window with **[A]** gun, then **[HE]** put **[THE]** gun to my head?

- BUT saying: **[HE]** appeared at the window with **[A]** gun is normal but then **[HE]** put **[A]** gun to my head **is NOT**.

I assume in normal questioning which requires a straight and nearly spontaneous answer, first it would be [A] gun then it would be [THE] gun... But not using [A] gun twice.

What do you think gentlemen of the Jury?

***

(39'40) then further on:

(Police) "Did you tell your chaperone at the time that you had to get rid of e-mails from that account and you want to do that?"

LEES...I had to delete some e-mails because my account would close down otherwise because there were too many e-mails because obviously overseas friends and family were concerned about me and were e-mailing me a lot."

HIS WORSHIP... Were you on Hotmail?

LEES YES, then: "Were you concerned about police becoming aware of e-mails that you'd received from somebody called Steph?"

LEES NO

HIS WORSHIP... Who is Steph?

LEES....I don't know

HIS WORSHIP...Is not Steph the name of the pseudonym false name adopted to write to you through the e-mail by somebody called Nick?

LEES...YES

HIS WORSHIP...And who is Nick?

LEES....A friend

HIS WORSHIP...A friend from Sydney?

LEES....YES

HIS WORSHIP......A friend from Sydney with whom you had a relationship?

LEES....NO, I object to this question, sir, relevance, there's got to be some relevance for it Can you believe that? Well, when first asked who is

The Vanishing of Peter Falconio

Steph? She answered I don't know perfectly knowing that Steph is the pseudo for her lover. Then she said that Nick is a friend and then agreed that Steph is more than a friend from Sydney….

Can you see now that Joanne Lees is the biggest liar, can you tell that, she is not really up to the job at all, BUT she is a Good-Looking Sheila, and believes that she can outwit everybody because she truly believes that she is smart and everybody else stupid.

(Questioning was from the actual police video of the interview.)

At one stage on my computer screen as I am watching the video I can see that the name of a person speaking has been blocked…It was the Defence. The person says:

"The relationship as between this witness and Mr Falconio is obviously relevant in this case. I have reason to believe that there was another relationship either known or unknown to Mr Falconio at the time and it may be highly and at the end of the day as to the credibility of this witness, I should be permitted to explore it."

(40'43) Fraser talking with Victor Susman …we kept on digging and digging and finally found Joanne Lees 'phone records from police files. Files which never came up at the trial…it has here Nick Reilly then, on the 16 of June 2001 less than a month away from the incident 28 calls…the calls continued after they left Sydney… Even after the events.

Food for thought! The truth is out there, but where?

92 - Extra: An Analysis of DNA Evidence...Must Be Read

In 2005 Bradley John Murdoch was found guilty of the alleged murder of Peter Falconio and the assault on Joanne Lees as we know on the 14th of July 2001 at Barrow Creek. The only witness was the accuser who never saw the actual physical killing to the alleged crime. No murder weapon found. Falconio's Dead Body has never been found since, but reliable witnesses gave evidence in court that they saw Falconio alive about a week to ten days after the alleged shooting. Joanne Lees never saw the actual killing even being metre away from both men.

(Repeat) In his summing up to the jury, Defence counsel Grant Algie challenged the two assumptions underpinning the Prosecution case.

I said it before, the two assumptions that have been made very early in the investigation of this matter, and indeed which continue to form the foundation of the Prosecution's case'.

- **The first is**: If that if there was a bad guy at Barrow Creek he actually left his DNA or blood on Joanne Lees.
- **The second is**: If there was a bad guy at Barrow Creek that guy is the man at the Shell truck-stop which has been the foundation for the prosecution's case (Mildren p.35)

The Prosecutor, Rex Wild relied on identification and circumstantial evidence to bring the trial to court. By law, not all of the individual facts presented in circumstantial evidence must be proved beyond reasonable doubt in order for the jury to reach a guilty verdict. The Jury may infer from the combined strength of the facts that the accused is guilty. The metaphor used to describe this is "strands in a rope". The more strands the stronger the case –even if individual strands cannot be proven beyond reasonable doubt.

"The more circumstantial facts there are which bear upon the question and the stronger each fact individually may be, may give rise to a cumulative force of probity which increase the probability of guilt, although each fact looked at individually would not lead to such a conclusion itself" (Mildren p. xxiii)

However, if the evidence shows that there is clearly another inference from a fact that is consistent with innocence the jury should acquit (Mildren 2015 p. xxii)

Prosecutor Rex Wild, argued strongly that the DNA evidence, combine with the identification (being the CCTV man) evidence proved beyond reasonable doubt that Murdoch had murdered/killed Falconio at Barrow Creek. He presented the DNA analysis from samples taken from five pieces of evidence to support this: blood found on the road and rocks (road kill) – DNA on the Kombi' steering wheel and gear stick –and the manacles used to tie Lees (worn just for fun by the Assistant Police Commissionaire Dalby and his mate) wrists and the patch of blood on the back of Lees 'T-shirt, allegedly left by Murdoch during his assault on Lees.

Well, I disagree with the above. However, in 2011 Rex Wild who had retired in 2006, his report admitted that: "If Murdoch's DNA had not been on Lees' T-shirt, I would have advised against bringing him to trial (Watt 2011), mentioned in my chapter 86 The Inquisition (p.415).

- Interesting is that Rex Wild retired on 31 January 2006 five weeks after the trial. I wonder if he had second thoughts about his comment feeling that may be, it was time to vanish like Falconio for safety reasons. Perhaps having probably some bad thoughts about his comment hoping no one would find out,
- The same applying to our Chief Justice Martin and his daughter Joanna who had been in a relationship with a juror who sat on Murdoch's trial (Robin Bowles).

Chief Justice retired in 2010. He was questioned by a journalist asking him about the relationship of his daughter with the juror (strongly denied by the Chief Justice saying that: "it was after (Robin Bowles) After what?... The birth of a boy in the first week of May 2006. Well, his time will come!

I find this very intriguing circumstantial evidence. This alone should raise more than one question hey!

Is Wild admitting that, apart from the unknown source of blood found on the back of Lees' T-shirt, the identification and circumstantial evidence did not have enough probative value to warrant bringing Murdoch to trial?

The Vanishing of Peter Falconio

Could the DNA on Lees' T-shirt alone have constituted proof beyond reasonable doubt that Murdoch murdered Falconio at Barrow Creek? Was there an innocent explanation for how the DNA came to be on the T-shirt? Even when positively identified. DNA is only reliable evidence of an association with a crime scene or a victim of a crime. It is no prima facie evidence of guilt for a criminal offence.

Forensic scientist and DNA expert witness, Dr Brian McDonald assessed that the likelihood that the DNA on the T-shirt was Murdoch's could be high, but that it doesn't tell us how it got there but rather had been put there [?]

It certainly doesn't tell us that there was contact between Murdoch and this T-shirt (Murder in the outback episode 4).

Assuming that the DNA was Murdoch's there are several possibilities, all of which were addressed by Grant Algie (Defence Lawyer).

- It was transferred directly from Murdoch onto Lees 'T-shirt at Barrow Creek either during the alleged crime or for another reason.
- It was transferred directly from Murdoch onto Lees' T-shirt at another location
- It was the result of innocent primary or secondary transfer of DNA.
- It was the result of accidental contamination during the collection, storage, handling and testing of samples.
- It was the result of undiscovered laboratory errors and contaminated samples (Lighterwood p. 514)
- Was it a "set up" by police deliberate contamination?
- The LCN (Low Copy Number) DNA analysis method was inherently flawed.
- And also, that perhaps we are here debating the DNA of his brother where similar meaning the same [?]
- After all, proving that Murdoch is/was not the CCTV man definitely means something.

Algie presented a compelling argument that all of the DNA evidence was unreliable, as the Crown could not exclude the real possibility of contamination which may have given false results.

Also, he didn't not rule out that samples had been deliberately contaminated.

"...Could they have been contaminated intentionally members of the jury? Could it be...a "set up, a fit up? ...Is it possible that police or somebody who had access to these items could have fitted them up? It might depend...on whether the police or whoever might have done this, thought they were doing anything wrong, in the moral sense you know. I mean, If Murdoch's guilty...if the police think that he really did it, no harm done....it has been known, hasn't it, for police to fit people up, particularly if they really did it" (Algie in Mildren).

LCN (Low Copy Number) DNA testing

In 1999 Dr Whitaker, a senior forensic scientist with the UK-based Forensic Science Service at Wetherby, developed the Low Copy Number test (LCN) test designed for measuring extremely small quantities of DNA. LCN requires only 15-20 cells to yield a profile. Samples can be amplified 34 times instead of 28 times during testing. At the time of Murdoch's trial Dr Whitaker agreed that Wetherby was the only laboratory in the world using LCN (27 The Queen v Murdoch 2005 NTSC 76).

DNA testing has never been full proof but there is no doubt that at the time of the trial there was significant controversy in the forensic world about the reliability of the LCN DNA testing.

In her expert evidence Dr Katrine Both, part-time forensic scientist at the Forensic Science Service in Adelaide, said that she had "large numbers of concerns" about the LCN tests; that the method was very "dangerous" and pushed "science to the limits".

In cross examination by the Defence, forensic scientist Chris Pearman, gave evidence that there were [two] problems with the LCN methodology:

...Firstly, if you conducted two tests you would likely have two different results; and second the system is so sensitive that it will pick up background contamination. The consequence of these problems is that it makes interpretation difficult" (Mildren p 47)

The Vanishing of Peter Falconio

In 2007 Law Society president **Maria Saraceni** and Criminal Lawyers Association vice-president **Philip Urquhart** said they had grave concerns about reliability of Low copy DNA tests.

"…WA legal groups have called for an immediate review of a controversial forensic DNA test used to help convict outback killer Bradley John Murdoch after British police suspended their use of the technique amid serious doubts about its accuracy" (Urban 2020).

In 2008, three years after Murdoch's guilty verdict, Professor of Law and Criminal Justice at Leicester Law School, Dr Carol McCartney's opinion was that LCN DNA might prove to have some value in criminal investigations, but it had not yet reached the required standard for use as evidence.

The DNA evidence

The "crime scene" at Barrow Creek

Forensic scientist, **Carmen Eckhoff**, from the NT Forensic Science Centre, began her investigation at the Barrow Creek crime scene at 8.30 pm on Sunday 15 of July, the day after the alleged crime.

Blood on the road and rocks

Eckhoff found a small pool of blood by the side of the road, 60-40cm in dimension; two smaller stains to the south of which could have come from the larger stain and "dotting "to the west of the larger stain (Mildren 2015 p 6).

The largest pool was covered with a 15-20cm high "pyramid "of dirt. Vince Millar had seen the pile of dirt when he rescued Lees in the morning of the 15 July and thought it was strange. Eckhoff later identified the blood as Falconio's by using his DNA on the Ventolin inhaler found inside the abandoned Kombi and confirming this against his parent's DNA.

"[38] (j) the main stain on the bitumen and several other samples taken from the areas adjacent to it were found to be human blood, the DNA of which was identical in profile to that of Falconio" (Murdoch v The Queen [2007] NTCCA 1)

True crime writer, Robin Bowles, had access to Murdoch. Curiously, she suggests that someone might have upended a container of blood and flicked it to empty it out. Did Bowles have inside information that led to believe that a vial of blood could have been deliberately spilt on the bitumen perhaps to fake a crime as cover for Falconio's disappearance? (Bowles 2022 p52)

Eckhoff also found evidence of blood on the surrounding rocks which she collected.

"Every one of the samples produced a full DNA profile which matched that of Falconio…Eckhoff said they were good samples and relatively fresh" (Barker 2005).

However, according to Maynard these samples turned out to be animal blood most probably from a road KILL.

Aboriginal trackers that there was "old blood". Tracker Ronald Brown was surprised that there were no ants on the blood which would usually the case (Shears) the tracker did not give evidence in court. Was the animal blood mentioned in the court proceedings?

Detectives were puzzled by the lack of blood at the scene, which was inconsistent with the amount expected from a fatal gunshot. DNA expert, Professor Barry Boetcher is well known for having no doubt that a dingo killed Azaria Chamberlain not her mother also believed it was not enough to secure a conviction.

"If a body had been shot and then dragged somewhere you would expect a blood trail. There was no blood trail in this case…There was no blood spatter found at the alleged crime scene. In my opinion, based on that and blood evidence, I would not expect today to have a guilty verdict recorded against anybody" (Knight, K 2020).

The Kombi

The Kombi was found on the night of the 14th of July partly obscured about 100 metres or thereabouts from the alleged crime scene and murder.

"[50] Ms Eckhoff gave evidence for the purpose of the objection from the Defence to the DNA evidence. She understood that crime scene examiners had examined the Kombi before it was moved from the scrub. In particular the outside of the vehicle had been dusted for fingerprints and examined for signs of blood" (The Queen v Murdoch [2005] NTSC 76)

The Vanishing of Peter Falconio

Initial testing of the Kombi

Carmen Eckhoff stated that she understood that the Kombi was towed to Alice Springs on the 15th July 2001 and she started her examination on the 16th (Algie stated that the kombi was removed on the 17 of July). Eckhoff swabbed a substantial portion of the Kombi, Steering wheel – knob of the gear stick –the front seats – and other items found in the vehicle. She explained that all items were sent from Alice to Darwin in individual containers.

According to Bowles, Eckhoff inspected the kombi in Alice at 11.30 pm on the 15th, we assume this was after she inspected the blood on the road. She found blood under a wheel arch and front bumper bar.

"Its windows were shut and the passenger and side doors locked, but later she could not recall if the driver's door was locked…She swabbed the van from front to back and tested it ortho- toluidine a substance that shows the presence of blood not visible with the naked eye. Her report stated NO Blood was found in the vehicle. She also examined the rear bumper bar and engine cover for blood – brain matter –and gunshot residue. There was no blood under the front right wheel arch and more under the bumper. She took samples from the passenger seat using sticky strip of tape to lift off DNA or other particles" (Bowles p 52)

According to Bowles the blood was tested and found to be of animal blood origin –probably road kill.

Please note the discrepancy between dates: Eckhoff says 15 of July – Algie says 17 of July

Algie pointed out the opportunity for contamination of the Kombi.

"[48] The kombi was removed by police from the scrub and transported to Alice. In essence, counsel submitted that a jury could not conclude beyond reasonable doubt that there was no contamination at one stage in the process between removing the van from the bush on 17 July2001 and the handling of the samples to Dr Whitaker on 24th October 2003" (that is 28 months as I said many times before).

Similarly, Eckhoff expressed concerns about the potential for contamination of the Kombi.

[51] Eckhoff also understood that on 15th July 2001 the kombi was towed from the scene to Alice Springs. She made enquiries about how the vehicle was towed because she had been asked to take swabs of both the steering wheel and the gear stick. She was told that nothing had been touched. It was Eckhoff understanding that the Kombi was placed in the crime scene vehicle examination bay in Alice to which police officers generally do not have access. (The Queen v Murdoch [2005] NTSC 76)

Steering wheel

Despite this reassurance, Eckhoff observed a police officer touch the steering wheel without wearing gloves during the forensic examination in Alice Springs. This seems like an extraordinary mistake by the policeman.

[53] "As to the steering wheel, Eckhoff said that while she was waiting for the fingerprint examination to be completed, she saw a police officer touch the steering wheel. She could not say why he did so, but it did not appear to do it for the purpose of adjusting the steering wheel or driving the vehicle... Um! why would he drive the vehicle...The officer did not touch the gear stick. Eckhoff advised the officer that the forensic examination had not been completed and he and his team were to have nothing further to do with the vehicle"

Can we be sure that the officer had not touched the gear stick and other parts of the Kombi un-noticed?

Ultimately the steering wheel sample would be dismissed as having no probative value as it was a complex DNA mixture from at least three individuals. (The Queen v Murdoch [2005] NTSC 76).

[13] "In a report dated 9 December 2004 Dr Whitaker reported a mixed DNA profile in the extract from the steering wheel which, in his opinion, is best explained if there is a contributor of DNA from at least three individuals. On the basis of the DNA bands he observed, Dr Whitaker expressed the opinion that he was unable to exclude the deceased, (yes the deceased without a dead body [sic]) Lees or the accused as being one of the

potential contributors. A qualification was added, however, that even if the DNA for all these three individuals was present, this would not account for all the DNA bands observed, therefore another individual or individuals would have to be considered in order to account for all of the DNA bands observed. Dr Whitaker concluded that, the DNA mixture of that complexity was not suitable for meaningful comparisons. In Dr Whitaker's opinion, despite being unable to eliminate the accused as a contributor, the result lack any probative value." (The Queen v Murdoch [2005] NTSC 76)

Gear stick

[52] "Eckhoff commenced her examination on 16th July and completed it on 17th July 2001. She swabbed the knob of the gear stick. She tested the rest of the gear stick for blood, but did not swab it for DNA purposes (what does this means? Is it a joke or what? Did not swab it for DNA purposes …What for then? Using a small proportion of the swab from the gear stick knob Eckhoff carried out a presumptive for the presence of blood. The swab from the gear stick knob was the source of material which was subsequently examined by Eckhoff for the presence of DNA" (The Queen v Murdoch [2005] NTSC 76)

Megan Hibble extracted the DNA from the gear stick swab on 18th July 2001 (Mildren 2015 p 286)

[10] "As to the gear stick knob, Eckhoff reported obtaining a weak partial DNA profile of a male person, the components of which could be attributed to the accused. In evidence at the preliminary examination Eckhoff said the DNA on the knob was extremely weak, the small amount and the relative frequency of the identified components is approximately 1 in 678 individuals in the NT and includes the accused." (The Queen v Murdoch [2005] NTSC 76)

The gear stick swab was sent to Whitaker in the UK with the following result:

[38] "A forensic examination of the swab from the gear knob of the Kombi produced a partial DNA profile that, inter alia (among other things,

did not exclude the appellant (Murdoch). This material was sent to an expert scientist in the United Kingdom and subjected to a specialised technique known as Low Copy Number (LCN) with a view to obtaining additional results…" (Murdoch v The Queen [2007] NTCCA 1)

It was proposed that the chance of a second unrelated person producing the partial DNA profile obtained from the swab that matched that of Murdoch was less than one in 13,000.

However, Algie pointed out that Whitaker based his analysis on the assumption that only Falconio and Murdoch had touched the gear stick but we know that Lees had also been driving the Kombi (Of course we know).

…One in 13,000 of the population might be expected to share the alleles that were attributed to Murdoch. We know that Lees also drove the Kombi been in the mixture, why excluding her? Even Eckhoff didn't exclude her as a contributor when she did the very early preliminary testing of that material…Common sense…wouldn't exclude her. Looking at the exhibit] three of the alleles attributed to Murdoch could have come from Lees…then we have…a far less significant partial profile of only six alleles as opposed to nine… (Algie in Mildren p46)

Naughton and Tan…

At the time of the trial there was no universal consensus on how mixed DNA profiles should be interpreted. Naughton and Tan provide a useful analogy in describing the problem with analysing mixed DNA samples. They compare DNA alleles to the letters in a name and use their names as an example.

<u>(I need to get my head around this, so saying that I understand it …would be a lie, but needs to be mentioned because I truly do not understand it.)</u>

"As this relates to us, our full names are, respectively: "MICHAEL JOSEPH NAUGHTON" and "GABE SIHANTAN" "If our names/DNA alleles are mixed, the following full profiles can be obtained and these suspects cannot be excluded: CAIN and ABEL –JOSEPH STALINE – PLATO –TOM JONES and or JANE AUSTEN. If partial profiles were for, the following suspects cannot be excluded: TON(Y) BLAI(R) –AM(Y) (W)INEHOUS – and /or MOTHE(R) THE(R)ESA

<u>Well, I am far from understanding this, but it needs to be mentioned and read.</u>

Similarly, Jamieson asserts that a mixed DNA profile of two individuals with profiles AB and CD (notwithstanding that more than one person could have the same alleles) results in the mixed profile ABCD which could yield at least six different potential contributors; AB, CD, AC, BD, AD and BC.

[45] "Jamieson notes that across ten loci, with two alleles per contributor, there are over one million ways to interpret a mixture of two contributors, that is, a mixture of DNA from two people could produce a million possible profiles."

"It is frequently not obvious how a scientist derives the opinion that favours one of this option over any of the others. At the very least, the possibility of other interpretations should feature in reports but, sadly do not. In casework, we frequently come across DNA reports that all but ignore any other possible interpretation than the one that provides the best probative value against the accused. The most obvious explanation is that the scientist has been influenced by knowledge of the profiles of those involved, whether it is the complainer or the suspect."

(Naughton and Tan 2011 p 255) THIS IS SO VERY TRUE.

Police Commissioner orders retesting of the Kombi

On 21 February 2022 NT Commissioner of Police, Paul White, instigated a six weeks review of Taskforce Regulus' handling of the case. The Task Force was initially set up in September 2001 and comprised 15 officers under the supervision of Detective Sergeant Chalker of Alice Springs Police. One of the key issues investigated was how forensic evidence had been collected, in particular the testing on the Kombi.

Joy Kuhl managed the re-testing of the Kombi. Khul is the infamous NT forensic scientist who in the 1980s mistakenly concluded that there was a foetal haemoglobin on the inside of the Chamberlain's car. This ultimately led to Lindy Chamberlain's wrongful conviction for the murder of her baby Azaria.

Algie used the Chamberlain case to instruct the jury that experts can be wrong and they should not be overwhelmed by them (Mildren 2015 p45)

Freelance cameraman Chris Tangey was asked to film the re-testing of the Kombi in Alice Springs. He was initially alarmed when he walked into the police forensic compound and saw Falconio's and Lees' personal belonging and much of the Kombi interior furnishings piled up against a wall with no apparent protection (Maynard 2005 p 148)

Tangey believed he saw quite strong luminescence on the inside of driver's side door that revealed the shape of a partial handprint. There was also some luminescence on the dashboard. However, Khul and police dismissed this.

As **Tangey** was filming he saw **Khul** spray Luminol on a door and heard a detective with her, senior Constable Bill Towers ask her if the resultant glow was blood; "No it can't be I went right over it this afternoon she replied.

Investigative journalist Roger Maynard had viewed a copy of Tangey's tape and writes that he tended to agree with Tangey's interpretation of what he heard and saw that day. (Maynard 2005 p 149).

Tangey suspected that police officer Tower may have touch parts of the Kombi without the necessary hand wear.

It seems beyond doubt that Tower was not in fact wearing gloves in the examination and is seen to contaminate the interior light switch with his bare hand. (Maynard 2005 p 151).

Ultimately Police was cleared of any major mistakes but senior officers admitted that some aspects of the investigation could have been handled better

Well, do you believe that?

Clothing worn

Initial testing: Lees clothing was bagged on the morning of the 15th 2001.

The Vanishing of Peter Falconio

[59] On 17th July 2001 in Alice Springs the extraction of DNA from a sample of Lees' T-shirt was carried out by another member of the laboratory. Ms Eckhoff explained that all items were sent from Alice to Darwin in individual containers. (The Queen v Murdoch [2005] NTSC 76).

The initial swab of Lees' T-shirt revealed DNA of an unidentified male person. Eckhoff was unable to match a profile with any record on any of the databases in Australia etc. Clothing worn included her shorts. A re-enactment of the alleged assault conducted by Dr McDonald demonstrated that Murdoch's would have been all over Lees and her clothing. Lees did have a shower on the night, but was there only one spot of Murdoch's DNA found on her clothing and if so, why? (Program 4 Murder in the Outback)

Algie suggested that there was a very real chance that Murdoch's DNA on the back of her T-shirt could have been accidentally deposited in Alice without anybody knowing about it. Murdoch and the British couple were both in Alice on the same day at the restaurant where the DNA could have been transferred onto the T-shirt (already spoken many times however try proving it).

[313] "In January 2003 Eckhoff re-tested the T-shirt using the Profiler Plus which revealed more data. (Profiler Plus is a PCR test that analyses points in human DNA where short sequences of proteins are repeated a variable number of times.) In January 2003 she used a different test which confirmed the results previously obtained, being across ten sites, but which also provided results across an additional six sites. She therefore had a profile across 16 sites (Murdoch v The Queen [2007] NTCCA 1)

Once Murdoch's DNA sample was obtained and following LCN testing in the UK…

[8] "Blood staining was located on the left shoulder at the back of the T-shirt won by Lees. DNA was obtained from a sample taken from the stain which produced a profile identical to the DNA profile of the accused. Whitaker is of the view that statistical calculations indicate observing this DNA profile is at leat 640 billion times more likely if the blood came from the accused than from an unrelated person selected at random from the NT

population. No objection was taken to the admissibility of the evidence" (The Queen v Murdoch [2005] NTSC 76)

Of course, who would, who could?

However, it is interesting stuff about all those calculations about DNA that nobody understands at the exception of very few (certainly not the jury nor myself really), but one wonders why they were incapable of calculating who between the CCTV man and Murdoch was going to win the Alice Fitzroy race based on time and fuel usage.

Manacles

In his address to the jury, Algie highlighted the poor record keeping practices by police in the NT and in SA in relation to the movement of the manacles or pre-made cuffs. Who had access to them –when –for how long – and for what purpose [?] He detailed the multiple occasions when the manacles could have been contaminated.

"Sergeant Kerr in a memo or an email to other officers involved in the matter, had serious concerns about how the cuffs had been handled…that they hadn't been properly examined…[the serious concerns] might have been a result of concerns that they'd been improperly handled " (Algie in Mildren p 49) "… "You would certainly have some serious concerns about what reliance you can place on any of the records in terms of satisfying yourself that nobody could have had access to these cuffs and contaminated them either unintentionally." (Algie in Mildren p50)

Initial testing

July 2001

"[38] (k) initial testing by a forensic scientist based in NT revealed the presence of material bearing DNA profiles identical with those of Lees and witness Vince Millar on the ties and wrist bands of the manacles and the presence of material bearing a DNA profile identical to that of Joanne Lees on samples of tape ties" (Murdoch v The Queen [2007] NTCCA 1)

17th July 2001:

Laboratory Director Dr Thatcher had them in his possession for the purpose of a teleconference.

30th July 2001:

Dr Thatcher examined them in respect to the pink substance (lip gloss).

31th July 2001:

Dr Thatcher received an internal memo email from Crime Commissioner Hardman where Hardman said he wanted the handcuffs completely dismantled. [In his evidence] Dr Thatcher couldn't say whether that was done or not" (Mildren p 49)

Well, the logic tells you that if Hardman is ordering it most certainly means that it had not been done.

"After the manacles had been tested, Peter Thatcher took them to a command briefing where Assistant Commissioner Dalby and Commissioner Brian Bates, both tried them on (unbelievable, however remarkable! Clapping in the background).

"This caused some consternation as the manacles could now be contaminated" (here, the word used is "could". Well, it's not could but have been. The manacles have been contaminated.

…Command scoffed at the possibility and the two officers subsequently refused to supply the forensic lab with their DNA (Bowles p 68)

31st July 2001:

Eckhoff told the court she examined a layer of tape within the centre-links of the cable ties. (Barker 2005)

August 2001:

Constable Sandry had the manacles for about four or five days. He was cutting bits of tape off and looking at them and working out how they were made. He also endeavoured to make copies of them (Mildren 2015 p 51)

"Officer Sandry took them out for four or five days in August 2001, but it doesn't appear in the entry…What is the explanation for these records not telling us, because apparently if they don't leave the biology section, it's not recorded [?] We do have a record here of officer Sandry having them for two days from 25-27 February 2002, but [HE] doesn't know what he did with them, can't remember." (Algie in Mildren p 50) I think Sandry is like Joanne Lees…Can't remember hey!

8th October 2002

The Vanishing of Peter Falconio

NT officers including Senior Constable Tim Sandry and colleen Gwynne went to Yatala jail in SA to interview Murdoch who had been arrested in Port Augusta on a charge of rape. They took the manacles with them for the purpose of the interview (in a paper bag mind you, repeat I know.) They claimed that the manacles were at all times in the original sealed paper evidence bag and were not taken out. But **Sergeant Sheldon** examined them.

8th October 2002

Police also executed search warrants at Sedan property believed to be Murdoch's (Mildren 2015 p 51)

They photographed the manacles next to Murdoch's gear…(Do you know what that mean?)

Could they have obtained Murdoch's DNA (contaminated?)

Well things get no better….

In October 2002

"When they make what you might think is an extraordinary and unbelievable trip to Adelaide and then to Yatala in circumstances where you might think that a photo would have been more sufficient or a set mock ups…"(Algie in Mildren p49) They spend four days …in the physical evidence section of the Adelaide police, above the forensic Science buildings…officer Sandry said he was aware that Murdoch's property was over in one set of shelves and drew a little plan…he put the bag with the cuffs over on the desk on the other wall two -3 metres …away from Murdoch's property …he put it there because he was conscious that he was going out to search property at Swan Reach that might have belonged to Murdoch and he didn't want any risk of contamination…You wouldn't want to take the handcuffs with you when you were searching Swan Reach because e there is an obvious risk of contamination. But you need then…to consider the evidence of Sergeant Mackenzie who said that they were put …in a shelf underneath where all of Murdoch's property was in the physical evidence section." (Algie in Mildren pp49-50)

15th October 2002

The manacles going back to Darwin…

...We're told they're put back in the forensic science freezer...You wouldn't know because there's no entry in the log! Nobody appears to be making any record of their movements ...we don't know if anybody else could have gone to the forensic Science Centre and had access or examined the cuffs. The last entry is 8th October 2002 because the next entry relates to the central loop of the wrist bandage which goes to see Whitaker on 22 April 2005 (Algie in Mildren p 51)

Year 2004

"For two and a half years...Although they say these items were in the forensic Science Centre in Darwin, you have not got a who did or did not have access to them for what purpose under what circumstances and what, if any supervision was provided (Algie in Mildren p 51)

2nd May 2004

Sandry cuts the tape from the cuffs and some more DNA testing is done. There is no record in the log for Sandry's access. That's when **Dr Thatcher's** DNA is found on them. (Mildren 2015 p 51)

Forensic scientist's DNA found on the manacles

"Forensic biologist Carmen Eckhoff told the court that the manacles were a significant piece of evidence and she did not know how Dr Thatcher's DNA came to be on the cuffs but it would have been any number of ways, despite protocols being in place to prevent it happening."

Eckhoff said it was not ideal to take them out of the laboratory and did not agree with the cable ties taken to Yatala prison in Adelaide.

"I was unhappy about then leaving my possession, particularly if the forensic examination may not have been completed. She made her feelings known to Dr Thatcher, who gave the handcuffs to Senior Constable Tim Sandry so he could take them to Adelaide.

When asked about the possibility of deliberate contamination of the cuffs with Murdoch's DNA she said that the samples from him that were stored in the freezer were of a very high concentration (BBC 2 November 2005).

Year 2005

22nd April 2005 LCN analysis in the UK

"You'd have to wonder if forensic officers are looking for DNA …back in July/August 2001 whether they would have completely dismantled the handcuffs …that is a fair and reasonable possibility that that happened, how could you place any forensic reliance of integrity of the cuffs almost four years later?" (Agie in Mildren p 49)

There is no doubt in my mind that there is not one proof beyond reasonable doubt that could have been the foundation for the received verdict: Guilty on all charges. All or most of the Officials are/were corrupted.

Obtaining Bradley John Murdoch's DNA
James Hepi comes forward

In July 2001 the NT government offered a reward of $250,000 for information that could lead to the capture and conviction of the alleged gunman. (I took the photo of the poster at Aileron Roadhouse where I spoke to Gregory Dick. in 2018… Gosh, time flies).

Now, this is terrible and shocking: The government was also willing to offer indemnity from prosecution to any accomplice willing to turn in the suspect …Total disgrace. (BBC 26th July 2001).

James Hepi was as we know Murdoch's ex-partner transporting Cannabis and most probably other drugs from Sedan in SA to Broome in WA.

On 16th May 2002, Detective Sergeant Peter Jenal of WA police arrested Hepi as he was driving into Broome with 3.7kg of marijuana in gas cylinder in his utility. There is a suggestion that Murdoch had dobbed Hepi into police following a dispute.

On 31st May 2002. Hepi's solicitor arranged a meeting with Jenal concerning the disappearance of Peter Falconio. Jenal took notes of that conversation and passed the information onto Detective Sergeant Chalker of Alice Springs. (Mildren 2015 p 8)

Hepi had information to trade. He told his lawyer. "I know about a regular run from Perth to Broome –and I also know who did Falconio: It was Brad Murdoch." (Bowles p 154).

Hepi's information was that Murdoch:
- Was once seen with constructing cable ties apparently similar/identical to those used to bind Lees.
- Once detailed to Hepi how he would dispose of a body,
- Travelled through the NT on the weekend of 14/15 July 2001 on a drug run from SA, and on arrival in Broome, mentioned that he had experienced unspecified trouble
- Dramatically changed his and his vehicle's appearance in the following weeks, shaving his moustache, thoroughly cleaning his vehicle and replacing many parts, including the canopy: and often mentioned the Falconio case. (Gans 2007)

We assume that **Jenal's** note of 16th to Detective **Chalker** included this information. Given that Hepi's statement directly implicated Murdoch, why wasn't Hepi formally interview until 10th September 2002, almost four months later (Mildren 2015 p 8)

"Hepi admitted in court that if Murdoch he would apply for the reward. He also believed that dobbing in Murdoch would give him a get out of jail card. The proof is in the pudding as he later received a suspended sentence. Police withdrew the reward in March 2006."

There were around 2,000 on the taskforce Regulus list of persons of interest. Murdoch was on a register of owners of the comparatively uncommon 75 series Toyota Land Cruiser imported from overseas....(Land Cruisers at that time were not uncommon, on the contrary they were very common ..I like to mention it). He was on the list, [but he had an alibi].

OK what was the alibi? (Of course it has never been mentioned…Please don't ask).

According to Bowles, Murdoch told her that some Broome police had interviewed him in November 2001, but not as a suspect (Bowles 2022 p 177). However as soon as the NT had Helpi's evidence Murdoch's name went to the top of the list.

Police needed Murdoch's DNA to do a comparison with the smudge on Lees' T-shirt, so they put out a national police alert and began searching for him in NT –SA –and WA, but there was no sign of him.

Police obtain a DNA sample from Murdoch's brother Gary Murdoch

Full non-identical siblings share about 50%of the same DNA with each other.

On 14th August 2002,

Police took a blood sample from Murdoch's brother in Perth.

Note that this is after they had Hepi's information initially given on 16th May 2002 but before he was formally interviewed on 10th September 2002.

"When the national police alert failed to produce any sign of him police visited his parents and his brother Gary. They all said they had no idea where he would be. Police asked if Gary would be prepared to give a DNA sample to compare with the DNA on Lees' T-Shirt. It is unclear whether Gary agree purely to rule himself out of inquiries, or because he was so convinced is brother was innocent it would help him too. But on 14th August 2002 he had a swab taken. If the DNA on the T-shirt was Murdoch, Gary would show up as a close match (William p 224)

Gary's sample revealed a partial match to the unknown male's DNA on the T-shirt. Combined with Hepi's evidence and other information gathered by Taskforce Regulus, this narrowed the investigators' suspicions to Murdoch.

"However, Taskforce regulus eschewed (avoided) relying on this technique as a means of justifying the sampling of Murdoch. Instead, when Murdoch was located two weeks later in SA, none of the information gathered by the investigators up to that date was used to justify wither his arrest or the taking of his DNA sample. (Gans, Jeremy 2007)

Was it legal to take Gary's DNA and use it for the purpose of putting out an arrest warrant for Murdoch prior to Hepi's formal interview on 10th September 2002 [?]...Well, I let you be the judge on that hey!

Police arrest Murdoch –but not for the Falconio alleged murder

On 28th August 2002

Only 14 days after the NT police took sample of Gary's DNA, Murdoch was arrested in SA on charge of rape presumably unrelated to the Falconio case –but was it? But, please explain why police could not find Murdoch hoping to take his blood sample when in fact they had no problem finding him regarding the rape case?

On 30th August 2002 NT police put out a media release indicating that Murdoch was also a person of interest in the Falconio disappearance that is two days after police took Gary's blood sample…What do you think? Do you find this very suspicious?

"Acting Deputy Commissioner of NT Police, John Dalby said that South Australian Police have notified NT Police about a man arrested and charged in Port Augusta for the rape and unlawful imprisonment of two females. As with other persons that have been brought to our attention in respect to the disappearance of Peter Falconio this person is at this stage, no more than a person of interest, **Mr Dalby** said" (Bowles p 160)

Lees and Falconio's family were advised of the arrest and matching DNA.

At this stage police had Hepi's statement and Gary's DNA sample, but not Murdoch.

They requested samples of Murdoch's blood via a Forensic Procedures Application to SA authorities.

On 4th September 2002

SA Attorney General Michael Atkinson and **NT Minister for Police, Fire and Emergency Services**, signed an agreement saying that it was in the "public interest" to transfer the DNA (Maynard 2005 p 170).

Murdoch's lawyers challenged the transfer but on 6th September 2002 **SA Magistrate Gary Gumpi** issued a court order agreeing to the Forensic Procedures Application. Murdoch's lawyers appealed.

"It is fundamentally obvious that the purpose of testing the blood one would cynically suspect, is not in respect to these South Australian allegations. It is for the purpose of sending these samples to the Northern Territory. (Grant Algie cited in Maynard p170)

On 2th October 2002

Justice Ted Mulligan rejected the appeal from Murdoch's lawyers. Mark Twigg's immediately announced he would appeal that decision but on

The Vanishing of Peter Falconio

8th October 2002 decided not to take the matter further. <u>No reason was given.</u> (Williams 2006 p 234)

"On Tuesday, Murdoch abandoned his legal battle to prevent NT Police testing his blood. Neither Murdoch nor his lawyer gave any reason for the decision to drop the appeal. (BBC Online News 10th October 2002)

Was Murdoch's blood sample sent to the NT on or about 8th October 2002? The only reference I can find is that the NT received a "controlled sample" on 17th November 2003. Murdoch was not extradited to the NT until 14th December 2003 and the controlled was not analysed in NT until 31st December 2003.

WAS THIS A SET-UP?

Murdoch told Bowles that he was concerned that the police would set him up for the Falconio case. Could it have something to do with Murdoch's knowledge of police dealing with drugs? Murdoch had revealed to Bowles that some Broome police were selling hydro at $5,000 per kg and were upset that he had been undercutting them. (Bowles 2022 p 176)

"Privately the defendant also feared that his DNA sample could be interfered with between the time it left Adelaide and when it was eventually compared with the tiny spot on the back of Joanne Lees 'T-shirt now being kept in Darwin." (Maynard p 170)

"Gary had also heard that one of the <u>Coffin Cheaters</u> had put out a contract on his brother." (Bowles p 155) Note that Murdoch belong to the Gypsy Jokers for a while (Bowles p 174). Not surprising given his line of business.

On 9th October 2002

"Eleven [11] days before the rape trial was due to begin, NT police announced that DNA tests had identified a 44 years-old man who would be charged with murdering Peter Falconio. Police said that Murdoch was a positive "DNA match" in the Falconio case and had enough evidence to make him their "prime suspect".

For legal reasons Dalby couldn't say the DNA was an exact match, merely that Murdoch couldn't be excluded by the result. Everyone knew, however precisely what [HE] meant.

The Vanishing of Peter Falconio

(Williams p 236)

"Police said that for legal reasons they cannot confirm that Murdoch's DNA matches a sample recovered from Joanne Lees 'clothing. But detectives now say they have enough evidence to him the prime suspect." (BBC article).

***

"Eleven [11] days before the rape trial was due to begin, NT police announced that DNA tests had identified a 44 years-old man who would be charged with murdering Peter Falconio."

Well, I read English and I do understand the language very well even being my second language.

Let us break down this sentence: ...Announced that DNA tests had identified a 44 years old man...This is definitely very precise, we know the age!

- Ok, Question: Who did identify the man?
- Answer: The DNA TEST

It is the result of a DNA test, conducted by a forensic team of supposedly experts working for a forensic lab. The result of the DNA test itself doesn't tell the age of the person. It is the interpretation (GOOD or BAD) given by the team of the lab, depending on the agenda...Are you okay with that?

- Then, someone in high position working for the forensic lab got in touch with police to report the test results which were: From A 44 YEARS-OLD MAN...
- It is based on the interpretation of the test results, nothing else. The interpretation without any doubt is under human control as I said GOOD or BAD
  Whether an interpretation is; physically –scientifically –or even politically, it cannot give you the age if the person of interest could not be found on any data base; here it's Australia.
- Do you believe that any DNA test will give you the precise age of a human person, related to the DNA test results from that person?

You can only answer by YES or NO. Your answer should be: NO

The Vanishing of Peter Falconio

[IF] the interpretation of the test results can give you the precise age, can it also give you the name and the address –the name of the wife or husband – the type of car the person drives and most importantly the registration number of the vehicle?... (Clapping in the background).

Would any DNA test and its results give you the age and name of a person found dead somewhere on the roadside or elsewhere for example, not knowing any details about the deceased? The answer is a [BIG NO]

Murdoch was on the list of 2000 potentially persons of interest – Murdoch was not a suspect then, far from it, [HE] was not on any data base, [HE] had been actually questioned by WA police earlier and released because [HE] had an alibi… Alibi accepted by police, which was later on classified as not to be released, for unknown reason to us or anybody else for that matter, even up until now in 2024. Murdoch only came to the surface because of the rape case. The question still remains about his alibi [?]

I don't know if you have a short memory but, please go back in time…let me explain. It's about:

Former Assistant Commissioner of Northern Territory **John Dalby** said:

- Police would not rely on DNA evidence, well that the first thing they did even when **The High Court** said: <u>You cannot convict on DNA alone. It is not safe enough.</u>

Then:

- *"After the manacles had been tested, Peter Thatcher took them to a command briefing where Assistant Commissioner Dalby and Commissioner Brian Bates, both tried them on..."*

Then:

"…Dr Whitaker did not examine those handcuffs **until May 2005** that is May this year, almost four years after Barrow Creek." (Algie's address to the jury in Mildren p 44) and seven months before the trial.

This seems to indicate that the actual manacles were in Australia all that time (4 years), when we know they had been contaminated by "Our Dear" Assistant Commissioner Dalby and Commissioner Brian Bates, both tried them on" and most probably also by officer Sandry who held the manacles for two days from 25 to 27 February 2002 but doesn't know what he did with them, he can't remember... like Joanne Lees! (Laughter in the background).

This means and tells you that in May 2005, four years after the alleged crime and before the trial, the cuffs which were contaminated by those two individuals Dalby and Brian Bates were sent to Whitaker in England ...But no worries.

Do you think the same could have taken place with Lees T-shirt?

The words that a DNA tests had identified a 44 years old man, were meant to promote Murdoch's GUILT without any shadow of a doubt.

MURDOCH WAS A SCAPEGOAT, IT HAD TO BE HIM!

Now back to my train of thoughts.... Sorry for the interruption, but keep on reading

...Back where I was previously and above ok....

- Well, yes of course knowing that there were only two suspects; The CCTV Man and Murdoch,
- And knowing that we know now who won the race Alice –Fitzroy (Laughter in the background).

The rape trial began in the SA Supreme Court on 20th October 2003 (Bowles says 13th October p 289) Murdoch pleaded not guilty. Algie alleged that the charges were part of a police set-up.

"The alleged victims and their co-conspirators had failed to get the DNA evidence on Murdoch before the set-up so the rape had been devised...he suggested. Was he indicating that the police had been involved in a conspiracy (sorry plot...) Judge David asked... It could be Algie replied." (Maynard p 173)

Murdoch was found not guilty of rape on 10th November 2003.

Murdoch's lawyer Grant Algie had told the court the rape charges had been made up as part of an elaborate three states (WA –SA –and NT). Conspiracy to frame his client for Falconio alleged murder" (Shears p 149)

Murdoch was immediately arrested for the alleged murder of Faconio and held in Yatala jail until he was extradited to the NT arriving in Darwin on 14th December 2003.

Police engage Dr Whitaker to conduct LCN testing
24th October 2003 (First analysis by Dr Whitaker)
The samples/swabs were sent to Whitaker in the UK for the more powerful LCN testing. This is only four days after the SA rape trial began, which is extremely suspicious in my view and the views of others.

- Did Whitaker have Murdoch's DNA at this time?

However, it was not until 17th November 2003 that NT police obtained a "controlled sample" of Murdoch's blood from SA furthermore:

- What is a controlled sample?
- Then **it took six weeks** for it to be analysed in Darwin.
- This delay was not explained,
- But **Eckhoff** found that the DNA was an exact match across the 16 sites with the profile obtained from the back of the T-shirt **in January 2003**.

[313] The opinion expressed by Eckhoff was that such a match demonstrates that it is at least 150 quadrillion times more likely that the DNA on the T-shirt came from the appellant than from any other person in the population selected at random (Please refer to my chapter 57). Her opinion as to the statistical probability was shared by **Dr Buckleton** an expert in a statistical interpretation of DNA results, whose statement was admitted into evidence without objection [by the Defence] I wonder why. (Murdoch vs The Queen [2007] NTCCA 1)

Well, if you refer to what Jamieson said and concluded [45] p 448 of this chapter, again I let you be the judge…Who is truly lying?

This information was admitted into evidence (of course beyond any doubt and reproach) at the pre-trial Hearing which started on 17th May 2004 and ended in August 2004.

Given Algie's allegation that there was a possibility with tampering plus the six weeksed delay, why didn't the Defence challenge its admission?

9th August 2004 Committal Proceedings
18th August 2004
[11] "The preliminary examination concluded on 18th August 2004 and the accused was committed to the Supreme Court for trial … (The Queen v Murdoch [2005] NTSC 76)

28th October 2004 Second analysis by Dr Whitaker
Does Dr Whitaker have Murdoch's DNA sample?

[11] "In **October 2004 Ms Eckhoff** travelled to the United Kingdom where, on **28th October 2004**, she handed DNA samples extracted from swabs to Dr Whitaker of the Forensic Science Service lab at Wetherby. (The Queen v Murdoch [2005] NTSC 76)

- What samples extracted from swabs did Eckhoff take to the UK?
- This is over two years after the NT police announced that Murdoch was their "PRIME SUSPECT" (remember out of two prime suspects one failed to reach Fitzroy!)
- Algie strongly suggested that, the "new samples may have been contaminated; accidentally or deliberately in the nine months between the date Eckhoff received Murdoch's DNA and the date Whitaker received the samples in 2004.

21st April 2005 Voir Dire Hearing (from the French: The Judge rules on the admissibility of evidence to be put before the Jury. The Defence can challenge whether certain evidence should be admissible or not).

***

Let us go back in time for a moment.

We know that in **2001** the only evidence in possession of the investigators were:

1 The T-shirt with a small bloodstain of unknown source up until now –**2** the manacles –**3** the blood on the road and few rocks – **4** Lees 'footprints –**5** four unidentified footprints – **6** a piece of tape –**7** a tube of lip gloss with no lid found by Jeanette Kerr at the alleged crime scene three months –**8** some of the tape used by the alleged killer when trying to restrict Lee 'legs and feet –and around her mouth –**9** the exterior of the Kombi –**10** the steering wheel –**11** the gear stick knob –**12** a CCTV film of a man and his

Cruiser entering the Shell truck-stop, BUT NO DEAD BODY...Nothing else that could be analysed for DNA.

***

Steering wheel contaminated? YES

Gear stick knob contaminated? YES, if the steering wheel was touched by the officer I have great doubts about the knob; so, I say YES

Manacles contaminated? YES

***

Please remember that the second assumption challenged by Grant Algie is the assumption that the bad guy is the man at the truck-stop. This ALONE was the foundation for the case and the guilty verdict. Why?

Because: If Bradley Murdoch's DNA had not been on Joanne Lee's shirt, I would perhaps have advised against bringing him to trial." (Rex Wild the prosecutor)

As the French would say; "Les paroles s'envolent mais les écrits restent" Words fly away, writings remain, which is the translation of this Latin expression: Verbafly, scripta manent used during Antiquity.

***

Now back to 21st April 2005 Voir Dire Hearing

Voir Dire Hearing means the Judge rules on the admissibility of evidence to be put before the Jury. The defence can challenge whether certain evidence should be admissible or not. The two words Voir and Dire arefrom the French language meaning seeing and saying.

The trial was due to start in **May 2005**. On the evening of **20th April 2005,** the Prosecution sprung a surprise on the Defence saying that they wanted to send the actual manacles to the UK for Whitaker to test in his laboratory. Prior to this [we assume] that he had only had swabs [?] (Maynard 2005 p 239 and 241)

Dr Whitaker was already in the NT to give evidence in the case. So, on 22nd April 2005 he flew back to London to conduct further LCN tests on the manacles.

The Vanishing of Peter Falconio

"**Chief Justice Brian Martin** (don't forget his daughter was in a relationship with a juror who sat on Murdoch's trial) <u>agreed</u> that the swab samples from the manacles, which were still in Darwin (the manacles that is), should be flown to Britain that afternoon by **Dr Whitaker** who had only arrived in Australia a few days earlier." (Maynard p 241)

"Dr Whitaker said he could complete the necessary tests on the cable ties and electrical tape out of which the manacles had been fashioned within a few weeks. But because the Defence would also want to have their own independent examination it might take double that time for the exercise to be completed." (Maynard p 241)

"[16] Initially, objection was taken to evidence concerning the DNA from the steering wheel and the gear stick knob on the basis that all material had been destroyed in the testing by Dr Whitaker and was not available for testing on behalf of the accused. Dr Whitaker gave evidence gave evidence prior to the empanelment of the Jury. In the course of that evidence, it emerged that all the material had not been destroyed. As a consequence, this basis of objection was not pursued. (The Queen v Murdoch [2005] NTSC 76)

If the evidence wasn't destroyed why didn't the Defence test it? Was it because there were no LCN facilities in Australia at that time?

On 31st of April 2005 Justice Martin announced that the trial would be delayed until October 2005.

"…Dr Whitaker did not examine those handcuffs until May 2005 that is May this year, almost four years after Barrow Creek." (Algie's address to the jury in Mildren p 44)

This seems to indicate that the actual manacles were in Australia all that time (4 years), when we know they had been contaminated by "Our Dear" Assistant Commissioner Dalby and Commissioner Brian Bates, both tried them on" and most probably also by officer Sandry who held the manacles for two days from 25 to 27 February 2002 but doesn't know what he did with them, can't remember… like Joanne Lees! (repeat but Laughter in the background)

"[38] (o) The United Kingdom expert witness further examined the Cable ties restraints that had been applied to Lees and in particular a specific individual loop of them. He took a sample from the adhesive surface of the innermost layer of the tape that had been applied around the inside of the loop in question. This was an adhesive surface that was actually the inside of the cable tie. The samples gave a mixed DNA results that indicated that there had been two (2) contributors [?]…Suspicious…

The expert evidence was to the effect that the minor bands in the profile also exist in the profiles of both Joanne Lees and Peter Falconio. However, the major component was a substantial profile that was not entirely complete. That profile matched the relevant segments of the appellant's DNA profile" (Murdoch v The Queen [2007] NTCCA 1)

- Well, what does it means …*entirely complete*? What was missing?
- (Yes of course) it was the profile matching the relevant segments of the appellant's DNA profile."
- …And/but NO "**relevant segments** (I love these two words) of Assistant Commissioner Dalby or Commissioner Brian Bates or officer Sandry?
- I mean; we have already Lees and Falconio for the minor bands perhaps we could include **U2** the Irish Rock Band to complete *"The Farce?"* Is that okay?

However, one question remains:

When **Whitaker** flew to Britain on **22nd April 2005** with the manacles (I hope in a bag), had he already and previously handled the manacles in Australia? When was that if he did? We know the Officials love using the words DNA testing which is always mixed with the word swab or swabs.

- My understanding is that, when a swab is taken, the next procedure is to send it to a forensic laboratory to be analysed for any DNA profile. Only then one can argue the result not before.

The perfect example in this case is the one of **Chris Malouf** who was released "after DNA tests were carried out (they said). This, was said and done to deceive. Swabs had been taken most probably, but no DNA testing took place especially on the early morning of the **15th of July 2001** (I don't think that anybody would argue my point). His arrest and release were extremely suspicious and still are….and so is the whole story about the manacles which have been contaminated …We don't need to go through again but I will somehow…

From what I understand, yes swabs were taken from the manacles but no DNA testing on them unless **Eckhoff** is lying because: [11] "In October **2004** Ms Eckhoff travelled to the United Kingdom where, on **28th October 2004,** she handed DNA samples extracted from swabs to Dr Whitaker of the Forensic Science Service lab at Wetherby. (The Queen v Murdoch [2005] NTSC 76)

It says she handed DNA samples extracted from swabs means that swabs were analysed and she was in possession of some DNA results – profiles whatever you like to call it.

- So, she was physically flying to England with <u>DNA samples extracted from swabs</u> to Whitaker to be **[tested]**…I thought the actual manacles had already been tested [?]
- But she does not take the manacles. <u>One would think that she would take both ie DNA samples extracted from swabs and the actual manacles. Wouldn't you?</u>

- So, on the 20th April 2005 the Defence is saying that they wanted to send the actual manacles to the UK for Whitaker to test in his laboratory…Anybody reading this would assume Whitaker is in England. Well NO because…
- Whitaker was in Australia. He flew two days after on 22nd April 2005 and before the announcement on 31st April 2005 of the delay of the trial until October 2005, meaning the manacles were in Australia and so was Whitaker!

You would think that they could have given him the cuffs as he was flying two days after. But, no they did not…WHY?

- **The first examination** on the cuffs by Whitaker was on 24th October 2003 (26 months) after the alleged crime. It says on the cuffs [not] DNA results from swabs taken from the cuffs.

- **The second examination** by Whitaker not on the cuffs but on DNA tests results taken from swabs was on **28th October 2004** (handed to him by Eckhoff in person when she flew to England personally).

–Whitaker did not examine the [actual] cuffs until **May 2005** (he flew on **22nd April 2005**) so, if that is correct the third examination was done in his lab in UK.

Why all that "machination"? I do not understand it. Why such problem with a pair of cuffs. Why so much handling of the cuffs?

One day they are here, next day they are somewhere else, then they are back again. Why so much movement involving the cuffs and the number of people handling them? Did THEY know something we didn't?

- What is the real reason why the trial had to be delayed for five months, when in fact the cuffs had been in Australian for already four years, but there is now an emergency for the cuffs to be sent to England after four years?
- The trial is now delayed for five months just because of the cuffs, BUT now no news about the T-shirt [?] Did they also send Lees 'T-shirt with the cuffs so THEY can be fiddled with?

One would think also that Eckhoff flying to the United Kingdom on the **28th of October 2004** would have taken not only the [DNA samples], but also the manacles or the T-shirt or items relevant to the case…. I cannot get my head around this kind of stuff…Do you?

Now:

- Also, on 15th. October 2002 the cuffs are back in Darwin from SA and put in the freezer (refer to all of the above). **THEN** on **2nd October 2004**, **officer Sandry** cuts the tape. More DNA testing is done. It must have been done in Darwin because the cuffs were back to Darwin on 15th October 2002.
- I find extremely suspicious about; how many times the cuffs have been travelling – how many people handled them – how many people contaminated them –how many times tape has been cuts – how many people cannot remember what they've done with them –how many times people ignored signing any entry. The whole set up is a nightmare but nobody cares…Yes blame Murdoch but trust Lees –the Prosecution –trust Hepi and the forensic scientists (the list is too long).

And I cannot comprehend why Eckhoff did not take the cuffs in **October 2004** which cause the cuffs to be sent to England 12 months later **in 2005**, so they can delay the trial to **October 2005** giving them more time to play with the T-shirt which most probably fits Gary Murdoch's DNA [???]

Anyhow, taking the manacles to the United Kingdom so that they could be tested by Dr Whitaker four long years after the alleged event point out to only one direction: CORRUPTION.

The Vanishing of Peter Falconio

93 - The Barrow Creek Abduction Missing Person $250,000 Reward Poster July 2001

Dear reader you may be wondering why this chapter is presented to you at nearly the end of the story. Well simply because now after reading so many pages of my work you have have a fair idea about people –real facts –or misleading facts.

By people I mean: The accused –the accuser –the Chief Justice –the Prosecution – the Defence –the accused ex-partner in illegal drugs trafficking –the witnesses –the police – the officials like the Deputy Commissioner of police –the experts on DNA –members of social media – not forgetting the unknown driver of the unknown Land Cruiser where both have never been identified etc.

We have now an open window on what may have taken place or not in this alleged crime where no Dead Body has been found and no witnesses to the actual and physical killing of Peter Falconio where nothing not even "L'ARME DU CRIME" the weapon used in this alleged crime has been found.

How do posters help inform people?

"A poster is visual communication tool. An effective poster will get your main ideas across to many people and will assist you in engaging your colleagues in conversations. A well-designed poster will act as a source of information, be a conversation starter, and promote and summarize your work.26 Aug 2024" (from the internet).

Here in our case, it is a source of information used to finding the person or persons who allegedly may have committed a terrible crime. Remember that until a Dead Body is recovered it is still a disappearance case. The main goal is to collect more information from the public. The more information the better

However, if the case is a conspiracy towards a single person or a group of individuals, it is mission impossible. Then the poster becomes a tool to draw people's attention away from something like a thief who distracted the bystanders. The collective intention is then definitely not honourable on the

The Vanishing of Peter Falconio

contrary. If a group of individuals are involved it is definitely a plot... Remember, we don't have a Dead Body.

Here the amount of money is quite substantial. When, and if a reward poster advertised false information, the offer regardless the amount of money is meaningless ...Nobody gets it. However, the bad and distracting intention remains the property of the one who created it. Usually, it's not about money but to draw people away from the truth. As we know, watch out when drugs are involved and No Dead Body.

1- The first paragraph of the reward poster reads:
"The minister for police has approved a reward of $250,00- offered for information which leads to the apprehension and conviction of a person or persons responsible for the abduction of Peter Falconio "
This seems okay, nothing wrong with the wording

2- The second paragraph of the reward poster:
"In addition, an appropriate indemnity from prosecution will be recommended to the Director of Public Prosecution for any accomplice, not being the person who actually committed the crime, who first gives such information.

The grant of any such indemnity is at the sole discretion of the Director"
Well, here we have a huge problem, why?
[a] Use of the word [accomplice]. In paragraph 1 the author of the poster (police) is hoping that for the sum of $250,000 THEY WILL find a person or persons responsible for the UBDUCTION of Peter Falconio.

Reading paragraph 1 doesn't suggest that there is an accomplice. The alleged killer was ALONE according to the accuser Joanne Lees's story. Alone all the time until his departure towards Alice Spring.

Why not using the word witness which would be more appropriate. But strangely, according to the poster there is an accomplice, the one who did not commit the crime, not the alleged crime but the crime.

Knowing that a Dead Body has never been found, what could be the interpretation?

The Vanishing of Peter Falconio

The author of the poster could have used the word witness or kept the two words person or persons (singular or plural), BUT NO, the word now is accomplice, NOT EVEN WITNESS.

- **Who wrote the script for this poster?**
- Is it a cover up, right from day 1, what are they hiding?
- What is it that the public does not know?
- <u>The message is quite clear, from day one it is not an alleged crime, but a crime. That is what they want you to believe. The word alleged which should be associated with the word crime does not appear anywhere.</u>

In the drug smuggling, one does expect quite a few accomplices. In our case, our dear Monsieur James Hepi, the accused ex-partner in the drug business, is no less than one of them. He is the one who actually dobbed the accused. Do you see anything abnormal –unusual about that?

- The way the author or authors wrote the reward poster indicates that: firstly, **they** knew of Mr Hepi,
- Secondly is/was James Hepi already a police informer?

Then we have the words: *"Any accomplice, not being the person who actually committed le crime"* of course we cannot have the informer the person who committed the crime hey!

This sentence is in the singular form. It does read or says; *"not being the person"* in contradiction with paragraph 1 which reads *"person or persons"*

- My theory is: The accused –James Hepi –some members of WA police are involved with the selling of drugs. All competing against the Accused
- James Hepi *"not being the person who actually committed the crime"* dobbing the Accused (the accomplice in the singular form)
- All this needed to be in writing in the reward poster for future protection of some officials –Mr James Hepi.

The Vanishing of Peter Falconio

- The public is definitely unaware of the actors. This is a very clever way of doing business and by the same token getting rid of the opposition.

This was purposely pre-written by introducing and using the word accomplice. Anybody reading the poster would have no idea of the plot…Not conspiracy, but plot!

Then we have still in paragraph 2: The allocation of the $250,000 reward will be at the sole discretion of the commissioner of police.

- And who is the Commissioner of police: the Deputy Commissioner of police was no less than John Dalby,
- The man who could not wait to get a blood sample of the accused who was in hiding according to the officials, but who nevertheless was easy to find regarding when the rape case took place. Was the accused really in hiding?????

3-Third paragraph of the reward poster

"Peter Marco Falconio disappeared soon after sunset on Saturday 14th of July 2001 on the Stuart Highway near Barrow Creek, Northern Territory."

- This information intended for the public is false and purposely created to deceive and influence everyone getting too close.
- The accused did not disappear soon after the sunset…Why?

Because Joanne claimed watching the sunset at Ti Tree at 6.10pm on the 14th of July with Peter Falconio. According to a witness, she was alone. The claim made by the witness prevail according to police.

Dear reader, in the course of your reading Joanne Lees left Ti Tree at 6.30pm towards Barrow Creek after refuelling. She even provided a receipt showing the time for when she refuelled. Ti tree is 120km to Barrow creek, a two- hour drive, meaning that even if she arrived alone or not, she got there at 8.30pm. That is the time Falconio re-appears, just to be shot 15 minutes later, but resurrecting a week later in Bourke NSW.

The Vanishing of Peter Falconio

I am sorry, but 8.30pm is long time passed sunset. Lees even mentioned that when the alleged killer stopped them, parking his car behind the Kombi he had his head lights on. She even said that it was pitch dark…Remember!

Therefore, saying and writing that Peter Falconio disappeared soon after sunset is false, IT IS A LIE meant to deceive, it was night time.

This is the first lie in the third paragraph.

Then it reads: She later escape and raised the alarm which is not true.

- She did not raise the alarm, she was rescued there as you know, from what we still don't know
- This is the second **LIE** in paragraph 3

Then it reads:

Mr Falconio's blood was located at the scene, which is also not correct nor true.

- The blood of Peter Falconio according of the experts and the trackers was never found at the alleged crime scene. It was all roadkill.
- This is the third big **LIE** in paragraph three of the reward poster

My question is: WHY?

Contact details of the reward poster (contact).

It reads: Any person with information is ask to phone… which is normal

Perhaps the wording could have or should have been:

Any person or ACCOMPLICE with information IS ASK TO PHONE. Sorry for being sarcastic.

The Vanishing of Peter Falconio

94 - Key Events

This seems to indicate that Whitaker had the actual manacles previously.

Key events

14 July 2001	NT Comfit picture based on Lees' description of 'the man' - long hair & moustache.
17 July 2001	DNA of an 'unidentified male' found on Lees T-shirt. Suspect not found on any DNA database.
31 May 2002	Hepi gives evidence against Murdoch to Det. Sergeant Peter Jenal in WA after being arrested on 16 May.
14 July 2002	E-fit of the suspect as first described by Lees published online by BBC. *No stone unturned in Falconio case* BBC News World Edition Sunday, 14 July, 2002. http://news.bbc.co.uk/2/hi/asia-pacific/2127470.stm
14 August 2002	DNA sample obtained from Gary, Murdoch's brother.
21 August 2002	E-fit drawing in the media now looks more like a clean shaven Murdoch with short hair (see photo below). BBC News of the World article *Outback girlfriend Lees seeks damages* http://news.bbc.co.uk/2/hi/asia-pacific/2206730.stm
28 August 2002	Murdoch arrested in SA for rape 14 days after police take Gary's DNA.
30 August 2002	Police media release state they have a 'person of interest' in the Falconio case.

The Vanishing of Peter Falconio

8? October 2002	Is Murdoch's blood sample sent from SA to NT? See 17 November 2003 below.
8 October 2002	Dr Thatcher in NT forensics lab retrieved manacles from freezer & gave them to Mr Sandry to take to Yatala in SA for interview with Murdoch. This is the last entry in the movement log until the central loop is sent to Whitaker on 22 April 2005.
9 October 2002	NT police announced that they were 'unable to exclude Murdoch from the investigation into Falconio's death' but that he is the prime suspect. Media called it a 'DNA match'.
10 October 2002	Murdoch's property in Sedan SA searched by NT police. They take manacles with them.
10 October 2002	*DNA breakthrough* announced in media. 'Following DNA tests police in the Northern Territory said they were seeking an arrest warrant for Bradley John Murdoch, 44'. Lees sees photo online of Murdoch. BBC News of the World article *Falconio family relief at DNA link* http://news.bbc.co.uk/2/hi/asia-pacific/2315379.stm
15 October 2002	Manacles come back to Darwin from SA.
23 January 2003	Using a different DNA test (Profiler Plus test) Carmen Eckhoff finds that Murdoch's DNA profile is 'an exact match' across all 16 sites with the profile obtained from the back of the T-shirt.
10 November 2003	Murdoch acquitted of rape in SA & immediately arrested for Falconio's murder. He was held in custody in SA.

17 November 2003	NT police obtained a 'controlled sample' of Murdoch's blood from SA. It was not analysed until 31 December 2003.
14 December 2003	Murdoch extradited to NT.
31 December 2003	Murdoch's controlled blood sample is analysed in Darwin.
2 May 2004	Sandry cuts tapes from the manacles & Dr Thatcher's DNA found on manacles.
28 October 2004	Eckhoff hands DNA samples extracted from swabs to Whitaker.
22 April 2005	Central loop? Of the manacles is sent to Whitaker. He did not examine them until May 2005.

95 - My Lust for Justice Is Such...

...that I wish and hope that Justice will prevail and that "ONE DAY" Bradley John Murdoch will be cleared and absolved of the blame.

"...people who claim they are innocent despite forms of DNA evidence linking them to crimes for which they have been accused and/or convinced could well be telling the truth. The presumption of innocence that is claimed to lie at the heart of all criminal investigations and prosecutions dictates that this is more adequately recognised and acted upon by the criminal justice system to avoid causing wrongful convictions and to overturn those that have already occurred." (Naughton and Tan 2011 p 257)

Mark Godsey a former prosecutor and co-founder of the Ohio Innocence Project in the US writes that too many accused are the victims of faulty forensic evidence.

"The discovery of hundreds of wrongful convictions by the innocence movement in the past two decades has exposed deep problems in our forensic sciences. In fact, inaccurate forensic science testimony was a contributing factor in 154 of the first 325 DNA exonerations in the United States, second only to mistaken eyewitness identifications...49 percent- nearly half- of those involved bad forensics." (**Godsey** p 93)

Was this the case in Murdoch's trial? I strongly believe Murdoch was a scapegoat.

...and now, from the latest of the latest in The Weekend Australian (26th November 2023) another bombshell:

DNA lab's fake facts key "proof of its lies" by David Murray Hedley Thomas. It must be read. If you can't afford to buy the newspaper steal it, but read it.

96 - Conclusion

"SHOW ME THE MAN I'll SHOW YOU THE CRIME" could not be more appropriate"

Keywords:

Monopoly– Control –Ideology –Belief –Mistake–Ignorance– Negligence –Prime Suspects

***

I really believe that the bigger the lie the more people believe it

Algie in Mildren page 35

"…Algie now seeks to cast doubt on whether the Crown, even if it has proved that Falconio is dead, has proved that it was the defendant who was the killer…

Now when you're reflecting on that, if you get to that point, you would need to take into account what I suggest are two assumptions that have been made very early in the investigation of this matter and indeed which continue to form the foundation of the prosecution case. The first is this: it is assumed, I suggest, that if there was a bad guy at Barrow Creek, he actually left his DNA or blood on Ms Lees.

And the second assumption which I suggest has been the foundation of the investigation and the prosecution is that if there was a bad guy at Barrow Creek, that guy is the man at the truck-stop at Shell…."

(would recommend anyone to buy and read Mildren's book)

The Prosecution worked very hard promoting some misinformation regarding Bradley Murdoch and the CCTV man advocating that it was not two individuals but one and one only. Well, the Prosecution failed miserably. THEY purposely ignored the fact that there were two PRIME SUSPECTS. It is a logical fact that no one can deny.

There is also another fact that no one can dismiss knowing that the CCTV man has never been identified by police or anybody else, which raise a major question: Where did the CCTV man go after leaving Alice Springs? Can anyone prove with the greatest certitude that his intention was to drive to Fitzroy Crossing? This created another issue because if no one knows

The Vanishing of Peter Falconio

who he is or what he does how can you tell where he is/was going [?] As a result, he also may not be the alleged killer therefore it is mission impossible to proclaim what everybody assumed: Murdoch the alleged killer. It is a very uncertain future which has also been ignore raising more questions. Did Falconio really got killed and what would or could be the consequences if one day Falconio re-surface even after a very long absence?

As far as I am concerned, it is not a possibility for Falconio to re-appear after a long absence, BUT reflecting on the case for nearly six years and knowing what Gregory Dick said to me about drugs and drug Lords someone got to him

I believe that THEY GOT RID OF PETER FALCONIO QUICK SMART AND BLAMED BRADLEY JOHN MURDOCH……S.I.M.P.L.E

Murdoch will never confess to an alleged crime he could not have done. We need to re-open this can of worms and we need a miracle. Trusting the police may be, The Court NEVER.

Anyhow, the Prosecution –Judge Martin –Joanne Lees –Monsieur James Hepi and all the conspirators as I said above; THEY all failed miserably. THEY should all feel guilty, but I believe THEY DON'T

The crucifixion of Murdoch was successful because of the monopoly and control supported by this ideology to IGNORE and the belief that THEY cannot be wrong nor corrupt.

The willingness to ignore and purposely hid the truth is/was astonishing.

As you know, the CODE distinguishes between the physical and fault elements which define criminal Offences and Defences. The truth should have defeated any allegation of liability, unfortunately it didn't as you know.

This ideology is a set of ideas that constitute one's goal, and actions or a set of ideas proposed by the dominant class of a group –order –or society to all members or to a particular individual, in this case: Bradley John Murdoch

The proof beyond reasonable doubt that Bradley John Murdoch could not have committed the alleged crime he was accused of, is/was the obvious fact.

The Vanishing of Peter Falconio

The fact that Murdoch was successful in reaching Fitzroy Crossing within the time limit contrary to the CCTV, is a full proof indication that the **DNA DEBATE IS/WAS CORRUPT**.

Truly and logically the proof that Murdoch was not at the alleged crime scene which I definitely **PROVED** means that **HE COULD NOT HAVE KILLED PETER FALCONIO.**

a fact that THEY all purposely hid, ignored and denied for reason unknown to me and to all future readers. THEY all made sure the jurors would buy it, especially the one who sat on Murdoch's trial, the one who was in a relationship with the Chief Justice's daughter a fact which also was denied later on when questioned by a "journo" (Robin Bowles). THEY all kept your mouths shut believing that we are all stupid.

So, knowing this, please start questioning the irregularities surfacing about the DNA and ask yourself what was that all about -what was the case all about –was it a conspiracy?

It certainly looks and sounds like it.

The whole case is/was scandalous, it is/was not only a true miscarriage of Justice, it was more than that; it was a farce.

It is still my understanding and belief that the accused was chosen as a scapegoat and that

Bradley John Murdoch who was not there killed Peter Falconio who was not there!

The trial was a scam, a conspiracy, a trial by media, a miscarriage of Justice and a symphony of lies after lies after lies.

"YOU CANNOT SEND AN INNOCENT TO LIFE IN PRISON AND GET AWAY WITH IT"

…. To conclude using the words of Gary G. Kohls MD

WHAT GOOD FORTUNE FOR THOSE IN POWER THAT PEOPLE DO NOT THINK…IT GIVES US A VERY SPECIAL, SECRET PLEASURE TO SEE HOW UNAWARE THE PEOPLE AROUND US ARE OF WHAT IS REALLY HAPPENING…

New South Wales 1-February 2024

97 - NOW THAT MURDOCH IS DEAD…

This new chapter has been added on the 28 of July 2025 exactly two weeks after Bradley John Murdoch passed away at the hospital in Alice Springs after spending less than a month in palliative care suffering from throat cancer.

My book was officially published on the internet at the end of May 2025 just before police raised the reward to $500K. Since the death of Murdoch, the Social-Media – broadcasters and others have had a good feast releasing woke information.

This information is about: **[1] Gregory Dick** who was running the Aileron roadhouse. When we met in 2018 in reply to my question about Joanne Lees escaping, he said **"mate he is alive and doing well**, then adding stuff about drugs and drug lords. He also told me that **Joanne Lees told a BIG LIE at the trial** (I did mention previously that he testified at the trial but his testimony was dismissed). Gregory also strongly believed in Murdoch's innocence and also said that the man who spoke to Joanne Lees near the fuel pump didn't look at all like Murdoch, but shared however strong resemblance with Chris Malouf.

…**COULD** the follow up be a coincidence? Gregory was admitted in Alice Hospital at the same time as Murdoch. **He first was in Medical West bed 22**, but has since been moved to **the orthopaedic ward**…Very strange indeed.

I spoke with him for a very short time four days ago. Greg is 79 years old but when we spoke, he sounded like a very disoriented man, I could only speak him less than 3 minutes.

Reading the following will shock you. "Mr Dick is also one of the few men to publicly back Murdoch. Yet in an interview with the **Herald Sun** on Saturday, the 79-year-old said there was one thing he was sure of:

- **"HE DID IT. I think that's the case."**
- "He's a p**ck of a man, and that's it. That's all there is to say," Mr Dick said.
- "**He**'s just a bad, bad man"

The Vanishing of Peter Falconio

Do you believe that? Has he been intimidated - warned – threaten? Gregory was a key witness for the prosecution of Falconio's trial in 2005

Now it's the turn of Vince Millar the truck driver whom as you know rescued Joanne Lees and/but could not understand the reason why **SHE WAS WARM – CLEAN – NOT INJURED** after spending 5 hours in the cold.

You read it previous in one of the chapters...Well, last week, watching the late news on channel 9, (I videoed it),

- Vince appeared on the screen speaking about Joanne Lees 'rescue with these words; **SHE WAS COLD**...Wow!
- As well as speaking you could read the words written on the screen...

Well, for a man who had 2 pages missing from his declaration taken by police the morning after the allege crime, pages which later were replaced by 2 new ones <u>written by police</u> which he refused to sign, this man is now saying: **SHE WAS COLD**

- **Changing his statement after Murdoch death, just like that definitely raises some interesting questions.**
- **Has he also been intimidated – warned - threaten for the same reasons?**

Now a cherry for the cake:
Robin Bowles is being submitted to the same treatment. She said on National television...

- ... That she received 4 letters from lawyers advising her to proceed carefully when making statements.

***

<u>From Robin Bowles a strong supporter of Bradley Murdoch.</u>
"I feel compelled to respond to some of these comments asap, especially 'have we been had?'! before Brad's supporters run off in wrong directions! Firstly, I have not been personally privy to Brad's 'final bombshell' as the media has chosen to label it!

The Vanishing of Peter Falconio

But I do believe he will be making a deathbed statement*, definitely NOT a confession, but information the police know and haven't acted upon. I suspect it is something I was made aware of on a visit to Brad after his conviction then i tried my best to get into the public domain before I was blocked out first by the subject/s of the info and then by Fraser, who just wanted to use Brad for his own money-making ends. Sussmann still has some of Brad's papers and you can bet he'll come out of the woodwork after Brad goes.

...Secondly, in the media interviews I've done I have said he is innocent, he hasn't told anyone where the body is because he DOESN'T KNOW. That's in the live/radio interviews, but not TV, because they edit to suit themselves, as we all know!

Finally, Brad is in Alice Srings hospital. He is terminally ill... For the police to double the reward and Gwyn**n to pop up again after all this time as a 'self-styled expert' and for the NT police to be allegedly going in to the hospital to interview him while he's so sick are cynical and despicable acts and they should back off and leave him alone! Do they really think doubling the reward is going to encourage Brad to tell them Peter's location?? Who gets the reward if he dies? Answer; no one. Cheap outcome! Please read media reports with a grain of salt!*

There is one more thing I like to mention, it's about the Peter Falconio's family; Why are they still believing that Bradley Murdoch was the killer, when Joanne Lees' stepfather **Vincent James** believes that Murdoch is innocent.

Many questions should still be raised. You must understand now that:
IF MURDOCH WAS NOT AT THE ALLEGED CRIME-SCENE, HOW CAN HE BE THE KILLER?
As I said before: TRUSTING THE POLICE ...PERHAPS, THE COURT NEVER.

98 - REFERENCES

Barker, Anne. 2005. *Conflicting evidence in Falconio trial*. ABC PM Thursday, 24 November, 2005 18:30:00. [Accessed online 30.08.20 Available at https://www.abc.net.au/pm/content/2005/s1516281.htm

Bowles, Robin. 2022. *Dead centre: The inside story of the mysterious disappearance of Peter Falconio*. Hawthorn, Victoria: Lake Press.

DNA breakthrough: Falconio family finds relief. *BBC News World Edition*. Thursday, 10 October, 2002, 16:26 GMT 17:26 UK http://news.bbc.co.uk/2/hi/asia-pacific/2315379.stm)

Gans, Jeremy. 2007. Catching Bradley Murdoch: Tweezers, Pitchforks and the Limits of DNA Sampling
Jeremy Gans. *Current Issues in Criminal Justice Volume 19 Number 1*.

Gill, Peter. 2001. Application of Low Copy Number DNA Profiling. Forensic Science Service, Trident Court, Birmingham, UK. *Croation Medical Journal* 42(3):229-232

Godsey, Mark 2017. *Blind justice*. Oakland, California: University of California Press.Knight, Kathryn. 2020. Outback mystery: The unanswered questions in Peter Falconio's murder – from man bundled into red car to footprints in the undergrowth. *The Sun*. 5 Jun 2020, 12:11Updated: 8 Jun 2020, 9:52. Available online: https://www.thesun.co.uk/news/11783465/peter-falconio-joanne-lees-murder-outback/

Ligertwood, Andrew. 2011. Can DNA evidence alone convict an accused? *Sydney Law Review*. 33(847) pp 487-514. Available online at http://classic.austlii.edu.au/au/journals/SydLawRw/2011/21.pdf

The Vanishing of Peter Falconio

McCartney, Carole. 2008. LCN DNA: proof beyond reasonable doubt? *Nature Reviews Genetics* v. 9 p. 325 Accessed online at: https://www.nature.com/articles/nrg2362

Maynard, Roger. 2005. *Where's Peter? Unravelling the Falconio mystery.* Australia: Harper Collins.

Mildren, Dean. 2015. *R v Murdoch. The Falconio case. A study in identification and circumstantial evidence.* Chatsworth, NSW: Reed International Books.

Naughton, Michael & Tan, Gabe. 2011. The need for caution in the use of DNA evidence to avoid convicting the innocent. *The International Journal of Evidence & Proof* (2011) 15 E&P 245–257.

Shears, Richard. 2019. *Bloodstain: The vanishing of Peter Falconio.* Sydney, NSW: New Holland Publishers.

Waterstreet, Charles. August 23, 2014 4.35pm High Court puts DNA and experts in their place.
The judges' unanimous decision in the Fitzgerald v Regina case sweeps aside prejudice and irrational thinking. *Sydney Morning Herald.* Accessed online: https://shorturl.at/tAJK1

Watt, Bob. 2011. The Territory Inquisition(s)...A Play Reading produced by Rex Wild QC Tuesday 24 and Wednesday 25 May 2011. *Balance two & three 2011.* Pp 30-31. Accessed online: www.lawsocietynt.asn.au.

Williams, Sue. 2006. *And Then the Darkness: The disappearance of Peter Falconio and the trials of Joanne.* Sydney: ABC Books.

www.ingramcontent.com/pod-product-compliance
Lightning Source LLC
Chambersburg PA
CBHW081352070526
44583CB00020B/2525